German-American Names

German-American
N·A·M·E·S

George F. Jones

Genealogical Publishing Co., Inc.

Acknowledgments

I wish to thank Bertha Butler of the University of Maryland Computer Science Center for many years of expert and patient help in devising computer programs. One of these, a system of reverse-alphabetical listing, served to assemble the names in this book according to their last roots and thus shed much light on their meanings and relationships. I also wish to thank Carol Warrenton, likewise of the University of Maryland Computer Science Center, for composing the program for printing this book.

G. F. J.

Der Schmidt.

CHAPTER ONE

Given Names - Significance and Origin

Many Americans with German names know the dictionary meaning of the corresponding German word without realizing that their name, being a name, may have an entirely different meaning. For example, the German dictionary tells us that the word *Kuss* means "kiss," but it does not tell us that the name Kuss is most often a shortened form of Dominicus and that, while the word *Mass* means "measure," the name Mass or Maas is usually a shortened form of Thomas. (1)

Unfortunately, onomastics (the science of names) is not an exact science, as is proved when experts disagree as to the meaning of a name. Only the parents of a child know what they think a name means, and often they do not know. While interning in an obstetrics ward, an acquaintance of mine once delivered a worn-out mountain woman of her tenth child. When the grateful woman asked him to think up a name, he suggested Decimus Ultimus; and she was delighted with the choice, which she did not understand. The name meant "the tenth and the last." He was right: he had tied her tubes. (2)

When my wife's parents chose the name Joyce for their daughter, they probably associated it with "joy" and "rejoice," little realizing that it once denoted a Goth; and the same thing was repeated when Joyce named our daughter Jocelyn (little Goth). Such misunderstandings are called popular etymology or folk etymology, etymology being the study of *etym* or roots of words. A good example of folk etymology is the common expression "planter's wart," which suggests that planters were most exposed to it, whereas it is really a "plantar wart" or a wart on the sole of the foot, as I learned recently. (3)

Old Germanic names were misunderstood already a thousand years ago by scholars who tried to interpret them. For example, Ratmund was rendered as "counsel + mouth" instead of as "counsel + guardianship;" and Adalramus was rendered as "noble ram" instead of as "noble raven." This study will make every effort to avoid folk etymologies, but some are inevitable, and the author will appreciate hearing of any the reader might find. (4)

Sometimes the researcher must risk an educated guess. For example, the German-American name Hass could derive from

German *Hass* (hate) or from German *Has* (hare), most certainly (but not absolutely certainly) from the latter, which is found in many American names such as Hashagen (hare hedge) and Hasenjaeger (hare hunter). A half century ago one of my sisters had a gentleman caller named Hass, who had the misfortune of having the first name Jack. When Jack Hass was spoken quickly, it said just what we brothers thought of him.   (5)

It is easy to define the term "German-American name," once we decide on the meaning of "German name"; for a German-American name is any name derived from the German language or its dialects, even if changes in pronunciation and spelling have rendered it unrecognizable. For our purpose, both Beam and Dice are German-American names, even if we do not easily identify them with Boehm and Theiss.   (6)

Defining "German names" is somewhat more difficult. For example, the Netherlands were originally a part of the Holy Roman Empire (i.e. the German Empire); and the people there speak Low Franconian, Low Saxon, and Frisian. The first two of these are German dialects, while the third is an independent language, which is also spoken in Germany. Since Dutch is now a national language, we will not include obviously Dutch names such as de Gruyter and van Horn, even if they may have been borne for centuries by families in Berlin.   (7)

On the other hand, even though Dreyfuss was a loyal Frenchman, his name (meaning "tripod") was German and is therefore included. When I first visited Paris, I rented a room from a woman who pronounced her name Oh-mess-air, which I took to be French. I later discovered that it was Haumesser, an Alsatian word meaning "hackknife" or "meat-cleaver," so it is also included. Also included are the names Kirchhoff and Stockmann, even though they are best known to us as the names of a Russian physicist and of the protagonist in Ibsen's *Enemy of the People* and also (with one *n*) of a precocious American economist who ridiculed Reaganomics. In other words, we are interested in the linguistic origin of the name, not in the nationality of its bearers. The word "German" refers to the German language, whether the name in question came from West or East Germany, Alsace, Switzerland, Austria, the South Tyrol, or any other German-speaking areas of Europe.   (8)

It is not always possible to ascertain from which language a name is derived: Horn could be German, English, Dutch, or Scandinavian. Therefore some American names discussed below may actually have been brought here by non-German families, but all do exist in Germany. A few well-known Latin and Greek names like Astor, Faber, Melanchthon, Mercator, Neander, Praetorius, Sartorius, and Stettinius are included because they have now become German names. There are also a few names of French origin, like Tussing for Toussaints, and a few names of Slavic derivation, like Kretschmer, Lessing, and Nietzsche. (9)

Because the word "philologist" will appear many times in this book, now might be a proper time to explain the word, even if it is hard to explain the profession. As the Greek roots *phil* and *logos* suggest, a philologist is one who loves words, one who cherishes them for their own sake, not for the sake of gain. No philologist ever became rich, not one ever built a bridge, removed a tumor, or won a battle; and it is difficult to explain what good they serve, unless, perhaps, to disabuse us of much misinformation. Nevertheless, some of the world's greatest minds have devoted themselves to this unproductive study, two splendid examples being Jacob and Wilhelm Grimm, scholars known to the public for their fairy tales but to the scholarly world for their collection of legal antiquities and, above all, for the "Grimms' Law," an explanation of the development of the various Germanic languages. The observations made by the Grimm brothers and other philologists of their day make it possible for us to understand the origin of German names, and therefore their contributions will be described in some detail a bit later. (10)

Most philologists write for each other, affecting an arcane jargon to exclude everyone else. Unfortunately, this study will have to use a few technical terms, but these will be explained. At the Day of Judgement I shall have to confess to having devoted a half century of my life to Germanic philology, whereas I could have been serving my Maker in some more productive way. However, unlike most Germanic philologists in their ivory towers, I am aware that there are many perfectly decent, hardworking, lawabiding people out there who have never studied Germanic philology. It is for them that this book is written. (11)

"In the beginning was the word." St. John was not alone in this belief; it was the opinion of most of his contem-

poraries, especially of his Greek ones, who had a word for
everything. It was centuries before Goethe's Faust, as the
first Modern Man, refuted St. John and argued that "In the
beginning was the deed." Today most people would agree
with the *New English Dictionary* that a word is merely
"Speech, utterance, or verbal expression." The ancients, on
the other hand, and not only those of our culture, knew that
a word was more than a mere utterance. It was a living
spirit with inherent power to do good or evil, as is so evident
in the blessings and curses of the Old Testament. Noah's
curse of Canaan and Isaac's blessing of Jacob were not just
words but were forces direct from Jehovah. Words had power
not only for the ancient Hebrews but also for the ancient
Germanic peoples, for whom an insult was a malevolent
spirit, a relentless demon that clung to a man until washed
off with blood.   (12)

What has been said about words naturally holds for names
too, since they are proper nouns, even in the few instances
when they are formed like adjectives or verbs, as in the case
of Lionhearted or Lackland. The very term "proper nouns"
(*nomina propria*) is significant; for a name, be it given or
earned, is proper to, or the property of, the bearer. This is
especially evident in the German word *Eigennamen*, or "own
names." One's name is, of course, more than just a posses-
sion, like land or gold; it is the immortal part of the person,
as Othello's ensign Cassio avowed. It is the part that lives
after the body dies, possibly borne by children of the deceas-
ed, or perhaps by many children of his admirers. Or perhaps
his name is carved in stone or borne by a city or a sym-
phony.   (13)

Even the Old Testament taught the value of a good name,
and this is one reason that, during the Middle Ages, to be
"nameless" (*namenlos* or *ungenant*) was most tragic. Proverbs
22:1 tells us that "A good name is rather to be chosen than
great riches," and Ecclesiastes 7:1 preaches that "a good name
is better than precious ointment." (Cf "to leave a living name
behind," and "their bodies are buried in peace, but their name
liveth for evermore.")   (14)

It has been said that "your name is who you are." Indeed,
before social security numbers, a name was most people's only
identity. This attitude is deeply ingrained in the Christian
Church, which accepts a new member only when he receives
a Christian name and ignores his surname; and it helps
explain the emphasis on the Feast of the Holy Name on New

Year's Day. In some cultures a change of name indicates a change in nature: the Indian youth receives a new name when he becomes a brave, and a British commoner receives a more fitting name when he is ennobled. When Lawrence Olivier was knighted, he became Sir Lawrence, not Sir Olivier. (15)

That such obsession with names was only a holdover from ancient word-magic is suggested by the ease with which modern men can change their names, without any great metamorphosis in their person. Indeed, one does not even have to go to the legislature, as was necessary in my father's childhood. When his nextgate neighbors tired of being teased because of their name, which was Hogg, they changed it to Howard. The next day some jokester put a sign on their gate: "Hogg by name, and hog by nature, changed to Howard by legislature." What the public did not know was that Hog was a respectable name as long as it denoted the young of most animals, including sheep. A Highland lassie cared little whether her laddie called her "my little lamb" or "my little hog." (16)

There are many tales of name changes, usually apocryphal but sometimes illuminating. From the '30s comes the tale of Franklin Delano Stink. When the judge agreed to let him change his name and asked which name he had chosen, he answered "Theodore Roosevelt Stink." Then there was the Mr. Murphy of South Boston who wished to change his name to O'Reily. When the judge asked why he wished to exchange one Irish name for another, he answered: "Venn I say my name iss Murphy, people aks me vut it vuss before it vuss Murphy." (17)

The ancient Germans had no firm faith in a hereafter, despite what latter-day mythologists tell us about Valhalla, which must have developed late and probably through analogy with the Christian heaven. Long after they had become nominal Christians, Germanic warriors were far more concerned with their posthumous good name than with their souls. *Beowulf* is nominally a Christian poem; yet, when the hero dies, the poet is concerned not with his soul but only with his good name, for he eulogizes him as *leofgernost*, or "most eager for fame." (18)

This obsession with one's good name lasted throughout the Middle Ages. Despite Christ's injunction to turn the other cheek, men of honor preferred to risk their immortal souls in duels rather than risk their worldly honor by declining a challenge. Today we can say "Sticks and stones may break my bones but names can never hurt me," but in those days names hurt far more than mere broken bones. Turning the other cheek would have been incomprehensible to the ancient German, the medieval knight, or the Southern Gentleman, who knew that he would enjoy no respect or esteem if he failed to gain satisfaction for an insult.　　　　　　(19)

The New English Dictionary says that a name is "the particular combination of sounds employed as the individual designation of a single person, animal, place, or thing." It is to be noted that the name consists of sounds, not letters. Now that most people of the Western World are literate, we think of names as groups of letters, as in a signature. Yet even today the sound is foremost, extremely varied spellings are legally recognized only if they sound the same (*idem sonans*). MacIntire, McIntire, and McIntyre are the same name, even if differently spelled, as are Cramer, Craemer, and Kraemer.　　　　　　(20)

When the ancient Germans formed their names, they, like the ancient Hebrews, knew that a name was more than a mere designation: like a word, a name had inherent power and was part and parcel of the person himself. It was believed that a man's virtues were influenced by his name and were in turn transmitted to his namesake. This belief lasted long after the introduction of Christianity, and Christian parents continued to select godparents whose names would contribute to their children's virtue.　　　　　　(21)

Because the God of the Old Testament was created in man's image, He was a jealous God, especially jealous of His name; and it should be noted that He performed most of His great works "for His name's sake," or to enhance His reputation among the various tribal gods of the time. ("Thou shalt have none other god before me.") Woe unto anyone who took the name of the Lord in vain! In fact, the Hebrews dared not utter His name; they had to resort to all sorts of circumlocutions such as Adonai and Elohim. Sacred names are taboo in many other religions as well: for example, the Hairy Ainu of Hokaido are afraid to utter the name of the bear. The early Germans, who were also shamanists, must have shared this fear, for they avoided the inherited Indo-European name for "bear," which would have been similar to Latin *ursus*. Instead, they beat around the bush with words like *bruin* and *berin*, both of which meant "brown" and gave us names such as Bruno, Bernhard, and Bermann. It should be noted that the name Beowulf meant "bee wolf," a circumlocution for the bear, which relishes honey. (22)

With such a long tradition of name-magic behind us, it is not surprising that people are still so touchy about their names. Goethe was wise in saying that we should never make a play on a person's name. For some twenty-five years, whenever I have been introduced to someone, he was likely to answer with a hearty chuckle, "Oh, one of the Jones boys!" I have always tried to be diplomatic and laugh along with my tormentor, as if I had not been subjected to the same stupidity a thousand times before, realizing that he really thought he had said something clever and original. (Strangely enough, I still do not know who the Jones boys were.)

(23)

How did names arise? According to the Bible, after God created Adam:

> Out of the ground the Lord God formed every
> beast of the field, and every fowl of the air;
> and brought them unto Adam to see what he
> would call them: and whatsoever Adam called
> every living creature, that was the name
> thereof.

This occurred just before God created Eve from Adam's rib. When Eve heard that Adam had named the hippopotamus hippopotamus, she asked why he had done so; and he answered that it looked more like a hippopotamus to him than any other animal God had shown him. (24)

Just as one could injure his enemy by driving nails into his image, one could gain power over him by abusing his name. As Stith Thompson's *Motif-Index of Folk-Literature* proves, this belief has been strong in all cultures, including our own. For example, in the Grimm's tale of Rumpelstiltskin, the queen's daughter gains power over her captor by learning his name. Belief in the power over names still lingers in our subconscious as either a positive or a negative factor. In discussing Johann Adam Treutlen, the first elected governor of Georgia, Henry Melchior Muhlenberg praised him for having Adam's natural intelligence and ability to give a name to every animal. Despite St. John's faith in the precedence of the word, many medieval scholars agreed with Genesis that the thing preceded the name: *Nomina sunt consequentia rerum* (names are the consequence of things).

(25)

To understand early German names, we must keep in mind that the ancient Germans, like the Latins, Celts, Slavs, Greeks, and many more peoples, were descended from one speech community, one we now call the Indo-Europeans. When I was in college, we learned that this linguistic community had developed its language in India and had gradually spread it westward to Europe. However, during the Hitler regime, when the terms "Aryan" and "Indo-European" were confused and abused, German philologists began to argue that the Indo-Europeans, or Indo-Germans as they called them, first developed their language in eastern Central Europe, in what is now more or less East Germany and Poland, from where they gradually carried it eastwards into Iran (Parsee) and India (Sanskrit), as well as into all of Europe, except where Finnish, Estonian, Hungarian, and Basque are spoken.   (26)

The languages resulting from these Indo-European invasions in Europe were the Celtic languages in the west and south, Latin and Greek in the south, the Slavic languages in the east and south, and German in the old homeland and also to the north. Perhaps the least changed of all these languages were Old Prussian, Lithuanian, and Latvian, all of them near and just north of the old cradle. This new theory, which smacked of blatant racism, first met with ridicule; yet the linguistic evidence has now convinced most philologists, be they ever so anti-Nazi.   (27)

The Germanic tribes, which were among the last to leave the old homeland, were excellently described in the year 98 A.D. by the Roman historian Cornelius Tacitus in a little area-study called the *Germania*, which may have been the foreword to a never-written history of the German wars. Tacitus describes a barbarian culture centered mainly on war; and, as we shall see, early German names bear him out. The language of the ancient Germans was not recorded, but we can reconstruct it by comparing words from old and modern Germanic languages, and also by comparing Germanic names recorded in Greek and Latin writings. From these we can learn much about the ancient Germans' life-style. We know, among other things, that they had cattle, horses, wagons, plows, grains, cloth, and a means of inscribing words, names, and incantations.   (28)

All languages are in constant flux. Children do not speak exactly like their parents and grandparents; and today we have difficulty in understanding Chaucer, or even Shakespeare. The remarkable thing is not that languages change, but that they change so slowly. As the various Indo-European peoples left their homeland, their dialects developed independently until they became mutually unintelligible languages. It was the great work of the Grimm brothers, especially of Jacob, to comprehend and codify the mutations that distinguished the Germanic languages from all other Indo-European languages. These mutations are now known as the Germanic sound shift. (29)

The phrase "sound shift" sounds ominous, like the Andreas Fault, or the Tower of Babel, as if any moment we might not be able to communicate. Actually, sound shifts occur so slowly that the speakers who perpetrate them are unaware of the havoc they are wreaking. There even seems to have been a sound shift, although not yet recorded, since we Americans broke off from our linguistic motherland: we pronounce words like "latter" and "bitter" the same as "ladder" and "bidder." Some Americans deny obstreperously that they do so; but, if they didn't, they would sound like Englishmen with their "clipped accent." Imitating the Brothers Grimm, I will formulate the Jones law as follows: "In American English intervocalic voiceless dental stops have become voiced." Or, put simply, *t* has become *d* between vowel sounds. "Voiceless" stops like *p*, *t*, and *k* do not cause the vocal chords to vibrate as the voiced stops *b*, *d*, and *g* do. In "this" the *th* is voiced, in "thistle" it is not. A "stop" is a consonant that interrupts the breath, like *p*, *t*, and *k*, whereas a "spirant" is spoken while air is being exhaled as in the case of *th*, *f*, and *s*. An "affricate" combines a stop and its corresponding spirant, as in *pf* and *ts* (which is written as *z* in German). (30)

To explain the Germanic sound shift simply, yet sufficiently for our purpose, we might say that the voiceless stops *p*, *t*, and *k* became the voiceless spirants *f*, *th*, and *ch* (which soon became *h*), while the voiced stops *b*, *d*, and *g* became the voiceless stops *p*, *t*, and *k*, thus replacing the lost consonants. Consequently the Indo-European roots that gave the Latin words *piscis*, *tenuis*, and *cornus* also gave the English words *fish*, *thin*, and *horn* as well as the German words *Fisch*, *duenn*, and *Horn*, while Latin *turba*, *duo*, and *genu* are cognate with (related to) "thorpe," "two," and "knee."(31)

The language produced by the Germanic sound shift, which is called Proto-Germanic, was subsequently subdivided by various mutations into many Germanic dialects, including

Alemannic, Anglian, Bavarian, Danish, Dutch, Frankish, Hessian, Norwegian, Saxon, Swedish, and Thuringian, as well as by many extinct languages such as Burgundian, Cimbric, Gothic, Lombard, and Vandal. Of the modern dialects, some have become national languages, such as Dutch and Flemish (from Low Franconian), and English from Anglian and Saxon.   (32)

This might be a suitable time to remind the reader that one should distinguish between the words "German" and "Germanic" rather than confuse them as many genealogical societies do. The word "Germanic," like *germanique, germanico,* and *germanisch,* denotes all the languages resulting from the Germanic sound shift, including English, Dutch, Swedish, Pennsylvania Dutch, etc. Since English is a Germanic language, one cannot distinguish between the English and Germanic elements in Pennsylvania. The recent popularity of the word "Germanic" seems to have begun during the Hitler regime, perhaps because it sounded less Nazi than "German" did. Correctly speaking, the inhabitants of Tacitus' *Germania* should not be called "Germans," since the German nation did not develop until after the invasions of the fourth to the seventh centuries. However, since it is awkward always to say "Germanic" and "Germanic peoples," we will sometimes just say "Germans" and "ancient Germans."   (33)

A language is a culturally independent dialect with its own rules. Pennsylvania German and Afrikaans, with only a million or two speakers each, are languages, while Bavarian and Swabian, with many millions of speakers, are only dialects of German. No one can complain that the Pennsylvanians are speaking incorrect German or that the Afrikaners are speaking incorrect Dutch; yet a speaker of standard German can scold a Bavarian or a Swabian for distorting the German language. We will soon see that many German and German-American names were taken from dialects and do not conform to standard German spelling or pronunciation. The dialect form of the name might be much older than the standard language and is not really a deviation, merely an alternate form not chosen by Luther and other language standardizers. Behm is merely a dialect variant of Boehm (Bohemian), whereas the American form Beam is a new development in both pronunciation and spelling. Because the vowels, like the consonants, varied from dialect to dialect, the names Naumann, Niemann, and Neumann are one and the same.   (34)

The dialects sometimes caused differences in the meaning of names. Although *Fuss* means "foot" in standard German, the name Streckfus originally meant "Stretch leg," not "Stretch foot." Some South German colonists in Georgia told their pastor that one of his parishioners had suffered an injury to his *Fuss* when a bear he had treed and shot fell on him. The pastor reported in his journal that the man's foot had been injured, but later he was more specific, the man's thigh had been dislocated. I had a similar experience in Bavaria when a man's ski stuck in the wet snow and, with his foot held high up by the ski, he began screaming in his dialect *mein Fuoss ist gebroche, mein Fuoss ist gebroche.* In trying to loosen his foot from the ski, I handled it ever so gently, while quite ignoring his thigh, even though it was really his femur that was broken. (35)

Like the ancient Hebrews, but unlike the Romans, the Germans were content with one name, a name made of two syllables. We cannot call this name a "first" name, because there was no second one; and we cannot call it a "Christian" name, since the Germans were still heathens. Therefore we must call it a "given" name, or, for the present, just a "name." The Germanic system of name-giving seems to have been derived from Indo-European practices, for similar systems were used by the Celts and Greeks. Some scholars think this system was limited to the Celts, Greeks, and Germans; others think that it was once universal among the Indo-Europeans but was later discarded by many of the tribes after their dispersal. For our purpose such a dispute is irrelevant: it is enough to know that the ancient Germans, like the Celts and Greeks, chose names composed of two roots. For example, the Greek name Thrasybulos combines the concepts "brave" and "counsel," just as the German name Conrad does. The concepts, but not the Indo-European roots, were identical. (36)

The roots used in primitive Germanic names were general concepts. For example, *rik* (cognate with Latin *rex* and *regnum*) could mean either "rule" or "ruler," as could the root *wald* (cognate with English "wield"). Likewise, *athel* could mean "noble," "nobility" or "nobleman." The asterisks (*) in the above examples signify that the words have not been preserved in their given form but have merely been reconstructed or postulated from later linguistic evidence. A few Germanic name-roots survived intact long enough to be recorded more or less unchanged, for example, *athel* and

hrotho appeared in many Anglo-Saxon names such as Aethelraed the Unready, king of Wessex, Aethelstan, king of Mercia, and Hrothgar, the lord and kinsman of Beowulf.
(37)
If these last three names had been preserved in southern Germany instead of in England, they would have appeared as *Edelrat, Edelstein,* and *Ruediger.* To understand these changes, we must consider the High German sound shift, a second sound shift that followed the first almost a millenium later. This sound shift, also described by the Grimm brothers, distinguished the South German dialects from all the other Germanic languages. This High German sound shift, which altered most consonants, began soon after the Alemanni and Bavarians reached the Alps following the collapse of the Roman Empire.
(38)
The High German soundshift gradually spread northward into central Germany and affected standard German, while the North Germans clung to the unshifted consonants of the other Germanic languages such as Dutch and English. Thus the German dialects were divided into High German in the south and Low German in the north. Many of the names we shall discuss were North German and were therefore unaffected by the High German sound shift. On the other hand, with the increase of literacy and the spread of the High German written standard language into northern Germany, many Low German names have taken on standard spelling. For example, the spellings of Kock, Groote, and Schaper have often become Koch, Grosse, and Schaefer; and the names are pronounced accordingly.
(39)
Once a gentleman named Holthusen asked me the meaning of his name, and I explained that it meant "forest house," being the Low German form of Holtzhausen. He was highly indignant when I said "Low German" and assured me that his people had been perfectly respectable. What he did not understand was that "High German" refers to the southern highlands of Germany, while "Low German" refers to the low coastal plain in the north. Boats go down the Rhine in a northwesterly direction from Basel to Rotterdam and down the Elbe in a northwesterly direction from Dresden to Hamburg. Because maps often hang on walls with north at the top, we say "up north" and "down south," just as the Germans say "up in Schleswig" (*oben in Schleswig*) and "down in Bavaria" (*unten in Bayern*), so it is sometimes hard to

remember that High Germany is in the south and Low
Germany is in the north.   (40)

Of greatest interest to us in the High German sound shift
are the changes of the new voiceless stops *p* and *t* (when
initial) into the voiceless affricates *pf* and *ts* (written *z*) and
the changes of *p*, *t*, and *k* (when medial or final) into *f*, *s*,
and *ch* (pronounced as in Bach). Also important were the
changes of the voiced stops *b*, *d*, and *g* to the voiceless stops
p, *t*, and *k*. Because of this shift, the English words "plow,"
"hope," "toe," "water," and "break" are cognate with German
Pflug, hoffen, Zeh, Wasser, and *brechen*; and English "door"
is cognate with the High German word *Tor*. At the end of a
syllable *k* was shifted to *ch* in all dialects; but at the beginning of a syllable it was shifted only in Switzerland, and there
only in pronunciation, not in spelling, so it did not change
the standard spelling of names beginning with *k*. As a result,
"King" and *Koenig* are cognates, whereas in the Germanic
root **rik* the final *k* was shifted in High German to *ch* (*rich*).
This shift of *k* explains the different endings of English
"book" and German *Buch*. The *b* and *g* shifted only in the
Upper German dialects of the far south, where they are
reflected in variants such as Pichler-Buehler and Kugel-
Gugel.   (41)

Simultaneously with the sound shift in some areas, and
soon thereafter in others, the *h* was dropped before *l* and *r*,
as it was also in English. Likewise, *w* was dropped before *r*
as in English pronunciation, but not in spelling (Cf. "wretch"
and *Recke*). Starting in the south a short time later was the
change of *th* to *d* (*thing* became *ding*). The *th* in modern
German names should always be pronounced as *t* because the
h in the digraph *th* was introduced into spelling in the
sixteenth and seventeenth centuries in an attempt to gain
elegance, since *th* appeared in many words taken from the
Greek via Latin. Therefore the *h* should be ignored in
pronouncing German names like Walther and Goethe. (42)

Soon after the High German sound shift *sl*, *sm*, *sn*, and *sw*
became *schl*, *schm*, *schn*, and *schw* so that *schlecht, schmal,
schnee,* and *schwarz* are cognate with "slight," "small,"
"snow," and "swart." *St* and *sp* also acquired the *sh* sound,
but it is not indicated in the spelling. By chance, many
German-American names reverted to the older Germanic
pronunciation through the influence of English, which had
not gone through the High German sound shift. For example,
Schwartz sometimes became Swarts, Schnell sometimes

became Snell, and Stein was pronounced as Stein instead of as "Schtein." There were, of course, also changes in many vowels; but they played a lesser role in identifying names. Both the Germanic sound shift and the High German sound shift were infinitely complicated, with many apparent exceptions, most of which were explained by the Danish philologist Karl Verner. The simplified account given here serves only to clarify those changes that will help explain the present forms of German names. For example, as a result of the High German sound shift there are many pairs of German names that are similar except that one of them (or its roots) was altered by the sound shift, while the other was not. Examples are the Low German names Dormann, Dierdorp, and Timmermann as opposed to the High German names Thormann, Tierdorf, and Zimmermann. (43)

It would be impossible, and certainly unrewarding, to try to reproduce all names under discussion in the exact form they had at a given date in their given area, because the changes took place at different times in different places. We will therefore give all German names in their classical Middle High German form, the form in which they appeared in South German literature from the eleventh through the thirteenth centuries. As a result of the High German sound shift, the Proto-Germanic roots *athel*, *hari*, *hrotho*, *rik*, and *theod* became *edel*, *her*, *ruod*, *rich*, and *diet*. Therefore *Hludowics became Ludwig, *Hrothgar became Ruedeger, Hrothoberacht became Ruoprecht, Theodoric became Dietrich, and Hariman became Herman. (44)

Now that we have explained the origin of the roots used in German names, we might list some of them. It was mentioned that the Germans were a warlike people. Consequently, it is not surprising that their names often referred to war, weapons, and martial virtues, as well as to armies, victory, protection, and domination or rule. It is significant that the common German words *Schwert* (sword), *Schild* (shield), and *Speer* (spear), which were non-Indo-European, do not appear in old Germanic names. This confirms the theory that the old Germanic names were already composed in Indo-European times, before the Germans borrowed these three words, along with many maritime terms, from non-Indo-European neighbors. (45)

Among the name-roots designating battle were *badu*, *gund*, *hadu*, *hilti*, *not*, and *wic*, while *wal* designated a battleground. Among weapons we find *bart* (battle ax), *bil*, *brand,* and *ecke* (sword), *ger* (spear), *gies, giesel* and *ort* (point of spear or sword), *grim* (mask, helmet), *helm* (helmet), and *lind* and *rand* (shield). Among martial virtues we find *bald* (bold), *hart* (strong), *kuni* (brave), *mut* (courage), *neid* (hate), and *wille* (determination). *Macht* and *Megin* both meant "power" (as in "might and main"), as did *ellen* and *kraft.* *Liut* and *volk* both meant "people"; but, because all peoples were armed, they signified "army," as did *her.* It is to be noted that the ancient Germanic word for "folk" was the source of the Russian word *polk,* meaning "regiment."

(46)

Victory was expressed by *sieg,* protection by *burg, fried, wart,* and *wern,* and guardianship by *mund,* while mastery or rule was suggested by *wald* and *rich.* Pride in possessions is suggested by *arbi* (inheritance), *od* (treasure) and *uodal* (inherited lands). Since fame, the purpose of life, was best won on the battlefield, we find the roots *hruod* (illustrious), *mar* (renowned), *brecht* (bright), and *luod* (loud or illustrious). *Regin* (mind, intelligence) and *rat* (both council and counsel) can be classed as military terms, since councils were usually councils of war. *E* designated law, and *hein* designated home.

(47)

Certain predatory animals and birds also deserved name-sakes: *ar* or *arn* (eagle), *ram* and *hraben* (raven), *ber* (bear), *wolf* (wolf), and *lint* (dragon). Thus we get Arnold (*arn + hold*), Wolfram (*wolf + hraben*), Bermut (*ber + mut*). The wild boar (*ebur*), even though not predatory, was extremely brave and therefore offered the root found in Eberhart and many other names. Strangely, the harmless little hedgehog, the *igel,* also furnished the root in Igelhart, perhaps because of some shamanistic affinity, as was the case of *hirsch* (hart). The swan, although inoffensive, furnished the name-root *swan,* but at first only for women, as in Swanhild. The non-European lion, when finally introduced by the Bible and literature, and perhaps by royal menageries, supplied the first root in Leonhart, probably formed through analogy with Bernhart and Wolfhart. Among the few peaceful concepts we find *fruot* (wise), *hold* (feal to one's lord, cognate with "beholden"), *trut* (dear); and *win* (friend), and we also find *ans* and *god* (god) and *alb* or *alf* (elf).

(48)

From the small sample of name-roots listed above we can make innumerable compounds, such as Albwin, Ansgar, Anshelm (St. Anselmus), Baldwin, Dietbald, Dietmar, Friedrich, Gunther, Hadubrand, Helmbrecht, Helmut,

Heribrand, Hildebrand, Luther, Meinhart, Reinhart, Siegfried, Sigismund, Volker, Walther, Wernher, Willebald, and many more. Most of these roots could occupy either the first or the second place in the compound, for example, we find both Friedgund and Gundfried and Gundhild and Hildegunde. However, some, like *diet, edel,* and *sieg* could only occupy the first place, while some, like *mund* (guardianship), could only occupy the second. As a result, we find Siegmund and Dietrich but not Mundsieg or Richdiet. Two popular roots, *engel* and *land,* now mean "angel" and "land." If Engelhart was a pre-Christian name, then *engel* must have had another meaning, perhaps the tribal name "Angle." In Lambrecht (*landberacht*) and Roland (*Hrodoland*), the root *land* must have had some meaning other than "land," perhaps "brave," or else it may have been corrupted from *nand* (risk).   (49)

Not only men, but also women, bore warlike names, such as Gertraut (spear + beloved), Gerwig (spear + battle), Gundhilt (battle + battle), Hildegunde (battle + battle), Kriemhild (helmet + battle), Kunigunde (brave + battle), and Waltraut (battlefield + beloved). To be sure, Germanic women did not actually fight; but in his *Germania* Tacitus tells us how the women accompanied their men into battle and acted as cheer leaders, war being the chief sport of the time. Besides that, women could transmit warlike virtues to their sons through their names; for, as we have seen, names exerted a power of their own. Today most Germans assume that Rosamund, Roselind, and Roswitha mean Rosemouth, Rosegentle, and Rosewhite; but, in actuality, they are composed of the root *hros* (warhorse) combined with *mund* (guardianship), *lind* (dragon or shield), and *switha* (swift, brave). Familiar with Latin, the clerics assumed that Rosamunda came from *rosa munda* (pure rose) and referred to the Virgin Mary. We will, however, devote little time to feminine names because this study is concerned only with surnames, which patriarchal societies generally derive from male progenitors. Nevertheless, some feminine names and words did produce place names, which, in turn, formed surnames. For example, the Virgin Mary gave the city name Marienborn (Mary's spring), which in turn gave the surname Marienborner; and the Nonnengasse (convent alley) gave the surnames Nonngasser and Nunnengasse.   (50)

In ancient days the two roots of an Indo-European name had usually reflected some mental association as in Adelbrecht (illustrious through birth), Wolfhart (as strong as a wolf), Sigismund (guardianship resulting from victory), and Dietrich (ruler of the people). In some cases the root *fried* would seem to contradict its partner, for example in Gundfried (battle peace) and Friedgund (peace battle). However, we should remember that war was the normal state: as Tacitus put it, a nation not at war was stagnating. Therefore we should not think that **frithu* (the earlier form of *fried*) had anything in common with the Christian concept of peace, rather it meant "protection" and even "defensive alliance." Consequently, Gundfried would suggest "security won through battle" and Friedrich would suggest "ruler of an alliance." Today most people think that a *Friedhof* (cemetery) is a place of peace, but actually it is a "protected yard," the German word *fried* in this context meaning "walled," as in *bergfried* (belfry). When I was a graduate student in Zurich, I took a room at a pension called the Friedegg (pronounced freet eck and meaning walled field). The other Americans knew it only as the Fried Egg. (51)

Whereas the name roots had once been meaningfully combined, in time the roots were chosen with no thought of logical connection. Each family had its favorite roots, which it attached at random to other roots, perhaps to those featured by the family with whom it was being allied through marriage. If a man named Wolfhart married a woman named Gertraut, they might name their son Wolfger, even though wolves do not use spears. Likewise, we find names like Arnolf (eagle + wolf) and Wolfram (wolf + raven), even though these creatures had different virtues. Also, there were tautologies like Richwald (ruler + ruler) and Hildegunde (battle + battle). Eventually the roots were combined entirely mechanically. Some of the old Germanic roots eventually coalesced; both Gerwalt (spear + rule) and Gerhold (spear + loyal) became Gerold. (52)

While Germanic names originally consisted of two roots, they were often shortened. For example, Adolf, Arnold, Bernhard, Gerhard, and Konrad could be shortened to Alf, Anno or Arnd, Benno or Bernd, Gert, and Kurt or Kunz. Likewise, Dietrich, Eberhart, Rudolf, and Uodalrich could give Dirk, Ewert, Rolf, and Uozo. Often a shortened form could have derived from any one of several longer forms: Otto might come from Otfried, Otmar, or Otward; Brand could have represented Hildebrand, Hadubrand, or Heribrand; and Wolf could have derived from Wolfbrecht, Wolfhart, or Wolfram. Often the shortened form of a name provided compound names. For example, Benshoff (Bernhard's farm) was derived from Bernhard via Benno.   (53)

The shortened form was often a pet name (*Kosename*), yet it was officially valid even in the case of emperors. Surprisingly, Attila, the scourge of God, was known by a pet name, it being a diminutive of the Gothic word *Atta*, "father." After passing through the High German sound shift, it became the name Etzel, which has been brought to America as a surname. While Attila was a bogeyman in Western Europe, the Etzel of German legend was a generous overlord, whom it was an honor to serve, a sort of Arthur and Charlemagne combined. Pet names are often so far removed from their base forms as to be unrecognizable. One could hardly guess that Peg is a pet name from Margaret or that Ted and Teddy are pet names from either Edward or Theodore. Such metamorphoses did not occur in one fell swoop. Margaret was shortened to Marg, Marg became Meg, and then Meg became Peg. Similar steps occurred in forming pet names like Theiss from Matthias (via Thiass and Thiess) and Bartel from Bartholomaeus. In time these pet names became surnames. Sometimes the shortened form is not immediately recognizable because it went back to an earlier form of the name. The English name Hank and the German name Heink do not look like Henry and Heinrich, but they do look somewhat like the earlier forms Henrik and Heinrik.   (54)

The very terms "pet name" and "shortened form" must be used advisedly. When one says Bill instead of William, it may show affection, but it may also show mere laziness, in which case it is actually only a shortened form. It would be difficult to ascertain the precise nature and degree of affection expressed by the names in the well-known lines, "Father calls me William, Mother calls me Will, Sister calls me Willie, but the fellows call me Bill." Heintzelein can hardly be called a "shortened" form of Heinrich. In my childhood gang there was a boy named John, but we called him Johnny with the Nubbin on the End of his Nose "for short." In the early stages of this book I used the term "pet name," but gradually I replaced it with the symbol < , meaning "derived from," thus leaving it to the reader to decide whether or not the shortened form indicated affection.   (55)

As the Roman Empire crumbled in the fifth and sixth centuries and the northern barbarians invaded Britain, Gaul, Spain, and Italy, they brought their names with them to the lands they conquered. The names of the invaders, as the ruling class, were soon adopted by many of the conquered populaces, with dire results for the names. Most of all, the Romanized Celts in France could not master the harsh consonants of the invaders' names and dropped many of them. Thus Henrik became Henri, Theodoric became Thierry, and Willihalm became Guillaume. Most of the names that we consider typically French today were once Germanic: Albert (Athalbrecht), Arnaud (Arnhold), Bertram (Berachtram), Gautier (Walthari), Louis (Hludowics), Renault (Reginwald), Robert (Hrothoberacht), Roger (Hrothgar), Roland (Hrotholand), and Thibault (Dietbald). The same held for Italy, where we find Alberto, Arnoldo, Enrico, Gualtieri, Guido (Wido), Gulielmo, Leonardo (Leonhard), Ludovigo, Orlando, Ottone (Otto), Rinaldo (Reginwald), Ruggiero (Hrothogar), Umberto (Hunberacht or Helmbrecht), and a host of others. In Spain, the most common names, such as Alfonso (*athel* + *fons*, noble + ready) and Hernandez (*fardi* + *nantha*, journey + risk) were inherited from the Gothic invaders. (56)

After the Norman invasion of England in 1066, most Anglo-Saxon names (still clearly Germanic) were replaced by French cognates. These were no longer so clearly Germanic as they had been after being introduced into Gaul by the Frankish invaders. Instead of Hrothgar, Athelbrecht, and Reginwald, we therefore find Roger, Albert, and Reynold. (57)

CHAPTER TWO

Surnames - Their Need and Origin

As the population increased after the migrations, it became necessary to distinguish between the various individuals in the community who shared a common name. This could be done, among other ways, by reference to a person's parentage, his residence, a terrain or topographical feature near his dwelling, his profession, his employer, his appearance, or his behavior. (58)

In Scandinavia, a man was often designated as the son of his father. Niel, the son of Lars, would be called Niel Larson, but his son Peer would be Peer Nielson, not Peer Larson. The same system of patronymics was once common in Germany. Arnold's son Berthold might have been designated Arnolds Berthold or Berthold Arnolds, just as Hinrich's son Hans might have been called Hans Hinrichs or Hans Hinrichssen. In the case of names like Arnolds and Hinrichs, the *s* eventually became a fixed part of the name and no longer suggested first generation descent. In other words, Heinz Hinrichs may have been the son of Hinrichs and the grandson of Hinrich, just as Felix Mendelssohn was the son of Mendelssohn, not of Mendel. We shall see that names sometimes indicated employment rather than descent, as in the case of the ecclesiastical names Pabst, Bischof, and Moench. The same was sometimes true of other names that could be mistaken for patronymics. While Hubers Hans, or Hans Huber, was probably Huber's son, he might also have been Huber's hired hand, as everyone in the village would know. (59)

As family names became fixed, Huber's Hans may have adopted the surname Huber and transmitted it to his children, even if they served other families. A similar phenomenon occurred in the American South after emancipation. The slaves had no surnames; they were known as "the Pinckney's Jim" or "the Middleton's Jupiter." As freedmen, these two may have become Jim Pinckney and Jupiter Middleton, unless they preferred to choose the names of neighboring planters. The surname Hubers could possibly come from the place name Hubers, a shortened form for Hubershof (Huber's farm). Although patronymics were the rule, there were a few cases of metronymics, or surnames from the mother, perhaps from a widow or an unwed mother. Examples are Elsohn

(Else's son), Figge (Sophia's son), Grett (Margaretha's son), and Anneshansli (Anna's Hans).   (60)

Noble families customarily assumed the name of their chief castle, as was the case of the Hapsburgs and Hohenzollerns. The owners of Wolkenstein Castle were the von Wolkensteins, or the Wolkensteiners. However, if they sold Wolkenstein Castle and moved elsewhere, they dropped their old appellative and took on the name of their new seat. Even humble people could sometimes be identified by the names of their residences: for example, the Josef who lived in Straatmannshaus was sometimes called Josef Straatmann, but only as long as he lived there. If he sold the house, the buyer received the name Straatmann along with the house. Already in the thirteenth century a German poet named Heinrich Hessler explained that Heinrich was his right name and that Hessler was the name of his house. It is understandable that the inventor of moveable type wished to be known by the name of his house, Gutenberg (good mountain), rather than by his true name, Gensfleisch (goose flesh).   (61)

The name of the house sometimes appeared on a shield in front of the house with an illustration for the benefit of illiterates. These illustrations often had religious significance: not only the angel but also the eagle, lion, lamb, and ox had religious significance, they being the creatures that accompanied the four Evangelists in church art. If the house sign hung before a business establishment, it often designated the wares sold or the services rendered; and this explains many German names such as Fisch (fish) or Tuchscherer (cloth shearer).   (62)

Sometimes a man was named for his place of business. If a tavern were called *zum Goldenen Loewen* (to the Golden Lion), *zum Rothen Hirsch* (to the Red Stag), or *zum Schwarzen Adler* (to the Black Eagle), the proprietor might have been called Loewe, Hirsch, or Adler. Regardless of the name of the establishment, the proprietor (*Wirt*) might be called Wirt or Wirth, or else Krug, Krueger, or Krieger, since the word *Krug* (pitcher) often designated a pub. Regardless of what the dictionary might say about the word *Krieger*, the name Krieger did not designate a soldier. Since taverners hung out a sprig of greenery to announce the arrival of new wine, they might be called Zweig (branch), or Busch (bush). According to popular wisdom, such advertisement should be unnecessary because "good wine needs no bush."   (63)

Many years ago a German colleague of mine named Busch, seeing my interest in names, suggested that I run an advertisement in the *New York Times* offering to interpret names. I did so; and the first request I received was from a widow named Busch. Suspecting that she might not care to have had a husband descended from tavern keepers, I answered that the name Busch could be either the sprig hanging in front of a tavern or else the *Helmbusch*, or crest on a knight's helmet. It is easy to guess which interpretation she preferred. (64)

The words *Haus* (house) and *Haeuser* (the occupant of a house) provided many names. Since most people lived in houses, these simple words would have had little power of differentiation, so we can assume that the present names Haus, Haeuser, and Heuser are usually shortened forms of compounds such as Althaus (old house), Neuhaus (new house), or Scheraus (house where cloth or sheep are sheared). The American forester family Weyerhaeuser once lived in a house by a *Weiher* or fish pond (from Latin *vivarium*). Whereas the word *Haeuser* is now the plural of *Haus*, it used to denote the occupant, not the plural, of *Haus*. The plural used to be the same as the singular (*hus*), as is indicated by dative plural place names like Holthusen, Schaffhausen (sheep houses) and Niederhausen (lower houses). If one dwelled on a road, one might be called Gass, Gassner, or Gessner, or else Bahn or some name ending in *weg*. (65)

In parts of Germany *aeu* and *eu* are pronounced like English "eye" (remember the Tannenbaum, a branch of which *freut* [gives joy] even in winter when it *schneit* [snows]). Therefore Haeuser is often pronounced Hizer, as in the case of James Lighthizer (from Leithaeuser), a county executive in Maryland, and also in the name Anhaeuserbusch, which recalls the ditty:

A boy fell off Anhaeuserbusch
And tore his pants to Schlitz.
He rose a sad Budweiser boy.
Pabst yes and Pabst no.

The baseball player Orel Hershiser's name derived from Hirschhaeuser, or "stag houses." Since the American name Rukeyser would make no sense if divided into *ru* and *keyser*, it must have been Ruckheyser, meaning the occupant of a house on a ridge. (66)

As in the case of Rukeyser, families were often designated by the terrain features near which they lived, such as hills, dales, mountains, valleys, fields, and forests. If a Johann lived near a *buehl* (hill), he might be called Johann Buehl, or Buehler (and in America Beeler or Bealer). Or if, as was usually the case, the hill was more precisely defined, such as Kraehbuehl (crow hill), then the resulting name would be Kraehbuehl (in America, Craybill, Greybill, and some forty other forms). If a man lived at, but not on, the *Buehl*, he might be called Ambuehl (in America, also Ample). Another kind of hill is a *kofel*, a sort of monticule or projection jutting up from the slope of a mountain, which might give a man living on it the name of Kofler. If there were two such chimney-like projections, an upper one (*Oberkofel*) and a lower one (*Unterkofel*), they might furnish the names Oberkofler and Unterkofler Oberkaufer and Unterkaufer.(67)

Far more numerous, of course, are names derived from *berg*, the commonest name for mountain. In addition to many families named Berg and Berger, there were far more named for specific mountains, such as Oberberg, Unterberg, Gruenberg, Silberberg, Koenigsberg, Heidelberg, and hundreds of others. In Switzerland, Austria, and Bavaria, where there are many mountains, names in *berg* and *berger* are especially frequent. The peak of the mountain was the *Horn*, as in Berghorn and Matterhorn.   (68)

The surnames based on terrain features or place names had at first been preceded by the preposition *von*, as in von Oberberg; but in time the preposition was dropped in most of Germany by all but the nobility and became a sign of rank. Commoners were satisfied with the name Oberberg or Oberberger. Nevertheless, some people, especially in Switzerland and along the Netherlands border, retained the *von* with no pretensions to nobility, as in the case of Von der Weit and Vonholt. Other prepositions, like *in* and *zu* were also usually dropped, though they occasionally remain as in Indorf and Inhoff. In dem Winkel (in the wooded valley) became Winkel or Winkler, and zem Stege (at the sty) became Steg or Steger. The name Austermuehle means "out of the mill," not "Oyster Mill."   (69)

Sometimes the preposition was not entirely lost, as when zum Eichelsweg (at the acorn path) became Meichelsweg and when in den Eichen (in the oaks) became Neichen (just as in English "a nadder" became "an adder" and "an ickname" became "a nickname"). In the case of Admiral Zumwald the preposition has remained, as it has also in the names Vomberg (from the mountain) and Vormwald (before the

forest). The preposition and article have regularly remained in Dutch names like Vandergrift, Vanderbilt, and van der Ren. Similar phenomena appear in English names like Attenborough and Atterbury, both mean "at the borough."
(70)
Since most flat lands in Germany are cultivated, the forests are largely on mountain ranges. As a result, the word *wald* (forest) usually designates a mountain range, as is the case of the Schwarzwald (Black Forest), Boehmerwald (Bohemian Forest), and Thueringer Wald (Thuringian Forest). In and near Austria a steep slope is a *Leite*, a word giving the names Leite, Leitner (Lightner in America), Hangleitner, etc. This name has an exact English equivalent in the name Banker, which denotes not a financier but a man who lives on a bank or slope. A person occupying a house on a *Leite* would be a Leithaeuser (the previously mentioned Lighthizer). Other names for slopes are *Fuhr, Gaeh, Gand Halde, Ruetsche, Schief, Schrudde,* and *Stechen.* A man residing on or near a *Stade* (landing) might be called Stade, just as a man living near a bridge might be called Brueckner and a man living near a church might be called Kircher or Kirchner.
(71)
There are relatively few name roots denoting forests. The most frequent is the root *wald* (cognate with English "wold" as in the Cotswolds). While *wald* always means "forest" in later names like Waldhausen, it must be differentiated from the older root *wald* meaning "rule," as in Walther (rule + army). A low or scrubby forest was a *busch*, as in Buschmann or Buschkirch (dweller or church in the low woods). A *horst* (cognate with the place-name root *hurst* in Lakehurst and Pinehurst) was a general word for a small forest or grove, whereas now it suggests an aerie or even a small military airbase, as in *Fliegerhorst.* A *hain* or *hein* was a grove, as in Hainmueller and Heindorf.
(72)
A rocky summit or crag was a *Stein* (stone), which was a good position for a castle, so we find castles with names like Steinfels (stone cliff), Steinburg (stone castle), and Altenstein (old mountain). In most names of this kind the root *stein* refers to a mountain, and therefore it is so translated in our appended list even though, in some cases, the root *stein* could have referred to the castle itself, which was inevitably built of stone. Logic suggests that *Steinberg* means "stone mountain," whereas *Bergstein* means "mountain rock." A man

dwelling on or near a *Stein* might be named Stein or Steiner
(in America often Stine, Stone, and Stoner).   (73)
In the name Steinert the last consonant is not part of the
root: it is merely an excrescent *t*, that is, a *t* that formed to
interrupt the *r*, which was still trilled in Germany at the
time surnames were being introduced. In some names the
root *stein* does not designate a cliff or crag, but merely a
mineral substance, as in Steinhauer (stone carver) and
Edelstein (noble stone, jewel). Other terms for hills, mountains, peaks, and ridges are *Boll, Brink, Gipfel, Huebel,
Huegel, Kamm, Knoll, Kopf, Kuppe, Nase,* and *Stauf.*   (74)
This might be an appropriate time to explain why there is
so often a dative ending on the adjective describing a terrain
feature, such as the *en* suffixed to the *alt* in the name
Altenstein. This goes back to the previously mentioned days
when place names were still preceded by a preposition, as
was formerly the case in English tavern names such as "To
the Red Rose." Originally, one would have said "at the old
stone" (*zum alten stein* or *am alten stein*); and in both cases
the place name would end up as Altenstein. The same would
hold of Breitenbach (*zum breiten bach*, "at the broad brook")
and Neuemburg (*zur neuen burg*, "at the new castle.")   (75)
Names were suggested not only by hills and mountains,
but also by valleys, the most frequent root being the *Tal*
(formerly *Thal*) which is found in Rosenthal, Lilienthal, and
Thalmann. In Alpine regions a bowl-like valley is a *gruob*,
and a man dwelling in one might be dubbed Gruber. A
narrow gorge is a *Schlund*, so the Heinrich living in or near
one may have been called Heinrich Schlund.   (76)
People were often designated by the stream or creek on
which they lived. As in the case of the name Berg, the name
Bach (brook) was often a shortened form of a compound
name. The appended list of names contains scores of compounds containing *bach*, examples being Auerbach, Bacher,
Bachmann, and Rauschbach. In Pennsylvania the name Bach
and its compounds are often written as Baugh because the
English scribes knew the sound *ch* only in Scots names.
These still retained the sound and indicated it with *gh*,
whereas the sound had long since ceased in English and
survived only in the archaic spelling of words like "through"
and "though." Unfortunately, the first syllable of these
Pennsylvania names with *baugh* are often corrupted beyond
recognition. In Pennsylvania the names Bach and Bacher also
appear as Pack and Packer.   (77)

A *Bach* is sometimes larger than a brook: one would translate *Forellenbach* as "trout stream," rather than as "trout brook," just as a *Rauschbach* would be a "rushing stream" rather than a "rushing brook." An *Altmuehlbach* would surely be an "old mill stream" rather than an "old mill brook." In personal names, the ending *bach* was practically interchangeable with *becker*. A family living on the Winsbach could call itself either Winsbach or Winsbeker. (As we shall see, when standing alone, the name Becker most often meant a baker.) The foot-crossing through a brook was a *furt* or *fort*, as in Frankfurt. (78)

The word *Ach*, which is cognate with Latin *aqua* (water) and designates a river, is found in many place names such as Charlemagne's capital Aachen and in Achebach and Anderach. This ending *ach* has now coalesced with the ending *ach* from *achi* (terrain) as in Steinach (stone terrain) and Dornach (thorny area) and also with *ach* from Latin *acum* (estate) as in Breisach and Andernach. Other words for streams are *born* and *bronn*, both of which appear in American names such as Aalborn (eel stream) and Bornemann (stream man). The word *brunnen*, which designated either a spring or a well, is found in the names Brunner and Brunnholtz. Many people took the name of the river near which they resided, as in the case of Johannes Tauber and Rembrandt van Ryn. (79)

Although Germany has been well drained for the last few centuries, it was, as Tacitus reported, a land of vast swamps. As a result we find many name-roots referring to marshes, bogs, and swamps such as *Bruehl, Bruch, Lache, Mar, Mies, Moor, Moos, Ohl, Pfutze, Pfuhl, Schlade, Schlier, Siech, Seifen, Struth,* and *Sutte*. Unfortunately, it is not possible to translate names containing these roots precisely without knowing from which areas their bearers came. For example, the word *bruch* (in Low German spelled *brock, broek,* and *brook*, and cognate with English "brook" and "brake") had various meanings, but it usually meant a damp clearing in a swampy forest. Since that definition is too cumbersome, we will translate it as "brake" as in "canebrake." The same name, Bruch, can also designate a quarry. The root *mar* meaning "swamp," as in Marbach and Marburg, should not be confused with the root *mar* meaning "famous," as found in Dietmar and Marbold. It is to be remembered that a surname like Marbach may commemorate a place that had long been drained before the family name was assumed. (80)

A marsh or bog is often indicated by a root meaning reeds or bullrushes, as in the case of *riet* and *reth* in Riet and Rethmeyer. The concept of "marsh mountain" sounds contradictory, yet we find it expressed by the names Hallenberg, Kellenberg, Marberg, Mosberg, Morsberger, and Moersberger. The name suggests a hill rising out of a marsh or swamp, as is expressed by our Southern word "hammock" (for hummock). However, in some areas there are actually marshes (*moor*) on the tops of mountains, as in the Sauerland Mountains of Westphalia. The word *mor* should not be confused with English "moor," which usually denotes a dry heath, which in German is a *Heide*.   (81)

To drain the many marshes, one had to dig many ditches and build many dams and dikes (*dam*, *dick*, *diek*). The High German cognate *Teich* means not the dike but the pond behind it, or any pond. A *lache* can be a pond as well as a bog, and a *fizer* or *fuetze* (from Latin *puteus*) could be either a pond or a puddle. A *See* is not a sea, but a lake. In marshy areas the word *Berg* is only relative. In Alpine regions it designates a sizeable pile of rocks and earth, but on the North German coastal plain it might be more modest, as in the case of Koenigsberg and Wittenberg. Similarly the root *brink* is translated here as "hill," while it may mean an area in a marsh elevated just enough to remain dry and arable.   (82)

A large number of surnames may be based on river names even if they have other meanings as well. For example, the name Tauber could suggest the raiser or seller of pigeons, but it may also designate a dweller on the River Tauber. Like many other rivers in western and southern Germany, the Tauber may have derived its name from a Celtic word. Just as most American rivers have Indian rather than European names, many German rivers have pre-Germanic names, mostly Celtic, some of which, in turn, derived from earlier Ligurian names. The Germanic invaders learned the names of the streams, swamps, hills, etc. from the Celtic inhabitants of the areas they occupied, but they did not understand their meanings. Therefore they added the words for stream, swamp, and hill to the native name. This gave forms like *albach*, *ascbach*, and *erbach*, which were eventually folk-etymologized into Allenbach (eel brook), Eschbach (ash tree brook), and Erlbach (alder brook). Of course, some brooks named Allenbach, Eschbach, and Erlbach may have

first been named by German-speaking people and therefore
not be a case of folk-etymology. (83)
Many names were based on words for fields or pastures.
The words *Acker* and *Feld* (field) supplied many American
names such as Acker, Ackers, and Ackerman, as well as Feld,
Felder, Feldman, and Rheinfelder. Low land, usually lying
along a body of water, was an *au,* as in Reichenau on Lake
Constance and also in the surnames Aumann and Aumueller.
A man living on an *au* was an *auer,* as in Reitenauer and
Rheinauer. Another word for meadow was *Wiese,* and a man
living on it was a Wiessner or a Wiesmann. Only in Switzerland does one find *matt* (cognate with English mead and
meadow), which designated a meadow that was mowed and
is found in the surname Durrenmatt. The word *Weide*
denoted a pasture, as in the name Fuellenweide (foals
meadow); and so did the word *Anger,* as in names like Anger,
Angermann, and Angermeyer. Smaller than a field is a
Garten (garden), which may be a *Baumgarten* (orchard), two
words that furnish many names such as Gaertner and
Baumgaertner. (84)
There is one very common root that is hard to define,
namely, *eck* (corner), as in the previously mentioned *Friedegg.*
Although the meaning "corner" is often acceptable, the root
eck (or *egg*) often has a vague meaning of "place," as in the
expression *in allen Ecken* (cf. "In every corner under the
sun"), where no angle is implied. Therefore, it will be
rendered as "place" in the following list. (85)
The reader is reminded that onomastics is not an exact
science but sometimes requires an educated guess. While *eck*
clearly means "corner" in the word *Eckstein,* the name Eckhof
could mean either "corner farm," or more likely, "oak farm,"
the latter being more likely because of varients like Eichhof,
Eickhof, and Eykhof. In the old Germanic name Eckhard, *eck*
definitely means "sword." (86)
It will be noted that many surnames based on terrain
features end with the agent suffix *er* (from Latin *arius*). This
was especially common in South Germany, especially in
Austria, with the result that, when the Salzburger Pro-
testants were banished in 1731 and settled in East Prussia,
the natives there assumed that all people whose names ended
in *er* must be Salzburgers. Names like Acher, Bacher,
Gruber, Kofler, and Steiner usually implied that the bearer
was the proprietor of a farm at the said terrain feature: if he
sold the farm, he left the name with it and took on the name

of his new property. The *er* ending often developed an excresent *T*, as in Bachert and Steinert. (87)

In English it is easy to distinguish in writing between a terrain feature and a proper name, because only the latter is capitalized. For example, we say "he went to the white oaks," but also "he went to White Oaks." The difficulty in distinguishing between *Flurnamen* (terms for terrain features) and proper names is well illustrated in the boundary descriptions (*Markbeschreibungen*) found in medieval documents describing the lands donated to monasteries and other religious organizations. Most of these descriptions were written in Latin, only the terrain features and place names being left in German; the Wurzburg boundary descriptions are an exception, being written solely in German. In tracing the boundaries of the donated lands, these valuable documents name numerous terrain features that now appear in American names, including: *acha* (river), *berg* (mountain), *brunno* (spring), *buohha* (beeches), *clingo* (rapid stream), *furt* (ford), *gruoba* (round valley), *houc* (hill), *loh* (low forest), *ror* (reeds), *seo* (lake), *sol* (pond), *stein* (mountain), and *struot* (swamp). (88)

Rural people often derived their names from the kind of trees they lived among or near. If one of two Josefs lived near the oaks while the other lived near the linden, then the first might have been called Josef Eichner or Aichner and the second Josef Linde or Lindner. Similarly, a man named Erlenhaus must have lived in a house among the alders, while a man named Eschenbach may have lived on a brook with overhanging ash trees, if not one containing *Aesche* (graylings). A farmer living among the birches might be called Birkenmeyer, or just Birk, Birker, or Birkli. A man named Ulmer may have lived near the elms, unless possibly his forebears had come from the city of Ulm. The word *Tanne* (fir), which is found in names like Tannenbaum and Tanhoeffer, also appears as in Dannenbaum and Danhoeffer. Because firs are the dominant tree in some areas, the root sometime merely connotes a forest of any kind, not just of firs. Although the word *Kiefer* denotes both a pine tree and a jaw bone, the name Kieffer, as we shall see, most often meant a barrel maker. In the case of fruit trees and fruit, like Apfelbaum and Birnbaum, the name probably signifies the pertinent orchard owner or fruit dealer. (89)

When I was swimming on the University of Heidelberg swimming team shortly after the Berlin Olympics of 1936, the latest and most popular backstroke was the "Kieffer stroke." Seeing no connection with pine trees, we concluded that the stroke got its name from the fact that the swimmer had to thrust up his chin in order to lower his head and thereby raise his legs for a flutter kick. Years passed before I learned that the stroke was named for its innovator, an American swimmer at the '36 Olympics, who had inherited his name from some German barrel maker. And this leads us to names derived from professions. (90)

The two oldest professions, for men, were hunting and fishing, which have given the names Jaeger and Fischer (Yeager and Fisher in America). In the late Middle Ages, when surnames were first being assumed, the fundamental profession was agriculture, which occupied about ninety-five percent of the population, rather than the five percent it occupies today in the developed nations. Consequently, many families were named Ackermann (field man), Bauer and Baumann (farmer), Felder or Feldmann (field man), and Pflug or Pflueger (plowman). The farmer's name might have derived from the nature of his farm. If he had one *huob* (hide of land), then he was a Huber; if he cultivated a *Schweighof* (cattle farm), then he was a Schweiger, Schwaiger, Schweighof, or Schweighofer (in America Swiger, Swiggert, or Swaggert, again with excrescent *t*). The name is not related to the noun *Schweiger*, meaning a silent man. A husbandryman was often named for the kind of beast or fowl he raised: for example Gais (goat), Kalb (calf), Lamm (lamb), Ochs (ox), Stier (steer), Stehr (wether), and Ziege (goat) or Ante or Entemann (duck raiser), Huhn (chicken), and Gans or Goos (goose). (91)

Many families received their names from the word *Hoff*, which originally meant a farmyard. The ancient Germanic king, who was merely the foremost peasant of the kinship, also had a *Hof*, which was larger than the other *Bauernhoefe*. Eventually the king's court, or *Koenigshof*, became more elegant, with many a *Hofmann*, or courtier, in attendance, such as the *Hofmeister*, or steward of the royal household. These words are now spelled with one *f* to show that the *o* is long (as in "hope"); but they used to have double *f*, as still found in most American names derived from them, such as Althoff, Althoffer, Hoffmann, and Neuhoff. (92)

Perhaps the most common name designating a farmer was Meyer or Mayer, which also had many other meanings. The word derived from the Latin word *major domus*, or the

keeper of the household. At first it referred to an important
official who was more or less the business manager of the
kingdom or the castle. Later it also referred to the bailiff
who managed an estate or farm. Eventually it denoted any
large farmer. Since this was the most usual meaning at the
time that surnames were being formed, that is the way it is
rendered in the appended list of names. A thirteenth-century
Austrian tale called *Meier Helmbrecht* tells of a peasant lad
who wished to become a knight but met a sad end. The story
is misnamed, the lad is not a *meier:* his father, who is
casually mentioned at the beginning, is the *meier*, a position
the son would have inherited only at his father's death or
retirement.   (93)

The name Meyer was so common that it became the
equivalent of *mann*, in fact, even interchangeable with it, so
that a man could be called either Kuhlmann or Kuhlmeyer.
It will be seen that many Jews took the name Meyer,
perhaps because of its similarity with the Hebrew name
Meir, the name of a famous medieval scholar. Sometimes
mann had no significance at all: Til and Tilmann were the
same name, as were Litz and Litzmann, all of them having
been derived from Dietrich and Ludwig. Likewise, *mann* and
er were equivalent in names like Bacher--Bachmann, Felder-
-Feldmann, and Aicher--Aichmann. Names like Neumeyer and
Neumann do not imply that the farmer was new but rather
that he was the proprietor of the Neuhoff, or New Farm.
Likewise, a Waldmeyer or Waldbauer did not have to live in
a forest, he may have been the proprietor of the Waldhoff,
which had once been in the woods before the surrounding
forests had been cleared. Another word for farmer was
Hausmann, literally "house man." That this word meant
"farmer" was proved when the Dutch humanist Roelof
Huysman latinized his name as Agricola.   (94)

If a countryman owned no land, he may have been a
Schaefer (shepherd), *Hirt* or *Hirte* (herdsman), or, in
Switzerland, a *Senn*. Or else he many have been a
Holtzhacker (woodcutter), *Kohlenbrenner* (charcoal burner), or
Aschenbrenner (ash burner). There were many other professions open to landless people, such as finding wild honey
(Zeidler) or gathering faggot (Ast). But this leads to the
subject of more specialized trades. The ancient Germans lived
in large family units, which provided most of their domestic
needs. The non-warriors, meaning the women, children,
elderly men, and serfs, not only farmed but also produced

most of the goods and artifacts needed in their culture. Gradually, certain individuals became adept at certain crafts and supplied goods not only for their own family group but also for neighbors and even strangers, with the result that the craft became a full time profession. In this case the person practicing the profession often assumed the name of the trade he practiced. (95)

Because of constant warfare, smiths were essential for making and repairing weapons; and secret powers were ascribed to them so that the name Schmidt was held in awe. Later there were other smiths, such as the *Hufschmidt* (blacksmith), *Nagelschmidt* (nailsmith), *Blechschmidt* (sheet metal smith), and *Messerschmidt* (knife smith or cutler). As a consequence there were many names including the root *eisen* denoting the people who produced or sold iron. Among other surnames designating professions we find Brauer (brewer), Binder, Fassbinder, or Boettcher (cooper), Gerber (tanner), Reeper and Seiler (rope maker), Schneider and Schroeder (tailor), Schumacher (shoemaker), Wagner (wainwright), Weber (weaver), and Zimmermann (carpenter). In addition we find hosts and taverners (Wirth and Kruger) and musicians and entertainers such as Geiger (fiddler), Trommer (drummer), Harfner (harpist), Tanzer (dancer) and Gauckler (acrobat). (96)

As time passed, the trade could become more specialized, the brewer could be *Bierbrauer* (beer brewer) and the tanner could be a *Weissgerber* or a *Rotgerber*, depending on whether he cured white or red leather. This might be cut into straps or belts by a *Riemenschneider*, or strap cutter. As the weaver became more specialized, he might employ a *Scherer* or *Tuchscherer* (cloth shearer) to cut off the Irish pennants protruding from his cloth. While the tanner prepared raw hides, the *Kirschner* or *Kuerschner* (furrier) prepared fine furs. In all these cases the profession was originally in apposition to the person and required a definite article: Peter der Schuster (Peter the shoemaker), Hans der Schneider (Hans the tailor), etc. (97)

The ancient Germans built their houses of wood, as is proved by Germanic roots in American names like Ahle (awl), Hammer (hammer), and Naegel (nails). Other names from carpentry are Drexler or Drechsler (turner), Tischler (cabinet maker), and Zimmermann (carpenter). The *l* in *Tischler* is not part of the root as it is in *Drechsler* and *Sattler* (saddler), which are composed of *Drechsel* and *Sattel* and the agent ending *er*. By error, names (and words) like Drechsler and Sattler were wrongfully divided into Drechs-ler and Satt-ler, thus causing people to think that *ler* was a functional agent-ending to be added to other roots like *tisch* (from Latin *discus*). The same faulty division was made of names like Gaert-ner (from *Garten*) and Oef-ner (from *Ofen*), thus producing a new agent-ending *ner*, which appeared in the recently mentioned names Lindner and Kirchner. The same phenomenon occurred in English when "a nadder" was erroneously divided into "an adder" and "an ickname" became "a nickname." (98)

Whereas most carpentry terms were of Germanic origin, the Germans did borrow the Roman word *scrinarius*, which designated a skilled joiner and later became the word and name Schreiner. In old Germanic sagas and ballads, the *burg* or borough was always made of wood, with the result that many feuds ended in a *Saalbrand* (hall fire), when the defenders chose to die in the flames rather than come out and surrender. After suffering raids from the Magyars in the tenth century, the Germans learned how to build stone fortifications like those of the Mediterranean and Arabic nations. (99)

Masonry was one of the most important skills learned from the Romans. The Latin word *murus* (wall) gave German *Mauer*, which in turn gave the word for a mason (*Maurer*), who might also be called a *Steinmetz*. (On the other hand, Hans Maurer may not have been a mason, he may have just lived on, or against, the city wall, in which case he would first have been called Hans auf der Mauer.) The Germans did, however, coin words from their own language for these imported skills: a stone cutter was a *Steinhauer* (stone hewer), a quarryman was a *Steinbrecher* (stone breaker), and a brickmaker was a *Steinbrenner* (stone burner). (100)

Upon occupying old Roman territory, the barbarian invaders learned many other skills they had never known or had practiced only crudely; and they often kept the Roman word, which in many cases went through the High German sound shift along with their native vocabulary. This was the case of the Latin word *cuparius* (barrel maker), which gave the English name Cooper. Altered by the High German sound shift, it became Kuefer or, in southern dialects, Kiefer or Kieffer, as in the aforementioned "Kieffer stroke." When the Latin word *catila* (kettle) went through the soundshift, it came out as *kessel*, which gave the name Kessler (maker or repairer of kettles). Likewise, the Latin word *tegula* (tile) passed through the soundshift to become *Ziegel*, which gave the professional name Ziegler (tiler or brickmason). (101) Perhaps Roman cooks were more skilled than German cooks, for the present German word for cook, *Koch*, is derived from Latin *coquus*, just as the name Pfister (baker) is derived from Latin *pistor*. The Germans also acquired two new words for "butcher": *Metzger* (from *matiarius*) and Metzler (from *macellarius*). A *Kellner* was the keeper of the wine cellar (*Keller*, from Latin *cellarium*). Tacitus tells us that the Germans had no wine, so they must have acquired all their art of viticulture from the Romans. The German word *Wein* was derived from Latin *vinum*, and the word *Winzer* (vintner) from *vinitor*, while the seller of wine, the *vinumcaupo*, ultimately gave the names Weinkauf and Weinkop. Tacitus makes it clear that, while the Germans had no wine, they did have beer. Nevertheless, the German word *Bier*, like English "beer," is derived from Latin *bibere* (to drink). (102) The name Mueller (from Latin *molinarius*) also reflects the Romans' more advanced technology, for the ancient Germans still had only the *quirn* (English "quern") or hand mill. Because there were so many kinds of mills, the name Mueller was as common as the name Meyer. The millers often acquired their names from the spot along the stream where their mills were located, such as Aumueller (mill on the meadow), Waldmueller (mill at the forest), etc. Apparently meaningless miller-names may have been shortened forms. While a Weissmueller ground white flour and a Braunmueller ground brown flour, it is unlikely that Schwartzmueller ground black flour (even if his brown flour became blackbread). It is more likely that his mill stood on the Schwartzbach and that he had first been called the Schwartzbachmueller. (103) Before the advent of store-bought clothes and shoes, tailors and shoemakers were in great demand and supply. The word *Schneider* originally meant "cutter," being analogous with the Old French word *tailleur*, from which we get "tailor." Another word for tailor was *Schroeder*, so that there are many American families named Schneider, Snyder, Shroder, and Schroeder (usually pronounced, and sometimes written, as Shrader). The most usual word for a shoemaker (and the source of the English word) was *Schumacher*, while the words *Schumann* and *Schubert* were also common. The Latin word *sutor* gave the German word *Schuster*. A man trained only to repair shoes, but not to make them, was a *Flickschuster*, which gives the American name Flick. As in the case of surnames based on place names and house names, professional names were not fixed initially. If Hans Schuster's son Heintz became a baker, he would become Heintz Beck or Heintz Becker, not Heintz Schuster. In time, however, professional names, like other names, became fixed and the cooper Carl Zimmermann may have inherited his name from his great-grandfather, the last carpenter in the family. (104)

When we speak of "Roman" arts and crafts, we should remember that the word is used in a general sense of everything from the Roman empire. The Romans were not the world's best craftsmen; they let their slaves, mostly foreigners, do much of their work for them. Therefore the "Roman" skills or sciences we praise may have come from Egypt, Cappadocia, Greece, Spain, or any other part of the far-flung Roman empire. For example, the Roman traders who visited the ancient Germans often came from Syria or Greece. Traders from the Roman world dominated trade in ancient Germany, just as the English and Scots did among the American Indians, who, like the ancient Germans, were warriors and disdained mercenary pursuits. Hence it is not surprising that the Latin word *caupo* (merchant), in its High German form *Kauf*, served as a root in the word *Kaufmann* (merchant). Later on, small retailers were Haacker, Hackermann, Hoeker, Haendler, or Kraemer, and the shopkeeper on the corner (Winkel) might have been called Winkel or Winkler. (105)

Like the Roman wine seller (*vinumcaupo*), many medieval German merchants took their name from the wares they sold, for in the highly regulated and guild-minded commerce of the Middle Ages merchants usually specialized in a single item. A seller of pepper (from Latin *piper*) was Pfeffer or Pfeffermann, the seller of salt was Salzer, Selzer, or Saltzmann, and the seller of sugar was Zucker or Zuckermann, the word *Zucker* having come from Arabic via Spanish *azucar*. The seller of herrings (usually caught in the Baltic Sea and salted) was called Hering. Numerous items supplied names for the people who manufactured them, sold them, or used them. Typical of the resulting names are Beil (ax), Gabel (fork), Kamm (comb), Kunckel (distaff), Loeffel (spoon), Messer (knife), and Teller (dish). A Hutzler sold dried fruit. (106)

Men who served in the military often gained their surnames from their military occupation or rank. At the time surnames were first being taken, most recruits became pikemen (*Landsknechte*, lansquenets), whereas the more fortunate ones became *Reuter*, or cavalrymen. The word *Reuter* and its synonym *Reiter* both came from the verb to ride (*reiten*), whereas the word *Ritter* first meant "trooper," being a member of a *rit* or cavalcade. In time *ritter* became the equivalent of French *chevalier* (knight) and was used only of the gentry. Those who served for pay were *Soeldner* (mercenaries, from Latin *solidarius*). (107)

The crossbow (*Armbrust*, folk etymology from Latin *arca balestra*) was still an effective weapon and gave the name Armbruster to both the user and the manufacturer of the weapon. The same was true of the *bogener*, who could either shoot or make bows. The *panzer* and the *bruenner* were the makers, rather than the wearers, of armor. A soldier who excelled and survived might become a *Webel* (sergeant), *Faehnrich* or *Faenner* (ensign), a *Hauptmann* (captain), or *Oberst* (colonel), or even *Marschall* (*marah*, horse + *scalc*, servant). A man who served a knight was a *Schildknecht*, or squire (literally, "shield knight"). (108)

The foremost man in a rural village was the *Bauernmeister* or village head man, also called the *Schultz*, *Scholz*, or *Schultheiss*. A larger town would have a *Burgermeister* and council of *Ratherren*, which gives the American name Rather, as in the case of Dan Rather. A surname referring to the higher offices usually indicated not descent, but rather employment. A man named Kaiser (emperor) was probably in imperial service, while a man name Koenig (king) was probably in royal service, unless perhaps he was persistently the *Schuetzenkoenig*, or winner of the markmanship contest. Employment is also suggested by the names Herzog (duke), Graf (count), Vogt (governor), Probst (provost), and Witzthum (vice-governor), the last three of these being from Latin *advocatus*, *propositus*, and *vice-dominus*. In addition to the higher officials, there were many more modest public servants such as public criers (Bellmann), bell ringers (Glocke) and official weighers (Waeger or Wagemann). Some of these services were rendered by "dishonorable" people, those who had no legal standing, like the skinner (Schinder or Abzieher) and court bailif (Scherg). (109)

Employment obviously produced the names Pabst (pope), Bischof (bishop), Abt (abbot), Pfaff (priest), and Moench (monk), since clergymen did not leave legitimate children to carry on their names. On the other hand, the sextons Sigrist, Mesner, Kirchner, and Kuester (think of Custer's last stand) may have had families with surnames taken from their profession. A Kentucky gentleman once named his sons Bishop, Commodore, Dean, and Major, with the result that later generations respected his family for having had so many titled members. (110)

The name Gott (God) was most often a shortened form of some name like Gottfried, Gotthelf, Gotthold, Gottlieb, or Gottschalk; but in some cases it may have been the nickname given to the actor who regularly played the role of God in a miracle play. Miracle plays may have contributed to the popularity of the names Adam and Eva, Maria Magdalena, Caspar, Melchior, and Balthasar (the Three Kings who brought gifts to Jesus), and other favorite roles in the plays. This was surely true of Puntzius (Pontius Pilate), who was hardly an exemplary character. (111)

People often gained their surnames from nicknames. (As mentioned, the word "nickname" is a false division of "an ickname," or an added name.) A common type of nickname comes from hair color or style, such as Red, Curly, Goldy, etc. In German we find the names Schwarz (brunet), Braun (brown haired), Roth (red haired), Weiss (blond), Krause, Kraus (curly), and Kraushaar (curly haired); and the name Gold may have sometimes referred to hair color, just as the name Kahl (bald) betokened the absence of hair. The name Rotbart, like its Italian form Barbarossa, could designate a man with either a red or a blond beard. As in the case of names from professions, all these nicknames had once been preceded by a definite article: Hans der Schwarze (Hans the brunet), and Klaus der Kraus (Klaus the curly haired). Nicknames could also result from the clothes one wore, especially if they were unusual or indicated the wearer's profession or status. Examples are Lederhos (leather breeches) and Bundschuh (laced footwear), both meaning peasant, Weisskittel (white smock), meaning miller or baker, and Gelbrock (yellow gown), meaning a Jew. People could also be teased about the food they ate, especially if it revealed their social status or rural tastes as in the case of turnips (Rueb) or sour beer (Sauerbier). (112)

Physical stature gave names such as Kurtz (short), Lang (tall), Gross (large), and Klein (small). The physical cruelty of the Middle Ages is well attested by instruments of torture

and by the popular merriment caused when they were used
publicly, so it is not surprising that mental cruelty is suggested by some of the nicknames inflicted at that time. A
man with a twisted body might be called Krumm (crooked) or
Krumbein (crooked leg), one with arthritic joints could be
called Steiff (stiff), one with a misshapen head might be
called Breithaupt (broad head) or Groskopf (bighead), and one
who squinted might be called Schiele (squint).   (113)
Kropf (goiter) was a fitting name for anyone so afflicted,
and Spitznas suited anyone with a pointed nose, just as
Finkbein (finch leg) suited a man with skinny shanks. A fat
man might be called Feiss, Fett, or Dick (thick) or perhaps
Bauch (belly). In fact, any part of the anatomy might suggest
a nickname, provided it were sufficiently deformed or unusual, such as Nase (nose), Schnaebele (little snout, in
America Snaveley), and Kehl (throat, unless he came from
Kehl across the Rhine from Strassburg). Originally, such
names had been prepositional phrases such as *mit dem bart*
(with the beard), *mit dem bauch* (with the belly), and *mit der
nase* (with the nose).   (114)
Nicknames could also result from personal behavior: a man
might be serious (Ernst) or jovial (Froehlich), courtly
(Huebsch) or crude (Rauh, Grob); or, if he vacillated, he
might be called Wankel or Wankelmut. Even more vituper-
ative were Greul (atrocity), Greulich (dreadful), and Grausam
(cruel). Less frequent were positive terms, such as Schoen
(beautiful), Klug (clever), and Kuhn (brave). Comical nicknames could also be taken from our furry and feathered
friends, such as Fuchs (fox), Has (hare), Gans (goose), Fink
(finch), Amsel (ousel, blackbird), and many others. Names
were also suggested by fish, such as Aal (eel), Barsch (perch),
Hecht (pickerel). In some cases the names of such creatures
may have signified that the person involved trapped, raised,
or sold them. This was true even of songbirds, for it was not
unusual for four-and-twenty blackbirds to be baked in a pie,
and thrushes and finches fared no better. A man named
Kaefer (beetle) mayhave had the perseverence of that insect,
and a man named Frosch (frog) may have eaten frogs, as
Frenchmen do in American fancy.   (115)
Nicknames were sometimes imperatives, such as Bleibtreu
(Remain loyal!), Fuerchtegott (Fear God!), Haltdichwohl (Keep
well!), Hoerauf (Stop it!), Kaufdasbier (Buy the beer!),
Streckfuss (Stretch a leg!), Schwingschwert (Swing the
sword!), and Siehdichum (Watch out!). Such names were often

given to new guild members at their initiation. Some of these imperative names were commands given in tasks no longer known to us. For example, Schudrein means "Shove it in!," but we do not know what was being shoved into what. If Samuel Clemens had not told us, we would not know the meaning of "Mark Twain."   (116)

Some nicknames derived from a man's favorite expression, as was the case of Jasomirgott (so help me God!), as Henry II, the first duke of Austria, was called because he used that oath so often. Similarly derived names may include Garaus (bottoms up!), Fruehauf (early up!), Glueckauf (safe return!, probably a miner's term), Gottbehuet (God forbid!), Herr Gott (Lord God), and Amen. The names of small coins sometimes serve to suggest parsimony or miserliness, examples being Dreier (thrupence), Grosch (penny), and Heller (worthless coin).   (117)

Some nicknames lasted for a long time, long after the reason for them had been forgotten. One of my fellow Boy Scouts rightfully acquired the name Asparagus Tips, which plagued him for years but was, fortunately, not passed on to his children to the third and fourth generation. Having run out of supplies on a mountain hike and half starved, we resolved to send a relief party down to the valley to find food. With many empty stomachs and only a few dollars, we could not decide between baked beans and hominy grits with gravy. At that point our friend suggested asparagus tips.   (118)

Before the Germans borrowed and imitated the French words for grandparents, aunts, uncles, and cousins, they had their own very intricate vocabulary for blood relationships, bonds which were much more binding then than now. These relationships have left American names such as Ahn (grandfather), Base (female cousin), Eidam (son-in-law), Enkel (grandchild), Ohm and Oheim (mother's brother), Schnur (daughter-in-law), Schwager (brother-in-law), Schwiegermutter (mother-in-law), Tochtermann (son-in-law), and Vetter (male cousin, kinsman). Although *Kegel* now means ten-pin, it used to mean an illegitimate child, as in the misunderstood expression *mit Kind und Kegel*.   (119)

Since very few people traveled in ancient days, a stranger was most easily identified by his tribal origin, and therefore we have surnames such as Bayer (Bavarian), Francke (Frank), Hess (Hessian), Preuss (Prussian), Sachs (Saxon), Thueringer or Duerringer (Thuringian), and Schwab or

Schwob (Swabian, sometimes Swopes in America). Naturally, a person was not called by a tribal name until after leaving home, for such a name would not distinguish him as long as he remained among his nationals. Because dialects differed so strongly, a stranger's accent immediately identified him even a few miles from home. At first, the words Sachsen, Bayern, and Schwaben referred not to the provinces but to the tribes themselves, regardless of where they were at that moment in their migratory wanderings. The terms were dative plurals and meant "to or among the Saxons," etc. The same held true later in the American colonies: traders and missionaries did not go to Iroquoia, but to the Iroquois, who might have been in transit. (120)

Among other territorial names that have furnished American surnames are Baden, Brandenburg, Durlach, Holstein, Oldenburg, Pfaltz, Schweitz, Silesia (Schlesinger), and Wuerttemberg. The name Deutsch does not refer to a tribe or territory, it is the name of the common language spoken by the various German tribes. Originally it just meant the vernacular or the tongue of the people (*zunga thiudisca*), this being a translation of the Latin term *lingua vulgaris,* or the vulgar language, as opposed to the *lingua latina,* the Latin language. Any German-speaker in an alien land may have been named Deutsch, Duetsch, or Daitsch. In Russia, on the other hand, he was called Niemitz (the dumb one) because he could not speak (Russian). (121)

People often bore the name of the city of their origin. Some just took the name of the city itself, such as Rosenheim or Bamberg, but most took the designation of the inhabitants of the town, as in the case of New Yorker as opposed to New York. Consequently, we find the American names Basler, Bamberger, Berner, Bremer (Bremen), Frankfurter, Hamburger, Mainzer (and Mentzer), Posner (Posen), Rosenheimer, Strassburger, and legions more. A Frankfurter need not have come from the large city on the Main, he could have come from the smaller Frankfurt on the Oder or from any of many places where the Franks forded a stream. (122)

Not only cities, but even small hamlets and villages supplied surnames. Some of these ended in the Germanic roots *dorf* (village, compare English "thorp"), *heim* (homestead, hamlet, cf. English "ham"), *hagen* (enclosure, hedge), and *ingen,* a root referring to a group of followers, as in the case of Sigmaringen, the place where Sigmar's people lived. A secondary meaning of *ing* is a vague concept of belonging, for example, Huelzing (belonging to a forest) and Aiching (belonging to the oaks).   (123)

Whereas *dorf* and *heim* originally designated small clusters of dwellings, some so-named places have grown into large cities, like Duesseldorf and Mannheim. Among place names and surnames ending in *dorf* and *heim* we find Altdorf, Altdorfer, Pappenheim, and Pappenheimer. The root *heim* sometimes appears as *ham* as in English Birmingham, for example in Mosshammer, an inhabitant of Mossham, who has nothing to do with hammers. The ending *heimer* finally lost most of its meaning and just meant an inhabitant in general, and therefore Burgenheimer did not have to have come from Burgenheim but could have come from Burgen.   (124)

A *hag* or *hagen* was an outlying settlement protected by a hawthorn hedge. Single sons often lived in such enclosures, with the result that a bachelor is called a *Hagestolz*. The root *hag* (hawe) appears in many names like Hashagen (hare hedge), Hagenbeck (enclosure brook), and Hagedorn (hawthorn); and a man living in a *hag* might be called Hagen, Hager, Hagmann, Hagemann, or even Hackmann. The Low German root *rode*, meaning a clearing, is found in Minnegerode and Wernigerode, while its High German equivalents *reit* and *reut* are found in Reitenbach and Reutlingen.   (125)

A name often misunderstood is Roland, of whom there is a statue in Bremen holding a gigantic sword. Most people assume that it commemorates the hero of the *Chanson de Roland* (from **hrotho* and **land)*, but this was not the case. Roland was not a name: it was a corruption of the legal term *rodoland*, or "reclaimed land." If a ruler undertook to clear (*roden*) unclaimed and uncultivated land, he could assert jurisdiction over it. To attest his juridical rights over this *rodoland*, he might stake his claim by erecting a marker, often in the shape of a man holding a sword as a symbol of jurisdiction. Because of the popularity of the hero Roland, people supposed that the markers represented him; and thus we have another case of folk etymology. A whole category of names derived from the act of clearing land, among which are *brand*, *reut*, *rod*, *sang*, and *schwand*. The name Waldbrand does not denote a forest fire, but a clearing in the woods. In America the root *schwand* sometimes appears as *schwang*, as in the name Neiswanger and Neuswanger (new clearing).   (126)

In addition to the place names ending in *dorf, heim, hagen, rod,* and *reut,* there were also many towns, especially in Switzerland, that ended in *weil* (also written *weiler, wil,* and *wyler*). These derived from the Latin word *villa,* which meant a large farm or estate and gave us the word "village." The first component of names ending in *weil* was often the name of the owner. For example, Wittenweil was a Roman villa appropriated by a Germanic invader named Witto, whose descendants were later called Wittenweiler. Among American names stemming from *weil* we find Weil, Weiler, and Hofwyl. At some time, already in Switzerland, names like Ebers-wil were wrongly divided and resulted in forms like Eber-schwil or Eberschwyl. Another root designating a town that is largely restricted to Switzerland is *ikon* (from *inghofen*), which is found in Ruemlikon, Rueschlikon, Russikon, Stallikon, Fuellikon, and many more. A less common ending, found mostly in north central Germany is *leben,* originally meaning "inheritance" but later just meaning property in general, as in Eisleben. The Slavic root *witz,* meaning village, appears in names like Bonnewitz.   (127)

Inghofen is not the only ending that has been mutilated. By tracing successive documents mentioning a place, we find that they have often dropped many unstressed syllables, so that from Udilscalckesberge all that remains is Uschelberg. Similar contractions occur in England, even if not always indicated by the spelling. When an American stated that he was going to St. Magdalene Church to catch a bus for Lancashire in order to call on Lord Cholmondeley, his British friend corrected him, pronouncing the names as Maudlin, Lancsha, and Chumly. When the Englishman said he would like to see Niagara Falls, the American corrected him with "Niffels." Because some long German names like Hruod-inesheim, Autmundistat, and Heribrachtshusen have been shortened to Rudisheim, Umstadt, and Herbstein, we cannot always be certain of the etymology of place names unless they appear in very old documents.   (128)

As Tacitus mentioned, the ancient Germans did not care to live in cities; during the invasions they often camped around the old Roman settlements and left the inhabitants at peace. The result was that many South German cities, towns, and villages retained their names, even if these names were sometimes altered by the High German sound shift and by the inability of the invaders to pronounce them properly. Most of these names were Celtic names that had long been latinized, such as Turicum (Zurich), Tavernae (Zabern), and Moguntia (Mainz). These Romanized Celtic place names provided the American names Zuricher, Zaber, Maintzer, and Mentzer. (129)

There were also genuine Latin names such as Confluencia (Koblenz, at the confluence of the Rhine and Moselle) and Colonia Agrippina (Koeln, a colony named in honor of Nero's mother, which we call Cologne). (130)

CHAPTER THREE

Christian Names

As we have seen, early German names were all pagan and mostly warlike. Names containing the roots *ans* and *god*, like Ansgar (god + spear) and Godwin (god + friend), referred to pagan gods. While the Germanic names were the most popular ones in Western Europe throughout the Middle Ages, Christianity introduced new names, mostly of Hebrew, Greek, and Latin origin. These names, often those of saints, were first found in the monasteries, where the monks shed their warlike Germanic names in favor of names more pleasing to God. Gradually, some of these names were assumed by royalty also; and we find rulers named John (Jehan, Jean, Johann, Jan, etc.), Georg, Stephan, and Philip. Some Christian names joined the older pagan names more easily because they resembled them. For example, Philip could have been confused with Filibert (very bright), Simon with Siemund (*sigi*, victory + *mund*, guardian), and Pilgrim with Biligrim (*bil*, sword + *grim*, helmet). Later converts often received names such as Christ, Christian, Karst, Kirst, and Kressmann.   (131)

The names of saints gradually took root also among secular people who, following ancient pagan beliefs, wished to gain the personal support of certain saints by naming their children for them, since namesakes had a moral claim on the protection of the people for whom they were named. The Virgin Mary's name was so popular that it was even borne by men, as in the case, later, of Karl Maria von Weber, Rainer Maria Rilke, and Erich Maria Remarque. (Few people know that Voltaire's real name Marie François Arouet.)

(132)

Despite the intrusion of saints' names, the old Germanic names still predominated until the Counter Reformation of the sixteenth and seventeenth centuries. In a group of ballads by a thirteenth-century Austrian poet known as Neidhart von Reuwenthal, we find many rustic names. The first fifty-seven names are Adelber, Adelheit, Adelhune, Adelmar, Ave, Berchtel, Diethoch, Eberhart, Elena, Engelbolt, Engelmar, Engelprecht, Eppe, Ermelint, Etzel, Frideger, Friderich, Friedliep, Friderun, Gisel, Giselher, Gotelinde, Gozbrecht, Gumprecht, Gunthart, Gundrat, Hadwig, Heilken, Hilde, Hiltburg, Hiltrat, Holengaere, Irenwart, Irmgart, Kuenzel, Randolt, Kuenegunde, Kuenz, Megenbolt, Liuthart,

Megenwart, Richilt, Ruoze, Ruoprecht, Sibant, Sigehart, Uodalhilt, Uolant, Uoze, Vrena, Vriderun, Vromuot, Walfrit, Waregrim, Werenbolt, Wierat, and Willebolt. It will be noted that all but three of these peasants have old Germanic names, mostly expressing warlike concepts, and most of these names were composed of the roots discussed earlier. Only Ave, Elena, and Vrena (St. Verena) have any Christian significance. (133)

Among the most popular holy names were those of certain popes, including Adrian, Alexander, Benedict, Clement, Fabian, Hildebrand, Johannes, Mark, Martin, Nicholas, Paul, Stephen, Urban, and Victor. A modern German named Hildebrand probably owes his name to Pope Hildebrand rather than to the hero of the old German *Lay of Hildebrand*, who had to fight his own son. Many of these foreign names gave two sets of derivatives. The common people followed native speech patterns and stressed the first syllable, whereas the Church retained the Latin accent. Thus we get JOhann and JoHANNES, from which arose Jahn, Jahnke, and Jantz as well as Hans, Hannes, and Hansel. (134)

After Luther revolted against Rome, most of his followers limited themselves to the names of scriptural saints such as Andreas, Johannes, Marcus, Matthaeus, Lucas, Petrus, and Paulus, while dropping the names of local and otherwise dubious saints. In place of the discarded saints, they often chose the names of Old Testament characters such as Abel, Abraham, Adam, Benjamin, Daniel, David, Jacob, Joachim, Jonas, Samuel, and Solomon. All of these were the source of German-American surnames in numerous variants. Because Old Testament names began to smack of heresy, they were forbidden in 1574 by the Synod of Tournai in France. (135)

Meanwhile, during the Counter Reformation, the Roman Catholic Church required all parents to name their child for a saint, which was usually the saint on whose day it was born. Consequently, most of the old Germanic names fell into disuse, except for those of popular emperors such as Carl, Conrad, Friedrich, Heinrich, Leopold, Ludwig, Otto, Siegmund, and Wilhelm. Among the most popular masculine saints in Germany, as elsewhere in Europe, were Johann, Joseph, Matthaeus (or Matthias), Sebastian, and the archangels Michael and Gabriel. It is not clear why the archangels Raffael and Uriel were less popular. Once a child had a hagiographic name, the parents could add a secular one too;

and this custom continued in Protestant lands, as in the case of Johann Wolfgang Goethe.   (136)
While most of the saints had Aramaic, Greek, or Latin names, there were some Celtic and even a few Germanic names on the list. Among the latter the Germans cultivated Conrad (brave + counsel), bishop of Augsburg, Meinrad (power + counsel), abbot of Einsiedeln, Oswald (god + rule), an Englishman, Rupertus (usually Ruprecht, from *hrodo* + *beracht*, famous + bright), who established Christianity in Salzburg, and Hubertus (mind + bright), the patron saint of hunters. Very popular was St. Francis of Assisi, whose name, derived from Germanic *frank*, appears in German as Franz or Frantz, but is pronounced Frantz in both cases. Less popular was St. Anselmus (god + helmet), also an Italian. Among the saints who contributed names to many German-American families were Anthony (Thoeni, Denny), Bartholomaeus (Bart, Bartel), Marcus (Merk, Merkel), Martin (Marti, Maertens), and Matthias (Matt, Matz, Thiess, Thyssen, and, in America, Tyson and Dyson.)   (137)
Christianity brought a slight softening of manners: to use Nietzsche's terms, a *Herrenmoral* (master morality) gave way somewhat to a *Sklavenmoral* (slave morality); and the ethics of the monastery were gradually imposed on society at large. Old names took on new meanings, while new names were introduced. The adjective *vrum* had once denoted effectiveness, a *vrumer ritter* was a capable knight, a *vrumer bauer* was a productive peasant, and a *vrumer munich* was a pious monk. Gradually the word dropped its first two meanings and kept only the last, and thus the name Frommhold, instead of meaning "effective and feudally loyal," took on the new meaning "pious and dear" for all classes. *Tuechtig* and *bieder*, which once meant doughty in battle, acquired for some people the meaning of capable and diligent, for example in business. In the new bourgeois society, respectability was more important than fame, so people adopted names like Ehrenmann (man of honor), Ehrlich (honest), and Ehrsam (respectable).   (138)
Gutmann, like French *bonhomme* and English Goodman, first meant "landowner" but was gradually understood to mean "good man." Among these new Christian names were Sanftmut (gentle disposition) and Demut (humility), which had literally meant "servant-disposition" (from *thius*, servant, and *mut*, disposition). The name is pronounced "day moot" in German, but is pronounced mostly as DeMUTH in America.

This is one of the many cases in which the English sound *th* (thorn), long since dead in Germany, has been falsely introduced into German-American names. Since it is more Christian to serve than to be served, we begin to find names like Diener (servant) and Dienst (service). The christianizing of German culture is shown in place names like Marienborn (Mary's well) and Theresienstadt (Theresa's city), which in turn became surnames. The Swiss city and surname Frauenfeld, which is now interpreted as "Field of our Lady," may have originally been Fronfeld "the field of our lord," or field where the peasants could perform their corvée service, or *Frondienst* (cf. *Fronleichnam*, Corpus Christi). However, most names like Frauenmann, Frauenhof, etc. do designate men or farms belonging to a convent. (139)

The names Gottfried, Gotthelf, Gotthilf, Gotthold, Gottlieb, Gotthlob, and Gottschalk, which had once belonged to the monasteries, gradually crept out into the world and became especially popular in Lutheran parsonages, where they were joined by new coinages like Fuerchtegott (fear God), Ehregott (glorify God), Leberecht (live right), Christfried (Christ peace), and Himmelreich (kingdom of heaven). The old name Friedrich (ruler of the **frithu*) was interpreted as "Prince of Peace" and was equated with the Hebrew name Solomon. Ulrich Zwingli misinterpreted his first name as Huldreich (full of grace), whereas it had actually been Uodalrich and had meant "rich in allodial (inherited) lands," again a case of folk etymology. (140)

During the period of humanism in the sixteenth century, scholars often signed their Latin writings with Latinized names. Georgius Agricola, the great humanist, was actually named Bauer; and the ancestors of the pencil manufacturing family Faber derived their name from the Latin word for smith, their name having been Schmidt. The map maker Gerhard Kremer signed his Latin maps with his Latin name, Mercator, while Francis Praetorius, the founder of Germantown, bore a latinized form of Schultheiss. In like manner Fischer (fisherman), Weber (weaver), Schumacher (shoemaker), Jaeger (hunter), and Schneider (tailor) gained prestige by calling themselves Piscator, Textor, Sutor, Venatus, and Sartor, or, the even more elegant, Sartorius. (141)

Some Latinists latinized their names by retaining or adding the suffix ending *us*, which was still commonly used until modern times in Biblical names like Petrus, Paulus, Martinus, etc. It should be noted that the common German name Christ is not blasphemous, since it merely means "Christian," the Lord's epithet always being Christus. Hans, the son of Martinus was Hans Martini, that being the Latin genitive, not an Italian name as is sometimes believed. In like manner, Paulus' son Niklas was Niklas Pauli or Pauly, while Jacobus' son Heinz was Heinz Jacobi or Jacoby. Scholars with names ending in *e* preferred the ending *ius*. The pastor of the Georgia Salzburgers bore the name Boltzius, a latinization of either Bolte or Boltze, while a con-artist who fleeced him called himself Curtius, although his real name was Kurtz. A Moravian teacher who served in Georgia and Pennsylvania was named Schulius, surely from Schule. The name Stettinius came from Stettin on the Baltic Sea. (142)

Some scholars were not satisfied with mere Latin names but preferred Greek ones, such as Neander for Neumann (new man). This was the case of Luther's friend Melanchthon, who incorrectly interpreted his name Schwarzerd as "Black earth." Actually the name may have been only Schwarzer (brunet), to which an excrescent *T* had been added. Excrescent *T*s appear in numerous names, among which are Braunert, Craemert, Daubert, Dickert, Dobert, Pabst, Obst, and Schweigert. Some people were named for the day of their births, such as Freitag (Friday), Sontag (Sunday), Maytag (May Day), and Oster (Easter). Obviously, descendants of such people bore those names without being born on those days. It is possible that a man named Freitag received his name because he owed corvée service on Fridays. (143)

Many German names had originally been French, often Huguenot. Literate French immigrants could preserve the correct spelling of their names because they associated with educated people who understood them, as was the case of the family of the German author Friedrich Heinrich Carl de La Motte Fouqué. On the other hand, the names of the working-class and peasant immigrants were usually ger-manized, and one would scarcely recognize Tussing as a rendering of Toussaints. In one instance the reverse took place: the accent on the North German name Guder Jan (Good John) was shifted to the second syllable, forming the name Guderian, which is usually assumed to be of French origin. (144)

In the South German language area the Romance-speaking Celts survived the Germanic invasions and lived alongside the invaders, even to the present in the Engadin. The first

Celts the Germans met when crossing the Rhine were the Volcae, which gave them the noun *walch* and the adjective *welsch*. In England the Saxons gave the cognate word *welsh* to the Celts of Wales. When the Volcae became romanized, the Germans on the Continent began to use the word *welsch* to designate Romance-speaking people, as the German Swiss still call their French-speaking countrymen. Because the romanized Celtic pockets remained among the Germanic invaders, we find place names like Wallensee, Wallenstein, and Wallis, where the older inhabitants survived.   (145)

The number of germanized Slavic names is high everywhere east of the Elbe, which served as a linguistic frontier between Germans and Slavs after the latter had occupied the lands abandoned by the former during their migrations westward and southward. Ever since the thirteenth century there had been a persistent *Drang nach Osten* (drive toward the east), which was finally reversed in 1944 at the Battle of Stalingrad. During the drive toward the east the Germans had often retained, even if altered, Slavic names such as Bogatzky, Cernak, Kretschmer, Lessing, Nietzsche, and Leibnitz. They also kept many East German place names such as Berlin, Breslau, Danzig, Dresden, Fehrbellin, and Leipzig, which have given us American surnames.   (146)

There are not really any German-Jewish names. There are Hebrew names, such as Chaim, Cohen, Levi, and Me'ir, the last of which, as mentioned, may have predisposed some Jews to adopt the name Meyer. A few German-language names were borne mainly by Jews, such as Langrock and Gelbrock, which referred to the long and yellow garments they were required to wear. Otherwise, there is no distinction between the names borne by Christians and Jews, except that certain names were more frequently adopted by the latter. In many of our Eastern inner-cities, names like Evans, Davis, Robertson, White, Williams, Wilson, etc. are borne mostly by blacks; yet they remain British, not African, names.   (147)

Within the Jewish community, or ghetto, simple names usually sufficed; if not, the father's name could be added. When the Jews were emancipated at the end of the eighteenth and beginning of the nineteenth centuries, they were required to take surnames for the purpose of taxation. If they had their choice many chose common German names that began with the same consonant as their "holy" or "synagogue" name. Thus, Menachem might choose Mendel just for its initial sound, and Nathan might choose Nadler for the same

reason, not because he made needles. Some merely re-arrang-
ed the letters, so that Lewi became Weil. Even after assum-
ing gentile-sounding *Decknamen* (cover names), religious Jews
still considered their synagogue names to be their true
names, for which they felt an emotional attachment. When
given a choice, some Jews chose romantic names such as
Morgenthau (morning dew), Blumenthal (flower valley),
Lilienthal (lily valley), Rosenberg (rose mountain), Silberstein
(silver stone), and their like. Although Americans often
consider such names to be Jewish, they are straight German
names, for such names were current in sentimental novels at
the time that Jews were taking civil names. The name
Rosenkranz (rosary) is certainly more appropriate for a
Catholic than for a Jew, and the name Rosenberg was borne
by the Nazi ideologist who wrote *The Mythos of the Twentieth Century.* (148)
Like their gentile neighbors, the Jews often took the
name of their trade, so many bore names like Kuerschner or
Kirschner (furrier), Kraemer (shopkeeper), Schlechter (slaughterer), or Wechsler (money-changer). On the other hand, the
chosen name did not necessarily designate trades associated
primarily with the Jews, for we also find Ackermann, Bauer,
Forster, Gaertner, Gerber, Jaeger, Wirth, and Zimmermann.
When required to assume surnames for purposes of taxation,
the Jews often used their house names, by which many
families had been known for generations. Typical examples
were Adler, Drache, Fisch, Fuchs, Gans, Hecht, Mandelbaum,
Rose, Rosenstock, and Rothschild. Many Jews took the names
of cities, often of large and imposing cities like Frankfurt and
Hamburg, without having ever lived there. (149)
It is said that the Jews often had to bribe the officials to
obtain desirable names. A tale, surely apocryphal but no less
significant, tells of a Jew who was in the tax collector's office
for a long time while getting his name. When he finally
emerged, his friends asked what name he got. "Schweiss"
(sweat) was his answer. "Very good," his friends remarked.
"Yes, but the *w* cost me half my fortune!" Since puns cannot
be translated, the story should be altered in English: he
received the name Shirt, but the *r* cost him half his fortune.
To know what names the German Jews received or selected,
one has only to look at any list of donors to cultural and
charitable undertakings. When I was studying at Heidelberg,
the main building, which had been donated by American
benefactors, bore a large bronze plaque listing the names of

the donors, more than half of whom were clearly Jewish. When I arrived there in 1936, all Jewish professors had just been dismissed. (150)

CHAPTER FOUR

The Americanization of German Names

Possibly the greatest change in German-American names was not the High German sound shift but their naturalization in America, especially in the eighteenth century. When the immigrants boarded their ships at Rotterdam, the English captains had difficulty in writing their manifests or ships lists. Knowing no German, and unfamiliar with German dialects, the scribes wrote down the names as they heard them, sometime in the form of the English names most resembling the sound. In this way Theiss, Weiss, and Weidmann became Dice, Wise, and Whiteman, while Albrecht, Leitner, and Leithaeuser became Albright, Lightner, and Lighthizer. The reason that so many eighteenth-century German immigrants could not sign their names and merely made an X was not that they were illiterate, because Protestant Germans had a higher literacy rate than their British contemporaries. The reason was that they could write only in German script, which the British authorities could not read. It occasionally appears that the immigrants tried to spell their names but did so with the German sounds of the letters. If a man named Diehl spelled his name as "*day, ee, ay, ha, ell*, the scribe may have understood it as Deahl.

(151)

In a few cases the writer of the ship list gave up and asked the meaning of the name; and thus Becker, Koch, Schneider, Soeldner, and Zimmermann became Baker, Cook, Taylor, Soldier, and Carpenter. Often the translation was advantageous. When two brothers named Zwetschen (plum) stood in separate lines at Castle Garden (prior to Ellis Island and therefore used by most German immigrants) they were handled by different clerks. One, being conscientious, struggled with the unfamiliar name and wrote it Tsvetshen. The other soon gave up and asked the meaning, and then he assigned the name Plum. It is not hard to guess which brother was more successful in business in America.   (152)

In the eighteenth century it was customary to translate Christian names, just as we still do today in the case of royal names when we say Frederick the Great and William the Second instead of Friedrich der Grosse and Wilhelm der Zweite. Common names like Johann, Georg, and Wilhelm were regularly anglicized into John, George, and William; but the scribes failed to recognize the roots of some names.

Therefore they failed to see that Ruprecht was the equivalent
of Robert and that Ludwig was the equivalent of Lewis, and
the result was that they sometimes rendered them as
Rubright and Ludowick. The same situation could occur in
the case of surnames that were identical with Christian
names: Paulus Franz might become Paul Francis and Johann
Wilhelm might become John Williams.   (153)

Only a few German first names have taken root in the
United States, most of them still being found in families who
cherish their German heritage. Among those that are still
popular are Carl, Ernst, Herman, Hubert, and Otto, all of
which also serve as surnames. Among girls' names we find
Heidi, Gretchen, Liese, and Minna. A test of whether or not
such names have really taken root is their presence or
absence in non-German families, for example, among our
African-American populace.   (154)

It should be noted that, while the first few generations of
Germans in America continued to choose German first names
to honor their parents and grandparents, later generations
joined the mainstream in naming their children for national
heroes and non-German friends. The reverse was also true:
the black mayor of Baltimore is named Kurt Schmoke, and
a lovely black bank teller in Savannah, Georgia, is named
Zeagler (from Ziegler). My own grandfather, who had no
German blood and bore the surname Meldrim, was christened
Peter Wiltberger in honor of his father's commanding of-
ficer.   (155)

In a few cases the German immigrant willfully changed his
name for professional reasons. The dancer Frederick
Austerlitz preferred to perform under the stage name Fred
Astaire, which sounded more elegant to American ears after
World War I; and Allan Konigsberg and Doris Kappelhof
acted under the names Woody Allen and Doris Day. It has
been mentioned that religious Jews cherished their synagogue names more than their cover names, and that explains
why it was easy for some of them to discard their cover
names and choose more suitable ones after reaching
America.   (156)

Some Germans tried to gain prestige by giving a French
flavor to their names, French being fashionable at the time.
August Schoenberg, a Jew, translated his surname to
Belmont and thus entered circles formerly closed to him.
Some people merely shifted the accent to the second syllable
to make it sound French. A few North Germans whose names

ended in an *e*, like Bode (messenger) and Gode (good), had already added an acute accent (Bodé, Godé) so that South Germans would not drop the final vowel. In America such names were thought to be French and were pronounced, and sometimes written, as Boday and Goday. In Charleston the early Lutheran silversmith Johann Paul Grimké left many "Huguenot" descendants. (157)

A name like Dusel (pronounced DOOzel and meaning "silly") sounds very French when the accent is shifted to the second syllable and the name is pronounced as DuSELLE, and the same is true of Mandel (almond) and Mantel (coat) when they are pronounced ManDELLE and ManTELLE (which Mickey Mantle did not choose to do). The same principle was at work in the change of accent in the word "tercel," meaning a thrice-moulted male falcon. The word should be accented on the first syllable, but the automobile manufacturer knew that the car would be more stylish if pronounced TerCELLE. Even the seventeenth-century English composer Purcell suffers his name to be murdered by Francophiles as PurCELLE. (158)

Some immigrants altered the spelling of their names to preserve the correct pronunciation, which would have been mispronounced if they had kept the original spelling. Families named Erhardt, Gerhardt, and Igelhard saved the correct sound (the true component of a name) by changing the spelling to Earhardt, Gearhard, and Eagleheart. Sometimes the corruption of a German name was due to a false breaking of the name, as we have seen in the case of Ebers-wyl and Eber-schwyl. Roth-schild (red shield) has become Rothschild, which has no meaning. Rat-her (council gentleman) has become Ra-ther, a rather meaningless name; and the Kraushaar (curly hair) Auditorium in Baltimore is often pronounced Kraw-shower. (159)

World War I extinguished, or hopelessly disguised, many German names. Because British propaganda convinced most Americans that the Germans cut off the hands of all Belgian boys and impaled little girls on the projections of the Gothic cathedrals, some German Americans renounced their origins in order to escape public opprobrium, and even sauerkraut had to take on the name "liberty cabbage." I was born during "the War to End all Wars," and for years afterwards we knew scarcely any Germans. Among our acquaintances the Ottos were Norwegians, the Balls were Alsatians, the Altstaetters were Swiss, and the Holsts were Danish. Some others had rectified their spellings from Schmidt to Smith and from Henrichsen to Henderson. Strangely, German shepherd dogs remained German, except when they were called police dogs, and Dachshunds remained "dash hounds." (160)

The chief value of the appended list of German-American names for genealogists is to help them continue their search of a family's antecedents when the line seems to come to an end. A friend of mine in Atlanta was proud of his descent from a prominent New England family named Capp. However, when he tried to document the descent, the line came to an abrupt halt in the mid-nineteenth century in Ohio and could not be pursued until it was discovered that the father of the earliest known Capp had previously been named Kapp. Therefore, if a genealogist comes to the end of an Anglo-Saxon line, it may be worth his while to search under the nearest German names. (161)

To be sure, not every Miller used to be a Mueller, in fact the spelling Miller was common in South Germany and Switzerland, as in the case of Johnny Weissmiller, the original Tarzan. In many cases the source of an apparently Anglo-Saxon name must have been Continental, usually German, because the name does not appear, or seldom appears, in England. Among these are Albright (Albrecht), Fulbright (Vollbrecht), Height (Heyd, Heid, or Heidt), Lightner (Leitner), Lighthizer (Leithaeuser), Yonce (Jantz), and Youngblood (Juengbluet, not young blood but young blossom). It is generally known that Firestone was an anglicization of Feuerstein, but it has not been mentioned that Firestone's greatest rival, Goodyear, may have had a similarly formed name. I have never known an Englishman named Goodyear, but Johannes Gutjahr of Linzingen arrived in America aged sixteen in 1864, just as Rudolf Feuerstein had done one year earlier; and it is likely that other Gutjahrs had arrived before Charles Goodyear vulcanized rubber. (162)

CHAPTER FIVE

Suggestions for Using the Name-list

In searching for a German-American name, particularly an early one, the reader should keep several things in mind. Being unfamiliar with German names, the English ship captains sometimes wrote them phonetically. Thus they sometimes spelled the sound represented in German by *ie* as "ee" or "ea", as was the case with Keefer and Keafer for Kiefer and with Reeser and Reaser for Rieser. Unfamiliar with the trigraph *sch*, the scribes usually wrote only "sh" as in English. Thus Schneider appears as Shnyder (or Snyder), Schultz as Shults, and Schueler as Shiele. In searching for a German-American name beginning with *sh*, the reader is advised to search under the *sch* spelling, since the *sh* list has been greatly shortened to avoid unnecessary duplication.
(163)

The digraph *pf*, unfamiliar to the scribes, appeared as *f*, as in Fleeger and Fleager for Pflueger and in Fister for Pfister. Whereas there had been only a few German surnames ending in *s* (indicating the genitive case), the English scribes often added a spurious *s* to German surnames, so that Bauer, Meyer, and Hyde (Heidt) also appeared as Bauers or Bowers, Meyers or Myers, and Hydes. Perhaps the scribes heard of these families mentioned in the plural, as in the case of the Smiths or the Blacks, and thought the *s* to be part of the name.
(164)

Umlauts, the diacritical marks over *a*, *o*, and *u*, were seldom used by German Americans and therefore do not appear here. They were originally the letter *e* superimposed over the vowel to modify its pronunciation, changing an *a* to *e* (rhyming with "say"), an *o* to the vowel sound in "girl" or "hurt," and the *u* to the sound of a French *u* (or, in South German names, to the sound *ee*). Instead of being superimposed, the *e* could follow the vowel, as in names like Goethe and Goetz; and that is the method used in the following list, even when the Standard German name has umlaut, as in the case of Schoen instead of Schön. In many cases the umlaut was eventually dropped. Therefore, when seeking a name with an *ae*, *oe*, or *ue*, the researcher should also search under *a*, *o*, and *u*, and vice versa.
(165)

The following compilation was begun in the naive belief that it could be complete, or even almost complete. Although not of German descent, I have competed for half a century against German thoroughness and have striven for *Voll-*

staendigkeit, or completeness. Innocently expecting to find all German-American names, I have added list after list; yet, like Achilles, whenever I have almost caught up with the tortoise of completion, the tortoise has moved on; and now the list, still incomplete, is as much as my readers, or my publisher, will bear. While this is a partial list, I cannot claim that it is an impartial list, for I have included all eligible friends, acquaintances, and colleagues lest they think I did not have them in mind while compiling the list. Originally based on eighteenth- and nineteenth-century ship manifests, this list also includes German names from American telephone books, newspapers, and TV programs.   (166)

Although this study cannot pretend to list all the thousands of American variants of German names, it is hoped that the reader can deduce most unlisted names by observing the various roots and the way they are combined in the names that are listed. For example, the name Auerstein is not listed (because I have found no American by that name), but the roots are found in Auerbach and Steinfeld and many other names so that the reader should be able to ascertain the meaning without finding the exact name itself. Likewise, the index sometimes refers to paragraphs (not pages) in the introduction that do not list the precise name in question but which do explain related names.   (167)

If the researcher cannot find a name where it belongs alphabetically, he should look for several lines above and below. Also, he should remember that, because of the High German sound shift, *b*, *d*, and *g* are sometimes interchangeable with *p*, *t*, and *k* and *p* and *t* are sometimes interchangeable with *pf*, *f*, and *z*. Also, many names can begin with either *C* or *K*, *T* or *Th*, or *Sch* or *Sh*.   (168)

The reader will note that the translations often do not concur with modern dictionaries. Since most surnames were adopted in the fourteenth to the seventeenth centuries, they were based on older meanings of the roots, often as they appeared in Middle High German. For example, since there were still no street cars, umbrellas, alarm clocks, or computers, the names Schaffner, Schirm, Wecker, and Rechner are rendered as "steward," "protection," "waker," and "teller" rather than as "conductor," "umbrella," "alarm clock," and "data processor." It will also be noted that many German-American names, especially of the earlier families, differ in spelling from modern German forms of the same names. This is because in the nineteenth and early twentieth centuries many German families altered the spelling of their names to concur with current orthographic reforms, which attempted to simplify and standardise spelling. The early immigrants, being safely in America, were unaffected by these reforms. Therefore many American families still use the older spellings; for example, we still find the spellings Carl, Schwartz, and Cunckel in place of the newer spellings Karl, Schwarz, and Kunkel. (169)

Every effort has been made to avoid folk etymology, or the popular but mostly incorrect interpretations of the names, but instances surely appear. The English renditions are merely transliterations, not interpretations. The reader is free to interpret a definition such as "marsh dweller" as "a person who lives near a marsh," " at a marsh," or "in a marsh," as he sees fit. The reader is reminded that fr means "from," the symbol < means "derived from," and OT and NT mean Old and New Testament. (170)

In the case of surnames derived from place names, space has sometimes been saved by explaining only the place name. The item "Altdorf, Altdorfer (old village)" explains the place name Altdorf as "old village"; it is assumed that the reader will understand that an Altdorfer is an inhabitant of that place. The same is true of "Frankfurter" (the Franks' ford), which explains only the name of the city, not that of the inhabitants. Places sufficiently populated to appear on maps and in gazeteers are marked with a raised 122, which follows the entry unless there may be confusion, in which case the 122 follows immediately after the pertinent name. It will be noted that old Germanic names like Eckhard and Anslem are rendered as (sword + strong) and (god + helmet) to indicate that there need be no conceptual relation between the two roots. Some names seem to be listed twice; for example, Forstreiter (forest rider, gamekeeper) is listed separately from Forstreiter (dweller in a forest clearing). Although the two appelations share the same spelling and pronunciation, they have different sources and different meanings and are therefore treated as separate names. (171)

Der Müller.

Aach, see Ach
Aachen (city) 122
Aal, Aahl (eel) 115, 116
Aal, Ahl (awl, cobbler)
Aalborn (nobly born) 46
Aargauer, Aargeyer (fr Aargau,
  Swiss region on the Aar) 121
Abaler, see Abele
Abbriter (from the clearing) 70,
  125
Abbuehl (from the hill) 70, 67
Abderhalden (from the slope)
  70, 71
Abel, Abell, Abels (brother of
  Cain) 135, 122
Abel < Albrecht 53, 54
Abele (poplar tree, fr Latin
  albus) 89
Abelmann (dweller near the
  poplars) 89
Abend (evening, one who lives
  toward the south)
Abendroth (evening red, Abbo's
  clearing) 125
Abendschein, Abenschein
  (evening glow)
Abendschoen, Abenschoen (as
  beautiful as the evening)
Aberbach, see Auerbach
Aberholt (hostile, offensive) 115
Aberle, Aberly < Albrecht, see
  also Aeberli
Abert < Albrecht
Abich (left, averse), < Albrecht
  53, 54
Abicht, see Habicht
Able, see Abel
Ableiter, Ableitner 122 (fr the
  slope) 70, 71
Abraham (OT name) 135, 122
Abram, Abrams (OT name) 135
Abscherer, see Scherer
Abschlag (steep slope) 71
Abschlag (excise collector) 109
Abt, Abts (Abbot) 110
Abtsreiter, Abstreiter (abbot's
  clearing) 110, 125, 126
Abzieher (skinner) 96, 109
Abzug (gully, drain)

Ach, Ache, Achen, Acher
  (river, cog. Latin *aqua*)
  79, 122
Achebach, Achenbach 122,
  Achenbacher, Achenback
  (brook coming fr a spring)
  79, 77
Achen (fr Aachen) 122
Acher (dweller on a river),
  see also Acker 79, 87
Achilles (Greek name)
Achmann (dweller on a
  river) 79, 94
Achsteller (stable on a stony
  terrain) 79
Achterholt (behind the
  forest) 70, 72
Achtermann (dweller behind
  [the village, hill, etc.]) 70,
  94
Achtung (attention) 117
Ackenbach, see Achebach
Acker 122, Ackers, Ackert
  (field) 84
Ackerhaus (house on a field)
  84, 65
Ackerhof (small farm) 84, 92,
  122
Ackerknecht (fieldhand) 84,
  95
Ackermann, Akermann
  (farmer) 84, 94
Ackmann, see Achmann
Adalmann, Addleman, see
  Edelmann
Adam, Adams (husband of
  Eve) 135, 111
Adami (son of Adam) 142
Adamsweiler (Adam's village)
  135, 127
Ade, Adde, see Adam
Adelbald (noble + bold) 46,
  46
Adelberg 122, Adelberger
  (noble mountain) 46, 68
Adelbert, see Albrecht
Adelbrich, Adelbrecht (noble
  + bright) 45, 47
Adeler, see Adler

Adelhart (noble + strong) 46,
46
Adelheid, Adelhyt (noble +
quality) 46, 133
Adelheim (noble hamlet) 46,
123, 122
Adelmann, Adelman (nobleman)
46, 94
Adelsberger (fr Adelsberg,
nobility mountain) 46, 68,
122
Adelsdorfer, Adelsdoerfer (fr
Adelsdorf, nobility village)
46, 123
Adelstein, see Edelstein
Ader (vein, well)
Ader (crossbow string) 108
Adich, Adichs, Adix < Adolf 53
Adler 122, Adeler (eagle, fr
noble + eagle, often a house
name 48, 63, 149)
Adolf, Adolph (noble + wolf) 46,
48
Adrian (Christian saint, name
of pope) 134
Advent (fr church calendar)
143
Aeberli, Aeberlj, Aberley, see
Eberle
Aebischer (dweller near ash
trees) 89
Aegidi (St. Aegidius) 131
Aelbragt, see Albrecht
Aeppli (little apple), see Apfel
Aeschbach (brook among ash
trees, or brook containing
aesche [graylings]), see
Aschenbach 89, 77
Aescher, Aeschlimann (dweller
near ash trees) 89
Afeld, Afeldt, Affeldt (river
field) 79, 91
Aff (ape) 115, 116
Affolter (apple tree) 89
Agatstein, Agetstein (agate,
magnet) 73
Agede, see Eigenter

Agilbert (sword + bright) 46,
46
Agricola (Latin for farmer)
140
Agtermann, see Achtermann
Ahl (eel, catcher of, or
dealer in, eels) 115
Ahl, see Ahle
Ahlbach (eel brook) 115, 77,
122
Ahlborn (nobly born) 46, 79
Ahlborn (eel spring) 79
Ahle (awl, shoemaker) 98
Ahle (honeysuckle)
Ahlemann, see Alemann
Ahler, Ahlers, Ahlert <
Albrecht
Ahlfeld (honeysuckle field)
84, 122
Ahlhorn (place name) 122
Ahlinger (fr Ahling) 122
Ahlmann (dweller at a fen
or swamp) 80, 94
Ahlstrom (eel stream) 115,
78
Ahn, Ahner (grandfather or
ancestor) 119
Ahn (dweller at a fen) 80
Ahn < Arnold 53
Ahorn (maple) 89, 122
Ahrbeck (eagle brook) 48, 77,
122
Ahrberg, see Arberg
Ahrenbeck (eagle brook) 48,
78
Ahrenberg 122, see Arberg
Ahrend, Ahrends, Ahrens,
see Arend, Arends
Ahrendorf, Ahrensdorf, see
Arendorf
Ahrenholtz, see Arenholtz
Ahrenhorst (eagle hurst) 48,
72
Ahrens, Ahrend, Ahrends,
see Arnd
Ahrensfeld (eagle field) 46,
84, 122

Ahrensmeyer, see Ahrens 48,
94
Aich 122, Aicher, Aichner
(dweller among the oaks) 89
Aichach (oak place) 89, 79, 122
Aichbichler (oak hill) 89, 67
Aichel, Aichele (acorn), see
Eichel, Eichelmann
Aichelberg (acorn mountain)
89, 68, 122
Aiching (belonging to the oaks)
89, 123, 122
Aichmann (dweller among the
oaks) 89, 94
Aidt, see Eid
Aigel, see Eigel
Aigner, see Eigne
Aik, see Aich
Aikenbrecher (oak cutter) 89,
95, 100
Ainbinder (cooper) 96
Airheart, Airhart, see Erhard
151
Aisenberg, see Eisenberg
Aisenstark (as strong as iron)
Aisner, see Eisner
Aist (place and river name)
122, 83
Aker, Akermann, see Acker,
Ackermann, also Eckert
Aker, Akers (metal container
for liquids) 106
Aland (a kind of fish) 115, 122
Albach, see Ahlbach
Alban (St. Albans) 131
Albaugh, see Ahlbach 151
Albeisser (cobbler) 104
Alber, Albers (poplar tree, fr
Latin *albulus*) 89
Alberg, Alberger, Albirger (fr
Adelberg, noble mountain)
46, 68
Albersheim (poplar hamlet) 89,
123
Albert, Albertus, see Albrecht
Alberti, Alberty, son of Albert
59, 142
Albinus (Latin: white)
Alborn, see Ahlborn

Albrand (noble + sword) 46,
46
Albrecht, Albracht, Albraecht
(noble + bright) 46, 47
Albrechtsdorf (Albert's
village) 46, 123
Albright, Albrite, see
Albrecht 151, 162
Aldag (weekday, also
Adaldag, noble day)
Alder, Alders, see Alter
Alderfer, see Altdorfer 151
Aldorf, see Altdorf 122
Aldorfer, Alldorfer (fr Aldorf
122), see Altdorfer
Aldhaus, see Althaus
Aleberger, see Alberger
Aleman, Alleman, Allman,
Alemann (a German, fr
French *allemand*) 121
Alexander (name of a pope)
134
Alf, Alfs, Alfing < Adolf 53
Alfers < Adolf 53
Algeier, Algeir, Algeyer,
Algire, Algyer (fr Allgaeu
in Austria) 121
Alkire, see Algeier
Allbach, Allenbacher, see
Ahlbach
Allbring, Albrink < Albrecht
53
Alldach, see Aldag
Alldorfer, see Altdorfer
Allemann 122, Allman,
Allimann, Allimang, see
Aleman
Allenbaugh (fr Allenbach
122, eel brook) 77, 151
Allendorf (old village) 123,
122
Allendorf (river village) 79,
123
Aller, Allers (name of river)
83
Allerheiligen (All Saints) 143
Allgeier, see Algeier
Allhelm, Alhelm (noble +
helmet) 46, 46

Allmang, see Aleman
Allmendinger (fr Allmendingen, public common 122)
Allp, see Alp
Allschbach, Allschpach, Allspach, see Alsbach
Alltstatt, Alstadt, see Altstatt
Allwin, see Alwin
Almann, see Aleman
Almende (common forest or pasture) 84
Almstedt (alpine meadow 84, Almsteadt 151)
Alp (fr Alpe 122, alpine pasture) 84
Alpenbaur (peasant on the mountain pastures) 84, 91
Alper, Alpers, Alpert, Alphart (elf + strong, see also Albrecht) 48, 46
Alperstein (Albrecht's mountain) 68
Alphart, see Alper
Alps, see Alp
Alsbach 122 (pre-Germanic river name + *bach*, brook) 83
Alspach (eel brook 122), see Ahlbach
Alsentzer (fr Alsenz) 122
Alstadt, see Altstadt
Alster (river at Hamburg) 83
Alster (magpie) 89
Alt, Altz, Ault, Alter (old man, the elder, senior) 113
Altbuesser (shoe repairer) 96
Altecken (old corner, old field) 85
Altemeyer, Altemayer (previous owner of a farm) 93
Altemueller (proprietor of the *Altmuehle*, old mill) 93, 94, 94
Alten (place name) 122
Altenbach (old brook) 77, 122
Altenberg, Altenberger (old mountain) 68, 122
Altenburg (old castle) 73, 122

Altendorf (old village) 123, 122
Altenhein (old grove, or old hamlet) 123, 122
Altenhoefer (fr Altenhoefen 122) 92
Altenhoff 122, Altenhoefer, see Althoff
Altenstein (old mountain) 73, 122
Alter, Alther, Alters, Alterman (old man, senior) 113
Altgelt (old money)
Althans (old Johnny, John the elder) 113
Althaus (old house) 65, 122
Altheinz (Heinrich the elder) 113
Altherr, Alther (old master) 113
Althoff, Althof 122, Althoffer (old farm, old court) 92, 122
Altholz (old wood) 72, 122
Althous, see Althaus 151
Altig, Altik, see Aldag
Altland 122, Altlandt (opposed to Neuland, or land recently reclaimed fr forest or swamp) 126
Altman, Altmann (old man) 113
Altmeyer (proprietor of the Althoff) 92, 94, see Altemeyer
Altmuehl (corruption of pre-Germanic word for "swamp water")
Altmueller, see Altemueller
Altona (fr pre-Germanic word for swamp, folketymologized to "all too near," town near Hamburg) 122
Altorffer, see Altdorfer
Altrith, Altruth (old clearing) 125

Alts, see Alt
Altschuh (old shoe, cobbler) 106
Altschul (old school, old
synagogue)
Altstadt, Altstaedt, Altstaetter
(old city) 122
Altvater (grandfather,
patriarch) 113
Altwobner (old weaver) 96
Altz (fr pre-Germanic river
name) 7, 83, see Alt
Alwin, Alwine (noble + friend)
46, 48
Alzheim, Alzheimer, Altesheim
(old hamlet) 123
Amacker (at the field) 70, 84
Aman, Amann, see Amman
Amand, see Amend and Aman
Ambach 122, Ambacher (on the
brook) 70, 77
Amberg 122, Amberger (on the
mountain) 70, 68
Amborn, Ambron (at the
spring) 70, 79
Ambros, Ambrose, Ambrosius
(St. Ambrose of Milan) 131
Ambrosi (son of Ambrose) 142
Ambrust, Ambruster, see
Armbrust
Ambuehl (at the Buehl or hill)
70, 67, 122
Amburn, see Amborn
Amecker (fr Amecke 122, at
the corner) 70, 85
Ameis, Ameise (ant)
Ameis (deforested area)
Amelsberg (mountain of the
Amelungs), see next entry
Amelung (a Germanic tribe or
dynasty) 120
Amen (Amen) 117, see Amman
Amend, Amende, Amendt,
Ament, Amment (at the end
of the road, field, etc.) 70
Ametsbichler (fr Ametsbichl,
ant hill) 67, 122
Amhyser (at the houses) 70,
65, 151

Amman, Aman, Ammeister
(Amtmann, official) 109
Ammen (nurses, see also
Amman)
Ammend, see Amend
Ammenhausen (the nurses'
houses, the officials'
houses) 65, 122
Ammer (yellow-hammer) 89
Ammer (pre-Germanic river
name) 83
Ammerheim (yellow-hammer
village) 89, 123
Ammerheim (village on the
Ammer) 83, 123
Ammermann (bucket maker)
96
Ammon, Amon (OT name)
135, see also Amman
Ampel (swinging lamp 106),
or see Ambuehl
Ample, see Ampel 151
Amrein, Amrhein (on the
Rhine) 70, 83, 122
Amsbacher (dweller on the
Amsbach, inhabitant of
Amsbach) 83, 122
Amsel (ousel, blackbird, fond
singer) 115
am Stein (on the crag) 70,
73, 122
Amtag (by day)
Amueller, see Aumueller
Amweg (on the path) 65, 122
Anacker (without a field, on
the field) 70, 84
Ancker (butter, butter
maker) 96
Anczel < Johann 134
Andenrieth (at the reeds,
marsh) 70, 81
Anderach (on the river) 70,
79
Andereas, Anders, see
Andreas
Andereck, Andereg, Anderich
(at the corner) 70, 85
Anders, Andersen (son of
Andreas) 59

Anderwiese (at the meadow)
70, 84
Andlau (pre-Germanic river
name in Alsace) 83
Andoni, see Anton
Andreas, Andrae, Andrea,
Andres (St. Andrew) 135
Andresen, Andresson,
Andrewsen (son of Andreas)
59
Anfeld (on the field, without a
field 70, 84; fr Anfelden) 122
Anfield, see Anfeld 151
Angebrant (field cleared by
fire) 84, 126
Angel, Angels, Angell (fishhook,
hinge, Angle), see Anger
Angel (pre-Germanic river
name) 83
Angelbach, Angelbeck (fishing
brook, or see Engelbach) 77
Angelberger (fr Amelberg 122),
see Engelberg
Angenendt (dweller at the end)
70
Anger 122, Angert (small
meadow, pasture) 84, 122
Angerbauer (farmer on or at
the pasture) 84, 91
Angermann (dweller on the
meadow) 84, 94
Angermayer (farmer dwelling
on or at a pasture) 84, 93
Angermueller (miller on the
field) 84, 103
Angersbach (meadow brook) 84,
77, 122
Angerstein (field marker) 84,
73, 122
Angst (fear) 115
Angst (dweller in narrow part
of valley) 76
Angstmann (executioner)
Angstmann (timid man) 115
Anhaeuser (fr Anhausen 122,
at the houses) 70, 65
Anhalt (German city and state)
121, 122

Anhorn (at the peak) 70, 68,
122
Anhut (without guard)
Anhut (hatless) 122
Ankerbrand (clearing on the
water) 126
Annacker, see Anacker
Annbacher (St. Anne's brook)
131, 77
Annen (short for Annenberg,
etc.)
Annenberg (St. Anne's
mountain) 131, 68, 122
Anneshansli (little Hans, son
of Anna) 60
Annewallt, see Anwalt
Anno < Arnold 53
Ansbach (fr Ansbach 122,
brook of the gods, or *ans*
pre-Germanic word for
"river") 48, 77, 83
Anschutz, Anschuetz (one
who turns on the water at
a mill)
Ansel, Ansell, Anssel, Ansler
< Anselm
Anselm, Anselmus (god +
helmet) 47, 48, 131, 137
Anselmi (son of Ansel) 142
Anske (little god) 47
Ansorge (without worry) 115
Anspach, Anspacher,
Anspack (fr Anspach 122,
god + brook)
Anstadt, Ansteadt, Anstet <
St. Anastasius 131
Anstadt (town on the *Ans*,
pre-Germanic river name)
83
Anstein (at the mountain)
70, 73, 122
Anstine (fr Anstein 122) 151
Answald (god + rule, god +
forest) 47, 46, 72
Ante, Antemann (dweller on
the boundary, at the end),
see Amend
Antemann (duck raiser) 91

Antenberg (duck hill) 115, 68
Antenbrink (duck hill) 115, 74
Anters, Antes, Anthes <
Andreas 53
Antley, Antli (little duck) 91,
115
Antlitz (face, countenance)
Anton, Anthon (St. Anthony)
131
Antoni, Anthoni (son of Anton)
142
Antwerck (siege machine,
mechanic) 108
Antzengruber (fr Anzengrub)
122
Anwalt (attorney)
Apel, Appel, Apelt (apple) 89,
105
Apelberg (apple hill) 89, 68
Apfel (apple) 89, 105, 122
Apfelbach (apple brook) 89, 77,
122
Apfelbaum (apple tree) 89
Apfelhaus (apple house) 89, 65
Apitz, Apitsch < Albrecht 53
App < Albrecht 53
Appel 122, Appelt, Appelbaum,
see Apel, Apfelbaum
Appel (pre-Germanic river
name) 83
Appelbome, see Apfelbaum
Appeldorne (apple thorn) 89,
122
Appelmann (apple grower or
seller) 89, 105
Appelstein (apple seed) 89, 151
Appenzeller, Appenzellar (Swiss
fr Canton Appenzell) 121
Appert < Albrecht 53
Apple < Adelbert, see Appel
151
Applefeld (apple field) 89, 84,
151
Applegarth (apple orchard) 89,
84, 151
Appler (apple grower or seller)
89
April (April) 143
Arb (heir, see Erb) 47

Arbaugh (fr Arbach 122,
eagle brook 48, 77 or fr
ar, pre-germanic word for
"river" 77, 83) 151
Arbegast, see Arbogast
Arbeiter (worker)
Arbengast, see Arbogast
Arberg (eagle mountain, or
mountain on the Aar) 48,
68, 83, 122
Arbogast (heir + guest, name
of a saint) 46, 131
Arbor, Arbort (Latin, arbor)
Arburg (eagle castle) 48, 73
Arcularius (Latin, casket
maker) 141
Arehart, see Erhard 151
Arenberg, see Arensberg 122
Arend, Arendt, Arens, see
Arnold
Arenholtz (eagle forest) 48,
72, 122
Arensberg, Arensberger
(eagle mountain) 48, 68,
122
Arenstein, see Arnstein
Arfmann (heir) 46
Argabright, Argenbright <
Erkanbrecht, genuine +
bright) 46, 151
Argire, see Aargauer 151
Arisman, see Ehrismann 151
Arlt < Arnold 53
Armbrust, Armbruester,
Armbreast, Armbreaster
(crossbow, fr Latin
arcuballista) 108
Armel, Aermel (sleeve, tailor)
104
Armenbeter (one who prays
for poor) 138
Armentrout (friend of the
poor) 138, 151
Armgast (poor stranger)
Arnau (eagle meadow) 46, 84
Arnbuehl (eagle hill) 46, 67
Arnd, Arndt < Arnold 53
Arndorf (eagle village) 46,
123, 122

Arndt, see Arnd
Arnheim (eagle hamlet) 46, 123
Arnhelm (eagle + helmet) 46, 46
Arnhoff (eagle farm) 46, 92
Arnholt, Arnholtz, see Arnold
Arno < Arnold 53
Arnold, Arnolt, Arnolds, Arnoldus (eagle + loyal or eagle + rule) 48, 58, 47
Arnoldi (son of Arnold) 142
Arnreich (eagle + rule) 46, 47
Arnsdorf, Arnsdorfer, see Arndorf 122
Arnstein (eagle mountain) 46, 73, 122
Arnulf (eagle + wolf) 46, 48
Arold, see Arnold
Aronstein, see Arnstein 151
Arzberger (fr Arzberg 122), see Erzberger
Arzt, Artz, Arts (doctor, fr Latin arciater) 96
Asbach (pre-Germanic as, meaning "water", + bach, brook) 83
Asch, Asche, Ash (ash tree, ash forest, see Esch) 89, 122
Asch (ashes, ash tree) 89
Aschbacher (fr Aschbach 122), see Eschbach
Aschberg, Ascheberg (ash tree mountain) 89, 48, 122
Aschemeier (farmer among the ash trees) 89, 93
Aschenbach (ash tree brook) 89, 77
Aschenbrenner (burner of ashes, perhaps for soap or potash) 95
Aschendorf (ash tree village) 89, 123, 122
Aschenmoor (ash fen) 89, 80
Ascher, Aschman, Aschmann (maker of tanner's lime, soapmaker's ash) 95
Asendorf (grazing village) 122

Ashauer (ash tree cutter, dweller on a meadow in the ash trees) 89, 95
Ashbaugh, see Aschbacher 151
Asher, see Ascher 151
Ashman, see Asher 151
Asmann, Assmann, Asmus, Assmus < St. Erasmus 131
Aspeck, Aschbeck (ash brook) 89, 77
Aspelhof (farm on a fen) 80, 92
Aspelmeyer (proprietor of the Aspelhof) 93, 94
Aspinwall < Espenwald (aspen forest) 89, 72
Assenmacher (wainwright) 96
Ast (branch, wood cutter, difficult person) 95, 115, 122
Astheim (east hamlet) 123, 122
Astholz (branch wood, faggot gatherer) 95
Astor (astor, fr the Greek 9, or perhaps Aster, magpie 89, or astore, Italian: hawk 89)
Astroth (branch clearing) 126
Aswalt, Answald, see Oswald
Atterholt (at the forest) 70, 72
Atz, Attz (donkey, also < Albrecht) 115
Atzbach (pre-Germanic at, river + bach, brook) 83, 77, 122
Atzelstein (magpie mountain) 73
Au, Aub, Aue (meadow, usually shortened fr compound word) 84, 122
Aubel < Albrecht
Aubitz < Albrecht

Auburg (castle on the meadow, or castle at Au) 84, 73, 122

Auch, Auchmann (night shepherd) 95

Auchenbaugh, see Achebach 151

Auchtmann, see Achmann 151

Aue, Auen, see Au

Auenbrugger (dweller near the bridge at the meadow) 84, 71

Auer (dweller on a meadow, usually shortened fr compound word) 84

Auerbach 122, Auerback (brook through meadow, possibly bison [*auerochs*] brook, or else based on pre-Germanic *ur*, muddy water) 84, 77, 122

Auerhahn (grouse) 89, 115

Auerswald (meadow wood) 84, 71

Auerweck (meadow path 65, or meadow village, fr Latin *vicus*) 84

Aufderheide (on the heath) 70, 81, 122

Auffahrt (Asension Day) 143

Auge, Augen (eye, eyes) 114

Augenstein (St. Augustine) 131

Aughinbaugh, see Achebach 151

Augsburg 122, Augspurg, Augsburger, Augspurg (Swabian city)

August, Augustus (Latin, Augustus) 141

Augustin (St. Augustine) 131

Aul, Auler, Aulner (pot, potter, fr Latin *olla*) 96

Aulbert, see Albert

Aule (jackdaw) 115

Aulebach, Aulenbacher (fr Aulenbach) 122

Aulenbaecker (potter) 96

Aulmann (potter) 96

Ault, see Alt

Aultland, see Altland

Aumann (meadow man) 84, 94

Aumiller, see Aumueller

Aumueller (proprietor of the Aumuehle) 84, 103

Aurich (place name) 122

Ausdermuehle (out of the mill) 69

Ausheim (outside the village) 69, 123

Auslander (outlander, foreigner)

Auspurger, see Augsburg

Aust, Austen, Austin (St. Augustine) 131

Austerlitz (town in Bohemia) 122

Austermann (easterner)

Austermuehle, see Ausdermuehle

Austrich, see Oestrich

Awert, see Eber

Ax, Axe, Axt, Axmann (ax, ax maker, carpenter) 96

Axel < Absolon (OT name, Absalom) 135

Axelbaum (axel shaft, wainwright) 96, 106

Axelmann (cartwright) 96

Axelrad, Axelrod (axle wheel, cartwright) 106

Ayd, Aydt, see Eid

Ayrer, Ayers, see Eier

Azenweiler (donkey village) 127

B

Baacke, Baake, see Baak

Baaden, Baader, see Baden, Bader 121

Baak (horse)

Baar 122, see Bahr

Baart, Baartz, see Bart

Baas (master, chief, boss)

Baasche, see Basch

Baase, see Base

Babst, Babest, see Pabst

Baccus, see Backhaus
Bach 122, Bache, Bachs (brook,
dweller on a brook) 77
Bacharach, Bachrach (city on
the Rhine) 122
Bachaus, see Backhaus
Bachdold, Bachdolt, see
Bechtold 151
Bachenheimer (fr Bachenheim
122, brook hamlet) 77, 123
Bacher, Bachert, Bachner,
Bachart (dweller on a brook)
77, 87, 122
Bacher (wild boar) 115
Bacher (Jewish, *bachur*,
Talmud student) 147
Bachhoffen, Bachofen 122, see
Backof
Bachhuber (farmer on the
brook) 77, 92
Bachmann, Bachman (dweller
on the brook) 77, 94
Bachmeyer, Bachmeier,
Bachmaier, Bachsmeyer
(brook farmer) 77, 93
Bachner, see Bacher
Bachrach, see Bacharach
Bachtel, Bachtell, see Bechtel
Bachthal (brook valley) 77, 76,
122
Bachus, see Backhaus
Back, see Baak
Back, Backe (jowl) 114
Back, see Bach
Backebrandt (baker's fire)
Backer, Backert, see Bacher,
Becker
Backhaus, Backhus (bakehouse,
bakery) 65, 122
Backhoffer, Backhofer, see
Backhof
Backler (baker) 96
Backman, Backmann (baker)
96
Backmeister (master baker) 96
Backner (baker) 96

Backof, Backoff, Backofen,
Backoven (baker's oven,
baker) 106
Backstrom (brook stream)
77, 78
Backus, see Backhaus
Bacmeister, see Backmeister
Badder, see Bader
Badecker, see Boettcher
Badedorfer (bath village) 123
Bademann (bath attendant)
96
Baden (baths, any one of
many South German
places) 121, 122
Badenhamer, Badenheimer
(fr Badenheim 122, bath
hamlet) 123
Bader (bath attendant,
surgeon) 96
Badertscher (surgeon) 96
Badmann, Badner, see
Bademann
Baecher, see Becher
Baechle, see Bechle
Baechtel, see Bechtel
Baeck 122, see Becker
Baecker 122, see Becker
Baedeker, see Boettcher
Baehler, see Buehler
Baehm, see Boehm
Baehr, Baehre (bear) 48
Baehring, Baehringer, see
Behrens
Baehrle (little bear) 48
Baehrmann, see Berman
Baehrwolf (bear + wolf) 48,
48
Baender, see Bender
Baeninger, see Peninger
Baenisch, Baensch, see
Benisch
Baenk (bench, bench maker)
96, 106
Baentzler < St. Benedictus
131
Baer, Baehr (bear, usually a
shortened form) 48

Baerenburg (bear castle) 48,
73, 122
Baerenreuth (fr Berenreuth
122, burned clearing) 126
Baerger, see Berger
Baerhold (bear + loyal) 48, 48
Baeringer, see Behrens
Baerley, Baerli (little bear) 48
Baerman, Baermann (bear
man, bear trainer) 48, 96
Baertlein (little beard) 114
Baesler, see Basler
Baetger, see Boettcher
Baetje, Baetjer, see Boettcher
Baetz, see Betz
Baeumer, Baeumler (expert on
fruit trees)
Baeurele, Baeurlein, Baeuerlein
(little peasant) 91, 122
Baeyerlein, see Baeuerlein
Baez, see Baetz
Bagger (dredger)
Bahl, Bahle, Bahls, Bahlmann,
Bahler < Baldwin 53
Bahn, Bahne, Bahnlein (path,
track, road) 65
Bahner, Bahnert (weaver's tool,
weaver) 106
Bahnke (little path) 65
Bahnmueller (miller on the
path) 65, 103
Bahr (bear) 48
Bahre (stretcher)
Bahremann (stretcher bearer)
Bahrenburg 73, see Barenburg
Bahrlein (little bear) 48
Bahsel, see Basler
Baier, Baierman, see Bayer
Baierlein, Baierline 151, see
Bayerle
Baiersdorf 122, see Bayersdorf
Bail, Baile, Bailer, Baylor, see
Beil, Beiler
Bain (leg) 114
Bair, see Baer, Bayer
Baisch < St. Sebastian 131
Baitmann, Baitz, Baizner
(falconer) 91
Bakenhus 122, see Backhaus

Baker, Bakker, see Becker
151
Balcer, see Baltzer
Balch (kind of game fish)
115
Balck, see Balk
Bald, Balde, Baldt, Balt
(bold 46, river name 83)
Baldauf, Balldauf, Balduf
(brave + wolf, or "soon
up," perhaps a greeting to
miners) 46, 48
Baldhauer, see Waldhauer
Baldinger 122 (fr Balding,
belonging to Baldwin) 46,
59
Baldwin, Baldewin (brave +
friend) 46, 47
Balk (beam)
Ball, Balls (ball, dance,
hunting sound)
Ball, Ballmann < Baldwin 53
Ballauf, see Baldauf
Ballenberg, Ballenberger (fr
Ballenberg 122)
Ballenger, Baller < Baldwin
Ballenhausen (town name)
122
Ballerstadt (fr Ballerstaedt)
122
Balling, Ballinger < Baldwin
53
Ballman, Ballmann <
Baldwin 53
Balmer, Ballmer, Ballmert
(dweller under a cliff, see
also Palmer)
Balmtag (Palm Sunday) 143
Balsam (balsam)
Balser, Balsor < Balthasar
Balsinger, see Bellsinger
Balter < Balthasar
Balthasar, Baltasar,
Balthhauser, Baltzar,
Baltzaer (one of the Three
Kings) 131, 111
Balthauer, see Waldhauer
Baltz, Baltz, Baltze, Baltzer,
Baltzel, Baltzell, Baltzer,

Baltzar, see Palts, Paulser, Balthasar, Baldwin

Bamberg, 122, Bamberger, Bamesberg (fr Bamberg)

Bancalf, see Bannkauf 151

Band (hoop maker) 106

Bandel, Bandell, Bandele, Bandli (ribbon maker) 106

Bandhagen, Bandhaken (cooper's hook, cooper) 106

Bandholt, Banholtz, Bandtholtz (wood for barrel hoops, cooper) 106

Baner, Banner, see Bahner

Bang, Bange, Bangs, Banger, Bangers, Bangert (timid) 115

Bangart, Banghart, see Baumgart

Banholtz (proscribed forest) 72

Bank 122, Banke, Banker, Banks (bench, workbench, bench maker) 106

Bankamper (field on a road) 65, 84

Bankard, Bankerd, Bankert (illegitimate child)

Bankwirt (taverner) 96

Bann (ban) 122

Bannat (Banat, German area in Hungary) 121

Banne, Bannmann (crowd, mob)

Banner (banner, ensign) 107

Bannertraeger (ensign) 107

Banninger (fr Banningen) 122

Bannkauf (proscribed sale)

Bansch, Baensche (pot belly) 114

Banse, Bansen (store room, granary, woodpile)

Bantel, Bantell, Bantle, Bantli (little band, ribbon maker) 106

Bantel < St. Pantaleon 131

Bantner (dweller in a fenced area)

Bantz, Banz, Banzel (small child)

Banwarth (road guard) 65, 47

Banzer, see Panzer

Baptista, Baptiste, Baptisto (John the Baptist) 131

Baranhardt, see Bernhard

Barb (kind of river fish) 115

Barbel, Baerbel < Barbara 60

Barbelroth (Barbara's clearing) 126

Barch (barrow hog) 91

Barchell (fr Barchel) 122

Barchmann (swineherd) 95

Bard, see Bart

Bardenhagen (halbard enclosure) 123, 122

Bardenwerter (halbard maker) 108

Barenbaum (bear tree) 48, 89

Barenburg (bear castle) 48, 73, 122

Barfuss (barefoot, Barefoot Friar) 114, 110

Bargar, Barger, see Berger

Bargfeld 122, see Bergfeld

Barghoff, see Berghoff

Bargmann, see Bergmann

Barhausen (bear houses) 48, 65

Barhorst (bear hurst) 48, 72

Baringer, see Baehringer

Bark, Barke 122 (birch tree) 89

Bark, Barke (ship)

Barkdoll, see Bergdoll

Barkewitz (mountain village) 127

Barkhaus, Barkhausen 122, Barkhauser (birch house, mountain house) 89, 68, 65

Barkheimer, see Bergheimer

Barkmann, see Bergmann

Barmann (half-free peasant), see Bermann

Barnd, see Bernd

Barner, see Berner
Barnhard, Barnhardt, see
    Bernhard
Barnhaus 122, Barnhauser
    (bear house) 48, 65
Barnheart, see Bernhard 151
Barnholt, see Bernholt
Barnhouse, Barnhouser, see
    Barnhaus 151
Barnscheier (bear barn)
Barnstein (fr Barnstein 122),
    see Bernstein
Barnstorf (bear village, or
    Bernhard's village) 48, 123,
    122
Baron, Barron (warrior, baron)
Barr (cash)
Barrabas (NT name) 111
Barringer < Berenger (bear +
    spear) 48, 46
Barsch, Barss (perch) 115, <
    Bartholomaeus
Bart, Barth, Barthel, Bartz <
    Bartholomaeus, Barthold,
    Bartolf, etc. 53, 54
Bart, Barth (beard, barber)
    112, 96
Barte (butcher's ax, butcher)
    106
Bartal, see Bertel
Bartasch (fringed purse) 106
Bartel, Bartels, Barthels,
    Barttel, Bartelmes <
    Bartholomaeus
Barth 122, see Bart
Barthel, see Bartel
Barthelm (battle-ax + helmet)
    46, 46
Barthelmes, see Bartoholmeaus
Bartholomaeus, Bartholomae,
    Bartholome, Bartholomes,
    Bartholomei, Batholomy,
    Bartholomus (St. Bartholo-
    mew) 131
Bartholt (battle-ax + loyal) 46,
    48
Bartkuss (beard kiss)
Bartle, see Bartel 151

Bartlebaugh (Bartel's brook)
    77, 151
Bartling (fr Bartlingen) 122
Bartmann (thick stone jug)
Bartmann (beard wearer)
    112
Bartol, Bartold, see Bartholt,
    Bartholomaeus
Bartolomaeus, see
    Bartholomaeus
Bartosch, see Bartasch
Bartram (battle-ax + raven)
    46, 48
Barts, see Bart
Bartsch < Bartholomaeus 53,
    54
Bartscher, Bartscheer,
    Bartscherer (beard shears,
    barber) 106
Barttel, see Bartel
Bartz, Barz, see Bart,
    Bartholomaeus
Barzmann < Bartholomaeus
    53, 54
Basch (sharp, as of spice)
Base, Basemann (cousin) 119
Basel, Basler, Bassel (fr
    Basel 122)
Bass (boss)
Basse (one-masted boat) 122
Basselmann, see Basel
Bassler, see Basel
Bast, Bastian, Bastien < St.
    Sebastian 131
Bastert (bastard)
Bate (help), see also Pate
Bates, see Betz 151
Bateman, see Bethmann 151
Bath, see Bad
Bathmann, Batmann (bath
    attendant) 96
Batt (emolument), also St.
    Beatus 131
Batten, Battenberg,
    Battenfeld (place names fr
    bat, swamp water) 122
Battermann (wooden spade)
    106
Battermann (boaster) 115

Battist (John the Baptist) 131
Batts, Batz, Batze, Batzer, see
Patz
Batty, see Battist
Bau (construction, cultivation)
122
Bauch (belly, glutton) 114, 114
Bauer, Bauers, Baur, Bauerdt
(farmer) 91, 149
Bauerfeld, Bauersfeld (peasant
field) 91, 84
Bauerle, Bauerlein, Bauerlien
151, Bauerline 151 (little
peasant) 91
Bauermann (same as Bauer)
91, 94
Bauermeister, Bauernmeister
(village head) 109
Bauernfeind, Bauernfiend 151
(peasant enemy, probably
initiation name) 116
Bauernschub, Bauernshub 151
(peasant overcoat) 112
Bauers, see Bauer
Bauerschmidt, Bauernschmid
(village smith) 91, 96
Bauersfeld, see Bauerfeld
Bauershaefer (peasant oats) 91
Bauerwein (peasant wine) 91,
102
Baugh, Baugher, Baughman,
see Bach, Bacher, Bachmann
151
Baughtall, see Bechtold 151
Bauhaus (shelter at
construction site) 65, 122
Bauholzer (seller of building
wood, builder in wood) 72,
105
Bauk, Bauker (drum,
drummer) 96, 106
Bauknecht (construction helper)
Bauknight, see Bauknecht 151
Baum, Baumes (tree) 89, 122
Baumann (tenant, see Bauer)
91
Baumbach (tree brook) 89, 77,
122

Baumberger (fr Baumberg
122, tree mountain) 89, 68
Baumbusch (tree busch) 89,
72
Baumeister (builder,
agricultural manager)
Baumel (little tree) 89
Baumer, Baumert
(horticulturist) 84, 143
Baumer (manager of, or
dweller near) a toll gate)
Baumgaert, Baumgaertner
(orchard, orchardist) 84
Baumgarden, Baumgarten
122, Baumgardner,
Baumgartner,
Baumgarthner,
Baumgartel, Baumgarner,
Baumgart (orchardist) 84
Baumhard (strong as a tree,
uncultivated tree-studded
area) 89, 46
Baumhof, Baumhoefer (tree
farm) 89, 92, 122
Baumiller (miller at a
Bauhof) 103
Baumler (tree guard), see
also Baumer
Baummer, see Baumer
Baumoehl (tree cutter), see
also Baumohl
Baumohl (olive oil seller)
105
Baumrin, Baumrind
(collector of bark for
tanning) 95
Baumstark (strong as a tree)
115
Baumstein (tree stone) 89,
73
Baumwoll (cotton) 105, 106
Baur, see Bauer
Baurmeister, Bauernmeister
(village mayor) 109
Baus, Bausch, Bauscher
(bolster) 106
Baus (bruise, swelling)
Bausch, see Busch

Bauschenberger (bush
mountain) 72, 68
Bauth, Bauthe, Bauthner
(building, beehive)
Bauthz (fr Bautzen) 122
Baverungen, see Beverungen
151
Bawman, see Baumann 151
Bayer, Bayr, Beyer, Bayermann
(Bavarian) 121
Bayerfalck (Bavarian falcon)
Bayerhoff (Bavarian farm) 122,
121, 92
Bayerle, Bayerlein (little
Bavarian, see Baeuerle) 121
Bayersdorf (Bavarian's village)
121, 123
Baylor, see Beiler 151
Bayrle, see Bayerle
Bazermann, see Patz
Beacher, see Buecher 151
Beachler, see Buechler 151
Beadenkof, Beadenkoef,
Beadenkopf, see Biedenkopp
151
Beagle, see Buegel 151
Beahm, see Boehm 151
Beahmesderfner (Bohemian
villager) 122, 123, 151
Beal, Beals, Beall, see Buehl
151
Bealefeld, Bealefield, see
Bielefeld 151
Bealer, Beeler, see Buehler 67,
151
Beam, Beamer, see Boehm,
Boehmer 151
Beamsderfer, Beamesderfer, see
Beahmesderfner
Bean, Beane, see Bohn, Bohne
151
Bear, Bearman, see Baehr,
Baehrmann 151
Beardorf (bear village) 48, 123,
151
Beaver, see Bieber 152
Bebel, Bebler, Beber
(something or someone
small)

Bechelmeier (proprietor of
the Bechelhof, little brook
farm) 77, 93, 92, 94
Becher, Bechermann, Bechler
(maker of mugs, fr Latin
bicarium) 106
Becher (tarheeler, tar maker,
fr Latin *pix*) 95
Becher (dweller on a brook)
77
Becher, Bechler (drinker,
tippler) 115
Bechlinger (fr Bechlingen
122)
Bechmann (tarheeler, tar
maker) 95
Bechold, see Bechthold
Bechstein (pitch stone) 73
Becht, Bechte, Bechtel,
Bechtler (New Year
revelry), see also
Bechthold
Bechthold, Bechtolt, Bechtoll,
see Berchthold
Beck (brook) 77, 122
Beck, Becks, Becke (baker)
96
Beck (snout) 114
Beck (basin, Latin, *bacinum*)
106
Beckel (helmet) 108
Beckelheimer, Beckelhimer
155 (fr Beckelheim 122,
little brook hamlet) 77,
123
Beckemeyer (brook farmer)
77, 93
Beckenbach (Becco's brook)
77
Beckendorf (brook village)
77, 123, 122
Beckenholt (brook wood) 77,
72
Becker, Beckert (baker) 96,
104, 143
Beckerbach, see Beckenbach
Beckermann, Beckmann
(baker) 96

Beckeweg (brook path) 77, 65
Beckhardt (Beghard, lay
 brother)
Beckler (tippler) 115
Becklin, Beckley, see Boekle
Beckman, Beckmann (baker) 96
Beckmann (dweller on a brook)
 77, 94
Beckner, see Becker
Beckolt, see Berchtold
Beckstein (brook stone) 122
Beckstein (brickmaker) 100,
 122
Beckstrom (brook stream) 77,
 78
Beech, see Buech, Buecher 151
Beechener, see Buechner 151
Beehler, see Buehler 151
Beek (brook) 77
Beeker, see Bacher, Buecher
 151
Beekmann, see Bachmann
Beel, see Buehl 151
Beeler, Beehler, see Buehler
 151
Beem, Beemer, see Boehm,
 Boehmer 151
Beer, Beermann, see Baer,
 Baermann, Bier, Biermann
 151
Beer, Beers, see Ber, Behr,
 Bier 151
Beerbach (bear brook, boar
 brook) 48, 77, 122
Beerbohm (pear tree) 89
Beerends, see Behrends
Beermann, see Baehrmann
Begabock, see Beckenbach 151
Begemann (dweller on the
 Bega) 83
Begstein, see Beckstein
Begtel, Begtoll, see Bechtel
Behagel (affable) 115
Behl, Behle, Behler, Behlert,
 see Buehl
Behling (fr Behlingen) 122
Behm, Behme, Behmer, see
 Boehm

Behn, Behne, Behner
Behnemann < Bernhard
Behnke, Behnken (little
 bear), or < Bernhard
Behr, Behre, Behrs (bear,
 boar), or < Bernhard
Behren, Behrens, Behrend,
 Behrendt < Bernhard 53
Behringer (fr Behringen) 122
Behrmann (bear + man, bear
 trainer) 48, 94
Behrman, Behrmann (beer
 handler) 96
Behrnhard, see Bernhard
Behse, see Besen
Beichel, Beichl (little belly)
 114
Beichler, Beichmann (slope
 dweller) 71
Beichter (confessor)
Beidel, see Beutel
Beidelmann, Beidelman, see
 Beutelmann
Beiderwieden (by the
 willows) 70, 89
Beier, Beiermann, see Bayer
Beierlein, see Baeuerlein,
 Bayerlein
Beigel, see Buegel 151
Beightel, Beightol, see
 Beichtel, Bechtol 151
Beights, see Beitz
Beil, Beiler (ax maker or
 seller) 106
Beilfus (ax foot) 114
Beiling (fr Beilingen) 122
Beilke (little ax) 106
Beilstein (ax stone, old
 hunting grounds)
Beimel, Beimler, see
 Baeumel, Baeumler
Bein, Beine, Beinn, Beinle
 (leg, bone) 114
Beinhauer (butcher, not leg
 hacker) 96
Beinhorn (river name,
 swamp corner) 80, 83
Beinike (little bee)

Beinkampen (by the fields) 70, 84

Beinstein (by the mountain) 68, 70, 122

Beisel, Beissel, Beissler (tool for splitting wood) 106

Beisner (one who hunts with falcons) 91

Beischwanger (adjacent clearing) 126

Beisser (falconer) 91

Beitel 122, Beittel, Beitle, Beitler, Beitelmann, see Beutel, Beutler, Beutelmann (purse maker) 106

Beitz, Beitzel, Beitzell (falconer) 91

Beker, see Becker

Bekmann, see Beckmann

Beler, Beeler, see Buehler

Belfield, see Bielefeld 151

Belitz (place name) 122

Bell, Belle (part of a ship)

Bell, Belle (white poplar) 89

Beller (watch dog, quarreler) 115

Belling, Bellinger (fr Belling) 122

Bellmann (public announcer) 96

Bellner (public announcer) 96

Belman, Bellmann, see Bellmann

Beltz, Belz, Beltzer, Beltzner, see Peltz

Beltzenhagen (place name) 123, 122

Bemer, see Boehmer

Bence, see Bentz 151

Benck, see Benk

Bendel (ribbon maker or seller) 106, 105

Bendel, Bendler (barrel hoop maker, cooper) 96, 106

Bender, Benders, Bendert (cooper) 96

Benderoth (swamp clearing) 80, 126

Bendewald (swampy forest) 80, 71

Bendex, Bendix < St. Benedict 131

Bendt < St. Benedict 131

Benedict, Benedick (St. Benedict) 131

Beneke, Bennecke < Bernhard 53

Bener < Bernhard 53

Benesch, Bensch, Benisch < Czech: Benedict

Bengel (club, fool) 115

Bengert, see Benkert

Benhof, Bennhoff (Bernhard's farm) 122

Benighoff, see Benninghoff

Benisch, see Benesch

Benjamin (OT name) 135

Benk, Benke, Benker, Benkert (bench, cabinet maker, from Benk 122) 96

Benkert, Benkart (bastard) 119

Benner, see Bender

Benning 122 < Bernhard

Benninghoff, Benninghof 122, Benninghove (peat bog farm) 80, 92

Benroth, Benrath 122 (a city, stream clearing) 126

Bensch, see Benesch

Bense, Bensen 122, Benser, Bensing, Bensinger (place where bullrushes grow) 81

Bensel, Benseler (dweller among the reeds) 81

Benshoff (reed farm) 81

Bensing, Bensinger, see Bentzinger

Benson, see Bentzen 151

Bentell, Bentels, see Bentler

Bentheim (name of city, marsh hamlet) 122

Bentler < St. Pantaleon 131

Bentley, Bentli, see Bantli 151

Bentsen, son of Bentz 59

Bentz, Benz, Benze, Benzel, Bentzel < Bernhard or Benedict

Bentzen, son of Bentz 59
Benzelius, see Bentzel 141
Benzenhof 122, Benzenhoffer,
Benzenhafer (reed farm) 81,
92
Bentziger 122, Bentzing,
Bentzinger (fr Bentzingen)
Benzinger 122, see Bentzinger
Beohmer, see Boehmer 151
Ber, see Baer
Berach (bear river) 48, 83
Berbisdorf (Berbi's village) 123,
122
Berch, see Berg
Berchelbach, Berckelbach (birch
brook) 89
Bercher, see Berger and
Bircher
Berchner, see Bergner
Berchtel, see Berchthold
Berchthold (bright + loyal,
bright + rule) 46, 46
Berck, see Berg
Berckhaeuser, Berckheiser,
Berckhyser (occupant of
mountain house) 68, 65
Bere, Berele < Bernhard 53
Berenbach (bear brook) 48, 77,
122
Berenberg 122, Berenberger
(bear mountain, berry
mountain) 48, 68
Berend, Berends, Berents, see
Baehrend
Berenger (bear + spear) 48, 46
Berenhaus (bear house) 48, 65
Berenholtz (bear forest) 48, 72
Berenstecher (boar castrator)
95
Berfeld (boar field) 48, 84
Berg, Berge, Bergs, Bergen
(mountain) 68, 82
Bergbauer (mountain farmer)
68, 91
Bergdoll (mountain valley) 68,
76
Bergdoll, see Berchtold

Bergenbach (mountain brook)
68, 77
Bergenslott (mountain castle)
68
Bergenstine (fr Bergenstein
122, mountain stone) 68,
73, 151
Bergenthal (mountain valley)
68, 76
Berger (mountain man) 68
Bergfeld (mountain field) 68,
84, 122
Bergh, see Berg
Berghaus (mountain house)
68, 65, 122
Berghauser, Berghaeuser,
Berkhaeuser, Berckheiser,
Bergheiser (fr Berghausen
122, house on a mountain)
68, 65
Bergheimer (fr Bergheim,
mountain hamlet) 68, 123,
122
Berghof, Berghoff,
Berghoeffer (mountain
farm) 68, 92, 122
Berghorn (mountain peak)
68, 68
Berghuis, see Berghaus
Bergk, see Berg
Bergkirch (mountain church)
68, 122
Bergland (mountain country)
68, 49
Bergler, Bergner (mountain
man) 68
Bergmann, Bergman (miner,
mountain man) 68, 94
Bergmeister (mine
supervisor) 68
Bergner (mountain man) 68
Bergschmidt (mountain
smith) 68, 96
Bergschneider (mountain
tailor) 68, 104
Bergstein (mountain stone)
68, 73, 122

Bergstrasser 122, Bergstresser, Bergstrosser (dweller on amountain road, fr Bergstrasse) 68, 65

Bergstrom (mountain stream) 68, 78

Bergtold, Bertoll, see Bergdoll

Bergweiler (mountain village) 68, 127, 122

Berhart, see Bernhard

Bering, Beringer (fr Beringen 122; see Behring)

Berk, Berke, see Berg and Birck

Berkelbach (birch brook) 89, 77

Berkemeyer, see Berkmeyer

Berkenbusch (birch bush) 89, 72

Berkenfeld (birchfield) 89, 84

Berkenhauer (birch chopper) 89, 95

Berkenkamp, Berkenkaempfer, Berkenkemper (birch field) 89, 84

Berkenmayer, see Berkmeyer

Berkenstock (birch trunk) 89

Berker, see Berger

Berkhausen, see Berghaus 89, 65, 122

Berkheim 122, Berkheimer (birch hamlet) 89, 123

Berkhof, Berkhoff, Berkoff (fr Berghof, mountain farm) 89, 92, see Berghoff

Berkholtz (birch wood, mountain forest) 89, 72, 122

Berkman, Berkmans, see Bergmann

Berkmeyer, Berkmeyer (proprietor of the Berkhoff) 68, 93, 92, 94

Berkner (mountain man) 68

Berkstresser, see Bergstrasser

Berlanstein (pearl mountain) 68, 151

Berlein (little bear) 48

Berlin, Berliner (German city) 122, 146

Berman, Bermann, Bermant (bear trainer, swineherd) 68

Bermut (bear + disposition) 68, 114

Bern 122, Berne, Berner, Berns (fr Bern)

Bernard, see Bernhard

Bernauer (fr Bernau, swamp meadow) 80, 84, 122

Bernd, Berndt, Berends < Bernhard 53

Berner (Swiss fr Bern) 122

Bernfeld (swamp field) 68, 80, 84

Bernhard, Bernhardt, Bernard (bear + strong) 68, 46

Bernhardi (son of Bernhard) 142

Bernheim, Bernheimer (swamp hamlet) 68, 123

Bernheisl, see Berninghaus

Bernholt (bear + loyal or bear + forest) 48, 48

Berning (belonging to the bear) 48, 59

Berninghaus (Berning's house) 65, 122

Bernsohn (son of the bear, son of Bern) 68, 59

Bernstein (amber)

Bernstein (bear mountain) 122

Bernt, see Bernhard

Bernwinkler (bear + wooded valley) 68, 76

Berodt (bear clearing) 68, 126, 122

Bersch, see Barsch

Berstein (bear mountain) 68, 73

Berstroser, see Bergstrasser

Bert, Bertz < Bertram, Berthold, etc. 53

Bertel, Bertell, Bertels < Berthold 53

Bertha < Brecht ...

Berthel, see Bertel

Berthold, Bertholdt, Bertold,
Berthhoud (brilliant + loyal)
46, 48
Bertling, see Bartling
Bertman, see Bartmann
Bertoldi, son of Berthold 142
Bertram, Berteram, see
Bartram
Bertrand (brilliant + shield) 46,
47
Bertsch, Bertschi < Berthold,
etc. 53
Bertz, Berz, see Bert
Berwage, Berwanger (fr
Berwangen, bear field) 48,
71, 122
Berwald (bear forest) 48, 71
Besch < Sebastian 131
Beschorner (shorn one,
clergyman) 112, 110
Besel (broom maker) 106
Besemann (broom maker) 96
Besinger, see Bessing
Besner (broom maker) 96
Besold, see Betzold
Besse (swamp) 80
Besser, Bessert (better,
collector of fines)
Bessing, Bessinger (fr
Bessingen) 122
Bessmann (repairman) 96
Best (best)
Best < Sebastian 131
Beste (river name, muddy
water) 83
Bestenholtz (for Westenholtz,
western forest) 72
Besterfeldt (west field) 84
Betenbaugh, see Bittenbach
151
Bethge, Bethke, Betke <
Bertram
Bethman, Bettmann (payer of
landlord's "requests")
Betram, see Bertram
Betrand, see Bertrand
Bettendorf (town name) 123,
122

Bettenhausen (tenant house)
65, 122
Better, Bettermann (rosary,
rosary maker) 106
Bettger, see Boettcher
Betz, Betts, Bates, Pates <
Bernhard 53
Betzinger, Betzner (fr
Betzingen) 122
Betzold, Petzold, Betzel,
Betzler < Peter 131
Beuchel (little belly) 114
Beucher, Beuchert, see
Buecher
Beuckelmann, see Buechner
Beuel, Beul (bruise) 122
Beuer, Beuermann (peasant)
91
Beuerle, see Baeuerle
Beuke, see Buche
Beul, Beuler, see Buehl,
Buehler
Beulshausen (place name)
65, 122
Beumler, see Baeumler
Beunde (private fenced-in
area) 84
Beurlein, see Baeuerlein
Beusch, see Baus
Beuschlag, see Beyschlag
Beuschlein (little bush) 89,
72
Beutel (purse, sack, purse
maker) 96
Beutel (wooden club)
Beutelmann (purse maker)
96
Beutelsbach, Beutelspacher
(fr Beutelsbach, sack
brook) 77, 122
Beuthler, Beutler (purse
maker) 96
Beutner (honey gatherer) 95
Beverung, Beverungen (a
city) 122
Beyder (possibly short for
name like Beiderwieden)
70

Beyer, Beyers, Beyern, see
Bayer

Beyerle, Beyerlein, Beyerling,
see Bayerle, Baeuerle

Beyermeister, see
Bauernmeister

Beyersdorf (Bavarian village)
121, 123, 122, see
Bayersdorf

Beyl, Beyhl, see Beil

Beylstein, see Beilstein

Beyrer, see Bayer

Beyrodt (adjacent clearing) 125

Beyschlag (small piece of a
field) 84

Beyschlag (illigitimate child of
a ruler) 119

Beyth (hesitation)

Bez, see Betz

Bezold, see Betzold

Bibelhimer (Bible hamlet) 123,
151

Biber, see Bieber

Bicher, Bichert, see Buecher

Bichell, Bichler, see Buehl,
Buehler

Bickel, Bickell < Burkhart, see
Pickel

Bicksler (box maker) 96, 151

Biddel, Buettel (beadle) 109

Biddenbach, see Bittenbach

Biddinger (fr Bidingen) 122

Biddle, see Biddel 151

Biderman, see Biederman

Biebel, Bieble, Biebel (Bible)

Bieber (beaver) 115

Bieberbach (beaver brook) 77,
122

Bieberbach (swamp-water
creek) 80, 77

Biecheler, Biechelar, see
Buechler

Biedekopp, Biedenkopf
(boundary lookout) 122

Biedenbach, Biedenback (fr
Biedenbach 122, boundary
brook) 77, 122

Biedenbuender (boundary
fence)

Biederkep, see Biedekopp

Biederman, Biedermann
(doughty man, respectable
citizen) 138

Biegel, Biegler (ax maker)
96, see Buegler

Biegeleisen (stirrup, pressing
iron) 96

Biehl, Biehler, see Buehl,
Buehler

Biehlmueller (hill miller) 67,
103

Biel, Bieler, Bieller, see
Buehl, Buehler

Bielefeld (city name) 122

Biemann (bee keeper) 95

Bien, Bienemann,
Bienemann (bee keeper)
95

Bienenfeld (bee field) 84

Bienert (bee keeper) 95

Bienfang (bee catcher) 95

Bienkorb (beehive) 95

Bienlein (little bee) 115

Bienstein (bee stone) 73

Bienstock, Bienenstock
(beehive, beekeeper) 95

Bier, Bierr (beer, brewer) 96,
106

Bierach (beaver river, bear
river) 83, 122

Bierbach (mud creek) 80, 77

Bierbaum 122, see Birnbaum

Bierbrauer (beer brewer) 97

Bierenbaum, see Biernbaum

Bierenberg (pear mountain)
89, 68

Bierhagen (bear enclosure,
pear tree enclosure)

Bierkenbeyl (birch ax) 89, 96

Bierley, see Bayerle 151

Bierman, Biermann,
Biermeyer, Bierwirth
(taverner) 96

Biersack (taverner) 96

Biersack (beer belly) 114

Biersdorf (beer village) 123,
122

Bierstadt (place name, swamp
city) 80, 122
Bierwage (beer wagon, beer
distributor) 96
Bierwirt, Bierwirth (beer host
96), also < Berwart (bear +
guardian 46, 47)
Biettel, see Buettel
Bigel, Bigler, see Buegel,
Buegler
Bihl, see Buehl
Bihlmeier, Beylmeyer, see
Buehlmayer
Bilauer (hill meadow) 67, 84
Bilderbach, Bilderback,
Bilderbeck, see Wilderbach
Bildstein 122; see Wildstein
Bile, see Buehle
Bilfinger (having six fingers)
114
Bilfinger (fr Bilfingen) 122
Bilger, see Pilger
Bilheimer, see Buehlheimer
Bilig, see Billig, Bille
Bill, Bills (hill) 67
Billauer (swamp meadow) 80,
84, see Bilauer
Bille, Biller, see Buehl, Buehler
Bille (battle ax) 108
Billerbeck (hill brook) 67, 77,
122
Billheimer, see Buehlheimer
Billhimer, see Buehlheimer 151
Billig (fair, as in *recht und
billig*) 115, 122
Billing, Billings, Billinger (fr
Billing 122, hill dweller)
Billman, Billmann, see
Buehlman
Billmann (maker or user of
battle ax) 107, 108
Billmeyer, Billmeier (hill
farmer) 67, 93
Billmire, Billmyer, see
Billmeyer 151
Billroth (hill clearing) 67, 126
Billstein (hill stone) 67, 73
Billstone, see Billstein 151

Bilse (henbane)
Biltz, Bilitz, Bilz, see Piltz
Bimeler, see Baeumler 151
Binau (bee meadow) 84, 122
Bince, see Bintz 151
Bindbeutel (fastenable purse)
96, 106
Bindel (bundle)
Binder, Bindermann, Bindler
(sheaf binder, cooper,
bookbinder) 96
Bindschaedler (cooper) 96
Bindseil (cord maker, roper)
96, 106
Binebrink (bee hill) 74
Bineke, Bineker, see Beneke
Binfield, see Bienefeld
Bingel, Bingle, Bingley, see
Bengel
Bingen, Binger (city on the
Rhein) 122
Binkert, see Benkert
Binning, Binninger, Bininger
(fr Binningen 122), see
Benning
Binnix < Benedict 131
Binstock (rush stem) 81, see
Bienstock
Binswanger (fr Binswangen,
reed field) 81, 126, 122
Bintz, Bintzel (fr Binz 122,
bull rushes) 81
Birbaum, Birenbaum, see
Birnbaum
Birch, Birchen, see Birk
Birchbauer, Birchbaver
(proprietor of the
Birchhof, birch farm) 89,
91, 94
Birchler, Birchner (dweller
among the birches) 89
Birchwil (birch village) 89,
123
Birck, Birk, Birke (birch) 89
Birckelbach (birch brook) 89,
77
Birdsong, see Vogelsang 152
Birely, see Bayerle 151

Birgel (place name) 122
Birger, see Berger
Birk, Birkel, Birkelein (little
    birch) 89
Birk < Burkhart
Birkborch (birch bark) 89, 73
Birkelien, see Birk 151
Birkenbach (birch brook) 89,
    77, 122
Birkenberg (birch mountain)
    89, 68
Birkenfeld (birch field) 89, 84,
    122
Birkenhauer (birch cutter) 95
Birkenstock (birch trunk) 89
Birkenthal (birch valley) 89,
    76, 122
Birkholt (birch wood) 89, 72,
    122
Birkholz, Birkholtzer (birch
    wood) 89, 72, 122
Birkle (little birch 89), or <
    Burkhard
Birkmann, Birkmeyer,
    Birkmaier, Birckenmayer
    (farmer among the birches)
    89, 94, 93
Birkner, see Birchler
Birman, see Berman
Birnbach (pear tree brook) 89,
    77, 122
Birnbaum (pear tree) 89, 122
Birner, see Berner
Birstaedt, see Bierstadt
Birtha, see Bertha
Birx, see Birck
Bisant, Biszant (Saracen coin)
Bischberg 122, see
    Bischoffsberger
Bischoff, Bischof, Bischop
    (bishop) 59, 110
Bischoffsberger, Bischopberger
    (bishop's mountain) 110, 68
Bishof, see Bischoff 151
Bisinger (fr Bising) 122
Bismark, Bismarck 122
    (bishop's boundary)
Bisschop, see Bischoff

Bissel, Bissler (bite, small
    quantity)
Bisser (fr Bissen) 122
Biswanger (adjacent clearing)
    126
Bitel, see Buettel
Bitinger, Bittinger (fr
    Bittingen) 122
Bitman, see Buettner
Bitner, see Buettner
Bittel, see Buettel
Bittenbach (barrel brook) 77
Bittenbender (barrel maker)
    96
Bitter, Bitterlich (bitter,
    bitterly)
Bitter (public announcer,
    beggar)
Bittermann (barrel maker)
    96
Bittle, see Buettel 151
Bittmann, see Buettner
Bittner, see Buettner
Bitz, Bitzel (fenced area) 122
Bitzelberger (fenced hill) 68
Bitzer (dweller on the Bitiz)
    83
Bixler (box maker) 96
Black, see Schwartz 152
Blacker, Blackert, Blackner,
    Blackman (bleacher) 96
Blackwelder, see
    Schwarzwaelder 152
Blaetterlein (little leaf)
Blahut (blue hat, show off)
    112, 115
Blaich, Blaicher, Blaik
    (bleacher) 96
Blakmann, see Blech
Blamberg (place name) 122
Blancke, Blank, Blanke
    (white, clean)
Blankemeier, see
    Blankmeyer
Blankenbaker,
    Blankenbeckler (baker of
    white bread) 96
Blanckenberg (white
    mountain) 68, 122

Blankenburg (white castle) 73, 122

Blankenheimer (fr Blankenheim, white hamlet) 123

Blankenhorn (white peak) 68

Blankensee (white lake) 83, 122

Blankfeld (white field) 84

Blankmann (white man, bleacher) 96

Blankmeyer (proprietor of the Blankhof, white farm) 93, 94

Blankner (bleacher) 96

Blass, Blasse (bald 112, pale 114), also < St. Blasius 131

Blasser, Blaser (bald) 112

Blatman, see Blatter

Blatt (leaf)

Blattberg (leaf mountain) 68

Blattberg (swamp mountain) 80, 68

Blatter, Blatterman, Blattermann, Blattner, Blatner (armor smith) 108

Blatz, Blatzer (wedge for breaking stone) 106

Blatz, see Platz

Blau, Blauer, Blauert (blue, credulous) 115

Blaufeld (blue field) 84, 122

Blaumen, see Blumen

Blaustein (blue stone, blue mountain) 73, 122

Blaxberg, see Blocksberg 151

Blay, see Blei

Bleacher, see Bleicher 151, 152

Blech, Bleche, Blecher, Blecker, Blechmann, Blecman, Blechschmidt (sheet metal, tinsmith) 96, 106

Bleck, Bleckmann, Bleckenschmidt, see Blech

Bleeker (bleacher) 96

Blei (lead, lead worker) 96, 106

Blei (kind of fish) 105, 115

Bleiberg (lead mountain, lead mine) 68

Bleibtreu (Remain true!) 116

Bleich, Bleicher, Bleichner (pale, bleacher) 113, 96

Bleier, Bleiler (lead worker) 96

Bleiker, see Bleicher

Bleistein (lead stone, pencil) 96

Blekmann, see Bleck

Blendermann (prestidigitator) 96

Blendermann (swamp dweller) 80

Blenker, Blenkner (dweller in a barren spot)

Blesch (blow)

Bless, Blesse (blaze, bald head), also < Blasius

Blessing < Blasius

Bleucher, see Bleicher

Bley, Bleyer, see Blei, Bleier

Bleystein (lead mountain) 151

Blimke, see Bluemke

Blimline (little flower) 151

Blimmer (little flower) 151

Blind, Blinder (blind) 114

Blitstein, see Blitzstein

Blitz, Blitzer (lightning)

Blitzstein (lightning mountain) 73

Blob, see Blau

Bloch, Block, Bloech, see Block

Blocher (jailer) 109

Block (block, trunk, stocks)

Bloede (weak, shy) 115

Bloem, Bloemen, Bloemer, Blom, Blohm (flower seller) 105

Blomeyer (flower farmer) 93

Blond, Blondell, Blonder (blond) 112

Bloom, Bloomer, see Bloem 151

Bloomberg, see Blumberg 151

Bloomfield, see Blumenfeld 151

Bloomgarden, see Blumgaertner 151

Bloomingdale, see Blumenthal 151

Bloss, Blosse, Blosser (bare, naked, unarmed), < Blasius

Blotenberg, Blottenberger (swamp mountain) 80, 68

Blotkamp (swamp field) 80, 84

Blough, see Blau 151

Blubaugh, Bluebaugh (blue brook) 77, 151

Blubaum (blue tree) 89, 151

Blucher, Bluecher (Slavic place name) 122

Bluefeld, see Blaufeld 151

Bluehe (blossom)

Bluehtner (flower seller) 105

Bluemel (little flower) 105

Bluementhal, see Blumenthal 76

Bluemke (little flower) 105

Bluestein, Blustein, Bluestone, see Blaustein 151

Bluh, see Bluehe

Bluhdorn (blossom thorn) 72

Blum, Blume, Bluem, Bluhm, Blumen (flower) 105

Blumbach (flower brook) 77

Blumberg, Blumenberg (flower mountain) 68

Blume, see Blum

Blumenauer (flower meadow) 84, 122

Blumenberg, see Blumberg 68, 122

Blumenfeld, Blumenfeldt, Blumfeld (flower field) 84, 147, 122

Blumenschein (flower brilliance) 147

Blumenstein (flower mountain) 73, 147

Blumenstiel (flower stem)

Blumenthal (flower valley) 76, 147, 122

Blumer, Blumert, Blummer (flower seller) 105

Blumingdale, see Blumenthal 151

Blumner (flower seller) 105

Blunt (blond) 112

Bluntschli (fat man) 114

Blusten, see Blaustein 151

Bluth (blood)

Bluth (blossom)

Bly, see Blei 151

Blyer, Blyler, see Bleier 151

Blyman, see Bleimann 151

Blyweiss (lead white) 151

Boarman, see Borman 151

Boas, Boaz (OT name) 135

Bobenheisser (upper house, see Oberhaeuser) 65

Bobenhyser, see Bobenheisser 151

Bobenrieth (upper marsh) 81

Bobst, see Pabst

Bock, Bocks, Bocker (buck, often a house name) 149

Bock (beach tree) 89

Bockhaus, see Backhaus 151

Bockman, Bockmann (dweller among beech trees) 89

Bockmiller (proprietor of a windmill) 89, 103

Bockner, see Buechner

Bod, Bode (messenger), see also Boede

Boday < Bode 157

Bodefeld (swampy field) 80, 84

Bodeke, see Boettcher

Bodemeyer (farmer in the swamp) 93

Boden (soil, bottom, valley)

Bodenbender (cooper) 96

Bodenberger (valley mountain) 68

Bodener (valley dweller, cotter), see also Buettner

Bodenheimer (valley hamlet) 123

Bodenschatz (duty on wine)

Bodensieck (valley swamp) 80

Bodenstein (valley stone) 73, 122
Bodiker, Bodker, see Boettcher
Bodmer (tabulator)
Bodmer (dweller on the plain)
Bodner, Bodnar, see Bodener
Bodtker, see Boettcher
Boeck, Boecker, Boeckh, Boeker, Boekel, Boekl, see Bock, Beck, Becker
Boecker, see Boettcher
Boeckman, Boeckmann, see Beckmann
Boede, Boedde (wooden tub) 106
Boedeker, see Boettcher
Boeger, Boegner, see Bogener
Boehl, Boehler, Boehling, Boehlke, see Buehl, Buehler
Boehler (cloister official)
Boehm, Boehme, Boehmer, Boehmlein, Boem (Bohemian) 34, 121, see also Baeumer
Boehme (pre-Germanic river name) 83
Boehne, Boehner, Boehnert (bean dealer) 105
Boehning, see Benning
Boehnisch, see Benesch
Boehnlein, Boehneke (little bean)
Boehringer, see Behringer
Boeke (beech) 89
Boekel, Boeckl, Boekle, Boeklin, Buckley (little buck)
Boeker, see Boettcher
Boekman, Boeckmann, see Beckmann, Buchmann
Boelker (howler, bellower), < Baldwin 53
Boellner see Bellner
Boender, see Bender
Boener, see Behner
Boening, Boenning, see Benning
Boer, Boeren, Boern, see Bauer
Boerger, Boergert (burgher)
Boerghausen, see Burghause

Boermann (peasant) 91
Boerner, see Berner
Boernstein, see Bernstein
Boerries < St. Liborius 131
Boesch, see Sebastian 133
Boese, Boesser (angry, mean) 115
Boessel (place name) 122
Boessner (repairman) 96
Boettcher, Boetcher, Boether, Boettge, Boettger, Boetjer, Boettiger (barrel maker, fr Latin *apoteka*) 96
Boettinger, see Boettcher
Boettner, see Buettner
Bogener, Bogner, Bognar (bowman or bow maker) 108
Bogensberger (bow mountain) 68
Bohde, see Bode
Bohl, Bohle, Bohlen, Bohls, Bolsen (plank)
Bohlander, see Polander
Bohlen, Bohler, Bohling, Bohlinger, Bohlmann < Baldwin 53
Bohltz, see Boltz
Bohm, Bohmer, see Boehm, Boehmer
Bohmann, see Baumann
Bohmfalk (tree falcon) 89
Bohn, Bohne, Bohner (bean dealer)
Bohn, Bohne < St. Urbanus 131
Bohnenberg (bean hill) 68
Bohnenstengel (bean stalk)
Bohnsack (bean sack)
Bohr < St. Liborius 131
Bohrer (borer) 96
Bohrmann, see Bormann
Bohrmester, see Bauernmeister
Bohse, see Boos
Bokmann, see Buchmann
Boland, Bolandt, Bolander, see Poland, Polander

Boldt (bold) 46
Boldt (bolt, crossbow bolt) 108
Bolenbaugh (fr Bolenbach,
swamp brook) 80, 77, 151
Bolender, see Polander
Boll, Bolle (hill) 67
Boll (river name, swamp water)
83
Bollack, see Pollak
Bolle (plump person) 114
Bollhorst (hill hurst) 67, 72
Bolling 112, Bollinger (hill
dweller) 67, see also Buhle
Bollman, Bollemann (small
heavy-set youth) 114
Bollmann (dweller on a hill) 67
Bollwagen < Baldwin
Bollweg (hill path) 67, 65
Bollwinkel, see Bullwinkel
Bolner (hill dweller) 67
Bolte, Bolter, Bolth, Bolten, see
Boltz
Boltz, Boltze, Bolz, Boltzius,
Poltz (bolt, maker of
crossbowbolts 108, also <
Baldwin
Bombach, Bomback, Bombeck
(swamp brook) 80, 77
Bomberg, Bomberger (fr
Bomberg 122, tree mountain)
89, 68
Bomert, see Baumer
Bomgartner, see Baumgaertner
Bomhardt (tree forest) 89, 72
Bomhoff (tree farm) 89, 92
Bomstein (tree stone) 89, 77
Bonacker (bean field) 84
Boner, see Bohner
Bongart Bongartz, see
Bomgartner
Bonhag, Bonhage (forbidden
enclosure) 123
Bonhoff (bean farm) 92
Bonmueller (bean miller) 103
Bonn, Bonner (inhabitant of
Bonn) 122
Bonner, see Bonn
Bonnewitz (place name, swamp
village) 127

Bonsack (bean sack)
Bontrager (bean carrier)
Bontz, see Buntz 151
Boode, see Bote
Book ..., see Buch ... 151
Bookhultz, see Buchholtz
Bookmiller, see Buchmueller
151
Bookstein (beech mountain)
89, 73
Boom, see Baum
Boone, see Bohne 151
Boor (peasant) 91
Boos (wicked, evil) 115
Booterbaugh, see
Butterbaugh
Booth, see Bote
Borch, see Burg
Borchart, Borchardt,
Borchert, see Burkhart
Borcher, Borchers, see
Burger, Burkhart
Borcherding (belonging to
Borcher) 59
Bordemann (lace maker) 96
Bordner (gate keeper) 96
Bordorf, see Borgdorf
Borenstein, see Bernstein
Borg, Borger, see Burg,
Buerger
Borg (swamp) 80
Borgdorf, see Burgdorff
Borgenicht ("Don't borrow,"
or "I don't borrow") 116
Borger (borrower)
Borger (castle dweller) 73
Borgfeld (castle field) 73, 84
Borggreve, see Burggraf
Borghard, see Burkhard
Borgholte (castle wood) 73,
72
Borgmann, Borgman (castle
man, burgher) 73, 94
Borgmeier (castle bailif) 73,
93
Boris, see Borries
Bork, Borke (bark)
Bork, see Burg, Burkhard
Borkholz (castle wood) 73, 72

Borkmann, see Borgmann 73, 94

Bormann < St. Liborius 131, see also Bornemann

Born, Borne, Borner, Borns (spring) 79

Borneman, Bornemann (spring + man) 79, 94

Bornfiend, see Bauernfeind 151

Borngesser (spring road) 79, 65

Bornhausen (spring house) 79, 65, 122

Bornheim (spring hamlet) 79, 123

Bornholtz (spring forest) 79, 72

Bornhorn (spring peak) 79, 68

Bornhorst (spring hurst) 79, 72

Bornkessel (spring kettle) 79

Bornman, see Bornemann

Bornscheuer (spring barn) 79

Bornsdorf (spring village) 79, 123, 122

Bornstein (spring mountain) 79, 73, see Bernstein

Borrus < St. Liborius 131

Borsch, Borscher < St. Liborius 131

Borsdorf, see Burgdorf

Borst (bristle) 114, 106

Bortner, see Pfortner

Bortz, Borz, see Portz

Bosch, Bosche (bush, brush, branch) 72

Boschert, Boschmann, Boschenmeyer (dweller in the bush) 72

Bose, see Boos

Bosemann (evil man) 115

Boskind (naughty child) 115

Bosler, see Basler

Bosman, see Bosemann

Boss (barrow hog) 91

Bossard, see Bussart

Bosse < Burckhart 53

Bosshard, Bosshart, Bossert (Strike hard!) 116, also see Bussart

Bossler, Bossle, see Basler

Bossner (striker, ten pin player)

Bote, Both, Bothe, Bott (messenger)

Bottcher, see Boettcher

Bottich, Bottiger (barrel, barrel maker, fr Latin *apotheca*) 96

Bottmann (court messenger)

Bottner, see Buettner

Bottomstone, see Bodenstein 151

Botts, Botz, Botzler (bogeyman) 115

Botzenhard, Botzenhart (scarecrow, bogeyman) 115

Botzmann (scarecrow, bogeyman) 115

Bouch, see Bauch 151

Bouerman, see Bauermann 151

Bough, see Bau, Bauch 151

Bougher, Boughers, see Bauer, Bauers 151

Boughman, see Bachmann, Baumann 151

Boughner, see Bachner 151

Boughtall, see Bechtold 151

Bouknight, see Bauknecht 151

Bouman, see Baumann 151

Bounds, see Buntz 151

Bouse, see Bauss 151

Bousman, see Baussmann 151

Bouthner, see Bauth 151

Bowden, see Boden 151

Bower, Bowers, see Bauer 151

Bowerfind, see Bauernfeind 151

Bowerman, see Bauermann 151

Bowermaster, see Bauernmeister 151

Bowersack, Bowersock, Bowersox (peasant bag) 91, 151

Bowker, see Bauker 151
Bowman, see Baumann 151
Bowmaster, see Baumeister 151
Bowsher, see Baus
Boyer, see Bayer 151
Bozman, Bozemann, see Botzmann
Braaten, Braatz (roast, cook) 96
Brabant (province in Belgium) 121
Brach (fallow land) 122
Brachfeld (fallow field) 84, 122
Brachmann (dweller on a fallow field)
Bracht (river name) 83, 122, see Brecht, Pracht
Brack, see Brach
Brackbill (fallow hill) 67
Brackhahn, Brachhahn (plover) 115
Brackmann (hunter leading hounds)
Bradenbaugh, see Breitenbach 151
Bradt, see Brot
Braeger, Brager, see Prager
Braendel < Hildebrand
Braeuer (brewer) 96
Braeuniger, see Brauninger
Braeutigam (bridgroom) 119
Braf, Brafman, Braffmann, see Bravmann
Brahm, Brahms (swamp) 80
Brahm, Brahms < Abraham 135
Braid, Braidman, see Breit, Breitmann
Brake, Bracke (fallow, brackish)
Brakebill, see Brackbill
Brakebusch (fallow scrub land) 72
Brakefield, see Brachfeld
Brakenhoff (fallow farm) 92
Brakhage (fallow enclosure) 123
Brakmann, see Brachmann

Brambeck (thorn brook, swamp brook) 80, 77
Bramer (hornet, see also Bremer)
Bramkamp (thorn field) 84, 122
Brammeyer (proprietor of the Bramhoff, thorn farm) 93, 94
Bramstedt (thorn place)
Brand, Brandes, Brandt, Brant, Brandes (sword, bran 46, also < Hildebrand
Brand, Brant, Brandt (forest clearing) 126
Brandau (clearing meadow) 126, 84, 122
Brandecker (fr Brandeck 122, clearing) 126, 85
Brandeis, Brandies, Brandis (cauterizing iron) 106
Brandel, see Brander
Brandenberg 122, see Brandenburg 151
Brandenburg, Brandenburger (fr Brandenburg) 121
Brandenstein (torch mountain) 73, 122
Brandenstein (burned-off mountain) 126, 68
Brander, Brandner (occupant of a clearing) 126
Brandes < Hildebrand 53
Brandhoff (cleared farm, burned off farm) 126, 92
Brandhorst (burned off hurst) 126, 72, 122
Brandjes, Brandl, see Brander
Brandland (burned off land) 126
Brandmueller (miller at the burned clearing) 103, 126
Brandner, Brandtner (occupant of a forest clearing, fr Branden) 126

Brandstaedter, Brandstetter
(cleared place, burned off
place) 126, 122
Brandstein (brick) 106, 122
Brandt, see Brand
Brandwein, Brandtwein,
Brantwein (brandy, distiller)
96, 106
Brandywine, see Brandwein
151
Branoff, see Brandhoff
Brant, Brantl, see Brand
Brasch (impudent) 114
Brasch < Ambrosius 131
Brasse (broom plant)
Bratfish (fried fish) 115, 105
Bratmann, see Brotmann
Bratt (roast, cook) 96, 106
Brauch (use, custom)
Braucht, see Pracht
Brauer, Braue (brewer) 96
Braukhoff (brake farm) 80, 92
Braumbart (brown beard) 112
Braumueller, see Braunmueller
Braun, Brauns, Braune,
Braunert (brown, fr
Braunau) 112
Braunbach (brown brook) 77
Braunbeck (brown brook) 77
Braunbeck (baker of brown
bread) 104
Braunberger (brown mountain)
68
Braunfeld (brown field) 84
Braungart (brown garden) 84
Braungreber, see Brungraeber
Braunhof (well farm) 92
Brauning, Brauninger (brown-
haird) 112
Braunmueller, Brownmueller
(miller of brown meal) 103
Braunscheidt (brown log)
Braunschweiger (person fr
Brunswick, "Bruno's village,"
fr Latin *vicus*) 121, 122
Braunspan (brown chip)
Braunstein (brown stone) 73

Brauntuch (brown cloth) 105,
106
Braunwald, Braunwalde
(brown forest) 72
Braus, Brause, Brausen
(noise, confusion)
Brautigan, see Braeutigam
Brautlacht (wedding,
wedding song)
Bravmann, Bravermann
(well-behaved man) 115
Brawner, see Brauning 151
Bray, see Brey 151
Braymer, see Bremer 151
Brech, Brecher (breaker, flax
breaker) 95
Brechbill, Brechbiel, see
Brackbill
Brecht (bright 47), usually <
Albrecht, also a clearing
125
Brechtel < Brecht, Albrecht
Brecker, see Brecher
Brede, Breden (swamp) 80
Bredehoef (marshy farm) 80,
92
Bredehoeft, Bredehoft, see
Breithaupt
Bredekamp (marshy field,
broad field) 80, 84
Bredemeyer (marsh farmer)
80, 93
Bredenburg (marsh castle)
80, 73
Bredhorst (marsh hurst) 80,
72
Bredt, see Brett
Bredthauer (board sawyer)
95
Breeback (marsh brook) 80,
77
Breemer, see Bremer
Bregenzer (fr Bregenz, town
and river name) 83, 122
Brehm, Brehmer (deer fly,
see also Bremer)
Breidenbach 122, see
Breitbach

Breidenbaugh, see Breitbach
151
Breidenstein 122, see
Breitenstein
Breier, see Braeuer
Breigher, see Braeuer 151
Breiner, Breighner (pottage
maker), see Breun 151
Breining, Breininger, see
Brauning
Breit, Breiter (broad)
Breitacker (broad field) 84
Breitbach 122, Breitenbach,
Breitenbaecher (fr Breitbach
122, broad brook) 77
Breitbart (broad beard) 112
Breitbart (broad battle-ax) 46
Breitenbach 122, see Breitbach
Breitenberger (fr Breitenberg
122, broad mountain 68)
Breitenbuecher (broad beeches)
89
Breitenecker (broad place) 85
Breitenfeld (broad field) 84
Breitenstein (broad stone) 73,
122
Breitfus (broad foot) 114
Breithaupt (broad head) 114
Breithof (broad farm) 92
Breitmann (fat man) 114
Breitmoser (broad marsh) 80
Breitschneider, see
Brettschneider
Breitschwerd, Breitschwerdt
(broadsword) 108
Breitstadt (broad city)
Breitstein (broad stone) 73
Breitwieser (broad meadow) 84
Brem, Bremer, Bremen,
Bremmer, Bremermann (fr
Bremen, swamp) 122
Bremhorst (gadfly hurst) 72
Brendel, Brendl, Brendler <
Hildebrand 53
Brenneisen (poker, brand) 106
Brenner 122, Brennermann
(burner of charcoal, etc., or
distillerof brandy) 95

Brennholtz, Brenholts
(firewood) 72, 105
Brennwald (burned forest)
72
Brentz 122, Brentzer,
Brentzel, Brentzinger
(dweller near the river
Brenz) 83
Breslau, Breslaw, Breslauer,
Bresslauer (fr Breslau
122)
Breslow, see Breslau 151
Bresler, Bressler, Bresslers,
see Breslau
Breth (board, board cutter)
98
Brethauer, Bretthauer (board
cutter, cabinet maker) 98
Brethholz (board, board
sawyer) 98, 105
Brethower, see Brethauer
151
Brett, Bretz (board) 105, see
also Bretzel
Brettschneider, Brettscheider
(board sawyer, cabinet
maker) 98
Bretzler (pretzel maker, fr
Latin *bracillum*) 96
Breuel (swamp) 80, see
Brauer
Breuer, see Brauer
Breun, Breune, Breuner, see
Braun, Braune
Breuning, Breuninger, see
Brauning, Brauninger
Breusscher (dweller on the
Breusch 83), see Preuss
Brewbaker, see Brombach
151
Brewer, see Brauer 151
Brey (pottage) 122
Breyer, see Braeuer
Breymayer, Breymeyer
(brewmaster) 93
Brezler, see Bretzler
Briar, see Braeuer 151
Brickbauer, see Brueckbauer

Brickel, Brickell (little bridge)
Bricker, Brickerd, see Bruecker
Brickhouse, see Brueckhaus
    151
Brickhus, see Brueckhaus
Brickmann, see Brueck
Brickner, see Brueck
Bridenbach, see Breitbach 151
Bridner (dweller on the Briede)
    83, see Breitner 151
Briedenstein, see Breitenstein
    151
Brieger (fr Brieg) 122
Briel, Brieler (fr Briel) 122, see
    Bruehl
Briest 122, see Priest
Brigenz, see Bregenzer
Briggeman, Briggemann,
    Brigermann, see
    Brueggemann
Brighoff (farm at the bridge)
    92
Bright, see Brecht 151
Brightbill (broad hill) 67, 151,
    see also Brechbill
Brightman, see Breitmann 151
Brightstein, see Breitstein 151
Brigmann, see Brueggmann
Brilhart, Brillhart
Brill (eye glass) 114, 106, 122
Brinckerhoff (farm on raised
    ground) 74, 92
Brine, Briner, see Braun,
    Brauner 151
Bringenberg (grassy mountain)
    68
Bringhurst (grassy hurst) 72,
    151
Bringmann, see Brinkmann
Brink 122, Brinck, Brinks,
    Brings (grassy raised
    ground) 72
Brinker, Brinkmann,
    Brinkmeyer, Brinkmayer,
    Brinkmeier (small farmer) 72
Brinkerhoff (small farm) 72
Brinkschulte (village mayor)
    72, 109

Britenstein (swamp
    mountain) 80, 73, see
    Breitstein 151
Brobeck (bread baker) 104
Brobeck, see Brombeck
Broberg, see Bromberg
Brobst, see Probst
Broch 122, Brochmann
    (brake dweller) 80
Brocht, see Pracht
Brock (brake, swamp) 80,
    122
Brockelhorst (Brockel hurst)
    122, 72
Brockelmann (fr Brockel)
    122
Brockhage, Brockhagen 122
    (brake enclosure) 72, 123
Brockhaus, Brockhausen 122,
    Brockhus (brake house)
    72, 65
Brockhoff (brake farm) 72,
    65, 122
Brockman, Brockmann
    (brake dweller) 72
Brockmeyer, Brockmeier
    (brake farmer) 72, 93
Brockner (brake dweller) 72
Brockschmidt (brake smith)
    72, 96
Brocksmith, see
    Brockschmidt 151
Brod, Brode, Brodt, Brodte
    (bread, baker) 96
Brodbaeker, Brodbeck (bread
    baker) 96
Broeder, see Bruder
Broening, see Brening
Broenner, see Brenner
Broich, see Brock
Brokhus, see Brockhaus
Bromann (swamp dweller) 80
Brombach 122, Brombeck
    (swamp brook) 80, 77
Bromberg, Bromberger
    (swamp mountain) 80, 68
Bromberg (thorn mountain)
    68, 122

Bromer (swamp dweller) 80
Bronner (dweller near a well) 79
Bronstein (spring stone) 79, 73
Brooker (brake dweller) 72
Brookhard (brake forest) 72, 72
Brookhover, see Brockhoff
Brookland (marshy ground) 80
Brookmann, see Brockmann
Brookmeyer, see Brockmeyer
Brosius < St. Ambrosius 131
Broth (bread, baker) 96
Brotmann, Brotzmann (baker) 96, 106
Broun, see Braun 151
Brouse, see Braus 151
Brower, see Brauer 151
Brown, Browner, see Braun, Brauner 151
Browning, see Brauning 151
Brownstein, see Braunstein 151
Brubach, Brubaker, Brubeck (swamp brook) 80, 77
Bruch (quarry) 122
Bruch (bog, swamp) 80, 122
Bruchmann (quarry worker)
Bruchmann (bog dweller) 80
Bruckhard, see Burkhard
Bruck 122, Brucker, Bruckmann, Bruckmeyer, Bruckner (dweller by a bridge) 71
Bruckbauer, see Brueckbauer
Bruder (brother) 119
Brueck, Bruecker, Brueckner (dweller by a bridge, bridge builder) 71
Bruecker, Brueckmann, Brueckner (dweller near bridge) 71
Brueckhaus (house near a bridge) 65, 122
Bruegge, Brueggemann, Bruegemann, Bruegger, see Bruecker
Bruehl (scrub-covered marsh) 80, 122

Bruekbauer, Brueckenbauer (bridge builder, farmer near bridge) 71
Bruening < Bruno
Bruennings (fr Bruening) 122
Bruenner (maker of burnies) 108
Bruens, see Bruns
Brugge, Bruggeman, Bruggemann, Brugger, see Bruecker, Brueckmann
Bruhn, see Bruno, Braun
Bruich, see Bruch
Brumback 112, Brumbaugh 151, see Brombach
Brumm, Brummer (loud noise, maker of loud noise)
Brune, Bruner, Brunert, see Braune
Brungard, Brungardt (well garden) 79, 84
Brungreber, Brungraeber, see Brunnengraeber
Brunhoefer (well farm) 79, 92, see also Braunhof
Bruning, Brunjes < Bruno
Brunk, Brunke, Brunken, Brunker < Bruno, see also Prunk
Brunkhorst (swamp hurst) 80, 72
Brunn 122, Brunner (person living near a spring), see Bruenner 79
Brunnengraeber (well digger) 79
Brunner (dweller by a well) 79
Brunner (burnie maker) 108
Brunnholtz, Brunnsholtz (forest by a spring) 79, 72
Bruno, Brunno (brown, bear) 22
Bruns, Brunsmann (brown), see also Bruno
Brunst (ardor, heat)

Bruschmueller (broom miller)
103
Bruschweiler, Bruschwiller
(broom village) 123
Brushwiler, see Bruschweiler
151
Brust (breast) 114
Bryl, see Brill
Bube (boy, servant)
Bubeck (butterfly)
Buberl (little boy)
Bubikon (town in Switzerland)
122
Bubp, see Bube
Buch, Buchs, Buchler, Buecher,
Buechner (dweller near the
beeches) 41, 89
Buchbinder (bookbinder) 96
Buchdahl (beech valley) 89, 76
Buchdrucker (book printer) 96
Buchel, Buchal, Buchle (little
beech) 89
Buchel, Buechel (little book)
106
Buchenmeyer, Buckenmayer,
see Buchmeyer
Buchenwald 122, see Buchwald
Bucher 122, see Buechner
Buchhagen (beech enclosure)
89, 123, 122
Buchhalter (bookkeeper) 96
Buchheimer, Buchhiem 151
(beech hamlet) 89, 123
Buchhoff (beech farm) 89, 92
Buchholtz, Bucholz (beechwood)
89, 72, 122
Buchler, see Buechler
Buchmann, Buchman, Buchner
(dweller near the beeches)
89
Buchmeyer, Buchmoyer
(proprietor of the Buchhoff)
89, 93, 94
Buchmueller (miller near the
beeches) 89, 103
Bucholz, see Buchholtz
Buchsbaum (boxwood) 89
Bucht (corral)

Bucht (bay)
Buchwald, Buchwalter (beech
wood) 89, 71, 122
Buck, see Bock, Buche,
Burkhard
Buckel, Buckelman
(humpback) 114
Bucker, Buckert < Burkhart
Buckhalter, see Burkhalter,
Buchhalter
Buckhard, Buckert, Bucker <
Burkhard
Buckholtz, Buckholz, see
Buckholtz
Buckler (shield) 108
Buckman, see Buchmann
Buckmeyer, Buckmeier,
Buckmeir, see Buchmeyer
Buckner, Bucknor, see
Buechner
Buckreus (beech branch) 89
Buckwalter, see Buchwald
Budde (cooper) 96
Buddemeier, Buddemeyer,
Buddemyer (bog farmer)
80, 93
Buddenbohm, Buddenbohn
(bog tree) 80, 89, 122
Buddenbrook (bog brake) 80,
80
Buddenhagen (bog enclosure)
80, 123, 122
Budecker, Budecker,
Budicke, Budke (cooper)
96
Budelman, Budelmann
(purse maker) 96
Buechel (little book)
Buechel (little beech) 89
Buechel, Buechler, Bichler,
Buehler (hill dweller) 67
Buechenau (beech meadow)
89, 84, 122
Buecher, see Buechner
Buechner, Buechler (dweller
among beeches) 89
Buecker, see Buechner
Buegler (stirrup maker) 96

Buehl, Buehler, Bueler, Bieler, Biehler (fr Buehl 122, hill) 41, 67

Buehlheimer (hill hamlet) 67, 123, 122

Buehlmayer, Buehlmeyer (hill farmer) 67, 93

Buehlman, Buehlmann (hill dweller) 67

Buehr, Buehre, Buehrer, Buehrmann, see Bauer

Buekler, see Buecker

Buel, Buell, see Buehl

Buenger, see Binger

Buerger (castle dweller, burgher) 73

Buergi, Burgy, see Birck

Buerhaus (peasant house) 91, 65, 122

Buerk, Buerkie (peasant) 91

Buermann, see Bauermann

Buesche, see Busch

Bueschel (bundle)

Bueschner (bush dweller) 72

Buetefisch (plaice, fishmonger) 115

Buettel (beadle) 109

Buettel (homestead)

Buettemeyer (householder) 93

Buettler, Buettner (barrel maker, fr Latin *buttis*) 96

Buetzel (scarecrow, bogeyman) 115

Bugher, see Bucher 151

Buhl, Buhle, Buhler, Buhlert, Buhlmann (lover, suitor, see also Buehl)

Buhr, Buhrmann (peasant) 91

Buick (beech) 89

Bulger (Bulgarian) 121

Bullerich (shouting, screaming)

Bullermann < Baldher (bold + army) 46, 46

Bullhausen (bull houses) 65, 91

Bullwinkel (attic space)

Bulman, see Buhlmann

Bultman, Bultmann (mattress seller) 105

Bultmann (dweller on a hill) 72

Bumann, see Baumann

Bumbaugh, see Bombach 151

Bumgardner, Bumgartner, Bumgarner, see Baumgaertner

Bummel (stroll, promenade)

Bunce, see Buntz 151

Bunde (fenced meadow) 122

Bundschuh (laced boot, peasant revolt) 112

Bungartz, see Baumgart

Bunger, Bungerts (drummer)

Bunt, Bunte (colorful)

Bunte (fish box)

Buntrock (coat of many colors 112, kind of crow 115)

Bunts, see Buntz

Buntz, Bintz (sleeping birth)

Buntz (fat man) 114

Burch, see Burg

Burchard, Burchhards, Burckhardt, see Burghart

Burck, see Burg

Burdorf 122, see Burgdorf

Buresch, Buresh (Slavic: peasant)

Burg (fortress, castle) 46, 73, 122

Burgard, see Burkhard

Burgdorf (castle village) 73, 123, 122

Burgemeister, see Burgermeister

Burger, Burgers, Burgert (burgher, castle dweller, townsman) 73

Burgermeister (mayor) 109

Burggraf (burgrave) 109

Burghalter (chastelain) 73, 109

Burghard, Burghardt, Burghart, see Burkhart

Burghauser, Burgheiser (fr Burghausen 122, castle houses) 73, 65

Burgheimer (castle hamlet) 73, 122, 123
Burghof (castle courtyard) 73, 92, 122
Burgholder, see Burkhalter
Burgman, Burgmann (burgher) 73, 94
Burgtorf, see Burgdorf
Burgunder (Burgundian) 121
Burgwin (protection + friend) 47, 48
Burhard, Burhart, see Burkhart
Burhorst (peasant forest) 91, 72
Burkard, Burkart, see Burkhard
Burker, Buckert, see Burger
Burkhalter, see Burghalter
Burkhamer, Burkheimer, see Burgheimer
Burkhard, Burkhardt, Burckhart (protection + strong) 47, 46
Burkhoff, Burkoff, see Burghoff
Burkholder, see Burkhalter 151
Burkhouse (castle house) 73, 65, 151
Burmann, see Bauermann
Burmeister, Burmester, see Bauernmeister
Burnemann, see Bornemann
Burrichter (village magistrate) 109
Burt (birth, burden)
Busch, Busche (bush, tavernkeeper) 72, 64
Buschel, Buschell (bunch, bundle)
Buscher, Busching, Buschling (dweller in the bush) 72
Buschgans (bush goose) 72, 115
Buschmann, Buschmeyer (farmer in the brushland) 72, 93, 94
Buse (pocket)
Bush ..., see Busch ... 151
Bushart, Busshart, see Bussard

Bushbaum (bush tree) 72, 89, 151
Bushman, Bushmann, see Buschmann 151
Bushrod (bush clearing) 72, 126, 151
Bushyeager (bush hunter) 72, 91, 151
Buskirk (bush church) 72
Buss, Busse (penitence, penance, fine, see also Busch)
Bussard, Bussart (soaring hawk) 115
Busse < Burkhard 53, 54
Busser (one doing penance)
Busser, Bussler, Bussmann (repairman) 96
Bussman, Bussmann (heavy drinker) 115
Bussmann (handyman) 95
Butke, see Boettcher
Butner, see Buettner
Butt (plaice, fishmonger) 115
Butter (butter dealer) 105, see also Butz
Butterbaugh, Buterbaugh (butter brook) 77, 151
Butterbaum (butter tree) 89
Butterbrot (butter on bread)
Butterfuss (butter foot) 114
Butterhof, Butterhoff (butter farm) 92
Buttmann (paice dealer) 115
Buttner, see Buettner
Butz, Butze, Butzer, Butzner, Butts (scarecrow) 114, also < Burkhard
Byer, see Bayer 151
Byerly, Byerley, see Baeuerle 151
Byler, Beyler, see Beiler 151
Byrle, see Bayerle 151

C

Note that most early German American names that formerly started with "C" are now spelled with "K" and appear accordingly in this list. A few Upper German names beginning with "C" begin with a "G" in standard German and are so listed.

Cabel, Cabell, Cabler, see Kabel, Gabel
Caemmerer, see Kaemmerer
Cagle, see Kegel 151
Cahler, see Kahl, Koehler
Cahn, see Kahn
Calb, see Kalb
Caldmeyer (proprietor of the Kalthof) 93, 94
Call, see Kall, Gallus
Callbaugh, see Kaltenbach 151
Callenius (Latin for Callen) 142
Calp, see Kalb
Camman, see Kamm
Campe, Campen, see Kampe 151
Canisius (probably Latin for Hund) 142
Cantor (Latin, singer)
Cantzler, see Kantzler
Canz, see Ganz 151
Capehart, see Gebhard 151
Caplan (chaplain) 110
Capp, Cappe, Cappes, see Kapp
Cappel, Cappele, Cappelmann (person fr Cappel, probably the one in Switzerland) 122
Carbaugh, Carbauh (possibly carp stream) 115, 77, 151
Carber, see Gerber 151
Carcker, see Karcker
Carl, Carle, Carel, Carll, Carolus (man)
Carlsen, son of Carl 59

Carsten, Carstens, Carstensen (Christian) 131
Carthaeuser (Carthusian 110, or fr Carthausen 122)
Cartman, see Gaertmann 151
Casch < Karl
Casman, see Kaesemann, Gasmann 151
Casner, see Gessner
Caspar, Casper, Caspers (one of the Three Kings) 131, 111
Caspari (son of Caspar) 142
Cassel, Casseler, Castle (fr Cassel, fr Latin *castellum*) 121, 122
Castner, see Kastner
Castor (Latin, beaver, patron sait of Koblenz) 141, 131
Caufman, Cauffmann, see Kaufmann 151
Caulberg, see Kalberg 151
Caulk, see Kalk 151
Caup, see Kauf
Caylor, Cayler, see Kehler, Koehler 151
Cedarbaum (cedar tree) 89
Cellarius (Latin, cellar master) 141
Chorengel (choir angel)
Chresman, see Kressmann 151
Chrisman, see Christmann
Christ (Christian) 131
Christbaum (Christmas tree) 143
Christer (Christian) 131
Christfried (Christ peace) 139
Christgau (Christian district)
Christi, Christy (son of Christian) 139, 142
Christian (Christian) 131
Christiani (son of Christian) 142
Christmann (Christian), see Kressmann 131

Christof, Christoph (St.
  Christopher) 131
Chrypfius (Gryphius, griffin)
Chrysler, see Kreisel
Chur (person fr Chur in
  Switzerland) 122
Claas, see Clas
Clabaugh, see Kleebach 151
Clain, see Klein
Clap, Clapp, see Klap, Klapp
Clas, Class, Clasen, see
  Nicolaus
Clattenbaugh, Clatterbaugh,
  Clatterbuck, see Gladbach
  151
Claus, see Klaus
Clause, Claussen (hermitage,
  cell) 122
Clausenius, see Klaus 141
Clauser, see Klause
Clawes < Niklaus
Claybaugh, see Klehbach 151
Clayman, see Klehmann 151
Cleh, see Klee
Clem, see Klemm 151
Clemens, Clementz, Clement
  (name of pope) 134
Cleve (fr Cleves) 121
Clever, see Kleber
Click, see Glueck 151
Cline, Clien, see Klein 151
Clinedienst, Clinedinst, see
  Kleindienst 151
Clinefelter, see Kleinfeld 151
Clingenpeel, see Klingenbuehl
  151
Clinger, see Klinger
Clingman, Clingermann, see
  Klingmann
Cloates, see Klotz 151
Clocke, Clocker, see Glocke,
  Glocker
Clodfelter (log field) 84
Clontz, see Glantz
Closs, Closse, see Kloss, Klosse
Clostermann, see Klostermann
Clouse, Clouser, see Klaus 151
Clutts, Clutz, see Klott 151

Coal, Coale, see Kohl 151
Cobach, Cobaugh 151 (cow
  brook) 77
Cober, see Kober
Coberg (German principality)
  121
Coblenz, see Koblenz
Coen, Coene, Coenen <
  Conrad 53
Coerper, see Koerber
Coffelt (cow field) 84
Coffer, see Koffer
Coffman, see Kaufmann 151
Cohen, Cohn (Hebrew:
  priest) 110, see also Kuhn
Colb, see Kolb
Coldiron, see Kalteisen 152
Cole, see Kohl
Colefelt (cabbage field) 84,
  151
Colehaus, Colehouse, see
  Kohlhas 151
Coleman, see Kohlmann,
  Kuhlmann 151
Colflesh, see Kalbfleisch 151
Colhower (coal digger) 151
Collar, Coller, see Kohler,
  Koller 151
Collin < Nickolaus
Collin (place name) 122
Collitz (place name) 122
Collmann, see Kohlmann 151
Collmeyer, see Kohlmeyer
  151
Colmar (fr Colmar in Alsace)
  122
Comb, see Kamm 152
Conrad, Conrads, Conradt,
  Conrath (brave + counsel)
  36, 46, 46, 136
Conradi, Conrady, son of
  Conrad 142
Conselman, see
  Kuenzelmann 151
Conz, see Kunz 151
Cooble, see Kuebel 151
Coogle, see Kugel 151
Cook, see Koch 152

Cool, Cooll, see Kuhl 151
Coolbaugh, see Kuhlbach 151
Cooler, see Kuhler 151
Coolmann, see Kuhlmann 151
Coon, Coons, Coonce, see
   Kuhn, Kuhns 151
Cooper, see Kupfer, Kuper 151
Cooperman, see Kupfermann
   151
Cooperstein (copper mountain)
   151
Coopman, see Kaufmann
Coos, see Kuss 151
Copeman, see Kaufmann 151
Copenhaver, Copenheaver (fr
   Copenhagen) 122
Copman, see Kaufmann
Coppel, see Koppel
Corber, see Koerber
Cordes, see Kordes
Cornbach (corn brook) 77
Cornberger (fr Cornberg 122,
   grain mountain) 68
Cornblath, Cornblatt, see
   Kornblatt
Cornbrook, Cornbrooks (grain
   brake) 80
Cornelius (Roman name [crow],
   name of pope) 134
Cornell, see Cornelius
Cornfield, see Kornfeld 151
Cornman, see Kornmann
Cornmesser (grain measurer)
Corthes, Cortes, see Cordes
Cost, see Kost 151
Coster, see Kuester 151
Cott, see Gott 151
Cotz, see Goetz 151
Coughman, see Kaufmann 151
Couler, see Kuehler 151
Coulter, see Kolter 151
Coun, see Kuhn 151
Counsul, Council, see Kuenzel
   151
Countryman, see
   Guenthermann 151
Counts, see Kuntz 151
Couts, Coutts, see Kauz 151
Crable, see Kraehbuehl 151

Craemer, Cramer, Cramert,
   see Kraemer 20, 105, 143
Craesman, see Kressmann
   151
Craft, see Kraft 151
Cram (retail trade,
   huckster's cart) 105
Cramer, see Kraemer 20,
   105
Crance, see Krantz 151
Crass, see Grass 151
Cratsar, see Kratzer 151
Cratz, see Kratz
Craumer, see Kraemer 151
Craus, see Kraus
Craver, see Grueber 151
Craybill, Crebil, see
   Kraehbuehl 151
Creager, see Krueger 151
Creamer, see Kraemer 151
Crebbs, see Krebs
Creger, Cregar, see Krueger
   151
Creiner, see Greiner 151
Creitz, Creytz, Creitzer, see
   Kreutz, Kreutzer
Cress, Cresse, see Kress,
   Kresse
Cressman, Cressmeyer, see
   Kressman
Creutz, see Kreutz
Crever, see Grueber 151
Crickenberger,
   Crickenburger, see
   Krueckenberger 151
Crider, Cridler, see Kreider
   151
Crimm, see Grimm 151
Criner, see Greiner 151
Crisman, Crissmann, see
   Kressmann 151
Crist, Criste, Cristner, see
   Christ
Critz, Critzer, Crizer,
   Critzman, see Kreutz,
   Kreutzer, Kreutzmann 151
Croesman, Croessman, see
   Kressmann
Croft, see Craft 151

Croll, see Groll, Kroll 151
Crombach, see Grumbach 151
Crombholts, see Krumbholtz
151
Cromer, see Kraemer 151
Cromm, see Krumm
Cron, see Kron, Krone
Cronauer, see Gronau 151
Cronberger, Cronenberg,
Cronenberger, Croneberge,
see Kronberg
Cronemeyer (royal bailiff) 93,
109
Cronk, see Krank 151
Cronkite, see Krankheit 151
Cronmiller (crown miller) 103
Croo, Crow, see Kroh 151
Crossbart (big beard) 112, 151
Crosse, Crossman, see Grosse,
Grossmann 151
Crossman, see Kressmann 151
Crouse, see Kraus 151
Crouthamel (herb hamlet) 123,
151
Croyter, see Kraeuter 151
Crueger, see Krueger
Crull, see Krull
Crum, Crumm, see Krumm
Crumbacker (crooked brook) 77
Crump, see Krumm
Crytzer, see Kreutzer
Cugel, see Kugel
Cuhn, see Kuhn
Culler, see Koller 151
Culman, Cullmann, see
Kuhlmann 151
Cunkel, see Kunkel
Cunrad, Cuonrad, Cunred, see
Conrad
Cunradi, son of Cunrad 142
Cuntz, Cunz, see Kuntz
Cunzeman, see Kuntzemann
Cuper, see Kupfer
Curland, Curlander (fr the
Kurland) 121
Curtius, see Kurtz 141
Custer, see Kuester 151
Cyphert, see Seyfert 151

D

A name beginning with "D"
in one dialect may begin
with a "T" in another and
be so listed here.

Daab (swamp) 80
Dachenhausen, Dachhausen
(thatched houses) 65
Dacher (roofer) 96
Dachhausen, see
Dachenhausen
Dachler, see Dacher
Dachler (swamp dweller) 80
Dachs (badger, badger
hunter) 115, 91
Dachslager (badger lair)
Dackerman, Dackermann,
Dackmann, see Dacher
Daegen, see Degen
Daehnert < Degenhard
Daehnick, Daehnike,
Daehnke < Degenhard 53,
54
Daeneke < Degenhard 53, 54
Daengler, see Dengler
Daescher, see Taescher
Daeuber, see Taeuber
Daeubler, see Taeubler
Daffner (taverner, fr Latin
taberna) 96
Dagenbeck (baker who bakes
daily) 96
Dagher, see Dacher
Dahl 122, Dahle 122, Dahl-
er, Dahlmann, Dallmann
(valley man, see
Thalmann) 76
Dahlberg (valley mountain)
76, 68
Dahlheimer (fr Dahlheim
122, valley hamlet) 76,
123
Dahlhoff, Dalhoff (valley
farm) 76, 92
Dahlke (little valley) 76

Dahlmeyer (valley farmer) 94, 93

Dahm, Dahms, Dahme, Dahmer < Adam, Damian 135, 131

Dahm (dweller near the Dahme River) 83, 122

Dahn, Dahne (forest) 72

Daichler, see Deigler

Daigel, see Deigler

Daimler (thumb screwer)

Dalhoff, see Dahlhoff

Daller (moist, cool place) 80

Dallwig, see Dalwig

Dalman, see Thalmann

Dalmeyer, see Dahlmeyer

Dalwig (valley village) 76, 123

Dam < St. Damian 131

Dam, Dame, Damser < Adam 135

Daman, Damen, see Dahm

Damewald, see Dannewald

Damkoehler (forest collier) 89, 95

Damm, Damme, Dammes (fr Damm 122, causeway, dike) 81

Dammann, Dammermann (dweller on or near dike) 81, see Thomas

Dammermut (dike, causeway, dweller on the dike) 81

Dammeyer, Dammeier, Dammyer (farmer on or at the dike) 81

Dampf (steam)

Damrosch (forest slide) 89, 71

Danaker, see Danecker

Danbach (brook through firs) 89, 77

Danecker, Danegger (place in fir trees) 89, 85, see Tannecker

Daneman, Danemann (forest dweller) 89

Danenhauer, Danhaur (fir chopper, wood cutter) 89, 95

Dange < St. Anthonius 131

Dangel < Daniel 135

Danhower, see Danenhauer 151

Danick, Danicke, see Danecke

Daniel, Daniels (OT name) 135

Dankelmann (marsh dweller, cf. English "dank") 80

Dankelmeyer (marsh farmer) 80

Danker, Dankers, Dankert < Dankwart 48, 47

Dankmar (thought + famous) 48, 47

Dankmeyer, see Dankelmeyer

Dankwart (thought + guard or watch) 48, 47

Danmeyer, Danmyer (forest farmer) 89, 93

Danmiller (forest miller) 89, 103

Dannecke, Dannecker, Dannegger, see Danecker or Denecke

Dannenbaum 122, Dannebaum, see Tannenbaum 89

Dannenberg (forest mountain) 89, 68, 122

Dannenfeld, Dannenfelder, Dannenfeltzer (forest field) 89, 84

Dannenfelser (wooded cliffs) 84

Dannenmann (forest dweller) 89, 94

Danner, Dannermann (forest dweller) 89

Dannewald, Damewald, see Tannenwald

Dannewitz (fr Danewitz 122, forest village) 89, 127

Dannhaeuser 122, see Tannhaeuser

Dannhoeffer, see Tannhoeffer

Danninger (fr Danningen 122)

Dannwolf (forest wolf) 89, 48

Dansler, see Densler
Dantzenbecker, Tanzenbecker
  (dancing brook) 77
Dantzler (dancer) 96
Danz, Danzer, Danzel (dancer)
  96
Danzig, Danziger (German city)
  122, 146
Dapfer, see Tapfer
Darmstadt, Darmstaet,
  Darmstaedter (person fr
  Darmstadt) 122
Dasch, Dascher, Dashner, see
  Taescher
Dasinger (fr Dasing) 122
Dattelbaum (date tree) 89, 149
Daub, Daube, Dauber, Daubert,
  Daubner, see Taub
Daubenberger (dove mountain)
  115, 68
Dauberman, see Taubermann
Daublein (little dove) 115
Daudt (swamp, reeds) 80
Dauer (duration, barrel-stave
  maker) 95
Dauernheim (place name) 122
Daum (thumb, short person)
  114
Daumenlang (thumb long) 113
Daumer (thumb-screw, torturer,
  tool for cutting rock) 106
Daun, Daunn (goose down,
  dealer in feathers) 105
Daun (down, swamp) 80, 122
Dauner (swamp dweller) 80
Dausch (mother swine) 91
David, Davit (OT character)
  135
Davids, Davidssohn (son of
  David) 59
Deagler, see Diegler 151
Deahl, see Diehl 151
Dealbone < Thiel Bohn 151
Deardorf, Deardorff, see
  Tierdorf 43, 151
Dearholt, animal forest 72, 151
Dearstine (animal mountain)
  73, 151

Deatrich, see Dietrich 151
Debald, Debold, Debolt, see
  Dietbald
Debelbesin, see Teufelbiss
  151
Deboer (the peasant) 91
Debs < Matthias 131
Dechan, Dechant (tithing
  man, tithe collector) 109
Decher, Dechert (roofer) 92,
  143
Decher (set of ten, tenth
  child)
Deck, Decke (blanket) 106
Deckdenbron (Cover the
  well!) 116
Decker, Deckert, Deckner
  (thatcher, roofer) 96
Deckler (maker of
  bedclothes) 96
Deckmann (thatcher) 96
Dedekind < Dietrich
Dedemeyer (Dietrich +
  farmer)
Dederer (stutterer) 114
Dederick, Dedrich, Dedrick,
  see Dietrich
Deeck, Deeken < Dietrich 53
Deemar, see Dietmar 151
Deener, see Diener 151
Deer ..., see Tier ...
Deering, see Thueringer 151
Dees, see Thiess 151
Deeter, see Dieter
Deetje, Deetjen < Dietrich 53
Deets, Deetz < Dietrich 151
Defenbau, Defenbaugh,
  Defibaugh, Deffibaugh,
  Deffinbaugh, see
  Tiefenbach 151
Defriece, see Devries 151
Degen (thane) 46
Degen (dagger) 108
Degenhardt, Degenhart
  (thane + strong) 46, 46
Degenkolb (hero + club) 46
Degering, Degerink <
  Degenhard

Degner, Degener (dagger maker) 108

DeGraffenried, see Graffenried

Degrote, Degroot, DeGroat (the large) 113

Dehle, Dehles, Dehls, Dehler < Dietrich 53, 54

Dehlenbeck (Dietrich's brook) 77

Dehlke < Dietrich 53

Dehm, Dehmann, Dehmert < Thomas, Damianus 131

Dehn, Dehne, Dehner, Dehnert < Degenhard

Dehrenbach (animal brook) 77

Dehrenkamp (animal field) 77

Deibel (devil)

Deibert < Dagebert

Deibler, see Teubler

Deich (dweller on a dike) 81

Deichgraeber (ditch digger, dike digger) 81

Deichman, Deichmann, Deickmann, see Teichmann

Deichmueller (pond miller, miller on the dike) 81, 103

Deigler (maker of wooden water pipes) 96

Deinert, Deinhart, see Degenhard

Deininga, Deininger < Degenhard

Deinlein < Degenhard

Deis, see Theiss

Deisinger (fr Deising in Bavaria) 122

Deisler (wainwright) 96

Deisroth (manure clearing) 126

Deiss, see Theiss

Deissel (wainwright) 96

Deist, Deister, Deistler (wooded ridge) 72

Deisterberg (wooded mountain) 68

Deistermann (dweller on a wooded ridge) 72

Deisteroth (clearing on a wooded ridge) 125

Deitch, Deitsch, Deitschman, see Deutsch

Deitelbaum, see Dattelbaum

Deiter, Deitrich, see Dieter, Dietrich 151

Deitz, Deitzel, see Dietz, Dietzel 151

Deken < Dietrich 53, 54

Dekher, see Decker 151

Delinger, Dellinger, see Dillinger

Demke, Demeke, Dempke < Thomas 53

Demm, Demme < Thomas 53

Demmler, Demler (glutton) 115

Demuth (humility) 139

Dencker, Denker (thinker, left-handed person)

Denecke, Denicke < Degenhard 53

Dengler (one who repairs blades by hammering them) 96

Denhard, Denhardt < Degenhard 53

Denk (left, left handed) 114

Denker, see Dankwart

Denmeyer (proprietor of the Denhoff, forest farm) 89, 92, 94

Dennard < Degenhard 53, 54

Denneger < Degenhard 53, 54

Dennelein, Dennerlein (little fir tree) 89

Dennemann (dweller among the firs) 89

Dennenberg 122, see Tannenberg

Dennewitz 122, see Dannewitz

Dennstedt, Daennstaedt (forest place) 89

Denny (sometimes fr Thoeni) 151

Densler (dancer) 96

Dentz, Denz, Dentzer, Denzer, see Tants, Tantz

Dentzel, Dentzler (dancer)
Deobald, see Dietbald
Depfer, see Tepper
Deppendal (deep valley) 76
Deppisch, Deppish (foolish) 115
Derenberger (animal mountain)
68
Derenkamp (animal field) 84
Derflinger (villager) 123
Derhammer (fr Derheim) 122,
123
Derheim (animal hamlet) 123
Derick, Derrick, see Dietrich
Derling, see Deuerling
Derrenbacher (animal brook) 77
Derrenberger, see Derenberger
68
Derring, Derringer, see
Thueringer 151
Dersch (foolish) 115
Derwart (game warden) 96
Desch, Descher, Deschner, see
Taescher
Deschler, Deschner, see
Taescher
DeShong (French, Deschamps,
fr the fields) 144
Dessau, Dessauer (German
city) 122
Dester, see Textor, Dexter
Deter, Detert, Dettermann,
Detterer < Diethard
Detje, Detjen, see Dietrich
Detmer < Dietmar
Detmold (place name, "people's
assembly" or else "swamp
place") 46, 80, 122
Detner, Detters, see Dettner
Detrich, see Dietrich
Dettelbach (swamp brook) 80,
77, 122
Dettmann (swamp dweller) 80,
94
Dettmar, Dettmer, see Dietmar
Dettmeyer (swamp farmer) 80,
93
Dettner (swamp dweller) 80

Dettweiler, Dettwiler (swamp
village) 80, 127
Detzel < Dietrich 53, 54
Detzner (manurer) 95
Deubel (devil)
Deuber, Deubler, Deubert,
see Tauber, Taubert
Deubner, see Taubner
Deuchler (maker of wooden
water pipes) 96
Deuerling (darling) 115
Deurer, see Duerer
Deutsch, Deutscher,
Deutschman,
Deutschmann, Deutch
(German) 121
Deutschendorf (German
village) 121, 123
Devilbiss, see Teufelbiss 151
Devriend (the friend)
Devries (the Frisian) 121
Dewalt, Dewald < Dietwald
(people + rule) 46, 46
Dewitz (Slavic place name)
122
Dexter (Latin, right hand),
see also Textor
Deys, see Theiss 151
Dice, see Theiss 151
Dick 122, Dicke 122, Dicks,
Dix, Dicker, Dickert,
Dueck (dweller near a
thicket) 142
Dick, Dicker, Dickert (fat,
thick) 114, 143
Dickerhoof, see Dickhoff
Dickhaut, Dickhout (thick
skin) 114
Dickhoff, Diekhof, Dieckhof,
Dyckhoff (dike farm) 81,
92, 94
Dickman, Dickmann,
Dickermann, see
Teichmann
Dickmer, see Dickmeyer
Dickmeyer (dike farmer) 81,
93
Diebald, see Dietbald

Dicks < Benedictus 131
Diebel, see Teufel
Diebold, Dietbolt, see Dietbald
Dieck, Diecks (dweller on or
near the dike) 81
Dieckhaus (dike house) 81, 65,
122
Dieckmann, Diekmann, see
Teichmann
Diederich, see Dietrich
Diefenbach, Dieffenbach,
Dieffenbacher, see
Tiefenbach
Diegel, Diegler, Diegelman
(potter) 96
Diegmann, see Teichmann
Diehl, Diehle, Diehlmann, Diel
(wall or floor of planks), or <
Dietrich 53, 54
Diehlbeck, see Dillenbeck
Diehm < Dietmar
Diekmann, see Teichmann
Diel (swamp brook) 80, 77
Diele (board, board sawyer) 95
Diemer, see Dietmar
Diener (servant) 138
Dienhart < Degenhard
Dienst (service, servant) 138
Dienstag (Tuesday) 143
Diepolt, see Dietbald
Dier, see Tier
Dierauer (animal meadow) 84
Dierbaum (animal tree) 89
Dierdorf 122, Dierdorff (swamp
village) 80, 43, 123 see
Tierdorf
Dierenberger, see
Duerrenberger 151
Dierhoff (animal farm) 92, 43
Diering (Thuringian) 121
Dierk, Dierks, Dierkes,
Dierksen, Dierchs < Dietrich
Diermann (animal man)
Dierstein (deer mountain,
animal mountain) 73
Diesbach (swamp stream) 80,
77
Diesel < Matthias 53
Diess, see Theiss

Diestelhorst (thistle brake)
80
Dietbald, Dietbold (folk +
bold or folk + rule) 46, 46
Dietel, Dietle < Dietrich 53,
54
Dieter, Dieder, Diether,
Dieterle, Dietermann <
Dietrich or Diethard
Diethard (folk + strong) 46,
46
Diethof (swamp farm) 80, 92
Dietmann (folk + man) 46,
94
Dietmar (folk + famous) 46,
47
Dietrich, Dieterich,
Diederich, Dietrichs,
Dietrick (folk + rule) 46,
47
Dietsch < Dietrich 53
Dietter < Dietrich 53
Dietwald (folk + rule) 46, 47
Dietz, Dietze, Diez, Dietzel,
Dietzer < Dietrich
Dietz (swamp) 80
Dietzius, latinized form of
Dietze 141
Diffenbaugh, Diffenbach, see
Tiefenbach 151
Diffendal, Diffendall (deep
valley) 76, 151
Diffenderfer, see Tiefendorf
151
Diffrient, see Devrient
Digler, see Degeler
Dihm, see Thiem
Dikhoff, Dikoff (proprietor of
the Dickhoff) 81, 92, 94
Dilger (son of Ottilie) 60
Dill, Diller (board, board
sawyer) 95
Dill, Diller (fr Dill 122)
Dillenbeck (board creek) 77
Dillenberger (board
mountain) 68
Dillfelder (board field) 84
Dillinger (fr Dilling 122)

Dillmann, Dillman < Dietrich 53
Dimler, Dimling (acrobat) 96
Dingbaum (council tree) 89
Dingedal (council valley) 76
Dingelmann, see Dengler
Dinger (judge, arbiter) 109
Dingfelder (parliament field) 84
Dingler, see Dengler
Dinkel (spelt, see also Duenkel)
Dinn, see Duenn 151
Dinsman, see Dienstmann 151
Dippel, Dipple, Dipper,
    Dippmann, Dippold, see
    Dietbold
Dirk, Dirks, Dircks, Dirkes,
    Dirksen < Dietrich 53
Dirzuweit (too far from you)
    116
Disch, see Tisch
Discher, Dischler, Dischart, see
    Tischler
Dischman, Dischner, see
    Tischmann, Tischner
Dischong, see DeShong
Ditmann, see Dietman
Ditmar, Dittmer, see Dietmar
Dittenbrand (swamp clearing)
    80, 126
Dittenhafer, Dittenhoefer,
    Dittenhoffer (swamp farm)
    92
Dittmann (swamp dweller) 80
Dittmann, see Dietmann
Ditter, see Dieter
Dittmar, Dittmer, see Dietmar
Dittrich, see Dietrich
Ditz, Ditzel, Ditzell, see Dietz,
    Dietzel
Divilbiss, Divilbess, Divilplease,
    see Teufelbiss 151
Diwall, see Dietbald
Dix < Benedictus, also see Dick
Dober, Doberer, Dobert (pigeon
    raiser or seller) 115, 143
Doberstein (dovecote mountain)
Dobert < Theodoberacht (folk +
    bright) 46, 46

Dobler, Dobeler, Doebeler,
    see Tobler
Dochman, see Tuchmann
Dochterman, see
    Tochtermann
Dock (kind of fish,
    fishmonger) 115
Dock (dry dock)
Dockstade (fish landing) 71
Dockweiler (marsh village)
    80, 127
Doctor (doctor)
Dode (swamp, reeds) 81
Dodenhof (swamp farm) 81,
    92
Doderer (stutterer) 114
Doebberstein, see Doberstein
Doebler, Doebling, see Tobler
Dorf (village, villager) 123
Doefler, see Dorfmann
Doehl, Doehle, Doehlen,
    Doehler < Adolf 53
Doehl 122, Doehle 122 (place
    names)
Doehling (fr Dehling in
    Wurttemberg) 122
Doehrer, Doehrling, see
    Thueringer
Doelfel < Adolf 53
Doell, Doelle, Doeller (marsh
    water, dweller in a marsh)
    80
Doelling (kind of perch,
    fishmonger) 115
Doellinger (fr Doelling 122),
    see also Doehling
Doellinger, see Doehling
Doemling < Domarich
    (judgment + rule) 46
Doenges (fr Anthonius) 131
Doeninger (dweller on damp
    terrain) 80
Doepfer, Doepner (potter) 96
Doerer < Theodor 131
Doerflein (little village) 123,
    122
Doerfling, Doerflinger
    (villager) 123

Doering (Thuringian, "herring nose" attributed to Thuringians) 121, 113
Doerle (little door, dweller by city gate)
Doermer (tower keeper, fr Latin *turris*)
Doerner (thicket dweller) 72
Doerr (dry)
Doerrer, Doerrmann (dryer) 96
Doescher (fr Doerscher, thresher)
Doetsch, see Deutsch
Doggendorf (bulldog village) 123
Dohl, Dohle 122, Dohlen (daw) 115
Dohmke < Thomas 131, 53
Dohnke < Anton 131, 53
Dohrman, Dohrmann, see Thormann
Dohrn, see Dorn
Dolch (dagger) 108
Dold, Dolde < Berthold
Dolf, Dolfi, Dolfs < Adolf
Doll, Dolle (mad)
Doll (valley) 76
Dollenberg (valley mountain) 76, 48, 122
Doller (valley dweller) 76
Dollfuss (club foot) 114, or < Adolphus or Rudolfus
Dollinger, Dolinger (fr Dolling 122)
Dollmann (madman) 115, see Tollmann
Dollmann (valley dweller) 76
Dolmetsch (Slavic: interpreter)
Dom, Dohm, Dohme, Dohmer (dweller near a cathedral)
Domaas < Thomas 131
Dome, Domes, Dohm, Dohme < Thomas 131
Domhoff (cathedral court) 92, 122
Donath < St. Donatus 131
Donge, Donges, Dongis < St. Anthonius 131
Donner (thunder, thunderer)

Donnewitz, see Dannewitz
Dopmann (potter) 96
Doppler (gambler)
Doremus < Adoremus (Let us adore [Him]!) 117
Dorenfeld (thorn field) 72, 84
Dorfman, Dorffmann, Dorfler (villager) 123
Dorman, see Thormann 43
Dorn (thorn, thicket) 72, 122
Dornbach (thorny brook) 72, 77, 122
Dornburg (thorn castle) 72, 73, 122
Dornbusch, Dornbush (thorn bush) 72, 72, 122
Dornfeld (thorn field) 72, 84
Dornheim (thorn hamlet) 72, 123, 122
Dorp (village) 123, 122
Dorsch (codfish seller) 115, 105
Dorwarth, see Thorwart 43
Dosch, Dosche (bush, tavern keeper) 96
Doster (thyme seller, spice seller) 105
Dower, see Dauer 151
Downer, see Dauner 151
Drach, Drache (dragon, house name) 149
Drachsel, Drachsler, see Drechsler
Drake, see Drach
Drakenfeld (dragon field) 84
Drayer, see Dreher 151
Dreber < Andreas 131
Drechsel, Drechsler, Drexler (turner) 98
Drees < Andreas 131
Dreher (potter) 96
Dreher, see Drechsler
Dreier (thrupence) 112
Dreier (potter) 96
Dreifus, Dreifuss, Dreyfuss (tripod) 8
Dreifus, Dreyfuss (fr Trier) 122

Dreisbach, Dresbach, see
Troestbach
Dreiss (swamp water), 80,
Dreiser, Dreist (audacious) 115
Dresch, Drescher (thresher) 95
Dresden, Dresner (fr Dresden)
122
Dresselhaus (fr Dresselhausen
122, turner's house)
Dressler, Dresler, see Drechsel
Dreus, Drewes, Drewing <
Andreas 131
Drexel, Drexler, see Drechsel
Dreyer, Dryer (turner, see
Dreier) 96
Dreyfus, Dreyfuss, see Dreifuss
8
Driebenbach (murky brook) 77
Driehaus (fr Driehausen) 122
Dries < Andreas 131, 53
Driesch (uncultivated field) 84,
122
Drieschbach (pasture brook) 84,
77
Driessheim (pasture hamlet)
84, 123
Driessler, see Drechsel
Droege (dry)
Drommelhausen (drummer
houses) 65
Drost, Droste (steward) 109
Drucker, Druecker (cloth
presser) 96
Drucker (printer) 96
Drusch (uncultivated, as of
land)
Drussel (trunk, snout) 114
Drutz (defiance) 115
Dryer, see Dreier, Dreyer
Dubendorffer, Diebendoerfer
(swamp village) 80, 123
Ducker (diving duck, devil)
Dude (bagpiper) 96
Duden (blockhead) 115, or <
Ludolf 53, 54
Dueffenbach, see Tiefenbach
Duehring, see Duering
Duensing (Duden's swamp) 80

Duerenberger (region in
Austria, dry mountain)
121
Duerer (door keeper)
Duering, Dueringer
(Thuringian) 121
Duermueller (water miller)
103
Duerr (dry, skinny) 114
Duerrbaum (dry tree) 89
Duerrenmatt (dry meadow)
84
Duesenberg (silent mountain)
68
Duetsch, Duitscher, see
Deutsch
Duffner (fr Teufen in
Wurttemberg) 122
Dulde < Berthold 53
Dumbaugh (fr Dumbach 122)
77, 151
Dumler (inexperienced) 114
Dunge < St. Anthonius 131
Dunger (manure)
Dunger (dweller on a
hummock)
Dunkel (dark) 113
Dunkelberg (dark mountain)
68
Dunker, see Dunkel
Dunkhorst (low-hill hurst)
68, 72
Durcholtz (through the
forest) 70, 72
Durenberger, see
Durrenberger
Durer, see Duerer
Durlach (dry pond) 80
Durlach (principality on
Rhein) 121, 122
Durman, see Thurmann
Durnbaugh (dry creek) 77
Durner, see Turner
Durrenberger, see
Duerenberger
Durst (thirst) 115
Durst (daredevil) 115

Dusel (silly, cf. English "dizzy")
115
Dusenberry, see Dusenberg 151
Dussel, Dussler (stream near
Dusseldorf) 83
Dusseldorf (German city), 122,
124
Dussing (ornamental belt 106),
see also Tussing
Dusterhoff (dreary farm) 92
Dutweiler 122, see Dettweiler
Dyson, see Theissen 151
Dyssgen < Dietrich

E

Eagel, Eagle (*igel*, hedgehog)
48, 159
Eagleburg (hedgehog castle) 48,
73, 159
Eaglehart, see Igelhart
Eakel, see Eichel 151
Earhart, see Erhard 159
Earl, Earle, Earley, see Erle
151
Earlbeck, see Erlenbach 151
Earman, see Ehrmann 159
Earnest, see Ernst 152
Earp, see Erb 151
East, see Ost 152
Eastberg, see Ostberg 152
Easter, see Oster 152
Eastwood, see Ostwald 152
Ebbeke, Ebbeling < Eggebrecht
Ebbert, Ebberts < Eggebrecht
Ebbinger, Eppinger (fr
Ebbingen, plain), also see
Eggebrecht
Ebbinghause, Ebbinghauser
(house on the plain) 65
Ebel, Ebele, Ebell, Ebeling,
Ebelt < Albrecht
Ebelding (belonging to Ebel) 59
Ebeling, Ebelke < Eber 59
Eben, Ebener, Ebner
(whiffletree)
Eben, Ebener, Ebner (fr Eben
122, dweller on a plain)

Ebenhack (level enclosure)
123
Ebensberger (mountain on a
plain) 68
Eber, Ebers, Ebert 143 (wild
boar) 48, or < Eberhard
Eberbach, Ebersbacher,
Eberbeck (reed brook) 81,
77
Eberding (fr Eberding 122,
belonging to Ebert 59)
Eberhagen (wild boar
enclosure) 48, 123
Eberhard, Eberhardt,
Eberharde, Eberhards,
Eberhart (wild boar +
strong) 48, 46
Eberl, Eberle, Eberlet,
Eberli, Eberlein, Eberlin,
Eberling (little wild boar
48, < Eberhard)
Ebersbacher, Eberspacher (fr
Ebersbach 122, boar
brook) 48, 77
Ebersberg, Ebersberger (fr
Ebersberg 122, boar
mountain) 48, 68
Eberschwein (wild boar) 48
Eberschwyl (boar village) 48,
127
Ebersmann (Eber's vassal)
48, 94
Eberstein (boar mountain)
48, 73, 122
Ebert, Eberth, see Eber,
Eggebrecht
Ebertsbach (Ebert's brook)
48, 77
Eberwein, Eberwine (boar
friend) 48, 48
Ebinger (fr Ebing 122, see
also Eppinger)
Ebinghausen (place name)
65, 122
Ebler < Albrecht
Ebner, see Eben, Ebener
Ebrecht (law + brilliant) 47,
see also Eggebrecht
Ebright, see Ebrecht 151

Ebstein, see Epstein
Eccard, see Eckhard
Eccles, see Eckel 151
Eche, Echeman, see Eiche,
　Eichmann
Echerd, Echard, see Eckhard
Echt (lawful, genuine)
Echternacht (name of Swiss
　town) 122
Eck, Ecker (fr Ecke 122,
　corner, place) 85
Eckard, Eckhart, see Eckhard
Eckbert (sword + bright) 46, 47
Ecke, see Eckehard
Eckeberger (oak mountain) 89,
　68
Eckeberger (sword + protection)
　89, 68
Eckel, Eckell, Eckels, see
　Eickel
Eckel, see Ekel
Eckelhof (oak farm) 89, 92
Eckelmann (dweller among the
　oaks) 89, 94
Eckelmeyer (proprietor of the
　Echelhof) 89, 93, 94
Eckenauer (oak meadow) 89,
　84
Eckensberger, Eckensbarger,
　see Eckeberger
Ecker (river name) 83, see
　Acker
Eckerle (little field) 84
Eckermann (dweller on the
　Ecker) 83, see Ackermann
Eckert, see Eckhard
Eckes, see Eck
Eckfeld, Eckfield 151 (oak
　field) 89, 72, 122
Eckhard, Eckehard, Eckhardt,
　Eckert (sword + strong) 46,
　46
Eckhaus (corner house) 85, 65,
　122
Eckhoff (oak farm) 89, 92, 122
Eckholt, Eckholdt (oak forest)
　89, 72, 122
Eckholt (sword + loyal) 46, 48

Eckinger, Eckler, Eckner,
　Eckmann (dweller on the
　corner) 85
Eckmann, see Eckinger,
　Eichmann
Eckmeyer (proprietor of the
　Eckhoff) 89, 93, 94
Eckner, see Eckinger,
　Eichner
Eckrich (sword + rule) 46,
　47
Eckrodt, Eckrote, Eckroth
　(oak clearing) 89, 126
Eckstein (corner stone) 89,
　73
Eckwart (sword + guard) 46,
　47
Edel, Edele, Edeler, Edler,
　Edeling, Edling (noble) 47
Edelberg (noble mountain)
　47, 68
Edelblute (noble blood) 47
Edelbrock, Edelbrook (noble
　brake) 47, 80
Edelen (noblemen) 47
Edelheiser (noble houses) 47,
　65
Edelman, Edelmann
　(nobleman) 47
Edelmeyer (proprietor of the
　Edelhof) 4, 93, 94
Edelmut (noble disposition)
　47, 115
Edelsberg (noble's mountain)
　47, 68, 122
Edelstein (jewel) 47, 74
Edenbaum (tree of Eden)
　135, 89
Edenfeld, Edenfield 151
　(Eden field) 84
Eder, Ederle, Edert (dweller
　on barren soil) 122
Eder (dweller near the Eder)
　83
Edgar (treasure + spear) 47,
　46
Eding, Edinger, see Ettinger
Edler, see Edel

Edward, Eduard, Edwards
(treasure + guardian) 47, 47
Efeldt (place name) 122
Effert < Everhard 122
Effinger (fr Effingen) 122
Effler, Effner, Effland (dweller
among the elms) 89
Effler (smith, tool repairer) 96
Efland, see Effler
Egbert (sword + brilliant) 46,
47
Ege, Egge (harrow) 106
Egel (leech, bloodsucker)
Egelberg (swamp mountain) 68
Eger 122, Egert (fr the Eger)
83
Eggebrecht (sword + bright) 46,
47
Eggelmann < Eggebrecht
Eggemann, Eggermeyer
(harrower) 95, see also
Eckmann
Eggenberger 122, see
Eckeberger
Egger, Eggers, Eggert
(harrower) 95, or < Agiheri
(sword + army) 46, 46
Eggert, see Eckhard and
Eggebrecht
Eggs, see Eck
Eghard, see Eckhard
Egiloff (sword + wolf) 46, 48
Eginhard (sword + strong) 46,
46
Egli, Eglin (kind of perch) 115
Egli (a place in Switzerland)
122, see Egloff
Eglisau (perch meadow, place
in Switzerland) 84, 122
Egloff, see Egiloff
Egloffstein (Egloff's mountain)
68, 73
Egmont (sword + protection)
46, 47
Egner, Egnert, see Eigen,
Eigner
Egolf, see Egloff
Ehard, see Ehart
Ehardi (son of Ehard) 142

Ehart (law + strong 46), see
also Erhard
Ehebrecht (law + bright 47,
46), see also Eggebrecht
Eheman, Ehemann (lawful
husband) 47
Ehinger (fr Ehingen 122)
Ehle, Eheln, Ehles, Ehly
(alder) 89, see also Ehrler
Ehler, Ehlers, Ehlert,
Ehrlermann (sword +
army) 46, 46
Ehrlerding (belonging to
Ehrler) 59
Ehling, Ehlinger (fr Ehlingen
122)
Ehman, see Ehemann
Ehnert < Eginhard
Ehninger (fr Ehningen 122)
Ehr, Ehren (honor, honors)
47
Ehregott (Glorify God!) 116,
140
Ehrenbeck, Ehrbaker (honor
brook, swamp brook) 47,
80, 77, 151
Ehrenberg, Ehrenberger (fr
Ehrenberg 122, honor
mountain, swamp
mountain) 47, 68, 80
Ehrenbrink (honor hill,
swamp hill) 47, 74, 80
Ehrenfeld (field of honor) 47,
84
Ehrenfried (honorable peace)
47, 51
Ehrenhard (honor + strong)
47, 46
Ehrenmann (man of honor)
47, 94
Ehrenpforten (glory portals)
47
Ehrenpreis, Ehrenpries
(prize of honor) 47
Ehrenreich (rich in honor,
realm of glory) 47, 46
Ehrenspeck, see Ehrenbeck
Ehrensperger, see
Ehrenberg, Ahrensberger

Ehres, Ehresmann, Ehrismann,
see Ehrenmann
Ehrhard, Ehrhardt, see Erhard,
Erhardt
Ehrich, Ehrichs, see Erich,
Erichs
Ehrig, Ehrick, see Erich
Ehringer (fr Ehringen 122)
Ehrle, see Erl
Ehrlich, Ehrlichs, Erlicher,
Ehrlick (honest) 138
Ehrling, Ehrlinger (fr Erlingen)
Ehrmann, see Ehrenmann
Ehrmannstraut (honored man's
beloved)
Ehrmannstraut (the beloved of
Irmin, the chief god)
Ehrreich (rich in honors) 47,
46
Ehrsam (respectable) 138
Ehrstein (honor stone) 47, 73
Ei (egg)
Eib (yew, crossbow) 89, 108
Eibach (fr *ib*, pre-Germanic
word for brook) 83, 122
Eibel, Eibl, Eibner, Eibling <
Albrecht
Eiben (yew tree) 89, 122
Eiberger (yew mountain) 89, 68
Eich, Eiche, Eicher (oak) 89
Eichach, Eichacher (fr Eichach
122, oak river, oak forest)
89, 79
Eichacker (oak chopper) 95
Eichbach (oak brook) 89, 77,
122
Eichbauer (oak farmer) 89, 91
Eichbaum, Eichelbaum (oak
tree) 89
Eichberg 122, Eichenberg,
Eichberger (oak mountain)
89, 68
Eichborn (oak spring) 89, 79
Eichel (acorn)
Eichelberg, Eichelberger (fr
Eichelberg 122, acorn
mountain) 68
Eichelhart (acorn forest) 89, 72

Eichelkraut (acorn herbs) 89
Eichelmann (acorn gatherer)
89, 94
Eichelstein (acorn mountain)
73
Eichen (oaks) 89, 122
Eichenauer (oak meadow)
89, 84, 122
Eichenberg 122,
Eichenberger, see
Eichberg
Eichenbrunn 122,
Eichenbrunner (oak well)
89, 79
Eichenfeld (oak field) 89, 84,
122
Eichenfels (oak cliffs) 89
Eichengruen, Eichengrien
(oak green) 89
Eichenlaub (oak foliage) 89
Eichenmeyer, Eichenmoyer
(proprietor of the Eichhoff)
89, 93, 94
Eichenmueller (miller at the
oaks) 89, 103
Eicher, Eichert, Eichler
(dweller near the oaks) 89
Eichfelder (oak fields) 89, 84,
122
Eichhacker (oak chopper) 95
Eichhammer (oak hammer
89, fr Eichheim 122)
Eichhauer (oak chopper) 95
Eichhoff (farm surrounded
by oaks) 89, 92, 122
Eichholtz, Eichholz (oak
wood) 89, 72, 122
Eichhorn (squirrel) 115
Eichhorst (oak hurst) 89, 72,
122
Eichler, Eichinger,
Eichlinger, see Eicher
Eichmann, Eichermann, see
Eicher
Eichmeyer (proprietor of the
Eichhoff) 89, 93, 94

Eichmueller, Eichmiller (miller
in the oaks) 89, 103
Eichner, see Eicher
Eicholz, see Eichholtz
Eichorn, see Eichhorn
Eichstadt, Eichstedt (oak city,
oak place) 89
Eichstein (oak mountain) 89,
73
Eichwald (oak forest) 89, 72
Eick ..., see Eich
Eick, Eicke, see Eich, Eiche
Eickel, see Eichel
Eickelberg (acorn mountain)
89, 68
Eickenberg (oak mountain) 89,
68
Eickhammer, see Eichhammer
Eickhoff 122, see Eichhoff
Eickholt 122, see Eichholtz
Eickmann, see Eichmann
Eickmeier, see Eichmeyer
Eid, Eide (oath)
Eidam, Eydam (son-in-law) 119
Eidel, see Eitel
Eidelberg 122, see Heidelberg
Eidelmann, see Edelmann
Eidemiller (miller on the Eide)
83, 103
Eidenberg (mountain on the
Eide) 83, 68
Eidenwald (forest on the Eide)
83, 72
Eidenweil (village on the Eide)
83, 127
Eidinger (fr Eidingen) 122
Eidler, see Edler
Eier, Eiers, Eyers, Eierman,
Eiermann (egg seller) 105
Eif, Eife (fr Eife 122)
Eifel (fr the Eifel region) 121
Eifert, Eiffert (zeal) 115
Eigel, see Egel
Eigelbach (leech brook) 77, 122
Eigen, Eigner (fr Eigen 122),
see Eigenmann
Eigenbrod, Eigenbrode,
Eigenbrodt (one's own bread)
Eigenbrun (private well) 79

Eigenheer (independent
landowner, freeholder)
Eigenholt (vassal + loyal) 48
Eigenholt (private forest) 72
Eigenmann (serf, vassal) 94
Eigner, Eigert (smallholder)
Eik ..., see Eich ...
Eike (oak) 89
Eikenberry, see Eickenberg
151
Eiker, see Eicher
Eikhoff, Eikof, Eickhoffe, see
Eichhoff
Eikmann, see Eichmann
Eikmeyer (proprietor of the
Eikhoff) 89, 93, 94
Eikner, see Eichner
Eikstein (oak mountain) 89,
68
Eilbach, Eilbacher (rapid
stream) 77
Eilbach (swamp brook) 80,
70
Eilberg (place name) 122
Eildeberger, see Eidelberger
Eiler, Eilers, Eilert,
Eilermann (hurrier), see
also Euler, Eilhart
Eilertsen (son of Eilert) 59
Eilhart (sword + strong) 46,
46
Eimer (bucket, fr Latin
amphora) 101, 106
Eimer (sword + famous) 46,
47
Eimke (little bucket) 101
Einaugler (one-eyed) 114
Einberg (place name, swamp
mountain) 122
Einbinder (book binder) 96
Einbrod, see Eigenbrod
Einegger 122, Einecker
(owner of private field) 84
Einert, see Einhardt
Einfalt (simplicty) 115
Einfeldt, Eigenfeld 122
(private field) 84
Einhardt (sword + strong)
46, 46

Einhaus (private house) 65,
122
Einholt, see Eigenholt
Einhorn (unicorn, a house
name) 149
Einig (united)
Einiger (single, solitary)
Einmueller (independent miller)
103
Einolf (sword + wolf) 46, 48
Einsiedler (hermit 110, fr
Einsiedeln, hermitage 122)
Einspruch (objection, protest)
Einstein (place encompassed by
a stone wall)
Eirich, see Eurich
Eis (ice)
Eis (ironmonger) 96
Eischberger (ice mountain) 68
Eischberger (iron mountain) 96,
68
Eisdorfer (ice village) 123, 122
Eise, Eisele, Eiseley, Eiseler,
Eiselen, Eiselt, Eiseman
(iron monger) 96
Eiseman, Eisenmann, see Eise
Eisen (iron, ironmonger) 96
Eisenach 122, Eisenacher
(German city, iron springs)
Eisenauer (fr Eisenau 122), see
Eisenhauer
Eisenbach (iron brook) 96, 77,
122
Eisenband (iron band) 106
Eisenbart < Eisenberacht (iron
+ bright) 96, 46
Eisenbeil (iron axe) 96, 106
Eisenbeis, Eisenbeiss (iron bite,
bully) 115
Eisenberg, Eisinberg,
Eisenberger (fr Eisenberg
122, iron mountain) 96, 68
Eisenbiss, see Eisenbeis
Eisenbrand (iron fire, smith) 96
Eisendraht (iron wire) 96, 106
Eisenfeld (iron field) 96, 84,
122
Eisenfels (iron cliff)

Eisenfress (iron eater,
turbulent person) 115
Eisengrein (iron + mask,
helmet)
Eisenhard, Eisenhardt,
Eisenhart (iron + strong)
96, 46
Eisenhaub (helmet) 108
Eisenhauer (iron hacker,
perhaps based on Fr.
Taillefer)
Eisenhauser (iron house) 65
Eisenhaut, see Eisenhut
Eisenhoefer (iron yard) 96,
92
Eisenhour, Eisenhower, see
Eisenhauer 151
Eisenhut, Eisenhuth,
Eisenhueter (fr Eisenhut,
iron hat, helmet, helmet
maker) 96, 108
Eisenklam (iron clamp) 106
Eisenkolb (iron club)
Eisenloeffel (iron spoon) 106
Eisenlohe (iron flame, smith)
96
Eisenman, Eisenmann
(ironmonger) 96
Eisenmann (jailer)
Eisenmenger, Eisenmenger
(ironmonger) 96
Eisenmeyer (proprietor of
the Eisenhof) 93, 94
Eisenrauch (iron smoke,
smith)
Eisenreich (rich in iron)
Eisenring (iron ring) 106
Eisenschmid, Eisenschmidt
(iron smith) 96
Eisenstadt (iron city, iron
place) 122
Eisenstein (iron stone, iron
mountain) 73
Eisentraut, Eisentrout <
Isandrut, iron + beloved)
60
Eiser, Eisert (iron worker)
96

Eisermann, see Eisenmann
Eisfeld, Eisfelder, Eisfeldt (ice field) 84, 122
Eisgrau (iron grey) 112
Eisgruber (iron miner) 96
Eisinger (fr Eising) 122
Eisler, see Eiser
Eisloeffel, see Eisenloeffel
Eisman, Eismann (ironmonger) 96
Eisner (ironmonger) 96
Eiswald (iron forest) 72
Eiswald (ice forest) 72
Eit, Eith (oath)
Eitel, Eitler (empty, having no first name)
Eitemiller (miller an the Eite) 83, 103
Eitermann (dweller among the nettles)
Eiting, Eitner (fr Eiting 122)
Eitner (burner, stoker, smelter) 96
Ekard, Ekhard, Ekhardt, Ekert, see Eckhard
Ekel 112, Ekels (disgust)
Eken (oaks) 89
Ekenhoffer (oak farm) 89, 92
Ekenroth, Ekerroth (oak clearing) 89, 126
Ekert, Ekhard, see Eckhard
Ekestein, see Eckstein
Ekman, see Eckmann
Elbe, Elbthal (German river, Elbe valley) 83
Elbeck (alder brook) 89, 77
Elberg (alder mountain) 89, 68
Elbers, Elbert, Elberth, Elbrecht (sword + bright) 46, 47
Elbing (fr Elbingen 122)
Elbrecht, see Elbers
Eldemann, see Eltermann
Elenzweig (alder branch) 89
Elermann, see Ellermann
Elers, see Ehlers
Elert, see Eller
Elfers, Elfert < Alfheri, elf + army) 48, 46

Elflein (little elf) 48
Elfring, Elfringer (son of Elvert)
Elg, Elger, Elgert (foot path) 65
Elhardt, see Eilhart
Elias (OT name) 135
Elich (lawful) 115
Eliel (OT name) 135
Eling, Elinger, see Elling
Elkmann (elk + man)
Elkmann (swamp man) 80
Ell, Ells (yard, measure)
Ellbrecht, see Elbrecht
Elldorfer (alder village) 89, 123
Ellekamp, see Ellenkamp
Ellemann, see Ellermann
Ellen (prowess) 115
Ellen (alders) 89, 122
Ellenbach, Ellenbeck (alder brook) 89, 77
Ellenberg, Ellenberger (fr Ellenberg 122, alder mountain) 89, 68
Ellenbogen (elbow) 114, 122
Ellenburg (alder castle) 89, 73
Ellenkamp (alder field) 89, 84
Eller, Ellern, Ellert (dweller by the alder trees) 89, 122
Ellerbrock, Ellerbrake, Ellerbruch (alder brake) 89, 80, 122
Ellerkamp, see Ellenkamp
Ellermann (grandfather) 119
Ellerrot (alder clearing) 89, 126
Ellestad (alder place, alder shore) 89
Ellewin, see Alwin
Ellg, see Elg
Ellgass (alder street) 89, 65, 122
Elling 122, Ellinger (foot path)

Ellinghaus, Ellinghausen,
Ellinhuyzen (fr Ellinghausen
122, house on foot path) 65
Ellner (dweller among the
alders) 89
Ellrich (prowess + strong) 46
Ellroth (alder clearing) 89, 126
Ellwanger (fr Ellwangen) 122
Ellwanger (alder field) 89, 84
Ellwanger (fr Ellwangen, elk
trap)
Elm, Elms (dweller among the
elms) 89
Elm (swamp) 80
Elmendorf (elm village) 89,
123, 122
Elmer (sword + famous) 46, 47
Elmer (noble + famous) 46, 47
Elmshaeuser (swamp houses)
89, 65
Elpert, see Albrecht
Elrich (noble + rule) 46, 46
Elsass, Elsasser, Elsaesser,
Elsassor (Alsatian) 121
Elsbach, Elsbacher (shad brook,
swamp brook) 80, 77, 122
Else, Elsen, Elser, Elsner
(dweller on the Els) 83
Elsenheimer (alder hamlet) 89,
123
Elserode (clearing on the Els)
83, 126
Elserode (clearing in the
alders) 89, 126
Elsfeldt (alder field) 89, 84
Elshof, Elshoffer (alder farm)
89, 92
Elshorst, Elsinghorst (swamp
hurst) 80, 72
Elsinger (fr Elsing, alder place)
89, 122
Elsner, see Else
Elsohn (son of Else) 60
Elsroad, see Elserode
Elstein (alder mountain) 89, 73
Elster (magpie, talkative
person) 115

Elster, Eltester (village
senior) 113
Elterman, Eltermann (senior)
113
Elteste (village senior) 113
Eltzroth, see Elserode
Elvers, see Elfers
Ely (OT name) 135
Emanuel (OT name) 135
Embach (beyond the brook)
70, 77, 122
Emberger (beyond the
mountain) 68, 70, 122
Embs (ant)
Emde, Emden 122, Emder
(German city)
Emer, Emert, Emmer,
Emmert < Emerich
Emerich, Emerick (fr
Amelrich, ruler of the
Amelungs, or fr Irmin,
"world king") 46
Emmel, Emmelmann <
Emerich
Emmen (place name) 122
Emmendorf (place name)
123, 122
Emmerich, Emmrich,
Emmerik, see Emerich
Emminger (fr Emmingen)
122
Emrhein, see Amrhein
Emrich, see Emerich
Ems 122 (fr the Ems River)
83
Emshof, Emshof (farm on
the Ems) 83, 92
Emsweiler (village on the
Ems) 83, 127
Enck (accurate,
perspicacious) 115
Enck (hired hand) 95
Enckhause (hired hands'
shelter) 65
Ende, Ender, Endemann, see
Amend
Endelman, Endelmann <
Andreas 53

Ender, Enders, Endres,
Endress, Endris, Enderis <
Andreas 53
Enderich (drake) 115
Enderle, Enderli, Enderly,
Enderlin, Endler, Enderlein
< Andreas 53
Endlich (Finally!) 117
Endrich, see Enderich
Eng, Enge, Enger, Engermann
(narrow)
Engbart (narrow beard) 112,
122
Engbert, see Engelbert
Engeberg (swamp mountain)
80, 68, 122
Engebrecht, see Engelbrecht
Engel, Engeln, Engels, Engeli,
Engeler, Engler (angel,
probably house name) 149
Engeland (England) 121
Engelbach (angel brook) 77,
122
Engelberg (angel mountain) 68,
122
Engelbert, Engelberth,
Engelberts, Engelbrecht
(angel + bright, Angel +
bright) 49, 47
Engeler, see Engler
Engelfried (angel + peace) 138
Engelhart, Engelhardt,
Engelhart, Engelharth,
Engelhaart (angel + strong,
Angle + strong) 49, 46
Engelhaupt (angel head) 149
Engelhaus, Engelhausen (angel
house) 65, 149
Engelhoff (angel farm) 92, 122
Engelke, Engelken, Engelking,
see Engelbert
Engelkraut (angel herb)
Engelman, Engelmann
(occupant of Engelhaus 65 or
Engelhoff 92, or else <
Engelbert)
Engelmann (Englishman) 121
Engelmeyer (proprietor of the
Engelhoff) 93, 92, 94

Engels, see Engel
Engelskirche (angel church)
71, 122
Engemann (dweller in a
narrow valley)
Engenhoefer (narrow farm)
92
Enger, Engers, Engert (fr
Engen 122)
Engermann, see Engemann
Engesser (dweller on a
narrow street) 65
Enghause, Enghausen,
Enghaussen, Enghauser
(narrow house) 65
England, Englander,
Englaender (Englishman)
121
Engle..., Engle..., see Engel...
Englehaupt, see Engelhaupt
151
Engler, Englert, Englerth
(Angle + army) 46, 49
Engler (dweller in house
zum Engel) 149
Engli (little angel)
Englischer (Englishman) 121
Engman, Engmann, see
Engemann
Engmeyer (proprietor of the
Enghof) 93, 92, 94
Engnoth (difficult straits)
Engwall (narrow wall)
Enk, Enke, Enker (hired
hand) 95
Enkel (grandchild) 119
Ennesfeldt (Enno's field) 84
Enninger (fr Enning 122)
Enrick, see Heinrich
Ensel, Enslin, Ensslin,
Enslein < Anselm 131
Ensinger (fr Ensingen) 122
Enten, Entemann,
Entenmann (duck raiser)
91
Entermann (duck raiser) 91
Entner, see Enten
Entstrasser (dweller across
the road) 70, 65

Entz, Enz (fr Enz of fr the Enz) 122, 83
Entzbacher, Entzenbache (fr Enzenbach 122)
Enzinger (fr Enzingen) 122
Ep, Epp < Eberhard
Epelbaum, see Apfelbaum
Epenstein, Eppenstein, Epstein, Eppstein, see Epstein
Eple, Epple, Eppli (little apple) 89
Eppel, Epple, Eppler, Epler, Eppelmann, see Appel, Apfel
Eppelsheim, Eppelsheimer (fr Eppelsheim 122, apple hamlet) 89, 123
Epperle < Eberhard 53
Eppert < Eggebrecht 53
Epping, Eppinger (fr Epping 122)
Epps < Eberhard 53
Eprecht, Epprecht (law + bright, see also Eggebrecht) 46
Epstein (wild boar stone) 48, 73, 151
Epsteine, Epstien, see Epstein 151
Erard, see Erhard
Erasmi (son of Erasmus) 142
Erb 122, Erbe, Erber, Erbin, Erben (heir, inheritance) 47, also < Erwin
Erb, Erbes, Erbsen (pea) 105
Erbach 122, Erbacher (swamp brook) 80, 77, see Erdbach
Erbsland (inherited land) 47
Erck, see Erk
Erd < Erhard 53
Erd, Erde (earth, or fr *ard*, swamp) 80
Erdbach, Erdesbach (earth stream, swamp stream) 80, 77, 122
Erdbrink (earth + grassy hill) 74
Erdel (arable land) 84

Erdenbrecht (earth + brilliant) 47
Erdheim (swamp hamlet) 123
Erdmann (earth man, modeled on Hebrew *Adam*) 135
Erdmeyer (swamp farmer) 93
Erdroth (swamp clearing) 126
Erfmeyer, Erffmayer (farmer on the water) 80, 93
Erfurt 122, Erffurth (German city)
Ergelet (grape bucket, fr Latin *arca*) 106
Ergenbright < Erkanbrecht (genuine + bright) 46, 151
Ergler (grape picker) 95
Ergott (Glorify God!) 117, 140
Erhard, Erhart, Erhardt (honor + strong) 47, 46
Erich, Erichs, Erig, Erick (law + rule) 47, 47
Eriksen (son of Erick) 59
Erischmann, see Ehresmann
Erismann, see Ehresmann
Erk < Erkenbrecht 53
Erkenbrecht (genuine + brilliant) 47
Erkmann < Erkenbrecht
Erl, Erle (alder) 89
Erlach (swamp pond) 89, 81, 122
Erlanger (fr Erlangen) 122
Erlebach, Erlbeck (alder brook) 89, 77, 122
Erlemann (dweller among the alders) 89
Erlen, Erler (alder) 89, 122
Erlenbach 122, see Erlebach
Erlenheiser (inhabitant of house among the alders) 89, 65
Erlewyn, Erlwein (freeman + friend) 48

Erlich, Erlichman, see Ehrlich,
Ehrlichmann
Ermann, see Ehrmann
Ermattinger (fr Ermattingen)
122
Ermel, Ermling, Ermeling
(sleeve, tailor) 96, 106
Ermut (honor + disposition)
115
Erna, Erne < Arnold 53
Ernest, see Ernst
Ernesti (son of Ernest) 142
Ernhut (guardian of hnor)
Ernsperger, Ernsberger, see
Arnsperger
Ernst, Ernest (vigor,
earnestness) 115
Ernstein 122, see Arnstein
Ernsthausen (Ernst's houses)
65, 122
Ernte (harvest)
Erp, see Erb
Erpenbach, Erpenbeck (heirs'
brook) 47, 77
Erpenstein (heirs' mountain)
47, 68
Errmann, see Ehrmann
Ertel, Ertell, Ertle, Ertelt <
Ortlieb
Ertzberger (ore miner, man fr
Erzberg) 122
Ervin, see Erwein
Erwein, Erwin (honor + friend)
47, 48
Erz (ore, miner) 106
Erzbischof (archbishop) 110
Erzgraeber (ore miner) 96
Esbach 122, see Eschbach
Esbrandt (clearing in the ash
trees) 89, 126
Esch (ash tree) 89, 122
Eschauer (fr Eschau 122, ash
meadow) 89, 84
Eschbach, Eschenbach,
Eschbacher, Eschelbach,
Eschbeck, Eschelbeck (fr
Eschenbach 122, ash tree
brook, or fr pre-Germanic

river term 83) 89, 77, see
Aeschbach
Eschborn (ash tree spring, or
see Eschbach) 89, 79, 122
Eschelmann, see Escher
Eschenbrenner, see
Aschenbrenner
Eschenfelder (fr
Eschenfelden 122, ash tree
field) 89, 84
Eschenhagen (ash tree
enclosure) 89, 123
Eschenmosen, Eschenmoser
(ash bog) 89, 80
Escher, Eschler, Eschmann
(fr Escher 122, swamp) 80
Eschmeyer (farmer among
the ash trees) 89, 93
Eschrich (rich in ash trees)
89
Eschwege (path through the
ash trees) 89, 122
Esenberg (ash mountain) 89,
68
Esendal (ash dale) 89, 76
Eser (back pack, also see
Escher)
Eshbach, see Eschbach 151
Eshelmann, see Eschelmann
151
Esher, Eshler, see Escher
151
Eshman, see Escher 151
Eslin, Esslin (jenny) 91
Esner, see Eschner
Espen (aspen) 89, 122
Espenhain (aspen grove) 89,
72, 122
Espenscheid, Espenschied
(aspen log) 89
Espich (aspen bush) 89
Ess (forge, hearth, smith) 96
Essel, Esselmann (fr Essel)
122
Essendorf (forge village,
chimney village, swamp
village) 80, 123, 122
Essenfeld (forge field, swamp
field) 80, 84

Essenhaven (forge farm, swamp farm) 80, 123
Esser, Essers, Essert (axel maker, wainright) 96, 106
Esser (glutton) 115
Esserwein (wine drinker) 115
Essig (vinegar, fr Latin *acetum* 105, or pre-Germanic word for swamp) 80
Esslin, see Eslin
Essling, Esslinger (fr Esslingen 122)
Essner (forge worker, hearth worker) 96
Ester, Esters (OT name) 135, 122
Esterling (easterner)
Estermann (field man)
Estermann (Ashkenazic metronym for Esther's husband) 60
Estermyer (proprietor of the Esterhof, eastern farm) 93, 151
Estinghausen (eastern houses) 65, 122
Estreicher, see Oestreich
Etchberger, see Etschberger
Etel ..., see Edel
Etsch, Etschmann (Adige, dweller on the Adige) 83
Ettenhoffer, Ettenhuber 122 (farmer on the Ett) 83
Etter (dweller on the Ett, dweller in a wattled enclosure) 83
Ettinger (fr Ettingen, village on the Ett) 83, 122
Ettlinger (fr Ettlingen, village on the Ett) 83, 122
Ettwein (Otwin, wealth + friend) 47, 48
Etzel, Etzler (pet name of Attila the Hun)
Eubel < Albrecht 53
Eugel (little eye) 114
Eulbacher (swamp brook) 77
Eulbeck (swamp brook) 77, 122

Eulberg (owl mountain) 68
Euler, Eulers, Eulert, Eulner (potter) 96
Eurich (sword + rule) 46, 47
Eva (wife of Adam) 135
Ever ..., Evers ..., see Eber..., Ebers
Everet, see Eberhard
Everhard, Everhardt, Everhart, see Eberhard
Eversburg (boar castle) 48, 73, 122
Eversmeier (proprietor of the Evershof) 73, 94
Everstein 122, see Eberstein
Evert, Everts, Evertz, see Ebert
Ewald, Ewalt (law + keeper, priest) 47, 47
Ewart, Ewartz (guardian of the law, priest) 47, 47
Ewers, Ewert, Ewertz, see Eber, Ebert
Ewig (eternal)
Exler, see Oechsler
Exley, see Oechsele
Eyb (pre-Germanic river name) 83, see Eib 122
Eyc, Eych..., see Eich...Eychler, see Eicher
Eyck (oak) 89
Eyckhof (oak farm) 89, 92
Eydam (father-in-law) 119
Eyder (eider) 105, 106
Eyer, Eyermann, see Eier, Eiermann
Eygenbrod, see Eigenbrod
Eyler, see Eiler
Eymann (egg man) 105
Eyrich, see Eurich
Eyring, see Eurich
Eysel (ironmonger) 96
Eysemann, Eysenman, see Eiseman
Eysen ..., see Eisen
Eytel, see Eitel
Eyth, see Eid
Ezell, Ezzel, see Etzel

F

Faas < Gervasius, Servatius
131, see Fass
Fabal, Fabel < St. Fabian 131
Faber, Fabert, Fabor (Latin:
smith) 141
Fabian (name of pope) 134
Fabricius, Fabritzius (Latin
name for Schmidt) 141
Fach (compartment, pigeonhole,
fishtrap) 106
Fach (swamp water) 80
Fack (swine) 91
Fackert, Fackeret (flax breaker)
95
Fackert (joyful)115
Fackler, Fakler (torch bearer)
Fackler (flax breaker) 95
Fadem (thread, tailor) 96
Fader (dweller on a fence)
Faecher (fan) 106
Faehner, Faehnrich (ensign)
107
Faelten, see Felten
Faerber (dyer) 96, 122
Faernbacher, see Farbach
Faesch, Faesche < St.
Servatius 131
Faessle, Faessler (cooper) 96,
106
Faeth, Faetke, see Fader
Faeustlin (little fist, little dog)
Faff, see Pfaff
Fahenstock, see Fahnenstock
Fahl, Fahle, Fahler, Fahler
(pale, swamp) 80
Fahlbusch (pale bush, swamp
bush) 80
Fahlteich (swamp pond) 80
Fahn (swamp) 80, or <
Stephanus (St. Stephen)
Fahn, Fahnen (flag) 108
Fahnestock (flag staff)
Fahr, Faehr (ferry landing) 122
Fahrbach, Fahrenbach,
Farenbach (*vornebach*, before
the brook) 70, 77

Fahrencorn (before the grain
field) 70
Fahrenhorst (before the
hurst 70, swamp hurst 80)
72, 122
Fahrenwald (before the
forest 70, swamp forest
80) 71
Fahrmann (ferryman) 96
Fahrmeyer (proprietor of the
Fahrhoff, ferry farm) 93,
94
Fahrner (fr Fahrn)
Faigel, Faigle (timid) 115
Fainberg, see Feinberg
Faiss, Faist, Faister, see
Feiss, Feist, Feister (fat,
corpulent) 114
Fakler, see Fackler
Falbausch, see Fahlbusch
Falk, Falke, Falck (falcon,
falconer, fr Latin *falco*)
115
Falkenau (falcon meadow,
swamp meadow) 80, 84,
122
Falkenberg (falcon mountain)
68, 122
Falkenburg 122, Falkinburg
(falcon castle) 73
Falkenhahn, Falkenhain
(falcon's grove) 72
Falkenheimer (falcon hamlet)
123
Falkenmeyer, Falenmayr
(proprietor of the
Falkenhoff) 93, 94
Falkenstein 122, Falkenstine
151 (falcon's crag) 73
Falkner, Falker, Falker
(falconer) 115
Fallentin (St. Valentine) 131
Falsenmayer (cliff farmer) 93
Falten < St. Valentine 131
Falter (butterfly)
Falter (apple tree, fr
apfelter) 89, 122
Falter (portcullis)
Falz, see Pfalz

Fandrich (ensign) 108
Fanger, Fangman, Fangmann (catcher)
Fannacht, see Fasnacht
Farabaugh, see Fahrenbach 151
Farb (color)
Farbach, see Fahrbach
Farbenblum (colored flower)
Farber, see Faerber
Farenholtz (before the forest) 70, 72
Farenhorst, see Fahrenhorst
Farinholt, see Farenholtz
Farn, Fahrne (fern)
Farnbacher, see Fahrbach
Farrenkopf (steer head) 113, 149
Farver, see Faerber
Fascher (bandager) 96
Fasching (Mardi Gras, Carnival) 143
Fasel (draft animal) 91
Fasenfeld (pheasant field) 84
Fasnacht, Fassenacht, Fastnacht (Mardi Gras, Shrove Tuesday)
Fass, Fasse, Faas (vat, barrel, barrel maker 96, also pet name for Servatius, Gervasius)
Fassbach (barrel brook) 77
Fassbinder, Fassbender, Fassbindler (barrel maker) 96
Fasshauer (barrel maker) 96
Fassler (barrel maker) 96
Fassnacht, see Fasnacht
Fatthauer, Fathauer, see Fasshauer
Fatz < St. Bonifatius 131
Fauch, Fauck, Faucker (bellows, smith) 96, 106
Fauenbach (peacock brook) 115, 77
Fauerbach, see Fauenbach, Feurbach
Faul, Fauler, Fowl (lazy) 115

Faulbach (stagnant brook) 77, 122
Faulert (dweller near stagnant water)
Faulhaber, Faulhaffer (noxious oat-like weed) 92
Faulhuber (farmer near stagnant water) 91
Faulkner, see Falkner
Faus, Fausel, Fauser (puffed up)
Fausnacht, Fausnaugh 151, see Fasnacht
Faust, Fausten (fist, little dog)
Faut, Fauth, Fautz, Fautzen, Fautzer, Fautter, see Vogt
Fawler, see Fauler 151
Fawst, see Faust 151
Fay < St. Sophia 131, 60
Fayler, see Feil
Fayst, see Feist
Fearer, see Fuehrer 151
Feaster, see Pfister 151
Fecher, see Faecher
Fechheimer (fr Fechheim 122)
Fechler, Fechner (furrier) 96
Fecht, Fechter, Feght, Feghtmann, Fegter (champion)
Feckel < Frederick, Friedrich 53
Fedder, see Vetter
Feder, Federler, Federmann, Feddermann (feather seller, goose down dealer, pillow maker) 105
Feder, see Fedder
Federbush (crest on helmet) 151
Federspiel (trained raptor, falconer) 91
Fee, see Vieh 151
Feer, Feehr, see Fehr
Feerer, see Fuehrer 151
Feger, Fegert (cleaner, burnisher) 108

Fegler, Feglear, Feggeler, see
　Feger
Fegt ..., see Fecht...
Fehl, Fehle, Fehler (swamp
　dweller) 80
Fehlbaum (swamp tree) 80, 89
Fehn (swamp) 80, 122
Fehr, Feehr, Feer (ferryman)
　96
Fehrenbach, Fehrenbacher,
　Fehrbach (fr Fehrenbach
　122, swamp brook) 80, 77
Fehrenkamp, Fehrkamp (fir
　field) 89, 84
Fehrhof (ferryman's homestead)
　92
Fehrlinger (fr Fehrlingen) 122
Fehrmann (ferryman) 96
Fehsenfeld (spelt field) 84
Fei < St. Sophia 131, 60
Feichtner, see Fechner
Feidler, see Pheidler, Fiedler
Feierabend (quitting time) 122
Feierstein, see Feuerstein
Feiertag (holiday) 143
Feig, Feige, Feigel, Feigelman
　(doomed to die, cowardly)
　115
Feigel, Feigl (violet)
Feigenbaum (fig tree) 89
Feight, see Veit 151
Feigmann (coward) 115
Feil 122, Feiler, Feilner, Feihl,
　Feillmann (file, file maker)
　96
Feilenschmidt (file smith) 96
Feilinger (fr Feilingen)
Fein (fine, elegant) 115
Feinberg (fine mountain) 68
Feinblatt (fine leaf)
Feinblum (fine flower)
Feind, Feindt (enemy)
Feinman, Feinmann (elegant
　man)
Feinstein (fine mountain) 73
Feinster, see Finster, Fenster
Feintuch (fine cloth) 106
Feirtag, see Feiertag
Feiss (fat) 114

Feist, Feister (fat, fertile)
　114
Feistenau (fertile meadow)
　84, 122
Feit, Feitel, Feith, Feitz,
　Feiz (St. Vitus) 131
Felbach (swamp brook) 80,
　83, 77
Felbaum (willow tree) 89
Felbinger (fr Felbing) 122
Feld, Feldt, Felder, Felders,
　Felden (field) 84
Feldbach (field brook) 84, 77
Feldbaum (field tree) 84, 89
Feldbausch, see Feldbusch
Feldberger (fr Feldberg 122,
　field mountain) 84, 68
Feldbursch (field lad) 84
Feldbusch (field bush) 84, 72
Felder, Feldner (fieldman,
　farmer) 91
Felderstein, see Feldstein
Feldhaus 122, Feldhausen
　(fieldhouse) 84, 65
Feldheim 122, Feltheim
　(field hamlet) 84, 123
Feldhofer (fr Feldhof 122,
　field farm) 84, 92
Feldkamp (field field) 84, 84,
　122
Feldman, Feldmann (field
　man, farmer) 91
Feldmeier (field farmer) 84,
　93
Feldmesser (surveyor) 84
Feldmuller (field miller) 84,
　103
Feldner, see Felder
Feldpausch, see Feldbusch
Feldstein (field stone) 84, 73
Felgemacher (felly maker,
　cartwright) 96
Felger, Felgenhauer (felly
　maker, cartwright) 96
Felhauer, see Felger
Felinger (fr Feling) 112
Felix (Latin, joyful) 115
Felk, Felkel, Felker, Felkner
　< Volkmar 53

Fell, Felle, Fellman, Fellmann,
Feller, Fellers, Felleret,
Fellermann (worker in hides)
96, 106
Fellenbaum (Fell the tree!,
lumberjack) 116
Fellenstein (Hew the rock!,
quarryman) 116
Felman, see Fell
Felmar < Volkmar
Felner, see Fell
Fels (cliff, crag)
Felsberg (cliff mountain) 68,
122
Felsch (false) 115
Felsenheld (cliff hero)
Felser, Felsing (fr Felsen 122,
cliff)
Felt, Feltz, see Filtz
Feltberger, see Feldberger
Felten, Feltikn < St. Valentin
131
Felter, see Felder
Felthaus (field house) 84, 65
Feltheim, see Feldheim
Feltmacher (felt maker) 96
Feltman, see Feld
Feltmeyer (field farmer) 84, 93
Feltner, see Felder
Feltz, see Filtz
Feltzmann, see Feldman
Feltzner, see Felder
Fendrick, see Faehnrich
Fenhagen (marsh enclosure)
80, 123
Fenkel (spice dealer, fr Latin
foeniculum) 105
Fenker (millet dealer) 105
Fenkhoff (millet farm, fr Latin
panicum) 92
Fenn 122, Fennemann (bog
dweller) 80
Fenner (ensign) 107
Fennhof, Fennhoff (fen farm)
80, 84
Fennigwerth (pennyworth)
Fenster, Fensterer,
Fenstermacher,

Fenstermaker (window
maker) 96, 106
Fensterwald, see Finsterwald
Fentz, Fenzel, see Wentzel
Ferber, Ferbert, see Faerber
Ferch (fir tree) 89
Ferdinand, Fernantz (Gothic:
journey + risk)
Feredag, see Feiertag
Ferembach, Ferenbach,
Ferenback, see
Fehrenbach
Ferg, Ferge, Ferger, Ferges
(ferryman) 96
Ferhman, see Fehrmann 151
Ferhorst, see Fahrenhorst
Ferkel, Ferkler (shoat) 91
Ferman, see Fehrmann
Fernbach, see Fehrenbach
Ferne (glacier)
Fernhaber, see Firnhaber
Fernholtz, see Fahrenholtz
Ferrenbach, see Fehrenbach
Fersch, see Pfirsich
Ferschbach (swamp brook)
80, 77
Ferst, see Fuerst 151
Ferster, Ferstermann, see
Foerster 151
Fertig (ready to travel)
Fertner (see Pfoertner)
Fesche, Feschner
Fesenfeld (spelt field) 84,
122
Fesmeier (spelt farmer) 93
Fessel, Fesseler (fetter
maker) 96, 106
Fessel (barrel maker) 96
Fest (firm, fat) 144
Fester, Festerling <
Sylvester 131
Feter, Fetter, see Vetter
Fett, Fette (fat, fertile) 114
Fetter, Fetters, Fetterle, see
Vetter, Vetterli
Fetterhof (fertile farm) 92
Fettig, Fetting, see Fett
Fetting (wing)

Fetz, Fetzer (executioner,
quarreler 115)
Fetz < St. Boniface 131
Feucht, Feuchter (damp, moist)
122
Feucht (fir tree) 89, 122
Feuchtner (dweller by the firs)
89
Feuchtwange (swamp field) 80
Feuer (fire)
Feuerbach 122, Feurbach
(swamp brook) 80, 77
Feuerberg (swamp mountain)
68, 122
Feuereisen (fire iron, poker)
106
Feuerhacken (poker) 106
Feuerhardt, see Feuerherd
Feuerherd (fire hearth, smith)
106
Feuerleim (fire clay) 106
Feuerlein (little fire)
Feuermann (fireman, stoker)
Feuermann (flint dealer) 105
Feuerstein, Feuerstine 151
(flint dealer) 105
Feurer (stoker)
Feurmann (stoker)
Feust, Feustel, Feustle, see
Faust
Fey, Feye, see Fay
Feyerabend, see Feierabend
Feyerbaugh, see Feurbach 151
Feyl, see Feil
Ficht 122, Fichtel, Fichter,
Fichtner (dweller among the
fir trees) 89
Fichtmeyer, Fichtemayer
(farmer in the fir trees) 89,
93
Fick, Ficke, Ficks, Ficken,
Ficker, Fickert < Friedrich
53
Fickenscher (purse cutter)
Fickus (fig, fr Latin *ficus*) 89
Fickweiler (Friedrich's villa)
127
Fidel, Fidler, see Fiedel,
Fiedler

Fieber (fever)
Fiebig, Fiebiger, see Viebig
Fiedel, Fiedler, Fiedeler
(fiddler) 96, 106
Fliederer (fletcher) 108
Fiege, Fiegner (overseer)
Fiegenbaum, see Feigenbaum
151
Fiehmann, see Viehmann
151
Fieken, Fiekers, Fiekert <
Sophia 60
Fieldhouse, see Feldhaus 151
Fienberg, see Feinberg 151
Fierer, see Fuehrer 151
Fierschnaller (four buckles)
Fierstein, see Feuerstein 151
Fiess (violent person) 115
Fiessler (womanizer) 115, see
Fuessler
Fietzen < St. Vincent 131
Fifer, see Pfeifer 151
Figge (son of Sophia) 60
Fikus (fig, Latin *ficus*) 89
Filbert (full + bright) 46, cf.
Vollbrecht
Filibs, see Phillips
Filtz 122, Filtzer, Filzer
(hatter, felt maker, course
farmer, cf. "wool hat" and
filtzgebur)
Filtzmeier (farmer by a high
marsh) 80
Finck, see Fink
Finckel, see Finkel
Finckelstein, see Finkelstein
Finckenstedt (finch city) 122
Findeisen (bloodletter) 96
Finder, Fintler (finder in a
mine)
Findling (foundling)
Fine, see Fein 151
Fineberg, Fineblum,
Fineman, Finestone, see
Feinberg, Feinblum,
Feinman, Feinstein 151
Finger, Fingern (finger 114,
also ring maker 106)

Fingerhut, Fingerhuth,
Fingerhood 151 (thimble,
tailor, thimble maker) 106
Fingernagel (finger nail) 114
Finister, see Finster
Fink, Finke, Fincke, Finken,
Finks (finch, carefree person)
115
Finkbein, Finkbeiner, Finkbiner
(finch + fenced area)
Finkel (blacksmith 96), see also
Fuenkel
Finkelstein (sparkling
mountain) 68
Finkemeyer, see Finkmeyer
Finkenauer, Finknauer (finch
meadow) 84
Finkenbeiner, see Finkbein
Finkenstein (finch mountain)
68
Finkernagel, see Fingernagel
Finkmeyer (proprietor of the
Finkhof) 93, 94
Finkstedt (finch city) 122
Finkweiler (finch hamlet) 123,
122
Finsterbusch (dark bush) 72
Finsterwald (dark forest) 72
Finzel < Wentzel, Vincentius
131
Firebaugh, see Feuerbach 151
Fireman, see Feuermann 151
Firestone, Firestine, see
Feuerstein 151
Firkel, Firker, Firks, see
Ferkel
Firmwald, see Vormwald
Firne, see Ferne
Firnhaber (last year's oats)
Firor, see Fuehrer 151
First (mountain ridge 68), see
also Fuerst
Firstenberg, see Fuerstenberg
Firstnau (ridge meadow,
prince's meadow) 84
Fisch, see Fischer
Fischauer (fish meadow) 84

Fischbach, Fischbeck (fish
stream) 77, 122
Fischbein, Fischbein,
Fishbein (whale bone, not
fish leg!)
Fischborn (fish stream) 79,
122
Fischel, Fischell, Fischelt,
see Fischer
Fischer, Fisscher (fisherman,
fishmonger) 91, 105
Fischgrund (fish bottom)
Fischhaber, see Fischauer
Fischlein (little fish)
Fischler (swamp dweller) 80
Fischner, see Fischer
Fischmann, Fischner
(fishmonger) 91, 105
Fischmeyer (proprietor of the
Fischhof) 93, 94
Fishbach, Fishbeck (fish
brook) 77, 155
Fishbaugh, see Fischbach
151
Fishbein, see Fischbein
Fisher, see Fischer 151
Fisler, Fissler, see Fuessler
Fister, see Pfister 151
Fitschner < Friedrich 53
Fitten (place name) 122
Fitts, Fitz, Fitzell, Fitzer,
Fitzner (artistic weaver,
tailor) 106
Fitzenberg, Fitzenberger
(pond mountain) 81, 68
Fitzenreiter (pond clearing)
81, 126
Fitzlert, see Fitts 143
Fizner (dweller near a pond)
81, see Fitts
Flach, Flacher (flat, plain)
Flachmueller, Flachmeyer
(miller, farmer on the
Flach) 83
Flachs (flax, flaxen-haired)
112
Flachs (flax grower or
dealer) 105

Flachsbart (flaxen beard) 112
Flacht (woven fence)
Flack, see Flach
Flack (swamp) 80
Flacks, see Flachs
Flad, Fladd, Flade (flat cake, cake baker) 96
Flaechsner (flax dealer) 105
Flaesch, see Fleisch, Flaschner
Flagel, Flagler, see Flegel, Flegler 151
Flagge (flag, colors)
Flaks, see Flachs 151
Flamholtz (fire wood)
Flamholtz (swamp forest) 80, 72
Flamm (flame, blacksmith) 96
Flammenkamp (swamp field) 80, 84
Flammer (smith) 96
Flanders (a Belgian province, a mercenary who served there) 121
Flanz (crooked mouth) 114, see also Pflantz
Flaschenriem (flask strap) 106
Flaschner (bottlemaker) 96
Flashhauer, see Fleishhauer 151
Flashman, see Fleischmann 151
Flashner, see Flaschner 151
Flath, Flather, Flater, Flathman, Flathmann (swamp dweller) 80
Flaum, see Pflaum
Flautt (flute player)
Flax, see Flachs
Fleager, see Pflueger 151
Fleagle, see Fluegel 151
Flechner (basket weaver) 96
Flechsenhar (flaxen-haired) 112
Flechsner, see Flaechsner
Fleck, Flecke (speck, spot, stain, cobbler, tailor) 96
Fleckenstein (spotted mountain) 68

Fleckner (cobbler, tailor, proprietor of the Fleckhof) 94, 96
Fleddermann (cake baker) 96
Fleegle, see Fluegel 151
Fleetmann (dweller by running water)
Fleg, see Pfleger
Flegel, Flegler (flail user or maker, thresher) 106
Fleig (fly, lively person) 115
Fleisch, Fleischer, Fleischmann, Fleischner (butcher) 96
Fleischbein (flesh leg, meat bone, butcher) 96
Fleischer (butcher) 96
Fleischhacker (butcher) 96
Fleischhauer, Fleischouer (butcher) 96
Fleischman, Fleischmann (butcher) 96
Fleischner (butcher) 96
Fleisener, see Fleischner
Fleisher, Fleishmann, see Fleischer, Fleischman 151
Fleiss (industry, diligence) 115, see also Fleisch
Fleissner (fr Fleissen), see Fleischner
Flekstein, see Fleckstein
Fleming, Flemming, Flemmings (Fleming) 121
Flender (flighty person) 115
Flensberg (fr Flensberg) 68, 122
Flersheim, see Floersheim
Flesche, Flescher, Fleschmann, see Fleisch, Fleischer, Fleischmann
Fleschner, see Fleischner, Flaschner
Flesher, see Fleischer 151
Flettner (dweller near rushes) 81
Flettner, see Floetner
Flexer, Flexner, see Flaechsner

Flick, Flicker, Flickner (patch, short for *Flickschuster*, cobbler) 104, 106
Flickinger (fr Flicking)
Flieder (elder, lilac)
Fliedner (bloodletter)
Fliegel, see Fluegel 151
Flieger (restless person) 115, see Pflueger 151
Flinchbaugh (pebble brook) 77, 151
Flink, Flinke, Flinkman (quick, nimble) 115
Flintenfeld (flint field) 84
Floch, Flock (flake)
Floerscheim (fr Floersheim 122)
Floetner (flute player) 96
Flohr, Flor < St. Florian 131
Florey, Flory < St. Florian 131
Florian < St. Florian 131
Florscheim, see Floerscheim 155
Florschutz (field guard)
Flott, Flotz (river, pond) 79, 81
Flottmann (dweller on a river) 79
Flougar, see Pflueger 151
Fluegel (wing, jutting piece of land)
Fluegge, Fluegger, Flueggert (fledged, lively) 115
Fluers, Fluhrer, Fluhres (field guard)
Flug, Fluge (flight), see also Pflug
Flugel, see Fluegel
Flugfelder (plowfield) 84
Fluh (steep stone slope) 71
Fluhr, Flur (meadow) 84
Flumenbaum (plum tree) 89
Fluth (flood) 77
Focht, Fochtmann, see Vogt
Fock, Focke, Focken < Volkwart, Volker, etc. 53
Fockeroth < Volkerodt, folk + clearing) 126
Fockhausen < Volkhausen (folk + houses) 65

Foederer (furtherer)
Foehr, Foehrs (fir tree) 89
Foelix, see Felix
Foelke, Foelker, see Voelke, Voelker
Foerg (ferryman) 96
Foerst (pre-Germanic river name) 83, see Fuerst
Foerstel, Foerstler, see Foerster
Foerster, Foerstner, Foerstermann (forester) 96
Foerstermann (fr Foerster in the Harz 122), see also Foerster
Foertsch, see Pfirsich 89
Fogel, Fogal, Foegel, Fogaler, Fogler, see Vogel, Vogler 151
Fogelman, see Vogelmann
Foght, see Vogt 151
Fohl (foal, young horse) 91
Fohlk, see Volk
Fohn, Foehn (south wind)
Fohr (fir) 89
Fohr (ferryman) 96
Forbach, see Fahrbach
Fohrbach (fir brook) 89, 77
Fohring, Fohringer (fir) 89
Foht, see Vogt
Folck, Folk, Folke, Folker, Folkert, see Volk, Voelker
Folendorf, Folenweide, see Fuellendorf, Fuellenweide
Folger (follower)
Folk, Folke, see Volk
Foll, Follen (foal) 91
Follendorf (foal village) 123
Foller, Foeller < Volkhart (folk + strong) 46, 46
Follhart, see Foller
Folmer, Follmer, Fulmer, see Volkmar
Folter (torturer)
Folter (portcullis)
Foltin < St. Valentin 131
Foltmann (torturer)
Foltz, Folz < Volkmar

Fooks, see Fuchs 151
Forbach 122, see Fahrbach
Forch, Forchel (fir) 89
Forchenbach (fir brook) 89, 77
Forchenbach (trout stream) 77
Forchheimer, Forchhenner (fr
    Forchheim 122, fir hamlet
    123)
Forchner (dweller among the
    firs) 89
Forcht (fear) 115
Forchtenicht, see
    Fuerchtenichts
Fordemfeld (in front of the
    field) 70, 84
Fordenbach, Fordtenbacher, see
    Vorbach
Forderer, see Foerderer
Forellun (trout) 115
Foremann, see Formann
Forhel (trout) 115
Forhoff, Fornnoff, Fornhof, see
    Vorhoff
Fork, Forke, Forkel (pitchfork)
    106
Formann (drayman) 96
Formhals (before the pass) 70
Formwalt, see Vormwalt
Fornadel (fir needle) 89
Forner (dweller among the
    ferns) 89
Forsberg, see Forschberge
Forsch, Forschlern, Forschner,
    see Forst
Forschberge, Forshberge (forest
    mountain) 72, 68
Forschlager (forest lair) 72
Forscht, see Forst
Forsh, see Forsch 151
Forst 122, Forster, Forstmann,
    Forstner (forester, dweller in
    the forest) 72
Forster (see Foerster)
Forstreiter (forest clearing) 72,
    126
Forstreiter (forest rider) 72
Fortenbaugh (brook with ford)
    78, 77, 155

Forthuber (farmer at the
    ford) 78, 91
Fortkamp (field at the ford)
    78, 84
Fortman, Fortmann (dweller
    at the ford) 78
Fortmeier (farmer at the
    ford) 78, 93
Fortmueller, Fortmuller
    (miller at the ford) 78, 93
Fortner, see Pfortner
Fortwengler, see Furtwanger
Fosbrink (fox hill) 74
Fosbrok, Fosbrook (fox
    brake) 80
Fosler, Fossler, see Vossler
Fosnaught, see Fasnacht 151
Foss, Fosse, Fosz, see Voss
Foster, see Forster
Fourhman, see Fuhrmann
    151
Foust, see Faust 151
Fout, Fouts, Foutz, see Faut
    151
Fowl, Fowle, see Faul, Faule
    151
Fox, see Fuchs 151
Fraas, Fraasch, see Frass
Frack (full dress) 112
Fraenkel, Fraenkle < Frank
Fraenzel < Franz 131
Frage, Frager (food dealer)
    105
Fraalich, Fraley, Fraleigh,
    see Froehlich
Frambach, see Frombach
France, Frances, Francis, see
    Frantz 151
Franck, Francke, see Frank,
    Franke
Franckfurther, see
    Frankfurter
Franckhauser, Frankhuyse
    (the Franks' house) 121,
    65
Frank, Franke, Franken
    (Franconian. Franken may
    be short for Frankenberg,
    etc.)

Frankel, Frankle, Frankl <
Frank
Frankenbach (Franks' brook)
77
Frankenberg, Frankenberger
(Franconian mountain) 121,
68
Frankenfelder (fr Frankenfeld
122, the Franks' field) 121,
84
Frankenfield, see Frankenfeld
151
Frankenheim (the Franks'
hamlet) 121, 123
Frankenstein (Franconian
mountain) 121, 73
Frankenthal (Franconian
valley) 121, 76, 122
Frankfelder, see Frankenfelder
Frankford, see Frankfurter 151
Frankfurter, Franckenfurther
(fr Frankfurt) 122
Frankl, Frankle, see Fraenkel
Frankland (Franconia) 121
Frankouse, Frankhouser (the
Franks' houses) 121, 65, 155
Franks, see Franck 151, 164
Franz, Frantz, Frantzen,
Fransen (St. Francis) 131
Franzmann (Frenchman) 121
Fras, Frass (glutton) 115
Fratz (grimace, rascal, glutton)
115
Frauenberg (Mountain of Our
Lady) 139, 122
Frauendienst (service of the
ladies)
Frauendoerfer (fr Frauendorf
122, Our Lady's Village) 139
Frauenfelder (fr Frauenfeld
122, "Field of our Lady," or
"corvée field") 139
Frauenknecht (servant to Our
Lady's convent) 139
Frauenpreis (praise of ladies)
Frauenschu (maker of ladies'
shoes) 96, 104

Frauenstadt (City of Our
Lady) 139
Frauke, Fraucke (little lady)
Fraumann (worker at a
convent) 139
Fraunfelder, see
Frauenfelder
Fraundorf, see Frauendoerfer
Fraunhoffer (convent farm)
139, 84
Fraunholtz (probably
Fronholtz, corvée forest)
139
Frayberg, see Freiberg
Fraylick, Fraylich, see
Froehlich
Frease, see Fries 151
Freburger, see Freiburger
151
Frech (impudent, bold) 115
Freck, Frecker, Freckmann
(bold), also < Friedrich
Frede, Freder (fr Frede 122,
swamp) 80, also <
Friedrich
Fredekin (little Friedrich)
Fredenstein (peace stone) 73
Frederic, Frederik, Frederica,
see Friedrich
Fredericki, son of Frederick
142
Fredericksen (son of
Fredrick) 59
Fredhoff, see Friedhoff
Fredrica, see Frederic
Freeberger, Freeburger, see
Freiberger, Freiburger 151
Freebour (free peasant) 151
Freed ... see Fried ...
Freed, Freede, see Friede
151
Freedlander, Freedlender (fr
Friedland) 121, 151
Freedman, see Friedmann
Freehauf, see Fruehauf 151
Freehof, see Friedhof 151
Freehold, see Freiholt 151
Freeland, see Friedland 151

Freehling, see Fruehling 151
Freemann, see Freimann 151
Freemire (free farmer) 93, 151
Frees, Freese, Freeze, Freesen,
Freesemann (Frisian) 121
Freesmeyer (Frisian farmer)
121, 93
Frei, Freie, Frey (free)
Freiberg, Freiberger (fr
Freiberg 122, tax exempt
mountain) 68
Freiburger (fr Freiburg) 122
Freid ..., see Fried ...
Freidag, see Freitag
Freidel, see Friedel 151
Freidenberger, see
Freudenberger
Freidenstein, see Freudenstein
Freier (wooer)
Freihauf, see Fruehauf
Freihof (independent farm) 84,
122
Freiholt, Fryholtz (public
forest) 72
Freihuber, see Freihof
Freilich (freely) 117
Freimann, Freiling (freedman)
Freimueller (tax exempt miller)
103
Freimut, Freimuth, see
Freyermuth
Freind, Freint, see Freund
Freinstein, see Freudenstein
Freis, Freise, Freisen (Frisian),
see Fries 151
Freistat (free city) 122
Freistueler, Freisthuhler,
Freistuler (official of
Vehmgericht)
Freitag (Friday) 143
Fremd, Fremder (stranger)
Fremdling, Froembdling
(stranger)
Frendt, see Freund
Frenkamp (swamp field) 80,
84, see Fehrenkamp
Frenkel, see Fraenkel
Frens, Frenz, Frenzel < Franz
Frenssen (son of Franz) 59

Frentz, Frenzel < Franz
Frerich, Frerichs, see
Friedrich
Frese, Fresen, see Fries
Fress (glutton) 115
Fretz, see Fritz
Freud, Freuden (joy)
Freudenberg, Freudenberger
(fr Freudenberg 122, joy
mountain) 68
Freudenburg (joy castle) 73,
122
Freudenhammer (fr
Freudenheim 122) 123
Freudenreich, Freudenrich
(joyful) 115
Freudenstein (joy montain)
73, 122
Freudenthal (joy valley) 76,
122
Freudhafer (joy farm) 92
Freudig (joyful) 115
Freund, Freundt (friend)
Freunlich (friendly)
Frevel (theft)
Frey, Freye, Freyer (free)
Freyberger (fr Freyberg 122,
free mountain), see
Freiberger
Freyburger (fr Freyburg 122,
free castle), see Freiburger
Freydel, see Friedel
Freyer, see Freier
Freyermuth, Freymuth,
Freymuht (free spirit) 115
Freyhofer (free court) 84
Freyling (free man)
Freyman (free man)
Freymeyer (free farmer) 93
Freysinger (fr Freising) 122
Freytag, see Freitag
Freyvogel (free bird, outlaw)
Frez, see Fritz
Friand, see Freund
Fric, see Frick 151
Frichi, see Fritschi 151
Frick, Fricke, Frickel <
Friedrich) 53

Frickenhaus (house on the
Frick) 83, 65
Frickenstein (mountain near
the Frick) 83, 73
Fricker, Frickert (dweller on
the Frick) 83
Frickinger (fr Fricking 122,
belonging to Friedrich) 59,
123
Frickmann (dweller on the
Frick) 83
Frickmann (follower of
Friedrich) 94
Fridag, Friday 151, see Freitag
Fridel, see Friedel
Fridley, see Friedlich 151
Frideric, Friderick, Friderich,
Fridrich, see Friedrich
Friebach (public brook) 77, see
Friedbach
Friebe (fr Slavic *vrba*, willow
tree) 89
Frieberger, see Freiberger 151
Fried, Friede, Frieds (peace),
also < Friedrich
Friedbach (foamy brook) 77
Friedbald, Friebald (peace +
bold) 47, 46
Friedberger (fr Friedberg 122,
peace mountain) 47, 68
Friedburg (peace castle) 47, 73,
122
Friedel, Friedle (friend,
sweetheart)
Friedemann, see Friedmann
Friedenheim, see Friedhaim
Friedensthal (peace valley) 76
Friedenwald (peace forest) 47,
72
Friederic, see Friedrich
Friedgen < Friedrich) 53, 54
Friedhaber (peacemaker)
Friedhagen (walled enclosure)
47, 123
Friedhaim (fr Friedheim 122,
peace hamlet, walled hamlet)
47, 123

Friedhof, Friedhoffer
(cemetery) 47, 92
Friedke > Friedrich 53, 54
Friedland, Friedlaender (fr
Friedland) 121
Friedle, Friedly, Friedler, see
Friedel 151
Friedlein < Friedrich
Friedlich (peaceful) 115
Friedman, Friedmann (peace
man) 115, also < Friedrich
Friedrich, Friederich,
Friedrichs, Friederick,
Friedericks, (peace +
ruler) 47, 46
Friedrichsson (son of
Friedrich) 59
Frieling, see Fruehling 151
Friemann, see Freimann 151
Friend, Friendlich, see
Freund, Freunlich 151
Friermood, see Freyermuth
151
Fries, Friess, Friese, Frieser,
Friesche, Friesner
(Frisian, often a false
plural of Frey) 121
Frieschknecht (Friesian
servant)
Friesenhahn (fr
Friesenhagen 122, Frisian
hamlet 121)
Frietag, see Freitag
Friethrick, see Friedrich 151
Frietsch < Friedrich
Frik, Frike, see Frick, Fricke
Friley, see Freilich
Frind, see Freund 151
Fring, Fringe, Frings < St.
Severin 131
Frisch, Frische (fresh, lively
115), also < Friedrich
Frischkorn (fresh grain)
Frischman, Frischmann, see
Frisch
Frischmut (fresh courage)
115
Frischolz (wood cutter) 95

Frishcorn, see Frischkorn 151
Fritchi, Fritsch, Fritschi,
Fritsche, Fritscher, Fritschel,
Fritschler, Fritschner,
Fritzsch < Friedrich 53
Fritz, Fritts, Fritze, Fritzel,
Fritzges, Fritzsche, Fritzius
< Friderizius, Latin for
Friedrich
Fritzmann, Fritzner <
Friedrich
Fritzweiler (Friedrich's villa,
peace village) 123
Froberg, see Frohberg
Froeb, Froeber (willow, fr
Slavic: *vrba*) 89
Froebel (undaunted) 115
Froehlich, Froehlicher,
Froehlig, Froelig, Froeli,
Froehly (joyful) 115
Froehling, see Fruehling
Froehlke, see Froehlich
Froembdling, see Fremdling
Froeschle (little frog) 115
Froese, see Fries
Froh (merry) 115
Frohbart (merry beard) 112
Frohberg (merry mountain) 68
Frohboese (quick to anger) 115
Frohlich, Frolic, Frolick,
Frohligh, see Froehlich
Frohman, Frohmann (merry
man) 115
Frohn, Frohne, Frohner,
Frohnert (court messenger,
corvée payer) 139
Frohnder, see Frohn
Frohsinn (merry disposition)
115
Frohwein (merry friend) 115
Frolich, Frohligh, see Froehlich
From, Frome, see Fromm
Froman, see Frohmann
Fromberg 122, see Frommberg
Fromm, Fromme, Frommer
(useful, pious) 138
Frommberg (swamp mountain)
80, 68

Frommeyer (industrious
farmer) 138, 93
Frommholt (pious dear) 138,
48
Fronacker (lord's field,
corvée field) 139
Froneberger (corvée
mountain) 139, 68
Froner, see Frohn
Fronfelder, Fronfelter (corvée
field) 139, 84
Fronheuser, Fronhyser
(corvée houses) 137, 65
Frosch (frog, house name)
149
Froschauer (fr Froschau 122,
frog meadow) 84
Frost, Frostz (frost)
Frostdorf, Frostdorp (frost
village) 123
Frowenfelder, see
Frauenfelder
Frucht (crop, fruit)
Fruchtbaum (fruit tree) 89
Fruchtel, Fruchter,
Fruchtmann (fruit dealer)
105
Fruden, see Freuden
Frueh (early riser), see also
Frey
Fruehan (early cockcrow)
Fruehauf (early riser 115,
child sired before
marriage)
Fruehling (spring)
Fruehsang, Fruesang (early
song)
Fruehwein (early wine)
Fruendt, see Freund
Fruetag (morning, Friday)
143
Fruetrank (early drink)
Fruh, Fruhling, see Frueh,
Fruehling
Fruhwirth (early host)
Fruke, see Frauke
Frum, see Fromm
Fruman (worthy man) 138
Fry, Frye, see Frey

Fusel (bad liquor, taverner) 96
Fuselbach (bad liquor creek) 77
Fuss, Fuess (foot, leg, foot of
mountain, see also Fuchs)
Fusselbaugh, see Fuselbach
151
Futerer, Futter, Futterer,
Futerman (feeder, fodder
dealer) 105
Fux, Fuxe, see Fuchs
Fuxmann, see Fuchsmann

G

Gaas, Gaass, see Gas
Gabble, see Gabel 151
Gabe (gift)
Gabel 122, Gabell, Gabeler,
Gabelmann (fork, fork maker
106, dweller at a road fork)
Gabelsberg (fork mountain) 68
Gaberle < St. Gabriel 136
Gabhart, see Gebhard 151
Gable, Gabler, see Gabel 151
Gabriel, Gabriels (an
archangel) 136
Gach (quick, turbulent) 115
Gack (silly, foolish) 115
Gackenbach (swamp stream)
80, 77, 122
Gackenback (shepherd's hut) 77
Gade, Gaden (chamber, room),
also < Gottfried, Gottschalk,
etc.
Gade (miner) 96
Gadermann (dweller by the
village gate)
Gadjohann (handsome John)
Gaeb (pleasant, welcome) 115
Gaebel (skull) 114
Gaebler, see Gabel, Gabler
Gaedeke, Gaedtke, see Goedeke
Gaehring, see Goering
Gaensebein (fenced yard for
geese)
Gaenslein, Gaensle, Gennsli
(gosling) 91
Gaerber, see Gerber

Gaerstener, see Gerstner
Gaertel (little garden,
gardner) 84, 98
Gaertner, Gaertener
(gardner, fr Garden or
Garten) 84, 98
Gaes, Gaesser, see Gaessner
Gaestel (little stranger, little
guest)
Gaetge, see Goetz
Gaetz, see Goetz
Gafke (little gift)
Gager (fr Gagen 122)
Gahl (fr Gahlen 122)
Gahr, Gahre, Garht <
Garmann, speer man) 46,
94, 53
Gahraus, see Garaus
Gaier, see Geier
Gaiger, see Geiger
Gail, Gailing, see Geil
Gainer, see Gehner 151
Gaisel, Gaiselmann, see
Geisel, Geiselmann
Gaiser, see Geiser
Gaister, see Geister
Galander (lark) 115
Gall, Galle < St. Gallus 131
Galler (servant at St. Gall)
139
Gallinger (fr Galling) 122
Gallman, Gallmann (servant
of St. Gall) 139
Gallmeyer (bailiff at St.
Gall) 93, 139
Gallster (incantation,
warlock)
Gallus (St. Gall) 131
Galm (noise)
Galster, see Gallster
Gambach, Gandbach (swamp
brook) 80, 77
Gamber, Gambert, Gampert
(acrobat, entertainer) 96
Gambler, Gambolt, see
Gamber
Gamble, see Gamber 151
Gamp, see Kamp

Gamper, Gampffer, Gampert,
see Gamber
Gams, Gamse (chamois,
chamois hunter) 91
Gamstetter (fr Gamsstaedt,
chamois place) 122
Gand, Gandel (pebble field) 71,
84
Gandenberg (stony mountain)
71, 68
Gander, Gandermann (swamp
dweller) 80
Gang, Gangl (stream) 77
Gangel (huckster) 105
Gangenmeyer (farmer on a
stream) 93
Gangloff, Ganglof (gait + wolf,
cf. Wolfgang) 48
Gangmueller (miller on a
stream) 77, 103
Ganke, Gankel < Janke
(Johann) 134
Gann (magic)
Gans, Ganss (goose) 91, 115
Gansberg, Ganzberger (goose
mountain) 68, 122
Gansburg (goose castle) 73, 122
Gansel, Gaensel (little goose)
91, 115
Ganser, Gansler, Gansner,
Gansert (goose raiser) 91,
115
Ganten, Gantner (goose raiser)
91, 115
Ganter, Ganther (auctioneer,
also see Guenther)
Ganz, Gantz, Gantze, Gantzer,
Ganzert (whole, complete),
see Ganser
Ganzemueller, Gantzenmueller
(goose miller) 91, 103
Gapehard, Gapehart, see
Gebhard 151
Gar (spear) 46
Garaus (Bottoms up!) 117
Garbe, Garben, Garbes (sheaf)
Garber < Garbrecht, see also
Gaerber

Garbrecht (spear + brilliant)
46, 47
Gardenhour (fr Gartenau,
garden meadow) 84, 84,
151
Gardenhour (garden digger)
84, 151
Gardner, see Gaertner
Garecht, see Garrecht
Garfinkel, Garfinkle 151,
Garfuenkel (carbuncle, fr
Latin *carbunculus*)
Garheart, see Gerhard 151
Garke, Garken < Gerhard 53
Garlach, see Gerlach
Garling, see Gerling
Garmann (spear + man) 46,
94
Garmes, Garms < Garmann
53
Garmhausen (Garmann's
houses) 65, 122
Garn (snare, yarn) 106
Garner (snarer, fish netter)
96
Garrecht (Quite right!) 117
Garreis, see Garaus
Garrel, Garrels, Garrelt,
Garrelmann < Gerhold
(spear + loyal) 46, 48, 53
Garrel (place name, swamp)
80, 122
Garst, Garster, see Karst
Garstener, see Gerstner
Gart, see Geert, Garthe
Gartelmann (gardener) 84
Gartenhoff (garden yard) 84
Gartmann (gardener) 84
Gartner, see Gaertner
Garz, see Geert
Gasel, see Gesell 151
Gasner, see Gass
Gaspar, Gaspars, see Caspar
Gass 122, Gasser, Gassner,
Gasmann, Gassmann
(dweller on a street,
shortened form) 65

Gassenheimer (hamlet on a road) 65, 123

Gassinger (dweller on a road) 65

Gassler, see Gass

Gassmann, see Gass

Gassmeyer (farmer on the road) 65, 93

Gassner, see Gass

Gast, Gastmann (stranger, guest)

Gasteier, Gasteiger (dweller on a steep mountain path) 71

Gastmeyer (newly arrived farmer) 93

Gastorf (village on the high land) 123, 122

Gastreich, Gastrich (hospitable) 115

Gattermann (dweller by a rail fence)

Gattling (kinsman, comrade) 119, 151

Gatz, Gatzke (fr Gatzen 122), see Katz

Gaubatz (Slavic place name) 146

Gauch (cuckoo, fool) 115

Gauckler, Gaukler (juggler) 96

Gaudenberger (one who has seen the *Mons Gaudium*)

Gauer (countryman)

Gauf, see Kauf

Gaug, Gauger (gadabout) 115

Gaugh, see Gauch 151

Gaughund (stray dog)

Gaul, Gauler (horse, carter) 96

Gaum (gum) 114

Gaum (man)

Gaumer (overseer)

Gaus, Gause, Gauss, Gauslin, Gaussmann, see Gans

Gausebeck (goose creek) 77

Gausepohl (goose pond) 80

Gautz, see Kautz

Gawff, see Kauf 151

Gaver, see Geber

Gayer, see Geier

Gayger, see Geiger

Gayheart, see Gerhard 151

Gayring, see Goering 151

Gearheart, see Gerhard 151

Gebaur, Gebauer (peasant) 91

Gebbe, Gebberd < Gebhard 53

Gebeke < Gebhard 53

Gebel, Gebele, Gebelein < Gottfried 53

Gebel, see Giebel

Geber, Gebers, Gebert, Geeber (giver, or < Godebrecht or Gottfried) 53

Gebhard, Gephardt, Gebhart (gift + strong) 46

Gebhauer, see Gebauer

Geble, see Gebel 151

Gebrecht (gift + bright) 47

Gecht, Gechter (impetuous person) 115

Geck, Gecke, Geckel, Geckler, Geckeler (fop, dandy) 115

Gedance (fr Danzig) 122

Geddoecke < Gottfried

Gedion (OT Gideon) 135

Geebel, see Gebel

Geeber, see Geber

Geehreng, see Gehring

Geel Haar, Geelhaar (yellow haired) 112

Geer, Geers, see Gehr

Geerdes, Geerdert, see Geert

Geerke, Geerken (little Gerhard) 53

Geerling < Gerhard 53

Geert, Geerts, Geertsen, Geertke < Gerhard

Gees, Geesman, Geesmann, see Gieseke

Geesler, see Giessler

Geest (dweller on high dry ground)

Gefeller (dweller by a waterfall)

Geffert < Gebhard 53

Geffinger < Gebhard

Geffken, Gefken < Gebhard
Gegenwart (presence)
Geger, Gegner (opponent,
    dweller outside of village or
    across the street)
Gehauf (Go up!) 116
Gehaut (Go out!) 116
Gehl, Gehle, Gehler, Gehlert,
    Gehlmann (yellow haired)
    112
Gehlbach (swamp brook) 80, 77
Gehmann, Gehner (dweller on
    a slope) 71
Gehr, Gehres < Gerhard,
    Gerwin, Gerbert
Gehrhard, see Gerhard
Gehrich, Gehrig, Gerick <
    Gerhard, Gerbrecht, etc.
Gehring, Gehringer, see
    Goering, Goeringer 53
Gehrke, Gehrken, Gehrlein <
    Gerhard, Gerbrecht, etc.
Gehrman, Gehrmann,
    Geermann (spear + man) 46,
    94
Gehrt, see Geert
Gehse (speer) 46
Geib, Geibe (filth)
Geidel (braggart, spendthrift)
    115
Geidt (greed, desire) 115
Geier, Gaier (gerfalcon, vulture,
    see Allgeier)
Geiersbach (vulture brook) 77
Geiershofer (vulture farm) 92
Geifuss, see Geilfuss
Geigel, Geiglein (little fiddle,
    little fiddler) 96
Geigenbach (fiddle brook) 96,
    77
Geigenberger (fr Geigelberg
    122, fiddle mountain) 96, 68
Geigenmeyer (proprietor of the
    Geigenhof, or farmer on the
    Geigenbach) 96, 73, 77, 94
Geigenmueller (miller on the
    Geigenbach) 96, 103, 83

Geiger, Geigert, Geigermann
    (fiddler) 96
Geigerheim (fiddlers' hamlet)
    96, 123
Geigermann (fiddler) 96
Geigmueller, see
    Geigenmueller
Geil, Geils, Geiler, Geilert
    (lively, wanton) 115
Geilenkirchen (swamp
    church) 80, 122
Geilfuss, Geilfuess (lively
    foot, lively person) 115
Geilhaar (yellow haired) 112
Geimer (spear-point +
    famous) 46, 47
Geis, Geise, Geiss (goat,
    goatherd) 91
Geisbert (noble scion +
    brilliant) 47, 47
Geisdoerfer (fr Geisdorf 122,
    goat village) 123
Geisel, Geisler, Geissler,
    Geisselmann (hostage)
Geisel, Geisler (whip,
    flagellant)
Geisemeyer (goat farmer) 91,
    93
Geisenheimer (fr Geisenheim
    122, goat hamlet) 123
Geisenrotter (goat clearing)
    126
Geisenstein (goat mountain)
    73
Geisfel (goat skin) 106
Geishirt, Geissert (goat
    herder) 91, 95
Geising, Geisinger (fr
    Geising 122)
Geisler (spear + army) 46,
    46
Geisler (goat raiser) 91
Geismann (goat man) 91
Geismar (swamp pond) 80,
    122
Geisreiter (goat clearing) 126
Geisreiter (goat rider,
    nickname for tailor)

Geiss, see Geis
Geissel, Geissler (hostage)
Geissendorfer (goat village) 123
Geissheimer (fr Geissheim 122,
goat hamlet) 123
Geissinger (fr Geissing 122)
Geissler (flagellant) 122
Geist (spirit) 122, see Geest
Geist (dregs, sediment)
Geister (spirits)
Geisthardt (spirit + strong)
Geistlich (spiritual, clerical)
Geisweiler (goat hamlet) 127
Geit, Geite, Geithe (greed) 115
Geitdorfer (fr Geitdorf 122,
goose village) 123
Geitz, Geiz, Geitzer (greed) 115
Geitzmann (greedy man) 115
Gelb, Gelber (yellow, blond)
112
Gelbach (swamp brook) 80, 77,
122
Gelbart (yellow beard) 112
Gelbert, Gelberdt, see Gilbert
Gelbke (little blond) 112
Geldemeister (guild master)
Gelder, Geldern, Geldermann,
Gelderlaender (fr Geldern in
the Netherlands) 121
Gelder (fr Gelden 122)
Geldern (province in the
Netherlands) 121
Geldhaeuser (money exchanger)
65, 96
Geldmacher (goldmaker,
alchemist, minter) 96
Geldmann (money man) 96
Geldreich, Geldrich (money
rich)
Gelerter (scholar, savant)
Gelfert < Gelfrat (merry +
counsel) 47
Gelhaus (yellow house) 65, see
Gellhaus
Gelinek, see Jellinek
Gelke < Gelmar (wanton,
cocky) 115
Geller (sacrifice + army) 46
Geller (town crier) 96

Geller, Gellert, Gellermann
(yellow haired) 112
Gellermann, see Geldermann
Gellhaus, Gellhausen (guild
house) 65
Gellinger (fr Gelling) 122
Gellmann, Gelman, see
Geldmann
Gellner, Gelner (goldsmith)
96
Gelpke (marsh brook) 80
Gelriche, see Geldreich
Geltner (goldsmith) 96
Gemeinbauer (farmer on the
common) 91
Gemeiner (private soldier)
107
Gemp, Gemper, see Gamper
Gems (chamois)
Genau (exact) 115, 117
Gender (auctioneer)
Gengel, Gengler (huckster)
105
Gens (goose) 91, 115
Gensel, see Gaensel
Gensheimer, Genshemer
(goose hamlet) 123
Gensler (goose raiser) 91
Gensli, Genslin, see Gaensel
Gentsch, Gentzsch, Gentz <
Johannes 131, 134
Genz, Genzler < Johannes
131, 134
Georg, George, Georges (St.
George) 131
Georgi, son of Georg 142
Gephard, Gephardt, see
Gebhard, Gebhardt
Geppel < Gephard
Geppert < Gebhard
Gerach, Gerack < Georgius
131
Geradwohl, see Gerathewohl
Gerald (spear + rule, or
spear + loyal) 46, 47
Gerard, see Gerhard
Gerathewol, Gerathewold
(Turn out well!, guild
name) 116

Gerbel < Gerbald (spear +
   bold) 46, 46
Gerben < Garwin, Gerwin
Gerber, Gerbert, Gerbler
   (tanner) 96
Gerbert, Gerbracht (spear +
   brilliant) 46, 47
Gerbrand (spear + sword) 46,
   46
Gercke, Gereke < Gerhard 53
Gerde, Gerdes, Gerts, Gerdts,
   Gerding < Gerhard
Gerecht, Gerichten, Gerichter
   (righteous, just, skillful) 115
Gerhard, Gerhards, Gerhardt,
   Gerhart (spear + strong) 46,
   46
Gerhing, see Gehring
Gerhold, Gerholz (spear +
   loyal) 46, 48, 52
Gerig, Gerich, Gerick, Gericke
   < Gerhard 53
Gering, Geringer < Gerhard or
   Gerold 53
Gerisch < Georg, Gerhard
Gerke, Gerken, Gerkens <
   Gerhard, Gerbod, etc. 53
Gerker, Gerkle < Gerhard 53
Gerlach (spear + play) 46
Gerland (spear + brave) 46, 49
Gerlicher, see Gerlach
Gerling, Gerlinger < Gerhard,
   Gerhold, etc. 53
Geerling, Gerlinger (fr Gerling
   122)
Germann, German (spear +
   man) 46, 94
Germanus (Latin, cousin)
Germar, Germer (spear +
   famous) 46, 47
Germershausen (swamp houses)
   80, 65
Germersroth, Germerroth
   (swamp clearing) 80, 126
Germeyer, Germyer (swamp
   farmer) 80, 93
Germuth (spear + disposition)
   46, 46

Gern, Gerne, Gerner,
   Gerners, Gerns, Gerndt,
   Gernt, Gernerdt (desirous)
   115
Gernand (spear + risk) 46,
   56
Gerngross (ambitious,
   aggressive) 115
Gernhard, Gernhardt,
   Gernhart < Gerner
   (desirous)
Gernot (spear + battle) 46
Gerold, Gerould, see Gerhold
Gerolstein (Gerold's
   mountain) 73, 122
Gerrard, see Gerhard
Gerrecht, see Gerecht,
   Garrecht
Gerring, Gerringer, see
   Gehring
Gerrsmann (Gerhard's
   follower) 94
Gersbach (Gerhard's brook)
   77, 122
Gersch, Gerschmann (barley
   farmer)
Gerschheimer (barley
   hamlet) 123
Gerschwiller (barley village)
   127
Gersdorf (barley village) 123
Gersh, Gershman, see
   Gersch 151
Gerst, Gersten (barley)
Gerstacker, Gerstaecker
   (barley field) 84
Gerstel, Gerstle, Gerstler,
   Gerstner (barley dealer)
   105
Gerstemeyer, Gerstenmeier,
   Gerstemeir, Gerstenmeyer
   (barley farmer) 93
Gerstenberg, Gerstenberger
   (fr Gerstenberg 122,
   barley mountain) 68
Gerstenblith (barley blossom)
Gerstendoerfer (barley
   village) 123

Gerstenfeld (barley field) 84
Gerstenhaber (barley farmer) 92
Gerstenschlaeger (barley thresher) 95
Gerstmann (barley dealer) 105
Gerstmeyer, see Gerstemeyer
Gerstner (barley dealer) 105
Gerteisen (goad) 106
Gertelmann, see Gartelmann
Gerth, Gerthe, Gertz < Gerhard 53
Gerthner, Gertner, see Gaertner
Gertz, Gertzmann < Gerhard 53
Gerung < Gerold 53
Gervinus (Latin for Gerwin) 141
Gerver, see Gaerber
Gerwig (spear + battle) 46, 46
Gerwin (spear + friend) 46, 48
Geschickter (envoy) 109
Geschke (clever, cunning) 115
Geschwind, Geschwinds, Geshwend (swift) 115
Gesell, Gesele, Gesell, Geseller (companion)
Gesinder (following)
Gesser, Gessler, Gessner, Gessel, see Gasner
Gestl, see Gast
Getrost (confident, optimistic) 115
Gettel, Gettle, Gettleman (kinsman, peasant youth)
Gettenberg (swamp mountain) 80, 68
Gettenmueller (miller near the swamp) 80, 103
Getter, Getner, Gettermann (caster, founder) 96
Gettman, Gettmann (caster, founder) 96
Getts, Getz, Getze, see Goetz
Getzandanner, see Giessendanner
Getzenberg (foundry mountain) 68

Geuter, Geutert, see Geit
Gevantmann (mercer) 96
Gewinner (winner)
Gewirtz (spice dealer) 105
Gex, see Geck
Geyer, see Geier
Geyger, see Geiger
Geyler, see Geiler
Geyser, see Kaiser
Gezelle, see Gesell 151
Gfeller, Gefeller (waterfall, steep valley)
Gibe, Giebe < Gilbert
Gibler, see Kuebler, Giebler
Gibrich < Giperich (gift + rule) 47
Gichtel (gout) 114
Gichtel (confession)
Giebel, Giebler, Giebeler (skull, head, gable)
Giebelhaus (gabled house) 65
Giefer, see Kieffer
Gielbert, see Gilbert
Gier, Gierer (desire), see also Geier
Gierhard, see Gerhard
Giering, see Gehring
Gierke < Gerhard 53
Gierlach, see Gerlach
Giers, Giersch, see Gerisch, Kirsch
Giesbert, see Giesebrecht
Giese, Gieseke, Giesecke, Gieske, Gieseking < Giesebrecht 53
Giesebrecht (scion, or hostage + brilliant) 47
Giesel, Giessel, Giesler, Gieseler < Gieselher (scion or hostage + army) 46, 53
Gieselbrecht (point of sword + bright) 46, 47
Giessbach (swamp stream) 80, 77
Giesselbrecht, see Gieselbrecht
Giesselmann, see Geisel
Giessendanner (swamp forest) 80, 72

Giesser (founder) 95
Giesshof (swamp farm) 80, 92
Giessler (dweller near a
swamp) 80
Giffert, see Gebhard
Giger, see Geiger 151
Gilbart (scion + battle ax) 46
Gilbert (scion + bright) 47
Gildemeister (guildmaster)
Gildhaus, Gildehaus
(guildhouse) 65
Gildner (guild member)
Gilfert, see Gelfert
Gilgen (St. Aegidius) 131
Gilgen (lilly)
Gille, Giller < Gilbert 53
Gilljohann (Gilbert-Johann)
Gillmann < Aegidius 131
Gilner, see Gildner, Geldner
Gilsdorf (Gilbert's village) 123
Gilsemann (dweller near the
Gilse) 83
Gilstein (swamp mountain) 80,
73
Giltner, see Gildner, Gelder
Gimpel, Gimbel (bullfinch) 115,
149, see also Gumprecht
Ginder, see Guenther
Ginrich, Gingrich, Gingerich
(Slavic for Heinrich) 146
Ginsberg (Guenther's
mountain) 68
Ginsburg (Guenther's castle) 73
Ginter, see Guenther
Ginthard (battle + strong) 46,
46
Gintling (belonging to
Guenther) 59
Girard, see Gerhard
Girbach (vulture brook) 77
Girdner, see Gaertner
Girke < Gerlach 53
Girsch, see Kirsch
Gissel, Gissler < Gieselbrecht
Gisselbrecht, see Gieselbrecht
Gisseldanner, Gissendanner,
Gissentanner, see
Giessendanner

Gisselman, see Geisel
Gissendanner, Gissentanner,
see Giessendanner
Gissner, see Giessler
Gisselbrecht (hostage +
bright) 47
Gist (dregs, sediment), see
also Geist
Gitting, Gittings, Gittinger
(fr Gitting 122)
Glaas, see Glas
Glaatz, see Glatz
Gladbach (swampy brook)
80, 77, 122
Glade, Gladen (shining)
Glade (swamp) 80
Gladfelder, see Glatfelder
Glaenzer (shining)
Glaeser, Glaesener,
Glaesmann, Glasman, see
Glas
Glahn (dweller on the Glan)
83
Glaiber, see Kleber
Glance, see Glantz 151
Glantz, Glanz (brilliance)
Glarner (fr Glarus in
Switzerland) 121
Glas, Glaser, Glaeser
(glazier) 96, 106
Glaskopf (glass cup, maker
of glass cups) 96, 106
Glass, Glasser, Glassler,
Glassner (glazier) 96, 106
Glassbrenner, Glassmann
(glass maker) 96
Glassmeyer, Glasmeier,
Glasmyer (manager of the
glass factory) 96
Glatfelder, Glattfelter (level
field) 84
Glatfelder (swampy field) 80,
84
Glatt (smooth)
Glatthaar (smooth hair) 112
Glatz, Glatzer (bald man)
112
Glaub (faith)

Glauber (believer, creditor)
Glaubitz (Slavic place name) 146
Glauch, Glaucher (fr Glaucha 122)
Glauer (clever) 115
Glauner (cross-eyed) 113
Glaus, Glauser, see Klaus, Klauser
Glaz, Glazer, see Glatz, Glatzer
Gleim (swamp) 80
Gleisbach (shiny brook) 77
Gleissner (hypocrite) 115
Gleit, Gleitsman, Gleitsmann, Gleitzmann (mounted guard)
Glendemann, Glindemann (fr Glinde 122, swamp) 80
Gleser, see Glaser
Glessner (glazier) 96
Glick, see Glueck
Glickman, Glicksman, Glicksmann (lucky man)
Glickstern, see Glueckstern
Glimph (sport, fun)
Glind (fenced area)
Glindeman (swamp dweller), see Glendemann
Glitman, see Gleit
Glitsch (spear) 46
Glock, Glocke, Glocker, Glockner (bell ringer)
Glockengeter (bell caster) 96
Glockmann (bell ringer) 96
Gloecker, Gloeckner, Gloekler, see Glock
Glor < St. Hilarius 131
Gloster, see Kloster
Glotz, Gloetzel, see Klotz
Gluckstern (lucky star)
Glueck, Gluck (luck, fortune)
Glueckauf (miner's greeting) 116
Glueckselig (blissful) 115
Glug, see Klug 115
Glut, Gluth (fire)
Gmeiner (commoner, community leader, private soldier) 107

Gmeinwieser (common pasture) 84
Gnade (mercy, grace)
Gnaedig (gracious) 115
Gnann, Knann (cousin, namesake) 119
Gnau, see Genau
Gob < Jacob 135
Gobel, Gobbel, see Goebel
Gobrecht < Godebrecht (god + bright) 47
Gochenauer, Gochenour, Gochnauer (fools' meadow) 84
Gockeler, see Gauchler
God, Godt, see Gott 43
Gode (good) 115, 43
Godebrecht (god + bright) 47
Godfried, Godfrey 151, see Gottfried
Godlove, see Gottlieb 151
Godman, see Gutmann
Godschalk, Godschalks, see Gottschalk
Godt, see Gott
Goebel, Goebbel, Goebels, Goebeler, Goebling < Godebrecht 53
Goecke, Goeckeler < Gottfried 53
Goedeke, Goedike < Gottfried 53
Goegel, Goegell (juggler, jokester) 96
Goehke < Gerhard 53
Goehl, Goehler, Goehlert (swamp dweller) 80
Goehmann (dweller on the Goe) 83
Goehre (swamp dweller) 80, see also Goehring
Goehring, Goehringer < Gerhard 53
Goeldener, Goeller, Goellner, Goellman (gold miner) 96
Goeller, Goellner, see Gellner
Goellnitz (place name 122)
Goeltner, see Goldener

Goeltz (animal castrator)
Goenner, Goeners (patron)
Goepel, Goepell, see Goebel
Goepfert < see Gebhard
Goeppner (jacket maker) 96
Goeppinger (fr Goeppingen 122)
Goerg, Goergen, Goerges, see
　Georg
Goering < Gerhard 53
Goerner, see Gerner
Goerres < St. Gregorius 131
Goertler, see Guertler
Goertz < Gerhard 53
Goertzhain (Gerhard's grove)
Goessling (gosling 91, 115, fr
　Goesslingen 122)
Goetche (barrel maker) 96
Goetel, Goethals, see Goettel
Goethe < Godfather
Goetsch, Goetsche < Gottfried
　53
Goetschalk, see Gottschalk
Goette (baptized child)
Goettel, Goettig, Goetting,
　Goettling < Gottfried,
　Gotthard 53
Goetz, Goetze < Gottfried, etc.)
　53
Goetzel, Goetzelman,
　Goetzelmann < Gottfried 53
Goetzendorf (Gottfried's village)
　123, 122
Goetzinger (fr Goetzing 122)
Goetzke < Gottfried 53
Gogel (relaxed, merry) 115
Gohde < Gottfried 53
Gohl (Slavic for bald), see also
　Kohl
Gohr, Gohrmann (fr Gohr 122),
　see Gormann
Gohring, see Goering
Gohs, Gohse, see Gos
Gold, Golde, Golden (gold)
Goldacker (gold field) 84
Goldbach, Goldbeck (fr
　Goldbach 122, gold brook) 77
Goldband (gold band) 106
Goldbaum (gold tree) 89

Goldberg 122, Goldenberg,
　Goldberger, Goldeberger
　(gold mountain) 148
Goldblatt (gold leaf,
　goldsmith) 96
Goldblum, Goldbloom (gold
　flower)
Goldcamp (gold field) 84
Goldeisen (gold iron)
Goldenbaum, see Goldbaum
Goldenblum, see Goldblum
Goldencrown (golden crown)
　151
Golder, Golderman
　(goldsmith) 96
Goldfarb (gold color)
Goldfeder, Goldfedder (gold
　feather)
Goldfine (gold fine) 151
Goldfinger (gold finger, ring
　maker) 96
Goldfuss (gold foot)
Goldhaber (gold possessor)
Goldhammer (gold hammer,
　house name 149, or yellow
　hammer 115)
Goldhirsch (gold stag,
　housename) 149
Goldhofer (proprietor of the
　Goldhof, gold farm) 92
Goldhorn (gold horn, house
　name) 149
Goldman, Goldmann (gold
　man, goldsmith) 96
Goldmeyer, Goldmeier
　(proprietor of the Goldhof)
　93, 94
Goldner (gold worker) 96
Goldreich, Goldrich (rich in
　gold)
Goldschmidt, Goldschmitt
　(goldsmith) 96
Goldstad (gold city)
Goldstein (gold stone, topas)
　73, 122
Goldstern (gold star, house
　name) 149
Goldstick (gold piece) 151

Goldstrom (gold stream)
Goldvogel (gold bird)
Goldwasser, Goldwater 151
(Danzig cognac) 106
Goldwein, Goldwyn (gold
friend) 48
Goll (bullfinch, fool) 115
Goller (collar) 106
Gollnitz (fr Golnitza 122, Slavic
place name)
Gollner, see Goeller
Gollstadt, see Goldstad
Golltermann (quilt maker) 96,
or fr Goltern 122
Goltze, Golz (fr Goltzen 122,
Slavic place name)
Gommel < Gumbert
Gompf, see Kampf, also Gump
Gonder, Gonderman, see
Guenther, Guenthermann
Gondorf (pre-Germanic place
name) 122
Gonter, Gontert, see Gunther
Good ..., see Gut...
Goodbrood (good bread, baker)
96
Goodhard, see Gotthard 151
Goodknecht, see Gutknecht
Goodman, see Gutmann 151
Goodnight, see Gutnacht 152
Goos (goose) 91
Goring, see Goering
Gorman, Gormann (dweller
near a bog) 80
Gorr < Gregorius 131
Gosdorfer (fr Gosdorf, goose
village) 123, 122, village on
the Gose 83
Gose (name of river) 83
Gosmann, see Goss
Gosner (goose raiser or dealer)
91
Goss, Gossmann (Goth)
Gosse, Gossen, Gosser
(drainage ditch) 81
Gossler, Gosseler (fr Goslar,
dirty water) 122
Got ..., see Gott
Gotcher, see Goettcher

Gothe, Gothen (place name)
122
Gotlib, see Gottlieb
Gotschall, see Gotschalk
Gott, Gotte (God, usually fr
Gottfried, etc., or actor in
miracle play) 111
Gottbehuet (God forbid!) 117
Gottberg (swamp mountain)
68, 80, 122
Gottdiener (God's servant)
140
Gotter < Gottfried
Gottesfeld (God's field, glebe
land) 84
Gottfried (God + peace) 140
Gotthard (god + strong) 46
Gotthelf, Godhelf (God +
help) 140
Gotthold (God dear, god +
rule) 140
Gottleben (life in God) 140
Gottleben (swamp village)
80, 127
Gottlieb, Gottliebs, Gottleib
(God + love) 140
Gottmann (man of God) 140
Gottschalck, Gottschalk,
Gottschall, Gottsalk (God
+ servant) 140
Gottsegen, Gottsagen 151
(divine blessing) 140
Gottskind (child of God) 140
Gottsmann, Gottesmann
(God's man, vassal or
employee of a monastery)
140, 139
Gottwald, Gottwalt, Gotwalt,
Gottwalts, Gottwals (God
+ rule) 140
Gotz, Gotze, Gotzen <
Gottfried 53
Gouchenauer, Gouchenour,
Gouchnour (fools' meadow)
84, 151
Goucher (dweller on a
meadow)
Gouldman, see Goldmann
151

Graaf, see Graf
Grab, Grabe, Grabs, Graben (grave, grave digger) 96
Grabau (grave meadow) 84, 122
Grabbe, Grabbe (grabber, seizer), see Grab
Grabel (rivulet) 79
Grabeman (grave digger) 96
Grabenheimer (ditch hamlet) 123
Grabenkamp (grave yard) 84
Grable, see Grabel 151
Grabenstein (gravestone) 73
Grabner (dweller near a ditch)
Graebe, Graeber, Graebner, Graebener (grave digger) 96
Graef, Graefe, Graeff, Graeffe, see Graf
Graefinstern (the count's star) 151
Graeul, Grauel (atrocity)
Graf, Graff, Graffe, Graef, Grave, Groff (count) 109
Graffenperger (fr Grafenberg, count's mountain) 68, 122
Graffenried (swamp marsh) 80, 81, 122
Graffenstein (count's mountain) 73
Graffmann (count's man) 109
Graft, see Kraft
Grahl, Grahls (chalice) 106
Graim, see Greim
Grall, see Grahl
Gram, Gramm, Gramer, Grammer, see Kraemer
Gramberg (fr Grambergen, muddy-water mountain) 68, 122
Gramm (angry), see Gram
Gramueller (grey miller) 103
Grandadam (big Adam)
Grandt (trough) 122, see Grant
Graniwette, Granwetter (juniper tree) 89
Grannemann (dweller near the junipers) 89

Grant (gravel, pebbles)
Grantmeyer (proprietor of the Granthoff, pebble farm) 93
Grantner (dweller on gravel)
Grantzau (gravel meadow) 84
Granz, see Grant, Krantz
Grap, see Grab
Gras, see Grass
Grasberger (grass mountain) 68
Graser (official mower) 95
Grashof (grass farm) 92
Grasmeher (grass mower) 95
Grasmick, Grasmueck (hedge sparrow) 115
Grass, Grasse, Grasser, Grassmann (grass, meadow guard) 95
Grassau (grass meadow, meadow guard) 84, 122
Grassman, see Grass 151
Grassmick, see Grasmick
Grat (ridge) 68
Gratz, Gratze (fr Graetz, Slavic for castle) 122
Gratz < Pacratius 131
Grau, Graue, Grauer, Graumann (graybeard) 112
Grauel, Graull, see Graeul
Graulich, Grauling (dreadful) 115
Graumann, see Grau
Graus (grey, see also Kraus)
Grausam (cruel) 115
Grave, Graves, see Graf
Graybill, see Kraehbuehl
Grayligh, see Greulich 151
Grayning, see Groening 151
Greb, Grebe, Greber, Grebner (official of a free community) 109
Grebill, see Kraehbuehl 151
Greef, see Graf
Green ..., see Gruen ...

Greenawalt, Greenwalt, see
Guenwald 151
Greenbaum, Greenebaum, see
Gruenbaum 151
Greenbeck, see Gruenbeck 151
Greenberg, see Gruenberg 151
Greenblat, Greenblatt, see
Gruenblatt 151
Greening, see Gruening 151
Greenspan, Greenspon, see
Gruenspan 151
Greenwald, see Gruenewald
151
Greesman, see Kressman 151
Grefe, see Graf
Grefenkamp (swamp field) 80,
84
Greger, Gregorius (St. Gregory)
131
Greif, Greiff (griffin) 149
Greifenhagen (griffin hedge)
123, 122
Greifenstein, Greyfenstein (fr
Greifenstein 122, griffin
castle) 73
Greim (helmet, mask) 46, 112
Greiner (quarreler, complainer)
115
Greip, see Greif
Greis, Greisel, Greiser
(graybeard) 112
Grell, Grelle (shrill, angry) 115
Grempel, Grempler (retailer)
105
Grendelmeyer (farmer at the
swamp) 80, 93
Grentzel, Grentzer (dweller on
a frontier)
Gresemeyer, see Gress
Greser, Gresser, see
Grassmann
Gress, Gressler, Gressmeyer,
see Grassmann 95
Gressmann, see Grassmann,
Kressmann
Grett, Gretter (son of
Margaretha) 60
Greul (atrocity)
Greulich (frightful) 115

Greuther (dweller in a
clearing) 126
Greutz, Greutzer, see
Kreutz, Kreutzer
Greve, Greven (swamp) 80,
see Graf
Grevenkampen (swamp
fields) 80, see Grafenkamp
Grewe, see Graf
Greybill, see Kraehbuehl 151
Greyder, see Kreider 151
Grider, see Kreider,
Kraeuter 151
Grieb (greaves)
Griebel, Griebner (dweller in
a hollow), see Gruber
Griefe, see Greif
Grieger, see Krieger, also <
Gregorius
Griem, Grieme (fr Griemen
122, mask, helmet)
Griep, see Greif
Gries (gravel)
Griesammer, Griesamer,
Griesemer, Grieshammer
(fr Griesheim 122, gravel
hamlet) 123
Griesbach (gravel brook) 77,
122
Griesbaum (gravel tree) 89
Griesbeck (gravel brook) 77
Griese (graybeard) 112
Grieshaber (rough-ground
oats)
Griesheim (gravel hamlet)
123, 122
Grieshoff (gravel farm) 92,
122
Griesing, Griesinger (fr
Griesingen 122)
Griesmeyer (proprietor of the
Grieshof, gravel farm) 93
Griess, Griesse, Griessler,
Griessmer (dweller on
sandy soil)
Griessmann, see Griesmeyer
Grievogel (griffin) 149
Griffe (marsh ditch) 122

Gril, Grill (cricket, whimsical
person) 115
Grillenberg 122, Grillenberger
(cricket mountain) 68
Grim, Grimm, Grimme (grim)
115
Grimbacher 122, see
Grumbacher
Grime, see Greim, Grimm 151
Grimm (grim, unfriendly) 115
Grimmiger (fierce) 115
Grindel 122, Grindler,
Grindlinger (swamp) 80
Grindelwald (forest in
Switzerland) 72
Grindle, see Grindel 151
Griner, see Greiner 151
Grinspun, see Gruenspan
Gripp, see Griepp
Grist, see Christ 151
Gritzner (grist maker) 96
Grob, Grobb, Grobe (crude) 115
Grobleben (swamp-water
settlement) 80, 122
Groegger < Gregorius
Groen, Groene, Groener,
Groenest (green)
Groenewald, see Gruenewald
Groenig, Groening (fr
Groeningen 122)
Groening (yellow hammer) 115
Groenwood, see Gruenewald
151
Groeschel (small silver coin)
Groessinger (fr Grossingen 122)
Groethausen, see Grosshaus
Groff, Groffe (crude, rough)
155, see also Graf
Groh (gray) 112
Grohmann (graybeard) 122
Groll (grassy marsh) 80
Groll, Grolle (grudge)
Groller (sulker) 115
Gromann (graybeard) 112
Grombein, see Krummbein
Gronau (green meadow) 84,
122
Grondt, see Grund

Gronemeyer (proprietor of
the Gronhoff) 94
Gronewold (green wood) 72
Gronhoff (green farm) 92,
122
Gronholz (green wood) 72
Groninger (yellow hammer)
115
Groon (swamp) 84, see
Gruen
Groote, see Gross
Grosch, Groschel (penny) 117
Grosh, see Grosch 151
Grosnickle, see Grossnickel
Gross, Grosse, Gros, Grosz,
Groos (large) 113
Grossenaker (large field) 84
Grossgebauer (big farmer) 91
Grosshart, Grosshard (large
forest) 72
Grosshaupt (bighead) 114
Grosshaus (fr Grosshausen
122, large house) 65
Grosskopf (bighead) 114
Grosslicht (big light, big
clearing) 126
Grossman (big + man) 113
Grossnickel (Big Nicholas,
Nicholas the elder) 113
Grossweiler (fr Grossweil
122, large hamlet) 127
Grote, Groth, Grotte, see
Gross
Groteyahn, see Grotjan 151
Grothaus, Grothhaus,
Grothusen (large house)
65
Grotheim (large hamlet) 123
Grothof (large farm) 94
Grotjan (Big John, John the
elder) 113
Groteyahn, see Grotjan 151
Grousaam, see Grausam 151
Grover, Groover, see Gruber
151
Grub, Grube (hollow, pit,
mountain cove)

Gruber, Grubert (dweller in a *Grube* or hollow)
Grubmeyer (farmer in the hollow) 93
Grueber, see Gruber
Gruel, see Greul
Gruen, Gruene, Gruener (green)
Gruenast (green branch)
Gruenau (green meadow) 84
Gruenbeck (green brook) 77
Gruenbaum (green tree) 89
Gruenberg (green mountain) 68, 112
Gruenblatt, Greenblat (green blade, leaf)
Gruendel (swamp) 80
Gruendelberger (swamp mountain) 80, 68
Gruene, Gruener (green)
Gruenewald 122, Gruenwalt (green forest) 72
Gruenfeld (green field) 84, 122
Gruenholt (green wood) 72
Grueninger (yellow hammer) 115
Gruenspan (green chip)
Gruenstein (green mountain) 73, 122
Gruenthal (green valley) 76, 122
Gruenwald 122, see Gruenewald
Gruenzweig (green + twig)
Gruess (greetings) 116
Gruetter (fr Gruett 122)
Gruhl (place name) 122
Grumbach 122, Grumbacher (swamp brook) 84, 77, see Krumbach
Grumbein (crooked leg) 114
Grunau (green meadow) 84, 122
Grunberg (green mountain) 68
Grund (bottom, valley)
Grundlach (valley lake) 80
Grundmann (valley dweller)
Grundmueller (valley miller) 103

Grundner, see Grundmann
Gruner, see Gruener
Grunewald 122, see Gruenewald
Grunsfeld, see Gruenfeld
Grupe, Grupp (grouper fisherman) 115
Gruss, see Gruesse
Gruve, Gruver, see Grube, Groover
Gruylich, see Greulich 151
Gryner, see Greiner 151
Grys, see Greis 151
Gschwandel (dweller in a clearing) 126
Gschwind (quick) 115
Guckel (rooster)115, 91
Guckelsberger (rooster mountain) 68
Gucker (lookout)
Gude (swamp) 80, see Gut
Gudekunst, see Gutkunst
Guderian (Good John) 144
Gudermuth, see Gutermuth
Guedemann, Guedermann, see Gutmann
Guelberth, see Gilbert
Gueldner (gilder)
Guelich (Juelich 122, principality on the Rhine)
Guempel, see Gimpel
Guendelach (battle play) 46
Guender, see Guenther
Guenst (favor)
Guenter, Guentert, see Guenther
Guenterberg (Guenther's mountain) 68
Guenther (battle + army) 46, 46
Guenz, Guentzer, see Guenther
Guenzburg (Guenther's castle) 73
Guering, see Goering
Guertel, Guertler (belt maker) 106
Guetemann, see Gutmann
Gueth, Guethe, see Gut

Gugel (cowl wearer or maker)
112, see Kugel

Guggenbuehler (fr Guggenbuehl
122, swamp hill or cuckoo
hill) 67

Guggenheim (swamp hamlet or
cuckoo hamlet) 123

Gugler (cowl maker or wearer,
fr Latin *cuculla*) 96, 110, see
Kogler

Guhl (fr Guhlen 122), see Kuhl

Gulde, Gulden (guilder)

Guldenfuss, see Goldfuss

Gulich, see Guelich

Gull (swamp dweller) 80

Gumbert, see Gundbrecht

Gumpel < Gundbold (battle +
brave) 46, 46

Gumpelman (acrobat) 96

Gumpert, see Gumbert

Gundacker < Gundwaker
(battle + brave) 46

Gundbrecht (battle + bright)
46, 47

Gundel < Gundolf, Gundrum,
etc.

Gundelach, see Gundlach

Gundelfinger (fr Gundelfingen
122, < Gundolf)

Gunderberger (Gunther's
mountain) 68

Gunderman, see Guentherman

Gundlach (battle play) 46

Gundlach (stagnant pond) 80

Gundolf (battle + wolf) 46, 48

Gundrum, see Guntram

Gunkel, Gunkelmann, see
Kunkel

Gunn, see Kuhn

Gunst (favor)

Guntermann (follower of
Guenther)

Gunteroth (Gunther's clearing)
126

Gunther (battle + army) 46, 46

Guntram (battle + raven) 46,
48

Guntrum, see Guntram

Guntzel < Gunther

Guntzenhauser (fr
Gunzenhausen 122,
Guenther's houses 65)

Gunzenheimer (fr
Gunzenheim 122,
Guenther's hamlet 123)

Gurth (girth, girdel) 106

Gurtner (girth maker) 96

Gurts, see Kurtz 151

Guss, Gusman, Gussmann
(founder, caster) 96

Gusstein (sink)

Gust, Gustl < Augustus

Gustav < Swedish, Gustaf
(for Gustavus Adolphus)

Gut, Guth, Gute (good,
property, estate)

Gutekunst (good skill)

Gutenberg (good mountain)

Gutenbrunner (fr
Gutenbrunnen 122, good
fountain) 79

Gutensohn (Guda's son) 60

Gutgesell (good fellow) 155

Guth, see Gut

Guthaber (estate owner)

Gutheim (estate hamlet) 123

Guthhard (good + strong) 46

Guthman, see Gutmann

Gutjahr (New Year's Day)
143

Gutknecht (landed knight)
107

Gutmann, Guthman,
Gutman Gutzler (good
man, man owning an
estate)

Gutschall, see Gottschalk

Guttenberger, see Gutenberg

Guttmann, see Gutmann

Gutwillig (affable) 115

Gutzel, see Gut

Gwinner (winner)

Gyger, see Geiger 151

H

Haacke, see Hacke
Haacker (retailer) 105
Haaf, see Haff
Haag, Haage, Haager, see Hag, Hager
Haak, Haake, Haackel (fr Haak 122, hook) 106
Haan, see Hahn
Haanecam (rooster field) 84
Haar, Haare, Haars (hair, flax)
Haarbleicher (flax bleacher) 106
Haarhaus (fr Haarhausen 122, marsh house) 80, 65
Haarmann (marsh dweller 80), see also Hermann
Haarmeyer (marsh farmer) 80, 93
Haart, see Hart
Haartz, see Hartz
Haas, Haase (fr Haas 122), see Hase 5
Haaseler, see Hassler
Haasmann, see Hasmann
Hab (possessions)
Habacher, Habacker (fr Halbach 122)
Habbeck, Habbecker (hawker) 91
Habbecker (fr Habbecke, swamp 122)
Habben < Hadebert (battle + bright) 46, 47
Habberle (oat grower) 91
Habecker, Habegger, see Habbeck
Habel (Slavic for St. Gall)
Habenicht (have not) 116
Haber, Habers, Habert (oats, oat dealer) 105
Haberbosch (oat bush)
Haberecht (Be right!, know-it-all) 116
Haberer (oat dealer) 105
Habergans (oat goose) 115
Haberger (fr Haberg 122)
Haberkamp (oat field) 84

Haberkorn (oat grain) 105
Haberl, Haberle, Haberly 151 (oat farmer) 91
Haberland (oatland) 122
Haberling 122, see Haberl
Haberloh (oat forest) 72
Habermaas (oat measure)
Habermann (oat dealer) 105
Habermehl (oat meal) 105
Habersieck (oat fen) 80
Haberstamm (oat stalk)
Haberstich (oat - steep slope)
Haberstock (oat stalk)
Haberstroh (oat straw)
Habich, Habicht, Hebicht (hawk) 115
Habight, see Habich 151
Habluetzel (Have little!) 116
Habmann, see Habermann
Hach, Hache, Hachen (youth)
Hachelbach (muddy brook) 77
Hachenberg (hawk mountain) 68, 122
Hachenburger (fr Hachenburg, hawk castle) 73
Hacher (flax hackler) 95
Hachlage (swamp water - lair) 80
Hachmann (dweller by swamp water) 80
Hachstein (swamp mountain) 80, 73
Hacht, Hachtmann, see Habich
Hachthal (swamp valley) 80, 76
Hack, Hacke (rake) 106, see also Hag
Hackenberg (swamp mountain) 81, 68, 122
Hackenmueller (swamp water - miller) 80, 103
Hackenschmied (rake smithy) 96
Hackenshmit (rake smith) 96, 151

Hacker, Hackert (raker, see
also Haacker)
Hackermann (huckster,
retailer) 105
Hackmann, see Hagmann,
Hackermann, Hakenschmied
Hackmeister (master of the
enclosure) 123
Hackstiel (rake handle)
Hadamar (battle + famous) 46,
47, 122
Hadamar (swamp marsh) 80
Hadd < Hadeward (battle +
guard) 46, 47
Hadel, Hadeler (bog dweller)
80
Hadepohl (swampy pond) 80
Hader, Haderle, Hadler,
Hadner (quarreler) 115, 122
Hadwig, Hedwig (battle +
battle) 46, 46
Haebbeler, Haeberle (young
goat) 91
Haebler (yeast dealer) 105
Haech (pot hook, cook) 96
Haechler (flax hackler) 95
Haeckler (vineyard worker) 95
Haefell, Haefele, Haeffele,
Haffeli, Hefley, Haeffler, see
Hafner
Haefer, Haefner, Haeffner, see
Hafner
Haefell, Haeffeli, Hefley,
Haeffler
Haeg 122, Haege, see Hag
Haeger, Haegler, Haegele,
Haegmann (dweller in an
enclosure) 123
Haehl, Haehle (swamp) 80
Haehler (fence for stolen goods)
Haehn 122, Haehner, Haehnert
< Haginher (master of the
enclosure) 123
Haehnle, Haehnlein (little
rooster) 115
Haekel, Haechel (hook, hook
maker, cook) 96, 106
Haelblein (ha'penney) 112

Haell, see Haehl
Haemel (sheep castrator) 95
Haemmer, see Hammer
Haemmerer, Haemmerle
(hammerer, smith) 96
Haen, Haenes, Haenle, see
Haehn
Haendel, Haendler (trade,
fight)
Haener, see Haehn
Haensel (little John) 131,
134
Haentschel, see Hensch
Haerdel, see Hert
Haering, see Hering
Haertel, Haertele, see Hert
Haerter, Haertter (communal
herdsman, communal
shepherd) 95
Haese, Haesle, Haesler,
Haeseler, Haessler, see
Hasel
Haeubt, see Haupt
Haeuser, Heuser, see
Haeusler
Haeusler, Haeussler
(householder, cotter) 65
Haeussli (little house) 65
Haf, Haff (harbor, bay)
Haf, Haff, Haffen (oats)
Hafemeyer (farm overseer)
93
Hafemeyer (oat farmer) 93
Hafen, Haffen, Hafenmeister
(harbor master)
Hafer, Haffer, Hafers, Hafert
(oats) 105
Haferkamm (oat field)
Haferkorn (oat grain, oat
seller) 105
Hafermann (oat dealer) 105
Haff, Haffen, see Haf
Haffentraeger (oat carrier)
Hafferstock (oat stalk)
Haffmann, see Hoffmann
Hafner, Haffer, Haffner,
Haeffner (potter) 96
Hafstaetter, see Hofstetter

Hag, Hage, Hagen (fr Hag 122, enclosure, hedge) 123

Hagebaeke (hedge stream) 77

Hageboek (hedge beech) 89

Hagebom (thornbush) 89

Hagedorn (hawthorn) 89, 122

Hagel, Hagele (fr Hagel 122, hail)

Hagelauer (hail meadow) 84

Hagelberg (hail mountain) 68, 122

Hagelgans (snow goose)

Hagelmaier (enclosure farmer) 93

Hagelstein (hailstone, a name for the devil) 122

Hagemann (enclosure dweller) 123

Hagemeier, Hagemeyer (manager of the enclo- sure) 123, 93

Hagemueller (miller by the enclosure) 123, 103

Hagen, Hagens (fr Hagen 122, enclosure, hedge) 123

Hagenbach (hedge brook; swamp brook) 80, 123, 77, 122

Hagenberg (enclosure mountain) 123, 68, 122

Hagenbruch (enclosure quarry) 123, 80

Hagenbuch, Hagenbucher, Hagenbucker (hornbeam)

Hagendorf (enclosed village 123, 123, village on the Hagen 83)

Hagendorn, Hagedorn (hawthorn) 89, 123

Hagenkotter (cotter in an enclosure 123, cotter on the Hagen 83)

Hagenmeyer, Hagenmayer (enclosure farmer 123, 93, farmer on the Hagen 183, 93)

Hagenmueller (miller at the enclosure 123, 103, miller on the Hagen 103, 83)

Hager, Hagers, Hagermann (dweller in an enclosure) 123

Hagerskamp (field belonging to a *Hager*) 123, 84

Hagius (latinized form of Hage) 141

Hagmann (dweller in an enclosure) 123, 94

Hagmauer (enclosure wall) 123, 100

Hahn, Hahne, Haan (rooster) 115

Hahnberger (rooster mountain, swamp mountain) 80, 68

Hahnstein (rooster mountain, swamp mountain) 80, 73

Hahr, see Haar

Hahrtman, see Hartmann

Haibler (hood maker) 96

Haid, Haidt, Haide, see Heid, Heide

Haidbrueck (heath bridge)

Haight, see Heid, Heide 151

Hail, Hailer, Hailler, Hailmann, see Heil, Heiler, Heilmann

Hailfinger (fr Heilfingen 122)

Hailgen, see Heiligen

Hain (grove), see also Hagen

Hainemueller (miller at the grove) 103, 72

Hainle, see Heinle

Hains, Hainz, Haintz, see Heinz, Heintz

Haiser, see Heiser

Haisler, see Heussler

Haiter (swamp) 80, see Heiter

Hake, see Haak

Haker, see Hoeker and Hacker

Halbach (swamp brook) 80, 77, 122

Halbauer (half-owner of a farm, sharecropper) 91

Halber (ha'penny) 112

Halberstadt (German city) 122
Halbfass (half barrel, tenant
farmer)
Halbfoerster (half-owner of
forest rights)
Halbgewachs, Halbgwachs (half
grown) 113
Halbmeyer (half-owner of a
farm) 93
Haldemann (dweller on a slope)
71
Halden (slopes) 71, 122
Halder (see Haldemann) 122
Halfadel (half-noble) 46, 151
Halfmann (share cropper) 95
Hall (Swiss town) 122
Hallbauer, see Halbbauer
Halle (hall, German city) 122
Hallebach, Hallenbeck (brook
along a slope) 71, 77
Hallenbach (swamp brook) 80,
77
Hallenberger (fr Hallenberg
122, swamp mountain) 81
Hallenburg (swamp castle) 81,
73, 122
Haller (fr Hall or Halle 122),
see also Heller
Hallick, see Heilig 151
Hallmann, see Hellmann,
Heilmann
Halls, see Hals
Hallwachs, see Halbgewachs
Halm (blade, stalk)
Hals (throat) 114
Haltemann, see Haldemann
Haltenhof (slope farm) 71, 84
Haltenmeyr (slope farmer) 71,
93
Halter, Haltermann (owner,
proprietor)
Halter, Haltmann (see
Haldemann)
Halwig, see Helwig
Hamann, Hamannt < Johann
134
Hambach, Hambacher (fr
Hambach 122, reed brook)

81, 77, see also
Hagenbeck
Hamberg, Hamberger (fr
Hamberg 122, reed
mountain) 81, 68, see also
Hagenberg
Hambrecht < home + bright)
124, 47
Hambright, see Hambrecht
151
Hamburg, Hamburger (fr
Hamburg 122, reed brook
castle) 81, 73
Hamel, Hamelmann (fr
Hameln, Hamlin) 122
Hamelgarn, see Hammelgarn
Hameyer, see Hammeyer
Hamm, Hamms (horse
collar) 106
Hammacher (horse collar
maker) 96
Hammann < Johann 134
Hammecker, see Hammacher
Hammel, Hammel (wether)
91, see Hamel
Hammelgarn (fish net) 106
Hammelmann, fr Hamlin
(Hameln) 151
Hammer 122, Hammers,
Hammermann, Hammerer
(hammer, hammer maker,
smith, carpenter) 96, 106
Hammer, Hammermann,
Hammerer (maker of
horse collars) 96, 106
Hammer < Hadumar (battle
+ famous) 46, 47
Hammerlein < Hammer
Hammerschlag (hammer
blow, smith) 96
Hammerschmidt,
Hammersmith (hammer
smith) 96
Hammerstedt (hammer city)
122
Hammerstein (hammer
stone, mountain) 73, 122
Hammeyer, see Halbmeyer

Hammler, see Hamelmann
Hammon, Hamon (OT name) 135
Hampe, Hampel < Hagenbercht (enclosure + bright) 123, 46
Hampf, see Hanf
Hampfling (hemp grower or dealer)
Hampsch, Hamscher
Haendler (merchant, huckster) 105
Han (reeds or swamp 81, also see Hahn)
Hanauer, Hannauer (fr Hanau, marsh meadow) 122
Hand (hand) 114
Handel, Handler (trade, trader) 105
Handschuh (glove, glover) 112, 106
Handschumacher (glover) 96
Handtke (little hand) 114
Handwerk, Handwercker (craft, craftsman)
Hanengrath (chicken bone)
Hanf (hemp) 105
Hanfeld (marsh field) 80, 84
Hanfling (hemp grower or dealer) 105
Hang, Hangg, Hanger (slope dweller) 71
Hangleiter (dweller on a steep slope) 71
Hangner (fr Hangen 122, slope dweller) 71
Hangstorfer (slope village) 71, 123
Hanitsch < Johannes 134
Hank, Hanke, Hankel < Johannes 134
Hanmann, Hannemann, see Hahnmann, Hahnemann < Johann 134
Hann, see Hahn
Hanna < Johann 134
Hannauer, see Hanauer
Hanner, see Haener
Hannes, Hanns < Johannes 134

Hannibal (Carthaginian general)
Hans, Hansi, Haensel, Hanselmann, Hansemann < Johann 134
Hansa (Hansa)
Hansberger (Hans' mountain) 68
Hanschel < Johannes 134
Hanschildt, see Hanschel
Hansel (little John) 134
Hanselmann (brownie, see Heinzelmann) 134
Hansen (son of Johann) 59, 134
Hanser, Hanssener, Hansser, Hanssers (member of Hanseatic league)
Hansing < Johannes 134
Hansle, see Hansel
Hanson (son of Hans) 59
Hanstein, see Hahnstein
Hanz, Hanzel, see Hans, Hansel 151
Hanzer, see Hanser 151
Hapacher (fr Happach 122, enclosure brook) 123, 77
Hapelbach (nightshade + brook) 77
Hapelfeld (nightshade + field) 84
Happel < Hadebold (battle + brave) 46, 46
Harbach, Harback, Harbeck, Herbach (fr Harbach 122, swamp brook) 81, 77
Harbarth, see Herbert
Harbaugh, see Harbach 151
Harbers, Harbert, Harberts, Harbrecht, see Herbert
Harburger (fr Harburg) 122
Harcke (rake) 106
Hard, Hardt, Hart, Harth (strong) 46
Hardekop (hardhead) 115
Harden, Hardelen < Hartwig, Hardeward (strong + guard), etc.

Hardenstein (forest mountain)
72, 73
Harder, Harders (forester) 96
Hardewig, see Hartwig
Hardmann, see Hartmann
Hardner, see Hartner
Hardt (forest) 72, 122
Hardt, see Hirsch
Hardtmann, see Hartmann,
Hirschmann
Harebeck (swamp creek) 80, 77
Haren (swamp) 80, 122
Harermann (swamp dweller)
80, 94
Harf (harp, harpist) 96, 106
Harf (man fr Harff 122 in the
Rhineland)
Harfner (harpist) 96
Haring (herring, herring
dealer) 115, 105
Harje, Harjes, Harjis <
Hermann, Herwig, etc. 53
Harkabus (harquebusier) 107
Harke, Harkmann (rake, raker,
rake maker) 96, 106
Harkel (little rake) 106
Harm, Harms (weasel, also <
Hermann)
Harman, see Hermann
Harmar (army + famous) 46,
47
Harmening, Harming <
Hermann
Harmsdorff 122, see Hermsdorf
Harmsen, son of Harm 59
Harnisch (armor, harness) 108
Harnischfeger (armor
burnisher) 108
Harniss (armor, harness) 108
Harpe (harp, harpst) 96, 106
Harpst, see Herbst
Harr, see Haarmann, Herwig,
etc.
Harsch (military troop) 107
Hart, Hardt, Harth (fr Hart
122, wooded mountain) 72

Hart, Harte, Harter, Hartel
(strong 46), also short for
names beginning in Hart.
Hart (stag)
Hartenbach (muddy brook)
80, 77
Hartenberg (wooded
mountain) 68
Hartenstein (wooded
mountain) 73, 122
Hartfeld, Hartfelder (fr
Hartfeld 122, stag field),
see Hirschfeld
Harth 122, see Hart
Harthkopf, see Hartkopf
Hartig, see Hartwig
Harting, Hartting, see
Hartwig
Harting (place name) 122
Hartje, Hartjen, see Hartwig
Hartkopf (hard head) 115
Hartlager (fr Hartlage 122)
Hartlaub (forest foliage) 72
Hartlieb (strong + legacy;
strong + dear) 46
Hartman, Hartmann (strong
+ man 46, 94, dweller on
a wooded mountain 72,
94)
Hartmann (strong + man)
46, 94
Hartmeyer (forest farmer)
72, 93
Hartmueller (forest miller)
72, 103
Hartmut, Hartmuth (strong
+ disposition) 46, 46
Hartner (forest dweller) 72
Hartog, see Herzog
Hartsock, Hartsook, see
Herzog 151
Hartstein (wooded peak), 72,
73
Hartstein (hard stone) 73
Hartung (strong man) 46
Hartway, see Hartweg 151
Hartweg, Hartway (path
through forest) 72

Hartwig (strong + battle) 46, 46

Hartz, Hartze (fr the Harz Mountains), see also Hart

Hartzel, see Hart

Hartzfeld (field in the Hartz) 84, see also Hirschfeld

Hartzog, see Herzog

Harwig (army + battle) 46, 46

Harz, see Hartz

Hasch, Hasche (Slavic for Johannes) 134

Hascher (policeman) 109

Hase, Has (hare) 115

Hasekamp, Hasenkamp (hare field) 115, 84

Hasel, Hasele (hazel) 89

Haselbach (hazel brook) 89, 77, 122

Haselbrug (hazel bridge) 89

Haselhorst (hazel hurst) 89, 72, 122

Haselman, Haselmann (dweller in the hazel) 89

Haselwander (hazel slope) 89, 71

Hasemann (hare mann) 115, 94

Hasemeyer (hare farmer) 115, 93

Hasenau, Hasenauer (hare meadow) 115, 84

Hasenberg (hare mountain) 115, 68, 112

Hasenclever (fr Hasenclev, rabbit clover) 122

Hasenfeld (hare field) 115, 84, 122

Hasenfus (hare leg) 114

Hasenjaeger (hare hunter) 115, 91

Hasenlauer (hare catcher) 115

Hasenpflug (Hate the plow!, guild name) 116

Hashaar (rabbit hair) 115

Hashagen (hare hedge) 115, 123

Hasler, Hassler (dweller among the hazels) 89

Hasli (little hare) 115

Haslinger, Hasslinger (fr Hasling 122)

Hasman (hare + man) 115, 94

Haspelhorn (turnstile arm)

Hasper, Haspert (swamp water) 80

Hass, Hasse (hare, hate) 5

Hassel (fr Hassel 122, swamp 80), see also Hasel

Hasselbach, Hasselbacher, Hasselbaecher (fr Hasselbach 122, brook running through hazel trees, swampy brook) 89, 80, 77

Hasselmann, see Haselman

Hasselwanger (hazel slope) 89

Hassenau, see Hasenau

Hassenpflug, see Hasenpflug

Hassinger (fr Hassingen 122)

Hassler (dweller among the hazel trees) 89

Hasslinger (fr Hasslinge 122)

Hassmann, see Hasmann

Hassner, see Hasmann

Hasso < Hartmann 53

Hatman, Hatmann, Hattsmann (dweller in the fen) 81

Hatt (fen, bog) 81

Hatto < Haduwulf (battle + wulf) 46, 48

Hattenberger (hill in a fen) 81, 68

Hatz, see Hetz

Haub, Haube (cap, hood, helmet) 106, 108

Haubeil (hewing axe) 106

Haubensack (clothing quartermaster) 107, see Hobensack

Hauber, Haubert (cap or hood maker) 96

Hauberger (deforested mountain) 68, see Heuberg

Hauch (breath, also < Hugo)

Hauck, Haucke < Hugo
Haudt, see Haut
Haueisen (mattock) 106
Hauenstein (Hew the stone!
116, 122), cf. Steinhauer)
Hauer, Hauers, Hauert (hewer,
chopper) 95
Hauf, Hauff, Haufmann (heap,
military detachment) 107
Hauf, Hauff (place names) 122
Haug, Haugg, Haugk, Haugs,
Hauk, Hauke < Hugo
Haukamp (deforested field) 84
Haumann (hay dealer) 105
Haumeister (hay ward)
Haumesser (hackknife)
Haupt, Haubt (head) 114
Hauptmann (captain) 107
Haus, Hauss, Hause, Haussen
(house, usually a shortened
form) 65
Hausberger (fr Hausberg 122,
house mountain) 65, 68
Hauschild (mercenary,
professional fighter) 108
Hausemann, Hausener, see
Hausmann
Hausen (houses, probably
shortened fr some name like
Hagenhausen) 65, 122
Hausenbeck (brook among the
houses) 65, 77
Hauser, Haeuser, Hausermann
(householder) 65
Haushalter (householder) 65
Hausknecht (domestic servant)
Hausleiter (house leader)
Hausman, Haussmann (house
owner) 65, 94
Hausner (house owner) 65
Hausrat, Haussrad (household
belongings)
Hausser, see Hauser
Hauswart, Hauswarth (house
guardian) 65, 47
Hauswirt, Hauswirth (master
of the house) 65

Haut, Hauth, Hautz (skin,
hide, skinner) 106
Haut, Hauth, see Hut, Huth
Havel, Havelmann (dweller
along the Havel, marsh)
80, 83
Havenner, see Hafner
Haver (oats)
Haverkamp (oat field) 84,
122
Haverle, see Haberle
Havermehle, see Hafermehl
Havervass (oat barrel)
Hawffman, see Hoffmann
151
Hayd, Hayde, see Heidt,
Heide
Hayl, see Heil
Hayler, see Heiler
Hayn, Hayns, see Hain
Hayser, see Haeuser, Heiser
Heartman, see Hartmann
151
Healer, see Heiler 151
Heavener, see Hafner
Hebbel, see Hebel
Hebeisen (crowbar) 106
Hebel, Hebeler (lever) 106
Hebel (sourdough, baker)
106, 122
Heber 122, Hebert,
Hebermann, see Hafer,
Hafermann
Heber (loader, carrier)
Hebermehl, see Hafermehl
Hebigt, see Habicht
Hech, Hechler (flax hackler)
95
Hechelberger (hackle
mountain) 68
Hecht (pickerel) 115
Heck, Hecke (hedge) 123,
122
Heckel (vineyard worker,
beater of flax, etc.)
Heckendorn (hedge thorn)
123, 72

Heckenlaub (hedge leaves) 123
Hecker, Heckert, Heckler,
    Heckner, Heckmann
    (enclosure dweller) 123
Heckscheer (hedge shears) 106
Hedrich, Hederich, see
    Heidrich
Hedwig, see Hadwig
Heer (army) 46, < Hermann 53
Heerdt, see Herd
Hefer, Hefler, Hefner, Heffer,
    Heffler, Heffner, Hefermann
    (yeast dealer) 105
Heffner, see Haefner
Heft (clasp maker, buckle
    maker) 96, 106
Hege, see Hag
Hegen (see Hecke)
Hegendorn, see Heckendorn
Hegelmaier, Hegemeyer
    (proprietor of an enclosed
    farm) 93
Hegl, Hegel, Hegler (enclosure
    dweller) 123
Heger, Hegner, Heggler,
    Hegmann, see Heckmann
Heger (gamekeeper, forester)
    109
Hehl, Hehle, Hehler (concealer,
    fence)
Hehr (sublime), see also Heer
Hehr (jay) 115
Hehrmann, see Hermann
Heiberger, see Heuberger
Heibly, see Hueble 151
Heicher, see Heucher
Heichler (hypocrite)
Heid, Heide, Heidt (heath,
    heathen) 81
Heidecker, Heideke <
    Heidenreich
Heidegger, see Heidecker
Heidel, Heydel (blueberry) 89
Heidelbach (blueberry brook)
    89, 77
Heidelbauer (blueberry farmer)
    89, 91
Heidemeier, Heidemeyer,
    Heidmayer (proprietor of the

Heidehof, heath farm) 81,
    93
Heidenreich, Heiderich,
    Heidrich (heathen?, heath?
    + rule) 81, 46
Heidt, Heidts, see Heid
Heier, Heiert, see Heger,
    Hauer
Heiger (heron) 115
Height, see Heid 151
Heil, Heill (fortune,
    prosperity, blessing)
Heiland (the Savior) 140
Heilbrunn, Heilbrun,
    Heilborn, Heilbronn 122,
    Heilbronner, Heilbrunner
    (holy + spring, a city)
Heilemann (healer)
Heiler (healer)
Heilig (holy)
Heiligenberg (holy mountain)
    68
Heiligendorf (holy village)
    123
Heiligentag (All Saint's Day)
    143
Heiligenthal (saints' valley)
    76
Heiliger (saint)
Heiligmann (holy man)
Heilmann, see Heilemann
Heim (home, hamlet, a
    shortened form) 123
Heimbach (hamlet + brook)
    123, 77, 122
Heimbaugh, see Heimbach
    151
Heimberger (fr Heimberg
    122, hamlet mountain)
    123, 68
Heimbert (home + bright)
    123, 47
Heimburg (home castle) 123,
    73, 122
Heimlich (furtive, secretive)
    115
Hein, Heine < Heinrich
Heindorf (grove village) 123,
    123

Heineke, Heinecke, Heinecken
< Heinrich
Heineman, Heinemann <
Heinrich
Heiner, Heinert < Heinrich
Heinhauser (fr Heinhaus 122,
grove house) 72, 65
Heinickel, Heinkel < Heinrich
Heining, Heininger < Heinrich
59
Heinke < Heinrich 53
Heinle, Heinlein < Heinrich 53
Heinmann, see Heinemann
Heinmeyer (farmer in the
grove 72, 93), see
Hagenmeyer
Heinmueller (miller at the
grove) 72, 103
Heinolt, Heinoldt (home +
loyal) 47, 48
Heinrich, Heinrichs, Heinrick
(home + master) 47, 46
Heins, Heinsmann, see Heintz
Heintz, Heintze, Heintzen,
Heinz, Heinze, Heintzler
(diminutive of Latin
Henrizius, for Heinrich)
Heintzel, Heintzler,
Heintzelmann, Heintzelmann
< Heinrich
Heinzmann < Heinrich
Heis, Heiss 122, Heise (hot),
see also Heidenreich
Heisel, see Haeusel
Heisenberg (scrub forest
mountain) 68, 122
Heisenbuettel (scrub forest
house) 65
Heisler, see Haeusler
Heisemann, Heissmann, see
Hausmann
Heisenstein (scrub forest
mountain) 73, 122
Heiser (hoarse 114), see also
Haeuser
Heiser < Heidenrich 53
Heiss, Heisse, Heisser (hot)
Heissler, see Haeusler

Heist, Heister (fr Heist 122,
young beech tree) 89, 122
Heit, Heith, Heitz, see Heidt
Heitkamp (heath field) 81,
84, 122
Heitmann, Heitzmann (heath
man) 81, 94
Heitmeyer, see Heidemeyer
Hekenturm (tower
surrounded by hedge,
turm from Latin *turris*)
123
Helbig, Helbing, Helbling
(ha'penny) 112
Helbrand, see Hildebrant
Held, Heldt (hero) 46
Heler, see Hehler
Helfenstein (Stone of Help)
140, 122
Helfer, Helfert (helper)
Helfrich, Hilfreich (helpful)
138
Helge (healthy, fortunate)
155
Hell, Helle (brilliant, bright)
Hellebrand, see Hildebrand
Helleman, Hellemanns, see
Heilmann, Helman
Heller, Hellert (small coin fr
Hall) 117
Hellerbran (hell's fire)
Helling, Hellinger (fr Helling
122), see Helbling
Hellinghausen (place name)
122
Hellmann (dweller on a
steep slope) 71, see
Heilmann
Hellmer, Hellmers (dweller
on a steep slope) 71, see
Helmer, Helmers
Hellwage (hell's chariot, the
Great Bear, the Big
Dipper)
Hellwege (army road, *strata
publica*) 122
Hellwig, see Helwig
Helm (helmet) 108

Helman, see Heilmann
Helman (devil)
Helmbacher (fr Helmbach 122,
helmet brook) 46, 77
Helmbarth (helmet + battle
axe) 46, 46
Helmbold, Helmboldt (helmet +
brave) 46, 47
Helmbrandt (helmet + sword)
46, 46
Helmbrecht (helmet + brilliant)
46, 47
Helmeister (the devil)
Helmer (helmet maker) 46, 108
Helmer < Hildemar (battle +
famous) 46, 47
Helmke, Helmken (little
helmet) 46, 108
Helmstaetter (fr Helmstadt
122)
Helmuth < helmet +
disposition) 46, 46
Helt, see Held
Heltzel (forest dweller,
woodman)
Helveti (Helvetian, Swiss) 121,
141
Helwig < Hiltiwic (battle +
battle) 46, 46
Hemd, Hemb, Hembt (shirt)
106
Hemelright, see Himmelreich
151
Hemmenger (fr Hemmingen
122)
Hemmer (swamp dweller) 80
Hemmerichs, see Himmelreich
Hemming, see Hambrecht
Hemminghaus (Hemming's
house) 65
Hemmingway < Hemmingweg
(Hemming's path) 65
Hemmler, Hemmerle, see
Himmler
Hempel, Hempele, Hemple,
Hempelmann < Hambrecht)
Hempel (hemp grower or
dealer) 105
Henchell < Johann 134

Hencke < Heinrich 53
Henckel, Henkel, Henckels,
Henckler, Hinkel <
Heinrich 53
Henckeljohann (Henry John)
Henckelman, Henckelmann <
Heinrich
Hendel, see Haendel
Hendrichs, Henricksmann <
Heinrich
Hendrick, Hendricks,
Hendriks < Heinrich
Heneger, see Heinecke
Henel < Heinrich 53
Hengel, Hengler, see Henkel
Hengstebeck (stallion brook)
77
Hengstenberg (stallion
mountain) 68, 122
Henig, Hening < Johannes
134
Henkel, Henkel, Henkels,
Hinkel (handle, see
Henckel)
Henn, Henne, Henny (hen,
or < Heinrich
Henne (place name) 122
Henneberger (fr Henneberg
122, chicken mountain,
Johann's mountain) 134,
68
Hennecke, Henneckes, see
Heinecke
Hennemann, see Heinemann
Hennes < Johannes 134
Hennig, Henning, Henninger
< Johann 134
Henrich, Henrichs, Henrick,
see Heinrich
Henrici (son of Henricus,
Latin for Heinrich) 142
Henry, see Heinrich 151
Hensch, Henschel, Henschen,
Henschle, see Hentsch
Hensel, Hensler, Henseler,
see Haensel, Haensler <
Johannes 134

Henss, Henssel, Henssler,
Henssmann < Johannes
134
Hentsch, Hentscher (glove
maker) 96, 106
Henz, Henze, Henzel, Henzell,
Hentzel, Henzler < Johannes
134
Hepel, Heppler (pruning knife)
106
Herald, see Herold
Herb, Herber (bitter), see
Herbert
Herbach (swamp brook) 80, 77,
122
Herberger (army + shelter) 46,
47
Herbert, Herberts, Herberth
(army + bright) 46, 47
Herbig, see Herwig
Herbold, Herbolt (army + bold)
46, 46
Herbrand, Herbrandt (army +
sword) 46, 46
Herbrecht (army + bright) 46,
47
Herbst (harvest, autumn) 143
Herd, Herde, Herdt, Herdte
(herd)
Herder (herder) 95
Herford, Herfurth (army
crossing) 46, 78
Hergenrother (fr Hergenroth)
122
Herger, Hergert (army + spear)
46, 46
Herget, see Herrgott
Hergott, see Herrgott
Herguth (army + wealth 46),
or see Herrgott
Herholt (swamp forest) 80, 72,
see Herold
Herich, Herig, see Hering
Hering (herring, seller of
herrings) 115, 105
Herl 122, Herle, Herlein <
Hermann 53

Herliberg (glorious mountain)
46
Herling, Herlinger <
Hermann 53
Herman, Hermann,
Hermans, Hermanus
(army + man) 46, 94
Hermsdorf, Hermannsdorfer
(Hermann's village) 122
Hernberger (the Lord's
mountain) 139, 122
Herold 122, Heroldt (army +
ruler 46, 46, herold at
miracle play 111)
Herr, Herre, Herrn (hoary,
senior, master)
Herrenbauer (the Lord's
peasant, monastery
servant) 139
Herrgott (Lord God) 117
Herrimann, Herrmann, see
Hermann
Herrnknecht (the Lord's
servant, monastery
worker) 139
Hersch, see Hirsch
Herschberger (fr Herschberg
122), see Hirschberg
Herschbrunner (stag
fountain) 79
Herschfeld (stag field) 122,
see Hirschfeld
Herschfenger (deer catcher)
Hersen (millet) 105
Hershy, see Hirschi 151
Hert, Herte, Hertel, Herthel,
Hertle < various names
beginning in *hart*)
Hertter, Hertler < Hartwig,
Hartlieb, etc.
Hertwig, see Hartwig
Hertz (heart)
Hertzel, Herzels (little heart,
see also Hert)
Hertzfeld (fr Herzfeld 122,
stag field) 84, see
Hirschfeld
Herwagen (army wagon) 46

Herwig (army + battle) 46, 46
Herz, see Hertz
Herzag, see Herzog
Herzberg, Hertzberger (fr
Herzberg 122, heart
mountain 68), see also
Hirschberg
Herzer (resin gatherer) 95
Herzfeld 122, see Hertzfeld
Herzig, Herzinger, see Herzog
Herzog, Hertzog (duke, army
leader) 46, 109
Herzogin (duchess, man in
duchess's employ) 109
Herzstein (heart mountain) 73
Hess, Hesse (Hessian 121), also
< Hermann
Hesselbach 122, see Haselbach
Hesselberg (hasel mountain)
89, 68, 122
Hessler, see Hassler
Hessling, Hesslinger (fr
Hesslingen) 122
Hetler, Hettler (goatherd) 91,
95
Hetman, Hettmann (captain)
107
Hetrich, see Heidrich
Hettel, Hettler (goat, goatherd)
91
Hettich < Hadebert, battle +
bright 46, 47
Hettinger, Hettner (fr
Hettingen 122)
Hetz, Hetzel, Hetzler (beater
on hunt, or < Hermann)
Heu (hay) 105
Heuberger (fr Heuberg 122,
hay mountain) 68
Heucher (dweller on a fen) 80
Heuer (this year's wine, fr
Heue 122)
Heuermann (vintner) 96
Heule (howl)
Heumann (hay man) 105
Heuse, Heuser, Heuss, see
Haus, Haeuser
Heusler, Heussli, Haeussler,
see Haeusler

Heuwarth (hay ward) 95
Hevener, see Hafner
Heyd, Heyde, Heydt,
Heyden, see Heid
Heydel, see Heidel
Heydrick, Heydricks, see
Heidrich
Heyer, see Heuer
Heyl, Heyler, see Heil,
Heiler
Heyland, see Heiland
Heylmann, Heylemann, see
Heilmann
Heyman, Heymann, see
Heinemann
Heyn, see Hain, Hein
Heyne, see Heine
Heynemann, see Heinemann
Heyser, see Heiser
Hibler, Hible, Hiblein, see
Huebler 151
Hibscher, see Huebscher
Hickelmann, see Huck
Hickman, see Heckmann
Hide, Hides, see Heidt 151,
164
Hiebel, Hiebler, see Huebler
Hieber, Hiebert, see Hueber,
Huebert
Hiebner, see Huebner
Hiegel, see Huegel
Hienreik, see Heinrich 151
Hiepler, see Huebler
Hierl (sword) 46
Hierl < Hermann 53
Hieronymus (St. Jerome) 131
Hiersfeld, see Hirschfeld
Highler, see Heiler 151
Height, see Heid 151
Hilberg, Hilberger (hill in
swamp) 80, 72
Hilbers, Hilbert, Hilbricht,
see Hildebrecht
Hilbrand, see Hildebrand
Hild, Hildt, see Hildebrand
Hildebrand, Hildenbrandt,
Hiltenbrandt (battle +
sword) 46, 46

Hildebrecht (battle + bright)
46, 47
Hildeger (battle + spear) 46, 46
Hildemar (battle + famous) 46,
47
Hildemut (battle + disposition)
46, 47
Hildesheimer, Hiltzheimer (fr
Hildesheim 122, marsh
hamlet) 80, 123
Hildihart (battle + strong) 46,
46
Hildt, see Held
Hildwein (battle + friend) 46,
48
Hile, Hiler, Hilmann, see Heile,
Heiler, Heilmann 151
Hilfrich (helpful) 138
Hilgartner (swamp garden) 80,
98
Hilgenberger, see Heiligenberg
Hilger 122, Hilgers, Hilgert <
Hildeger
Hill, Hille, Hiller < Hildebrand,
Hildeger, etc.
Hillebrand, Hillenbrandt, see
Hildebrand
Hillegas, Hillegass (swamp
road) 80
Hillenburg (castle in swamp)
80
Hillferding (fr Hilferding 122)
Hillgartner, see Hilgartner
Hilliger, see Heiliger
Hillmer, Hillmann <
Hildebrand, Hildebert, etc.
53
Hillmuth, see Helmuth
Hillsee (Holly lake, swamp
lake) 89, 81
Hillsinger (fr Hillsing 122)
Hillstrom (swamp stream) 80,
77
Hilpert < Hildebrecht (battle +
bright) 46, 47
Hilscher (swamp dweller) 80

Hilse (dweller near the holly
trees, or near the swamp)
89, 80
Hilseberg (holly mountain)
89, 68
Hilsenbeck (holly brook,
swamp stream) 89, 77
Hiltner (attic)
Hiltz (swamp) 80, 122
Hiltzheimer (swamp hamlet)
80, 123, see also
Hildesheimer
Himebaugh, see Heimbach
151
Himel, see Himmel
Himelfarb (sky color)
Himelmann, see
Himmelmann
Himelsbach, see
Himmelsbach
Himelright, see Himmelreich
151
Himler, see Himmler
Himmel (heaven, sky,
probably a house name)
149, 122
Himmelberger (fr
Himmelberg 122, heaven
mountain) 68
Himmelmann, see Himmler
Himmelreich (kingdom of
heaven) 140
Himmelsbach,
Himmelsbacher (swamp
brook) 80, 77
Himmelwright, see
Himmelreich 151
Himmer, see Hubmeier
Himmler (occupant of Haus
zum Himmel) 149
Himpel, see Hempel
Hinaman, see Heinemann
151
Hince, see Heintz 151
Hinck, Hincke (limper 113),
also < Heinrich
Hinckel, Hinkelmann (baby
chick) 115, 91

Hinde (hind)
Hindeleuthner (fr the
backslope) 71
Hinderberger, see Hinterberger
Hinderer, Hindermann (dweller
behind the village)
Hinderhoffer (proprietor of the
Hinderhoff, farm out back)
84
Hine, Hinelein, see Hein,
Heinlein 151
Hinebaugh, see Heimbach 151
Hines, see Heinz 151
Hinkel, Hinkle, Hinkelmann,
see Hinckel
Hinnen (dweller "back there")
Hinrich, Hinrichs, see Heinrich
Hinsch, Hinsche < Heinrich 53
Hintenach (in pursuit)
Hinterberger (fr Hinterberg
122, fr behind the mountain)
68
Hintz, Hintze, Hintzel, Hinz,
Hintzman, Hintzmann <
Heinrich
Hipner, see Huebner
Hipp, Hippe, Hippmann
(pruning knife 106, or <
Hildebert 46, 47)
Hippel, Hippler, Hippelmann
(waffel seller) 105
Hippenstiel (pruning knife
handle) 106
Hipsch, see Huebsch
Hipskind (well-mannered child)
Hirnschal (skull) 114
Hirsch (stag, hart) 48, 149
Hirschbein (deer bone) 48
Hirschberg, Hirschberger (fr
Hirschberg 122, stag
mountain) 48, 68
Hirschbiehl, Hirschbuhl,
Hirschbuehler (stag hill) 48,
67
Hirschfeld, Hirschfield (stag
field) 48, 84, 122
Hirschhausen (stag house) 48,
65, 122

Hirschheimer (stag hamlet)
48, 123
Hirschhizer, see
Hirschhausen 151
Hirschhorn (antlers, deer
horn) 48
Hirschi, Hirschy (little stag)
48
Hirschkind (little stag) 48
Hirschle (little stag) 48
Hirschler, Hirschner (stag
hunter) 48
Hirschman, Hirschmann
(stag man) 48
Hirschstein (stag mountain)
68
Hirse (millet) 105
Hirshauer (fr Hirschau 122,
stag meadow) 48, 84, 151
Hirshbein, see Hirschbein
Hirshizer, see Hirschhizer
151
Hirt 122, Hirth, Hirtz
(shepherd, herdsman) 95
Hirtzel, Hirzel, see Hirsch
Hisle, see Haeusle
Hiss, Hisser, see Heis and
Heuss
Hite, see Heidt 151
Hiter, see Heiter, Hueter
151
Hitner, see Huettner
Hitz (heat)
Hitz (goat) 91
Hitzelberger (fr Hitzelberg
122)
Hitzler, see Hutzler
Hixenbaugh (Hick's brook)
151
Hizer, see Haeuser 151
Hobach, Hobeck (high brook)
77
Hobell, Hobelmann
(carpenter's plane,
carpenter) 98, 106
Hobensack (hops sack, hops
dealer) 105
Hober, Hobert < Hadebracht
(battle + bright) 46, 47

Hobler (planer) 98
Hobman, Hobmann, Hobner,
see Hoffmann
Hoburg (fr Hochburg 122, high
castle) 73
Hoch (high, tall man) 113
Hochberg (high mountain) 68
Hochbrueckner (fr Hochbruck
122, dweller by the high
bridge)
Hochfelden (fr Hochfeld 122,
high fields) 84
Hochgenug (high enough) 115
Hochhalter (dweller on a high
slope) 71
Hochhaus (tall house) 65, 122
Hochheim, Hochheimer (high +
hamlet, a city and famous
wine) 122
Hochhiser (dweller in a high
house) 66, 151
Hochhut (high hat) 112
Hochkeppel (high cap) 112, 122
Hochlander (highlander)
Hochmann, see Homann
Hochnadel (high needle)
Hochrein (high path)
Hochreuter (fr Hochreute, high
clearing) 126
Hochschild (high shield) 149
Hochstadt, Hochstaedtler (fr
Hochstadt 122, high city,
high shore)
Hochstein (high crag) 73, 122
Hochstetter, Hochstettler, see
Hochstadt
Hochwald (high forest) 72, 122
Hochwart (high lookout) 122
Hock, Hocke, Hocken (retailer,
huckster) 105
Hockenbrock (fr Hockenbroich
122)
Hockhaus, see Hochhaus
Hodel (wagon cover, huckster
with wagon) 105
Hodler (huckster, ragman) 105
Hoebecke (from Hoebeck 122)
Hoebener, see Huebner

Hoeblich, see Hoeflich
Hoebling (courtier)
Hoechst (high place, name of
city) 122
Hoeck, Hoeckel (huckster)
105
Hoecker, Hoeckert (seller of
foodstuffs) 105
Hoef..., Hoeff...., see Hof,
Hoff
Hoefle (small court, small
farm) 92
Hoefler, Hoeffler, Hoefner
(farmer) 92
Hoeflich (courtly, courteous)
115
Hoefnagel, see Hufnagel
Hoefner, see Haffner
Hoeft, Hoeftmann, see Hoff,
Hoffmann
Hoeh, Hoehn, Hoehne
(heights)
Hoehenholtz (forest on the
heights) 72
Hoehl (cave)
Hoehler (dweller near a
cave)
Hoehn, see Hoeh
Hoehn (scorn)
Hoelscher (maker of wooden
shoes) 96
Hoeltz, Hoeltzer, Hoelter,
Hoeltzel, Hoeltzle, Hoelzl,
see Holtz
Hoener (scorner)
Hoenig, see Honig
Hoepfel, Hoepflinger (hops
dealer) 105
Hoepfner (hops dealer) 105
Hoeppel, Hoeppner, see
Hoepfner
Hoerauf (army + wolf 46, 48,
folketymology: "Stop it!")
116
Hoerder, see Herder
Hoerger, Hoeriger (serf, fr
Hoergen 122)

Hoering (place name 122), see
Hering
Hoerl, Hoerle, Hoerli, Hoerlein
< Hermann 53
Hoermann, see Hermann
Hoerner (horn maker) 96
Hoernle, Hoernlein (little horn)
Hoersch, see Hirsch
Hoerst (place name 122), see
Horst
Hoertz (place name 122), see
Herz
Hoesler, see Hessler
Hoetz (place name 122), see
Hetz
Hof, Hofe, Hoff (yard, court)
92, 122
Hofacker, Hoffacker, Hoffecker
(fr Hofacker 122, field
belonging to farm or court)
92, 84
Hofer, Hoffer (farmer 92, fr
Hof 122)
Hoffart, Hoffarth (pride,
arrogance) 115
Hoffart, Hoffwart (keeper of
the court) 109
Hoffbauer (peasant working for
court) 92, 91
Hoffberg, Hoffberger,
Hoffenberg (court mountain
92, 68, fr Hofberg 122)
Hoffecker, see Hofacker
Hoffeiser (farm houses) 92, 65,
151
Hoffeld (court field or high
field) 92, 84, 122
Hoffer, Hoffert, Hofferth,
Hoffhers (manager of a
cloister farm 92, fr Hofe
122)
Hoffheintz, Hoffheins (hired
hand) 95
Hoffherr (gentleman of the
court)
Hoffman, Hofmann, Hoffmanns
(courtier, manager of a
cloister farm) 92
Hoffmantel (court cloak) 112

Hoffmaster, see Hofmeister
Hoffmeyer (court farmer,
estate manager) 92, 93
Hoffnagel, see Huffnagel
Hoffner, see Hofer
Hoffstadel (farm stable, court
stable)
Hoffstatt, Hoffstaetter,
Hoffstaedler (fr Hoffstadt
122 (court city)
Hofius, Hoffius (latinized
Hoff) 141
Hoflich, see Hoeflich
Hofmann, see Hoffmann
Hofmeister (manger of
cloister)
Hofmiester, see Hofmeister
151
Hofnagel, see Hufnagel
Hofnar (jester, court fool) 96
Hofner, see Hoffner
Hofstadter, Hofstetter (fr
Hofstadt 122, farmstead)
92
Hofweil, Hofwyl (fr
Hofweiler, farm belonging
to court) 92, 127
Hogedorn, see Hagedorn
Hohemeyer (farmer on the
hights) 93
Hohenberger (high
mountain) 68, 122
Hohenbrink (high hill) 74
Hohenholtz (high forest) 72,
122
Hohenloh (high forest) 72,
122
Hohenschilt, see Hochschild
Hohenstein (high crag) 73,
122
Hohenthal (high valley) 76
Hohl, Hohler, Hohlmann (fr
Hohl 122, hollow), see
Hollmann
Hohlbein, see Holbein
Hohlsteiner (fr Holstein) 121
Hohlweg (sunken way) 65

Hohman, Hohmann (tall man, prominent man), see Hofmann
Hohmeyer, see Hoffmeyer
Hohn, Hohne (contempt)
Hohn (heights) 122
Hohnholz (high forest) 72
Hohr (place name 122), see Haar
Hohemeyer (farmer on the hights) 93
Hoit, see Heid 151
Holand, Holland, Hollander (Holander) 121
Holbach, Holback (swamp brook) 80, 77, 122, see also Hollebach
Holbein (bow-legged) 114
Holbrunner (elder tree spring) 89, 79
Hold, Holdt, Holt, Holder (loyal, beholden, dear) 48
Holderbaum (elder tree) 89
Holdermann, see Hollmann
Holdorf (elder village) 89, 123, 122
Holemann, see Hollmann
Holfeld, Holfelder (swamp field) 80, 84
Holl, Holle (elder tree) 89, 122
Holland, Hollandt, Hollander, see Holand
Hollebach, Hollenbach (swamp tree brook) 80, 77, 122
Hollenbaugh, see Hollenbeck 151
Hollenbeck (swamp brook) 80, 77, 122
Hollenschade (elder shade) 89
Hollenschein (elder sheen) 89
Hollenstein (elder mountain) 89, 68
Holler, see Haller
Hollerbach (elder brook) 89, 77
Hollinger (fr Hollingen 122, swamp dweller 80)
Hollman, Hollemann, Holloman, Hollomann

(swamp dweller 80, dweller among the elders 89)
Hollstein 122, see Holstein
Holm (cross-beam)
Holm (island) 122
Holmann, see Hollman
Holschuh, see Holtzschuh
Holst, Holste (forest dweller, fr Holstein) 72, 121
Holstein, Holsteiner, Hollstein, Holsten (fr Holstein) 121
Holster, see Holtzer, Holtser 151
Holston, see Holstein 151
Holt (forest) 72, 122
Holt, Holter, see Hold
Holthaus, Holthausen, Holthus, Holthusen (forest house) 72, 65, 122
Holthoff (forest farm) 72, 92
Holtkamp (forest field) 72, 84, 122
Holtman, Holtmann (woodman) 72
Holtmeyer (proprietor of the Holthoff) 72, 93, 94
Holtscher (wood dealer) 105
Holtschulte (forest magistrate) 109
Holtspan (wood chip, woodcutter) 95
Holtstein, see Holstein
Holt-Stone, see Holtstein 151
Holtz 122, Holts, Holtze, Holtzer (wood, wood dealer) 105
Holtzapfel, Holtzappel (fr Holtzappel 122, crabapple 89)
Holtzbender (barrel stave maker) 96
Holtzendorf (forest village) 72, 123, 122
Holtzer, Holtser, Holtzner (woodman) 72

Holtzhauer, Holtzhacker (wood cutter, woodpecker) 95, 115
Holtzhauser (house in forest) 72, 65, 122
Holtzinger (fr Holtzing 122, belonging to the forest) 72, 59
Holtzmann (woodman) 72, 95
Holtzschuh, Holtz-shoe (wooden shoe) 106
Holtzwarth (forest keeper) 72
Holtzworth (wooded river island) 72
Holweg, Holweck, see Hohlweg
Holz ..., see Holtz ....
Holzapfel, see Holtzapfel
Holzbauer (forest farmer) 72, 91
Holzberg, Holzberger (fr Holzberg 122, forest mountain) 72, 68
Holzborn (forest spring) 72, 79
Holzer, see Holtzer
Holzermann, see Holtzmann
Holzgang (fetching wood)
Holzhammer (wooden hammer) 106
Holzhausen 122, Holzhauser, see Holtzhauser
Holzheid (wooded heath) 72, 81
Holzknecht (lumberman) 95
Holzli (little forest) 72
Holzman, Holzmann, see Holtzmann
Holzmueller (sawmiller) 105
Holzschmidt (forest smith) 72, 96
Holzschneider (sawyer) 95
Holzschuh, Holzschu, see Holtzschuh
Holzworth, see Holtzworth
Homan, Homann, Homanns, see Hohmann
Homberg, Homberger (fr Homberg) 122
Homburg (fr Homburg) 122
Homeister, see Hoffmeister
Homeyer, Homeier, see Hoffmeyer

Hommel (bumble bee, restless person) 115
Homrighausen (town in Wittgenstein) 122
Honecke, see Hunecker
Honeyman, see Honig 151
Honig, Honigs, Hoenig, Honik, Hoenik (honey, beekeeper) 95
Honikberg (honey mountain) 68
Honnold, see Hunold
Honstein, see Hohenstein
Hooch, see Hoch
Hoofman, see Hoffmann 151
Hoofnagel, Hoofenagel, see Hufnagel 151
Hoohheim, see Hochheim
Hoop, Hoope, Hoopen, see Hoff, Hauf
Hoopengardner, see Hopfengaertner
Hooper, see Huber 151
Hoover, see Huber 151
Hopack, Hoppacher (hops brook)
Hopf, Hopfe (hops) 105
Hopfensack (hops sack)
Hopfgaertner (hop grower) 98
Hopfgarten, Hopfengaertner (hops garden) 98, 122
Hoppenfeld (hops field) 84
Hoppenstein (hops mountain) 73
Hoppler, Hoppner, Hoppmann (hops dealer) 105
Hora (Slavic: forest)
Horath (place name) 122
Horbach, Herbach (swamp creek) 80, 77, 122
Horberg (swamp mountain, wooded mountain) 80, 68
Hord, Horde (treasure)
Horein (high path)
Horenkamp (swamp field) 80, 84

Horenstein (swamp mountain
80, 73, see also Hornstein
Horich, Horichs, see Hoerger
Horlacher (fr Horlach 122,
swamp pond) 80
Horlander (swamp land) 81
Horn, Hoerner (fr Horn 122,
horn, mountain peak,
promontory 68, wedge of
field projecting into forest
84)
Hornbach, Hornbacher,
Hornback, Hornbeck,
Hornbecker (fr Hornbach
122, brook near peak,
swamp brook) 80, 68, 77
Hornberg, Horenberg,
Hornberger (fr Hornberg
122, peaked mountain 68,
68)
Horner, Hoerner, Hornemann
(horn blower 96, dweller
near mountain peak 68, at
end of field 84)
Hornig, Horniger, Horning
(probably fr Slavic *hora*,
mountain)
Hornle (little horn) 68
Hornsperger (peak mountain)
68, 68
Hornstein (peak mountain) 68,
73, 122
Hornung (frost, February,
bastard)
Horst (hurst) 72, 122
Horstmann (dweller in a hurst)
72, 94
Horstmeyer (farmer at a hurst)
72, 93
Horter, Hortmann, Hortel
(treasure keeper)
Hospelhorn, see Haspelhorn
Hoss, Hosse, Hossen, see Hess,
Has
Hossbeck (Hessian brook) 121,
77
Hosselrode (hazel clearing) 89,
126

Hossler, see Hassler
Hostetter, Hostetler, see
Hoffstetter
Hoth, Hotter, Hotler,
Hottmann (milliner, hat
maker) 96
Hotop, Hotopf (Hat off!) 116
Hottenbach, Hottenbacher
(swamp brook) 80, 77, 122
Hottenstein (swamp
mountain) 80, 73
Hotzinger (fr Hottzingen)
122
Houch, see Hauch 151
Houer, see Hauer 151
Houf, Houff, see Hauf 151
Hough, see Hauch 151
Houpt, see Haupt 151
House, see Haus, Hauss 151
Householder, see Haushalter
151
Houseknecht (domestic
servant) 151
Houseman, see Hausmann
151
Housen, see Hausen 151
Houser, see Hauser 151
Housewart, see Hauswart
151
Housewird, see Hauswirth
151
Housman, see Hausmann
151
Houtman, see Hauptmann
151
Houts, see Haut 151
Howarth, see Heuwarth
Howse, Howser, Howze,
Howzer, see Haus 151
Hoyden, see Heid
Hoyer (guard, watchman)
Hoylmann, see Heilmann
Hub, Hube, Huben (fr Hub
122, hide of land) 91
Hubbach, Hubacher (farm
brook) 91, 77
Hubbe < Hubert
Hubbel, Hubel (hill) 72

Huber, Hubers, Huberd,
Hueber (cultivator of one
hide of land) 91
Hubert, Huberts < St.
Hubertus (mind + bright) 47,
131
Hubmeier, see Huber
Hubner, see Huber
Hubsch, Hubscher, Hubschman
(courtly) 115
Hubschmidt (smith owning one
hide of land) 91, 95
Huch < Hugo
Hucht (thicket) 72
Huck, Huckel, Hucker (marsh
dweller) 80
Huckestein (marsh mountain)
81, 73
Hudepohl (hut pond) 81
Hudt, see Hut
Huebel, Huebler (hill) 67
Huebenthal (Hueben Valley 76,
Hueben 122, prehistoric
name of brook) 83
Hueber, Huebner, see Huber
Huebscher, Huebschert
(courtly, handsome) 115
Huebschmann (courtier)
Huegel (hill) 67, 122, see Hugo
Huegelmeier (hill farmer) 67,
93
Huelle (fr Huellen 122, swamp)
80
Huelsmann (swamp dweller) 80
Huelsmann (dweller among the
hollies) 89
Huemmelmann, see
Himmelmann
Huene (giant)
Huenecke (descendant of the
giants)
Huenemeyer (farmer near a
cairn) 93
Huepner, see Huber
Huerde (fence gate)
Huesmann, see Hausmann
Huessler, see Heussler
Hueter, Huether (keeper,
guardian)

Huette, Huettner (hut,
workplace)
Huettig (fr Huttingen) 122
Huff (hoof, probably short
for Huffschmidt)
Huff, see Hoff
Huffaker (small farm) 84
Huffer, Hufferet (blacksmith)
96
Huffman, Huffmann, see
Huber, Hoffmann
Huffschmidt, Huffschmit
(blacksmith) 96
Hufnagel, Hufnail (horseshoe
nail, blacksmith) 96
Hufschmidt, see Huffschmidt
Hug, Hugi < Hugo
Hugel, Hugele, Hugeles, see
Huegel
Hugelsheim (hill hamlet) 67,
123
Hugo (thought, mind)
Huhn, Huhner (chicken,
poultry dealer) 91, 105
Huhnebein (chicken leg,
chicken bone) 114
Hullstein, see Holstein
Huls, Hulls, Hulst (marsh,
holly) 89, 80
Hulsemann, Hulsmann
(marsh dweller, dweller in
the holly) 80, 89
Hulsheyser (swamp houses,
holly houses) 80, 89, 65
Hulshoff (marsh farm, holly
farm) 80, 89, 92
Hults, Hultz, see Holtz
Humbert (bear cub + bright)
48, 47
Humboldt (bear cub + loyal)
48, 48
Humburg (bear cub + castle)
48, 73
Hummel (bumble-bee,
restless person) 115, 122
Hummer (lobster)
Humpe < Humbert
Humperding < Humbert

Ihrlick, see Ehrlich
Ikeler, see Eichler 151
Ikels, see Eichels, Eichholtz
  151
Iler, see Eiler 151
Ilg, Ilgen (St. Aegidius or St.
  Kilian) 131, 122
Ilgenfritz (Fritz fr Ilgen)
Ilger (fr Ilgen)
Illich, Illig, see Ilg
Ilmen (dweller by the Ilm) 79,
  83
Iln (name of river) 83
Ilnau (meadow along the Iln)
  79, 84
Ilrich, see Ulrich
Imbach (in the brook) 70, 77,
  122
Imboden (in the valley) 70, 96
Imbs (beeswarm) 91, 95, 122
Imbsweiller (beeswarm village)
  123
Im Busch (in the brush) 70,
  72, 122
Imdahl (in the valley) 70, 76,
  122
Imgarten (in the garden) 70,
  84
Imhof, Imhoff (in the farmyard)
  70, 92
Imke < Irmin (powerful)
Immel < Emmerich
Immenhauser (fr Immenhausen
  122, bee house)
Immer (river name) 83
Immergut (always good) 115
Imthurn (in the tower, *thurn*,
  fr Latin *turris*) 70
Imwald, Imwold (in the forest)
  70, 71
Indergand (in the rubble field)
  84
Indermuhle (in the mill) 70,
  103
Inderwiess (in the meadow) 70,
  84
Indorf (in the village) 70, 123,
  122
Ingber (spice dealer) 105

Ingel, Ingels (swamp) 80, see
  Engel, Engels
Ingelhof (swamp farm) 80,
  92, see Engelhoff
Ingelmann, see Engelmann
Inhalter (proprietor)
Inhoff (in the court yard) 70,
  92
Insel 122, Insul (island, fr
  Latin *insula*)
Inselmann (island man)
Interlaken (between the
  lakes, place in
  Switzerland, fr Latin
  interlacus) 122
Irlbacher (swamp brook) 80,
  77, see Erlebach
Isaac, Isaacs (OT name) 135
Isberg, see Eisberg 151
Ischler (fr Ischel 122, or
  dweller by the Ische) 83
Ise, see Eise 151
Isemann, see Eisemann 151
Isenberg, Isenberger, see
  Eisenberg, Eisenberger
  151
Isengard, see Eisengard 151
Isenhard, see Eisenhard 151
Isenhour, see Eisenhauer
  151
Isenhut (helmet) 108
Isenminger, see Eisenmenger
  151
Isenring, see Eisenring 151
Isenschmidt, see
  Eisenschmid 151
Isenstadt, see Eisenstadt 151
Iser, see Eiser
Iser (dweller near the Iser)
  83
Isermann, see Eisermann
  151
Isler, see Eisler 151
Isner, see Eisner 151
Israel (OT name) 135
Issel, Isselmann (fr Issel)
  122
Ittenbach (place name) 122
Itzig < Isaac

Iunge, see Junge

J

Jaac, Jaaks, Jack, Jacke <
  Jacob
Jackel, see Jaeck
Jacker, Jackert (jacket maker)
  96
Jackle, see Jaeck 151
Jacob, Jacobs, Jacobes, Jacobus
  (OT name) 135
Jacobi, Jacoby (son of Jacob)
  142
Jacobsen, Jacobson, Jacobsohn
  (son of Jacob) 59
Jaeck, Jaecks, Jaeckel, Jaekel,
  Jaeckle, Jaeckli, Jaecklein,
  Jaegli (little Jacob)
Jaegemeyer (farmer with
  hunting rights) 91, 93
Jaeger, Jaegger, Jaegerl,
  Jaegermann (hunter) 91
Jaegerschmidt (smith with
  hunting rights) 91, 96
Jaekel, see Jaek
Jaeschke < Johannes 134
Jag (hunt, hunter) 91
Jager, Jagerman, Jagler,
  Jagmann, see Jaeger
Jahn, Jahns < Johann 134
Jahnke (little John) 134
Jahr, Jahren (year)
Jahrhaus < Gareis (wrought
  iron, smith) 96
Jakob, see Jacob
Jakobi (son of Jakob) 142
Jan, Jans < Johann 134
Jandorf (John's village) 134,
  123
Janing, Janning < Johann 134
Jansen, Janssen, Janssens,
  Janson (son of John) 59, 134
Jantz, Jantzen, Janz (son of
  John) 59, 134
Jasper < Caspar
Jauch (liquid manure)

Jauss < Josef, Jost
Jeckel, see Jaeckel
Jedermann (Everyman, in
  miracle plays) 111
Jegelhardt, see Igelhard
Jeger, see Jaeger
Jehle < Ulrich 53
Jehrling (yearling, annual)
Jelling (Slavic: stag, elk)
Jenner (January) 143
Jenning, Jennings < Johann
  134
Jensch, Jentzsch, Jentz <
  Johann 134
Jensel, Jensen < Johann,
  see also Gensel 134
Jentsch < Johann 134
Jergen, see Juergen
Jeschke < Johannes 134
Jeter, Jetter (weeder,
  gatherer) 95
Jingling, see Juengling
Jmhof, see Imhof
Joachim, Jochem, Johen (OT
  name) 135
Job, see Hiob 151
Jobst < Hiob (Job) 135
Joch (yoke, mountain pass)
Joder (Theodor) 131
Joel (OT name) 135
Joellenbeck (dirty brook) 77,
  122
Joerg, Joerge, Joerger,
  Joergens, Joerk, Joerke
  (George) 134
Johan, Johann, Johannes
  (John) 131
Johanknecht (John servant)
Johansen, Johanssen (son
  of John) 59
John < Johann 134
Johnsen, Johnson (son of
  Johan) 59
Johst, see Jost
Jonas (OT Jonah) 135
Jonck, see Jung
Joncker, see Junker
Jong, see Jung

Jonger, see Junger
Jontz < Johannes 134
Joost, see Jost
Jordan (OT name) 135, 122
Jorge, Jorgen, Jorgens, see
  Joerg
Joseph, Josef (NT name) 131
Jost (St. Jodocus) 131
Jucker (swamp dweller) 80, see
  Junker
Jud, Jude, Judd, Judmann
  (Jew) 121
Judenburg (Jew castle) 73
Juengling (youth)
Juengst (youngest) 113
Juergen, Juergens < Georg
Juergensen, son of Juergen 59
Juker, see Junker
Julig (fr Juelich) 121
Julius (Latin name) 141
July (July) 143
Juncker (young lord, squire)
Jung, Junge (young) 113
Jungandreas (young Andrew)
  113
Jungblud, Jungblut (young
  blossom)
Junge, Junges (youth)
Junger, Jungers, Jungert
  (youth, disciple)
Jungfermann (convent servant)
  138
Junghahn, Junghane (young
  rooster) 91
Junghans (John the younger)
  113
Junghaus (young house) 65
Junginger (young man) 113
Jungk, see Jung
Jungling, see Juengling 113
Jungman, Jungmann (young
  man) 113
Jungst (youngest) 113
Junk, see Jung
Junker, Junkermann, see
  Juncker
Jupp < Joseph 131
Jurgen, Jurgens, Juergensen,
  see Juergen

Juss, Jusse < Justus,
  Jodocus
Just, Justus (Latin name,
  "just"), see also Jost

K

Kaal, see Kahl
Kaatz, see Katz
Kabel (cable, lot for drawing,
  river name) 83, 122), see
  also Gabel
Kachel, Kachele (tile, tile
  maker) 106
Kachler, Kachner (tile
  maker, potter) 96
Kade (swamp) 122
Kaefer, Kafer (beetle,
  perseverant person) 115
Kaeferstein (beetle
  mountain) 73
Kaegel, see Kegel
Kaehle, Kaehler (see Kehle,
  Kehler, Koehler)
Kaelber, see Kalb
Kaemerlin, Kaemerling
  (court servant)
Kaemmel (occupant of house
  zum Kembel, "to the
  Camel") 149
Kaemmerer (chamberlain,
  treasurer) 109
Kaes, Kaess, Kaese (cheese)
  105, 106
Kaesemeyer (cheese farmer)
  93
Kaessler, see Kessler
Kaestner (chest maker) 98
Kaestner (manager of the
  granary)
Kaeufer (purchaser, see also
  Kofler)
Kafer, see Kaefer
Kafka (Czech: jackdaw) 115
Kagle, see Kegel 151
Kahl, Kahle, Kahler, Kahlert
  (bald, fr Latin *calvus*)

Kahlbach (muddy brook) 80,
77, see Kaltenbach
Kahlbaugh, see Kahlbach 151
Kahlberg (bald mountain) 122
Kahlenberg (bald mountain) 68,
122
Kahler, see Kohler
Kahm, see Kamm
Kahn, Kahns (rowboat)
Kahn, see Cohn
Kahnbach (rowboat brook) 77
Kail, Kailer, see Keil, Keiler
Kaiser, Kaisser (emperor, fr
Latin *caesar*)
Kalb, Kalbe (calf) 91
Kalbaugh, see Kahlbach 151
Kalberer (calf raiser or dealer)
91, 105
Kalbfleish (calf meat, veal,
butcher) 96
Kalbfuss (calf foot, butcher) 96
Kalbskopf (calf's head) 114, 149
Kalcher (chalk maker, fr Latin
calcarius) 96
Kalckbrenner, see Kalkbrenner
Kaldenbach, see Kaltbach
Kaler, see Kahler
Kalichmann (chalice maker, fr
Latin *calix*) 96
Kalkbrenner (lime burner) 96
Kalkbrunn (chalk spring) 79
Kalker, Kalkmann (lime
maker) 96
Kall, Kaller, Kallert, Kallner,
Kallman (dweller by a
stream) 77
Kallemeyer, Kallmeyer,
Kallmyer (farmer on a
stream) 77, 93
Kallenbach 122, see Kaltenbach
Kallenberg, Kallenberger,
Kallenstein (stream
mountain) 68, 73, 122
Kalman, see Kallmann
Kalmbach, Kalmbeck, see
Kaltenbach
Kalteisen (cold iron, smith) 96,
122

Kaltenbach, Kaltbacher,
Kaltenbacher,
Kaltenbacker, Kalterbach
(cold brook) 77, 122
Kaltenbaugh, see Kaltenbach
151
Kaltenborn (cold spring) 79,
122
Kalthof (cold farm) 92, 122
Kaltreider, Kaltrider (cold
clearing) 126
Kaltschmidt (coppersmith,
kettle smith) 96
Kaltwasser (cold water)
Kalwe (bald, fr Latin *calvus*)
112
Kamber (comb maker) 96
Kamerer, see Kammerer
Kamm (ridge of mountain,
comb, combmaker) 106,
122
Kamman (comb maker) 96
Kammer (chamber, fr Latin
camera) 122
Kammeraad (comrad)
Kammerdiener (valet)
Kammerer, Kammerle, see
Kaemmerer
Kammermann (chamberlain,
administrative official) 109
Kammermann (dweller on a
ridge)
Kamner (comb maker) 96
Kamp, Kampe, Kamps (field,
fr Latin *campus*) 84, 122
Kampenmueller,
Kampfmueller (miller with
a cogwheel) 84, 103
Kamper, Kampmann
(champion, fr Latin
campus)
Kampf, Kampfer (struggel,
struggler, fr Latin,
campus)
Kamphaus (field house) 84,
65, 122
Kampmayer, Kampmeyer
(field farmer) 84, 93

Kandel (pitcher) 106, 122
Kandlbinder (pitcher maker) 96
Kangiesser, see Kannengiesser
Kann, Kanne (can, pitcher, fr
Latin *canna*) 106
Kannenberg (pitcher mountain)
68, 122
Kannengiesser, Kannengieser,
Kannengieszer (pewterer) 96
Kant, see Gand
Kantor, see Cantor
Kantzler (chancelor, fr Latin
cancellarius) 109
Kapfer (gazer)
Kapfer (dweller at a mountain
peak)
Kaplan, Kaplon (chaplain) 110
Kapp, Kappe, Kapps,
Kappenmann (cowl maker,
Capuchin monk) 96, 106,
110
Kappel (chapel, place in
Switzerland) 122
Kappeler, Kappelmann (cap
maker) 96
Kappler (monk, occupant of a
chapel) 110
Kappus (cabbage farmer, fr
Latin *caput*)
Kaps, see Kappus
Karch, Karcher, Karchner
(carter, fr Latin *carruca*, see
also Karg)
Karg, Karger (clever, stingy)
115
Karl, Karle (man, Charles,
cloister servant) 139
Karlbach (Charles' brook) 77
Karli (son of Karl) 142
Karmann (basket maker) 96
Karp < St. Polykarpus 131
Karp (carp) 115
Karsch (lively, merry) 115
Karseboom, see Kirschbaum
Karsner, see Kirschner
Karst, Karsten, Karstner,
Karstmann (mattock)
Karst (bare alpine land)
Karst (Christian) 131

Kas, Kase, Kass, see Kaes,
Kaese, Kaess
Kaschenbach (cherry brook)
89, 77
Kasekamp (cheese field) 84
Kasemann (cheese dealer)
105
Kasemeyer (folk-etymology fr
Casimir), see Kaesemeyer
93
Kasmann, see Kasemann,
Gassmann
Kaspar, see Caspar
Kassebaum (chestnut tree)
89
Kassel, Kassler (fr Kassel)
121, 122
Kastendiek, Kastendyk
(chestnut dike) 89, 81
Kastner, see Kaestner
Kastor (Latin *castor*, beaver,
Bieber) 141, 122
Kat, Katt, Katte, Kattner,
Kathmann (cotter)
Katterfeld (fenced field) 84
Kattermann, see Gattermann
Katz, Katzen (cat)
Katz (fr Hebrew *Kahanzedek*
priest)
Katzenbach, Katzenbacher
(swamp brook) 80, 77, 122
Katzenberg, Katzenberger
(cat mountain) 68, 122
Katzenelnbogen (cat's elbow,
probably folketymolgy fr
Celtic) 3, 4, 122
Katzenmayer, Katzenmeyer,
Katzmeier (proprietor of
the Katzenhof, cat farm)
93
Katzenstein, Katzenstine 151
(cat mountain) 73, 122
Kaub 122, Kaubes
(bullrushes) 81
Kauder, Kauders (fr Kur in
Switzerland) 122
Kauf, Kauff, Kauffer
(purchase, merchant, fr
Latin *caupo*) 105

Kaufler, Kauffler (inhabitant of a *Kofel*) 67
Kaufmann, Kauffman (merchant) 105
Kaulbach (swamp brook) 80, 77, 122
Kaulfuss (clubfoot) 114
Kaup, Kaupp (merchant) 105
Kautz (screech owl) 115, 122
Kayler, see Kehler, Koehler 151
Kayser, see Kaiser
Kazmier, see Kaesemeyer 151
Keagle, see Kegel 151
Keane, see Kuehn 151
Keasel, Keasler, see Kiesel, Kiessler 151
Keaver, see Geber 151
Kebhart, see Gebhard 151
Keck (lively) 115
Keebler, see Kuebler 151
Keefer, see Kieffer 151
Keefover, Kefauver, see Kiefhofer
Keehn, Keehner, see Kuehn, Kuehner 151
Keeler, see Kuehler 151
Keen, Keene, Keener, see Kuehn, Kuehne, Kuehner 151
Keenaple < Kienappel (pine cone) 151
Kees, Keesen < Cornelius
Keesler, see Kiessler 151
Kegel, Kegelmann (illegitimate child) 119
Kehl, Kehle (throat, < Wolfskehl) 114
Kehl (narrow gorge)
Kehler (fr Kehl, swamp) 122, see also Koehler
Kehr, Kehrs, Kehrer, Kehrmann (dweller on the Kere) 83, 122
Kehs, see Kaes
Keibler, see Kuebler 151
Keichenmeister, see Kuechenmeister 151

Keicher (gasper, wheezer) 114
Keidel (course or misshapen person) 115
Keifer, see Kieffer 151
Keil (wedge, woodchopper) 95
Keiler (wild boar)
Keilhauer (boar tusk)
Keilhauer (woodcutter) 95
Keilholtz (wedge for splitting wood, wood chopper) 95
Keim (germ, sprout, < Joachim)
Keiper, Keipert (fish netter)
Keiser, Keisser, see Kaiser
Keisersmith (imperial smith) 110, 151
Keisler, see Kessler
Keiss, see Kies 151
Kelbaugh (swamp brook) 80, 77, 151
Kelberman (calf dealer) 91, 105
Kelch, Kelchner (chalice, calice maker, fr Latin *calix*) 96
Kell, Kelle (ladle, trowel, mason) 106, 122
Kelle (swamp) 80
Kellenberger (fr Kellenberg, swamp mountain), 80, 68, 122
Keller, Kellers, Kellner (cellar, cellar master, fr Latin *cellenarius*) 102, 122
Kellerhouse (cellar house) 151
Kellermann, Kellermeyer (butler, keeper of the cellar) 102
Kellner, Kelner, see Keller
Kelly, see Kell 151
Kelnoffer (swamp farmer) 80, 92
Kelsch, Koelsch (from Cologne) 122

Kelter, Keltner (winepress,
vintner, fr Latin *calcatura*)
96
Kem, Kemler, Kemmler,
Kemmer, Kemner,
Kemmacher (comb maker)
96, 106
Kemerer, see Kaemmerer
Kemmel (resident on a ridge)
Kemp, Kempe, Kempel, Kempf,
Kempfer, Kemper, Kemperle,
Kemphfer, Kemperly
(champion) 84
Kempt, Kempter (fr Kempten)
122
Kendel, Kendal (fr Kenel 122)
Kenner (connoisseur) 115
Kenpf, see Kemp
Kensler < Kentzler (chancelor)
151
Kentner (Slavic: stand for beer
and wine barrels)
Kentner (fr Kenten) 122
Kentzel (raised ground), see
Kuentzel 151
Kephart, see Gebhard 151
Keplinger, see Kepplinger
Keppel, Kepple, Keppler,
Kepler, Kepner (cap maker,
man fr Kappel) 96, 106, 122
Keppelhoff (chapel court) 156
Kepplinger (fr Kepplingen)
Kerbe (notch, score)
Kerber (basket maker) 96
Kerch ..., Kerck, see Kirch ...
Kerchner, see Kirchner
Kerg, Kerge, Kerger, see Karg
Kerhart, see Gerhard 151
Kerker (prison, fr Latin *carcer*)
Kerkhof 122, see Kirchhoff
Kerkhuis (church house)
Kerkner, see Kirchner
Kerl (fellow)
Kermes, Kermisch (kermess,
church festival) 143
Kern (kernel)
Kern (handmill) 122
Kernberg, Kernberger (mill
mountain) 68, 122

Kernebeck (swamp stream)
80, 77
Kernenbeck (miller of coarse
grain) 103
Kerner (carter), also see
Koerner
Kersch 122, Kerschner,
Kerschman, see Kirsch,
Kirschner, Kirschman
Kerschbaum (cherry tree) 89,
122
Kerschensteiner (cherry
stone) 89, 73
Kerschner, see Kuerschner
Kerse, Kerser (Christian)
140
Kershbaum, see Kirschbaum
151
Kerst, Kersten (Christian)
139, see also Gerst
Kerzner (candle maker) 96
Kesbauer, Kesemeyer
(swamp farmer) 80, 91
Kese, see Kaese
Keslar, Kesler, see Kessler
Kessel, Kessell, Kessels
(kettle, kettle maker or
burnisher, fr Latin
cattilus) 101
Kesselring (kettle hook, cook)
106
Kessler (kettle maker,
tinker) 96
Kestenbaum (chestnut tree)
89
Kestenberg (chestnut
mountain) 89, 68
Kestenholtz (chestnut wood,
cabinet maker) 89
Kester, Kesster, Kestner,
Kestler, see Kaester
Ketchindaner, see
Getzendanner 151
Ketelhut (kettle lid)
Kettelberger (kettle
mountain) 68
Kettenring (chain mail) 108

Ketter, Ketterer, Kettler,
Kettner (chain maker, fr
Latin *catena*) 96
Ketzer (heretic, fr Latin
Cathari)
Keuler (mallet maker) 96
Keusch (pure, virgin) 115
Keyl, see Keil
Keyser, Keysers, see Kaiser
Kibler, Kiebler, see Kuebler
151
Kiefer, Kiefere, Kieffer,
Kiefner, Kieffner, Kiefert
(cooper, fr Latin *cuparius*)
96, 100
Kiefhofer (proprietor of the
Kiefhof, pine farm) 89, 92
Kieger, see Geiger 151
Kiehl, Kuehl (cool)
Kiehn, Kiehner, see Kuehn
Kiehnle, Kienke (little pine) 89
Kienast (pine branch) 89
Kienholdt (pine forest) 89, 72
Kienz, Kientz, see Kuentz 151
Kies (pebbles)
Kiesel, Kiessel, Kiesling,
Kiessling (pebbles)
Kieselhorst (pebble hurst) 72,
122
Kieser, Kiersler (beverage
taster, weight tester) 109
Kiesewetter ("Check the
weather!") 116
Kiesselbach (pebble brook) 77,
122
Kiessling (dweller in the
pebbles or gravel) 122
Kifer, Kiffer, see Kieffer 151
Kihl, see Kuehl 151
Kihn, see Kuehn 151
Kilberg, see Kilchberg 151
Kilchberg (church mountain)
68, 122
Kilchenstein (church mountain)
73
Kilcher (chief cleric in a
church) 110
Kile, Kiler, see Keil, Keiler 151

Kilgen, Kilian, Killian (St.
Kilian, Irish monk) 131
Kimmel, Kimmel, Kimmell,
Kimmelman, see Kuemmel
Kimmerle, see Kuemmerle
Kimpel, see Guempel 151
Kince, see Kuentz 151
Kind, Kindt, Kindl, Kindle,
Kinder (child)
Kindermann (schoolmaster)
Kindsvater, Kindervater
(baptismal sponsor)
Kingel, Kinkel, Kinkler
Kinn (chin) 114
Kinsberger, see Guenzberg
151
Kinsbrunner (Guenther's
well) 79, 151
Kinsel, see Kuenzel 151
Kinnss, see Kuentz 151
Kinstler, see Kuenstler 151
Kintz, Kintzel, Kintzer, see
Kuentz, Kuentzel,
Kuentzler 151
Kinzinger (fr Kinzingen 122)
Kipp, Kippe, Kipper, Kippers
(dweller on the Kippe) 83
Kippenberg (marsh
mountain) 80, 68
Kippenbrock (brake on the
Kippe) 83, 80
Kirbach, see Kirchbach
Kirberger, see Kirchberg
Kirch (church, dweller near
the church)
Kirchbach (church brook) 77,
122
Kirchberg, Kirchberger
(church mountain) 68, 122
Kirchenbauer (church
builder, peasant on glebe
land) 91
Kircher, see Kirchner
Kirchgaessner, Kirchgesser,
Kirchgessner (dweller on
church alley) 65
Kirchhausen (church houses)
65, 122

Kirchhof, Kirchhoff, Kirkhof,
Kirchhoffer (church yard) 8,
92, 122
Kirchman (sexton) 110
Kirchmeier (glebe farmer) 93
Kirchner (employee of church,
dweller near church) 71, 110
Kirchoff, see Kirchhoff
Kirck, Kircke, Kirckner,
Kirkner, see Kirch, Kirche,
Kirchner
Kirk..., see Kirch
Kirn, Kirner (swamp) 80, see
Kern, Kerner, Koerner
Kirsch (cherry, fr Latin *ceresia*)
89
Kirschbaum, Kirschenbaum
(cherry tree) 89, 122
Kirschenhofer (proprietor of the
Kirschhof, cherry farm) 89,
92
Kirschensteiner (cherry stone)
89, 73
Kirscher, Kirschner, see
Kuerschner
Kirschermann, Kirschenmann,
Kirschman (cherry grower or
dealer) 89, 105
Kirschner, see Kuerschner
Kirschstein (cherry stone) 89,
73
Kirsh ..., see Kirsch ...
Kirsh, Kirshman, Kirsher, etc.,
see Kirsch etc.
Kirst, Kirtsen (Christian) 131
Kirts, Kirtz, see Kuertz 151
Kiselburgh (gravel castle) 73,
151
Kiser, see Kaiser 151
Kisner, Kissner, see Kistner
151
Kissinger (fr Kissing or
Kissingen, swamp area) 80,
122
Kister, see Kuester
Kister, Kistner, Kistler,
Kistenmacher (chest maker,
fr Latin *cista*) 96

Kitsintander, see
Getzendanner 151
Kittel, Kittle (smock, baker,
miller, etc.) 112, 106
Kittelmann, Kittleman
(smock wearer, smock
maker) 112, 96, 151
Kittner, Kittler (monk,
smock wearer, smock
maker) 112, 96
Kitz, Kitzer, Kitzmann (kid,
goatherd) 91, 95
Kitzing, Kitzinger (fr
Kitzing) 122
Kitzmiller (kid miller) 103
Klaas < Nikolaus
Klaff (gossip)
Klaeger (public prosecutor)
109
Klaffenbach (resounding
brook) 77, 122
Klag, Klage, Klager
(complaint, complainant)
Klamm, Klamman (dweller
in a gorge)
Klang (sound)
Klapf (cliff)
Klapp (shutter, trapdoor)
Klapp, Klapper, Klappert
(gossip)
Klapproth (clearing in the
Hartz Mountains) 126
Klar, Klaar, Klarr, Klahr
(clear)
Klarmann (man of rectitude)
115
Klas, Klaas, Klass, Klassen,
Klaus < Nikolaus
Klatthaar (tousel haired) 112
Klatzkopf (bald head) 114
Klaucke (wise man) 115
Klaue (claw) 114
Klauenberg, Klaunberg (claw
mountain) 68, 122
Klaus, Klauss < Nikolaus
122
Klause, Klausen 122,
Klauser, Klausener,
Klausmann, Klaussner,

Klausler (hermit's cell, hermit, fr Latin *clausum*)
Klausmeyer, Klausmayer, Klausmeier (farmer near hermit's cell)
Klausmier, see Klausmeyer 151
Kleamann, see Klehmann 151
Kleb, Klebe, Klebes, Kleber, Klebert (dweller in a damp place) 80
Kleber, Klebert (plasterer) 96
Klee < Nikolaus 53
Kleebach (clover brook) 77
Kleebauer (clover farmer) 91
Kleeberg (clover mountain) 68, 122
Kleefeld (clover field) 84, 122
Kleefisch (fr Cleves) 121
Klees < Nicklas
Klef (cliff) 122
Kleger, Klegermann, see Klaeger
Klehmann (plasterer) 96
Kleiber (clay plasterer) 96
Kleid, Kleidlein, Kleiderlein (clothing, clothier) 105, 106
Klein, Kleine, Kleiner, Kleines, Kleinert, Kleinle, Kleinlein, Kleinmann, Kleinmeyer (small, little) 113
Kleinbach (small brook) 77
Kleinbaum (small tree) 89
Kleinberg (small mountain) 68, 122
Kleindienst (corvée service)
Kleinfeld, Kleinfield 151, Kleinfeldt, Kleinfelder, Kleinfelter (small field) 84, 122
Kleinhammer (small hammer) 122
Kleinhans (Little John, John the younger)
Kleinhauf (small heap, small troop)
Kleinhaus (fr Kleinhausen 122, small houses) 65
Kleinheinz, see Kleinhans 113

Kleinhenn (small hen)
Kleinjohann (small John, John the younger) 113
Kleinknecht (secondary hired hand) 95
Kleinkopf (small head) 114
Kleinman (small man) 113
Kleinmichel (little Michael, Michael the younger) 113
Kleinpeter (little Peter, Peter the younger) 113
Kleinschmidt, Kleinsmith (locksmith) 96
Kleinschrot (small grain, groats, miller) 103
Kleinsteuber (fine dust)
Kleis, Kleiss < Nikolaus
Kleist, Kleistner (paster)
Klem, Klemm, Klement < St. Clementius 131
Klemann, Kleemann, Klehmann < St. Clementius 131
Klemm, Klemme (penurious) 115
Klemmer (stingy person), see Klempner
Klemmich, see Kleinmichel
Klempner (tinsmith) 96
Klenck, Klenk, Klencker, Klenkel (dweller by a marsh pool) 80
Klepp, Klepper, Kleppner, Kleppert (gossip, calumniator) 115
Klepper (nag, jade; tenant who pays in horses)
Klette (bur)
Kletter (hanger-on) 115
Kliebenstein (Split the stone!, quarryman) 116
Klimper, see Klempner
Klinbach, see Kleinbach 151
Klinck, Klincken (dweller by a marsh pool) 80
Kline, see Klein 151
Klinedienst, see Kleindienst 151

Klinefelter, see Kleinfeld 151
Klinejohn, see Kleinjohann 151
Kling, Klinge, Klinges (deep
   gorge with noisy stream) 122
Klingebuhl, Klingebuehl,
   Klingebiel (gorge hill) 84
Klingehoffer, Klingenhoffer,
   Klingenhofer, Klingelhofer,
   Klingelhoefer, Klingelover
   (proprietor of the Kingehoff,
   gorge farm) 92
Klingel, Klinkel (small bell)
   106
Klingelhofer, see Klingehoffer
Klingelschmidt (bell smith) 96
Klingemann (dweller in a
   gorge)
Klingemeyer, Klingenmeier
   (gorge farmer) 93
Klingenbach (resounding
   stream) 77
Klingenberg (resounding
   mountain) 68, 122
Klingenbuehl (resounding hill)
   67
Klingenhagen (gorge enclosure)
   123, 122
Klingenhofer (fr Klingenhof)
   122, see Klingehoffer
Klingenschmidt, Klingensmith
   (sword smith, cuttler) 96
Klingenstein (gorge mountain)
   73, 122
Klinger, Klingermann,
   Klingmann (swordsmith 96,
   gorge dweller)
Klinghoffer (fr Klinghof) 122,
   see Klingehoffer
Klingler (public crier) 109
Klingmann, Klingmeyer
   (occupant of a gorge) 93
Klink, Klinke (latch, locksmith)
   96
Klinkhamer, Klinkhammer
   (latch hammer, locksmith) 96
Klinsmith, see Kleinschmidt
   151
Klob (plump coarse person)
   114, 115

Klock, Klocke, Klocker, see
   Glock, Glocke, Glocker
Klockmann (wise man) 115
Kloekner, Klocker (bell
   ringer)
Kloepfer, Kloeper, Kloepper
   (knocker)
Kloes, Kloese (dumpling,
   cook) 96
Kloetzel, Kloetzli, see Klott
Kloosterhuis (cloister house)
   65
Klopfenstein (Strike the
   stone!, quarryman) 116
Klopfer (mallet) 106
Klopfinstern ("Beat your
   forehead" in remorse) 116
Klopp (flax swingle) 106, 112
Kloppenstein (stone for
   sharpening scythes, see
   Dengler) 73
Kloppmann (flax swingler)
   95
Klosmann, Klossmann,
   Klossner < Nikolaus
Kloss, Klosse (lump, clump,
   < Nikolaus)
Kloster, Klostermann
   (cloister, monk, fr Latin
   claustrum) 110, 122
Klott, Klotz (block, log,
   clumsy person) 115
Klotzbach (stream full of
   logs) 77
Klouser, see Klause 151
Klueg, Klug, Kluge, Kluger,
   Klugmann (clever) 115
Klung, Klunck, Klunk (tassel
   maker) 96
Knabe, Knapp, Knapp (boy)
Knabschneider (boy's tailor)
   96
Knann, see Gnann
Knapp, Knappe (page, boy,
   miner)
Knauer (course person) 115
Knauf, Knauff (nob, stub)
Knebel (crossbar) 106
Knecht (servant, hired hand)

Knechtel, Knechtle (little
  servant)
Kneemoeller, see Niemoeller
  151
Kneip (knife, shoemaker) 106,
  96
Kneip, Kniepe, Kneiper
  (taverner) 96
Kneiss (gneiss)
Knell, Kneller (noisy person)
  115
Knepper (button maker) 96
Knie (knee) 114
Knieper (users of pincers, such
  as cobblers and leather
  workers) 96
Knieriemen, Knierim 151 (knee
  strap, leather worker) 106
Knipe, Kniper, see Kneip,
  Kneiper 151
Knittel, Knittle (cudgel, crude
  person) 115
Knobel (round elevation) 74,
  122
Knoble, see Knobel 151
Knoblauch, Knobeloch (garlic
  seller) 105, 122
Knochen (bones) 113, 122
Knochenhauer (butcher) 96
Knode, Knodt (knot)
Knoechel, Knochel (knuckle)
  113
Knoedler (dumpling maker) 96
Knoepfler (button maker,
  button maker) 96
Knoll, Knolle (hill, mountain
  top) 67, 122
Knopf, Knopfle, Knopfler,
  Knoepler (button, button
  maker) 106
Knopp 122, see Knapp, Knopf
Knor, Knorr (nob, knot,
  hunchback) 113
Knor (hill) 67
Kobel, Kobler (fr Kobel,
  swamp, little shelter,
  birdcage) 122

Koben (hut, pig pen, pig
  raiser) 106
Kober (basket, back pack,
  fish trap, huckster) 105,
  106
Koblentz, Koblenz (Koblenz,
  a city) 122, 130
Kobler (back pack carrier,
  cotter) 105
Kobold (gremlin)
Koch, Koche (cook, fr Latin
  coquus) 102
Kochenburger (fr
  Kochenburg, castle on the
  Koche) 83, 73
Kochenderfer, see
  Kochendorf 151
Kochendorf, Kochendorfer
  (village on the Kocher) 83,
  123, 122
Kocher 122, Kochert (cook,
  dweller on the Kocher) 93,
  83
Kocher, Kochert, see Koecher
Kocherthal (Kocher valley)
  83, 76, 122
Kochheiser (occupant of a
  cook house) 65
Kochmann (cook) 102
Kock, Kocks, see Koch
Koder, see Koeder
Koeb, Koebel, Koebelin <
  Jacob
Koecher (quiver, quiver
  maker) 96
Koechli (little cook)
Koeder (bait)
Koefler (dweller on a Kofel)
  67
Koefler (trunk maker) 96
Koegel, see Kegel
Koegler (juggler) 96
Koegler (dweller on
  mountain top) 68
Koehl, Koehle, Koehler, see
  Kehl, Kehler

Koehler, Koeller, Koehlert
(collier, charcoal burner) 95, 122
Koehlerschmidt (charcoal
smith) 96
Koehn 122, Koehne,
Koehnemann, see Kuehn,
Kuehne, Kuehnemann
Koehten (fr Coethen, East
German city) 122
Koelbel, Koelbl, Koelble,
Koelber (battle club)
Koell, Koelle, see Kell, Kelle
Koellner, see Kellner
Koenemann, see Kuehnemann
Koenig (king) 41, 109
Koenigsbauer (royal farmer) 91
Koenigsberg, Konigsberg
(Prussian city) 122
Koenigsburg (royal castle) 73
Koenigsfeld (king's field) 84,
122
Koenigsmark (royal boundary)
122
Koepke < Jacob
Koeppel, see Keppel 122
Koerber (basket maker) 96
Koerner (user of handmill) 122
Koerner (granary supervisor)
Koerper, Koerpert (body, fr
Latin *corpus*)
Koerschner, see Kuerschner
Koestel, Koestle, Koestler
(boarder)
Koester, see Kuester
Koestner, see Kestner
Koetter (cotter)
Kofel, Koffel, Kofler, Koffler,
Kofer (projection on slope of
mountain, see Unterkofler)
67
Kofer, see Kofel
Koffer (trunk), fr Latin
cophinus, but often
corruption of *kofler*)
Kofman, Koffman, Koffmann,
see Kaufmann 151
Kogel, Kogler (cowl, monk,
hood maker, fr Latin
cuculla) 106, 122

Kogel, see Kugel
Kohde, see Gode
Kohl, Kohle (cabbage,
cabbage dealer, fr Latin
caulis)
Kohlbauer (cabbage planter)
91
Kohlbecker (swamp brook)
80, 77
Kohlberg, Kohlenberg,
Kohlenstein (coal
mountain) 68, 122
Kohlberg (cabbage mountain)
68, 122
Kohleisen (collier's poker,
collier) 95
Kohler, Kohlerman (collier)
95
Kohlhammer, see Kohlheim
Kohlhas, Kohlhaas <
Nikolaus
Kohlhas (cabbage hare,
nickname for peasant)
Kohlhauer (coal digger) 95
Kohlhaus, see Kohlhas 122
Kohlheim (cabbage hamlet,
coal hamlet) 123
Kohlhof (cabbage farm) 92,
122
Kohlman, Kohlmann (collier)
95
Kohlmeyer (proprietor of the
Kohlhoff) 93
Kohn, Kohne, Kohner, see
Kuhn, Cohen
Kolb (club, see Kalb)
Kolbacher, see Kohlbecker
Kolbe, Kolben (club) 122
Kolbecher, see Kohlbecher
Kolberger, see Kohlberger
Kolker, see Kalker
Kollenborn, see Kaltenborn
Koller (cape) 112, 106
Koller (giddiness, frenzy)
Kollman, Kollmann, Kollner,
see Kohlmann
Kolter (plowshare, fr Latin
culter) 106
Konder, see Gunther 151

Konig, see Koenig 151
Konigsberg, see Koenigsberg
    151
Konrad, see Conrad
Konradi, son of Konrad 142
Konts, Konz, see Kuntz 151
Konzelman, see Kuenzelmann
    151
Koobler, see Kuebler 151
Koogel, Koogle, Koogler, see
    Kugel 151
Kool, Kooler, see Kuhl, Kuhler,
    Kohler 151
Koon, Koons, see Kuhn 151
Koonce, Koons, see Kunz 151
Koontz, see Kuntz 151
Koopman, see Kaufmann
Kopald (cobalt)
Kopf (head, cup, fr Latin
    cuppa) 114
Kopp < Jacob, see also Kapp,
    Kopf
Koppel < Jacob
Koppel (common pasture) 122
Koppelberger (mountain with
    common pasture) 68
Koppenhafer, Koppenhaver,
    Koppenhofer, Koppenhoffer,
    Koppenhoefer (fr
    Koppenhoefen 122, farmer
    who pays rent in capons) 92
Kopper (bloodletter) 96, see
    Kupfer
Koppman, see Kaufmann
Korb (basket, basket maker
    106, child found in a basket,
    fr the Korb 83)
Korbach 122, Korbeck (swampy
    brook) 80, 77
Kordes < Conrad 53
Korenblit, see Kornblit
Korff, Korfes, Korfmann
    (basket, basket maker) 96,
    106
Korn (grain, wheat, grain
    dealer) 105
Kornblatt (corn blade)
Kornblit (grain blossom)

Kornblum (cornflower)
Korner, see Koerner
Kornfeld (grain field) 84
Kornhaus (granary) 65
Kornhauser (granary
    manager)
Kornman, Kornmann (grain
    raiser, grain dealer) 105
Kornmesser (official grain
    measurer) 109
Kornmeyer, Kornmayer
    (grain farmer) 93
Kornreich (rich in grain)
Kornscheuer (grain barn,
    granary)
Kornstein (grain mountain)
    68
Korper, see Koerper
Korte, Korten, Korter, Korth,
    Kortte, Kortz, see Kurtz
Korthals (short neck) 114
Kortjohann (short John) 113
Kortkamp (short field) 84
Kortschenkel (short legs) 114
Korz, see Kurtz
Koster, Kostermann (taster),
    see Kuester
Koth, Kothe (mud, filth)
Kotmair (mud farmer) 93
Kottenbach (granary creek)
    77
Koubek, see Kuhbach 151
Kougl, see Kugel 151
Kouns, Kountz, see Kuntz
    151
Koutz, see Kautz 151
Kowellentenz, see Coblentz
    151
Krabacher (crow brook) 77
Krabbe (crab, active person)
    115
Krack, Kracke (crow) 115
Krack (underbrush)
Krabacher (crow brook) 77
Kraeber, see Graeber
Kraehbuehl (crow hill) 67
Kraehe (crow) 115
Kraeher (crow catcher)

Kraemer (shopkeeper, retailer)
105
Kraenckel, Kraenkel (sickly)
115
Kraetzer, see Kratzer
Kraeuter, Kraeuther (herbs,
herb seller) 105
Kraff, see Graf
Kraft, Krafft (strength 115,
river name 83)
Krahe, see Kraehe
Krahenbuhl, see Kraehbuehl
Krahmer, see Kraemer
Kral, Krall, Kralle (claw) 114
Kral (Czech: king, fr Carl) 146
Krallmann (fr Krall) 122
Kram (retail trade, huckster's
pack, huckster) 105, 122
Kramer, Kramers, see Kraemer
Kramp, Krampf (cramp)
Kranck (sick) 115
Kranitzfeld (border field, fr
Slavic) 84
Krankheit (sickness)
Krannewetter, Krannebitter
(juniper forest) 89
Krantz, Kranz, Krans (wreath,
rosary) 106
Krapf, Krapfer (fritter) 106
Krapf (hooked nose, hunched
back) 114
Krass (crass, gross) 115
Kratz < St. Pankratius 131
Kratz, Kratzer, Kratzler,
Krazer (scraper, wool
comber) 96
Kraus, Krauss, Krause,
Krauser (curly haired) 112
Krausam, see Grausam
Kraushaar (curlyhead) 112, 159
Krauskob, Krauskopf (curly
headed) 112
Kraut, Krauth (greens, herbs)
105
Krauter, Krautler, Krauthman,
Krautz, see Kraeuter
Krauthammer (fr Krautheim,
herb hamlet) 123, 122
Kraybil, see Kraehbuehl

Kreager, see Krueger 151
Kreatchman, Kreatchmann,
see Kretschmann 151
Krebs (crab, crab catcher)
Kreek, see Krueg 151
Krefeld (swampy field) 80,
84
Kreger, Kregar, Kreeger, see
Krueger 151
Kreh (crow) 115
Krehbiehl, see Kraebuehl
Krehmeyer (proprietor of the
Kraehoff) 93
Krehnbrink (crow hill) 74
Kreider, Kreidler (chalk
maker or seller, fr Latin
creda) 96, 105
Kreideweiss (chalk white)
112
Kreis, Kreiss, Kreise (circle,
district), see Greis
Kreischer (screamer)
Kreisel, Kreisler (spinning
top)
Kreiter (quarreler) 115, see
Kraeuter
Kreitz (cleared land 126,
122), also see Kreutz
Kreitzer, see Kreutzer
Krell, Kreller (cross-patch)
115
Kremer, see Kraemer
Kremeyer (proprietor of the
Krehhof, crow farm) 93
Kremp, Krempf (hat with
turned up brim) 112
Krempe (swamp) 80
Krenkel, see Kraenkel
Krentz, Krenzmann, see
Grentzel
Kreps, see Krebs
Krepp, Krepner (dweller on
a sunken path) 65
Kress (cress, fr Latin *cresso*)
Kressmann (Christian) 131
Kretsch, Kretschmer,
Kretchmer, Kretschmann
(tavern keeper, fr Slavic)

Kretz, Kretzer, Kretzel,
Kretzler (collector of fines)
109, 122
Kreuder, see Kreider
Kreuder, see Kraeuter
Kreuger, see Krueger
Kreul, see Greul
Kreuscher, see Kreischer
Kreutz, Kreuz, Kreutziger,
Kreutzinger (crusader,
dweller on a cross road) 122
Kreutzer (a coin)
Kreuzberger (fr Kreuzberg 122,
cross mountain) 68, 122
Krey, Kreye, Kreyer (crow)
Kreyder, see Kreider
Kreyss, see Kreis
Krick, see Krueck 151
Kridler, see Kreidler 151
Krieder, Kriedler see Kreider
151
Krieg (war), see Krug
Krieger, see Krueger
Kriegmann, see Kruegmann
Kriegsmann (soldier) 107
Krieter (querulous person) 115
Krimm 122, see Grimm
Krimmel, Krimmell (crooked)
114, 122
Krimmelbein (crooked leg) 114
Krings < St. Quirinus 131
Krisfeller, Christfelder (Christ's
field) 140
Krisler, see Kreisler 151
Kritzer, see Kreutzer 151
Kroat (Croat) 121
Krob, Krobs, Krober, see Grob
Krock, Krocker (fr Crock or
Cracow) 122
Kroeder, Kroeter (toad)
Kroeger, see Krueger
Kroeher, see Kraeher
Kroemer, see Kraemer
Krog, Kroger (fr Krog 122), see
Krug, Krueger
Krohn, see Kron
Kroll, Krall (Slavic for king
[Carl])

Kroll (curly) 112
Kromer, see Kraemer
Krompholtz, see Krumholz
Kron, Krohne (crown)
Kronberg, Kronberger,
Kronenberg, Kronenberger,
Kroneberger (crown
mountain) 68, 122
Kronburger (fr Kronburg
122, crown castle) 73
Kronfeldt (crown field) 84
Kronk, see Krank
Kronmeyer (crown farmer)
93
Kronmueller (crown miller)
103
Kronsbehn (crane leg) 114
Kronstadt (crown city) 122
Kropf, Kropp (crop, goiter)
114
Krouse, Krouss, see Kraus,
Krause 151
Kroushour, see Kraushaar
151
Krout, see Kraut
Krueck (crutch)
Krueckeberg, Kruckeberg (fr
Krueckenberg 122, crutch
mountain) 68
Krueger (tavern keeper) 96
Kruegmann (tavern keeper)
96
Kruesy, see Kraus
Krug, Krugs (pitcher, tavern,
taverner) 96, see Krueger
Kruger, Krugman, see
Krueger, Kruegmann
Krull (curly) 112
Krum, see Krumm 151
Krumbach (crooked brook)
77
Krumbein (crooked leg) 114
Krumbholz, Krumholtz,
Krummholtz (bent wood
for wheel, wheelwright) 96
Krumhus (crooked house) 65
Krumm (crooked) 114
Krumpholz, see Krumbholz

Krup, Krupp (croup, crupper)
Kruse, Krusen, Kruser, see
    Kraus
Kruth, see Kraut
Krutmann, Krautmann (spice
    dealer) 105
Kruttschmer, see Kretschmer
Krygsman, see Kriegsmann 151
Kubach, see Kuhbach 122
Kubel, Kubler, see Kuebel,
    Kuebler
Kubel, Kubler (mountain ridge)
Kuche, see Kueche
Kuchenbeisser (cookie biter)
Kuchenmeister (chief cook) 102
Kuckuck (cuckoo) 115
Kuebel, Kuebele, Kuebler,
    Kuebeller, Kubler, Kiebler
    (tub, bucket maker) 96
Kuefer, Kuefner, see Kieffer
Kuefus, see Kuhfuss
Kuehl, Kuehler, Kuehling,
    Kuehlman (dweller near a
    pit or mine)
Kuehlwein (cool wine) 102
Kuehn, Kuehne, Kuehner,
    Kuehner, Kuehnert (brave
    man) 115
Kuehnemann (brave man) 115
Kuemmel, Kuemmelmann
    (carraway seed, fr Latin
    cuminum) 105
Kuemmerle (miserable
    creature)
Kuempel, see Kump
Kuenlin, see Kuhn
Kuenstler (artist, artisan) 96
Kuentzel, Kuenzel, see Kuntz
Kuenz, see Kuntz
Kuerschner (furrier) 96
Kuessnacht (city in
    Switzerland) 122
Kuester, Kuesterle (sexton, fr
    Latin custos) 110
Kuettner (cowl wearer, cowl
    maker, monk)
Kufel, Kufler, see Kieffer
Kuffner, see Kiefer

Kugel, Kugel (cowl, cowl
    maker, fr Latin cuculla)
    106
Kugel, Kugelberg (round
    topped mountain) 68
Kuhbach (cow brook) 77, 122
Kuhfuss (cow foot, club foot)
    114
Kuhhirt (cowherd) 95
Kuhl, Kuhle, Kuhler,
    Kuhlert Kool (pond, pit)
    81
Kuhlenberg (cool mountain)
    68
Kuhlmann, Kuhlman,
    Kuhlemann, Kuehlemann
    (dweller on a pond) 81
Kuhltau (cool dew)
Kuhlwetter (cool weather)
Kuhmann (cow man) 91
Kuhn, Kuhne, Kuhnen,
    Kuhns, Kuhner, Kuhnert
    (brave) 115, < Konrad
Kullenberg, Kullberg, see
    Kuhlenberg
Kullenthal (cool valley, pond
    valley) 76
Kulman, Kullmann, see
    Kuhlmann
Kulp (carp) 115
Kumet, Kummet, Kumeth,
    Kumith (horse collar) 106
Kummel, Kummelmann, see
    Kuemmel
Kummer (sorrow) 122
Kummerling (stunted tree)
    89
Kump, Kumpel, Kumper,
    Kumpf, Kumps,
    Kumpermann (barrel
    maker) 96, 106, 122
Kumpfmiller (miller with
    overshot wheel) 103
Kumpost (kind of sourkraut,
    peasant food) 112
Kunckel, Kunkel, Kunkele
    (distaff, fr Latin conucula
    106, relative on distaff
    side 119)

Kunert, see Kuehnert
Kung, Kunig, see Koenig
Kunisch < Conrad
Kunkel, Kunkl, Kunkelmann <
    Conrad, see Kunckel
Kunnert, see Kuehnert
Kuno, see Kuhn, Conrad
Kunolt, Kunoldt (brave + rule)
    46, 48
Kunrad, see Conrad
Kunsman, see Kunstmann
Kunst (art, skill, also <
    Constantius)
Kunstler, see Kuenstler
Kunstmann, Kuntzler,
    Kuntzman, Kuntzmann,
    Kuntzelmann (artisan) 96
Kuntsman, see Kunstmann 151
Kuntz, Kuntze, Kunz, Kunze,
    Kunzle, Kuhns < Conrad
Kuper, Kuperman, see Kupfer,
    Kupfermann
Kupfer, Kupfermann (copper
    dealer) 105
Kupferschmid (coppersmith) 96
Kupp, Kupper, Kuppert
    (dweller on a mountain
    peak)
Kuradi, Kunradi (son of
    Konrad) 142
Kurath < Conrad
Kurland, Kurlander (territory
    on the Baltic) 121
Kursner, Kurstner, see
    Kuerschner
Kurt, Kurth, Kurtz, Kurtze,
    Kurz, Kurts < Conrad
Kurtzman, Kurtzman,
    Kurtzmeyer (short man) 113
Kuss (kiss), or < Dominicus
Kussmaul, Kusmaul (not "kiss
    mouth" but Czech for
    "tousel-haired") 112
Kuster, see Kuester
Kutler, Kuttler (maker of cowls
    106, or fr Kutten 122)

Kutscher, Kutcher,
    Kutchermann (coachman,
    fr Hungarian)
Kutner, see Kuettner
Kyle, Kyler, see Keil, Keiler
    151
Kyser, see Kaiser 151

L

Lach, Lack (laugh)
Lach (blaze on a tree)
Lach, Lache (puddle, lake)
    81, 122
Lachberg (boundary
    mountain) 68
Lachenicht (Don't laugh!)
    116
Lachenmann, see Lachman
Lacher, see Lachner
Lacher (incanter, see
    Lachmann)
Lachman, Lachmann (leech,
    incanter) 96
Lachmann (dweller at a
    pond) 81
Lachner (dweller on a
    boundary or on a pond)
    81
Lack, Lacker (laquer,
    laquerer) 106, 122
Lacke, see Lach
Lackmann, see Lachmann
Lackner (meat pickler) 96
Lackner (dweller by a pond)
    81
Lademacher (chest maker)
    98
Laden (window, store) 105
Lader, Ladner (loader)
Laderer, see Lederer
Laechler (laugher)
Laemmer (lambs) 91
Laendler (countryman)
Laerch (lark) 115
Laessig (easy-going) 115

Laeuenstein (lion mountain) 73
Laeufer (runner, deer's leg)
Lage (flat area between
mountains) 122
Lager, Lagger (couch, lair,
camp)
Lahm, Lahme (lame) 114, 122
Lahner (wire maker) 96
Lahner (dweller on the Lahn)
83
Lahr (dweller on the Lahr) 83,
122
Laib, see Leib
Laibinger (fr Laibingen) 122
Lainhart, see Lehnert,
Leonhard 151
Lallemand, see Alleman
Lamb, Lambb (lamb) 91
Lambard, see Lampart
Lambert, Lampert, Lambrecht,
Lambrechts, Lamprecht (land
+ bright) 49, 47
Lambright, see Lambert 151
Lamm, Lamkin, Lamke,
Lampke, Lammlein (lamb)
91
Lamp, Lampe, Lampen (lamp,
see also Lambert)
Lampart, Lampert, Lombart
(Lombard, banker, also see
Lambert) 121
Lanck, see Lang
Land, Landes (land, shortened
form of certain names)
Landau, Landauer (name of
province and cities) 121, 122
Landbeck (land brook) 77
Landborn (land spring) 79
Landeck, Landecker (name of a
province) 121
Lander (picket fence) 122
Landfeld, Landfelder (land
field) 84
Landgraff, Landgrof, Landeraf
(landgrave) 109
Landhut (regional lookout)
Landman, Landmann
(countryman, compatriot)
Landmesser (surveyor) 96

Landolt (brave + loyal) 49,
48
Landsberg (place name) 122
Landschultz (village mayor)
109
Landsknecht (lansquenet,
pikeman) 107
Landskroner, Landskroener
(fr Landskron 122)
Landsman (countryman,
compatriot)
Landwehr, Landwehrmann
(militiaman) 107
Landzberg, see Landsberg
Lane, see Lehn 151
Lanehardt, Lanehart, see
Lehnert, Leonhard 151
Lang, Lange, Langer,
Langert, Langes (long,
tall) 113
Langbaum (tall tree) 89
Langbein (long leg) 114
Langenbach, Langenbacher
(long brook) 77, 122
Langenberg, Langenberger
(long mountain) 68, 122
Langenbrunner (long spring)
79
Langendorf, Langendorfer
(long village) 123, 122
Langenecker, Langeneker (fr
Langeneck 122, long field)
84
Langenfeldt, Langenfelder (fr
Langenfeld 122, long
fields) 84
Langenhagen (long hedge,
enclosure) 123, 122
Langenthal (long valley) 76,
122
Langenwalter (fr
Langenwald 122, long
forest) 71
Langer (tall mann) 113
Langfeldt 122, see
Langenfeldt
Langfield, see Langenfeldt
151
Langhaar (long hair) 112

Langhage (long enclosure) 123, 122
Langhals (long neck) 114
Langhans (tall Johnny) 113
Langhaus (long house) 65, 122
Langheim (long hamlet) 123, 122
Langheinrich (tall Henry) 113
Langhirt (tall herdsman) 113, 95
Langhoff, Langhoffer, Langenhoffer (long farm) 92
Langhorn, Langhorne (long horn)
Langhorst (long hurst) 72, 122
Langhutte (long hut)
Langloh (long forest) 72
Langman, Langmann (tall man) 113
Langmesser (long knife)
Langnau, Langenau, Lankenau (long meadow) 84
Langohr (long ear) 114
Langrock (long gown) 112
Langsam (slow) 115
Langschmidt (tall smith) 96
Lannert, see Lahner
Lansman, see Landsman
Lantz, Lants, Lans, Lantz 122 (spear, lance) 107, 108
Lantzer (pikeman) 107
Lapp (rag, fool) 115
Lasser < Lazarus 131
Laster (vice)
Laster (packman)
Lastinger (prunella weaver) 96
Lastner (burden carrier)
Latz (codpiece) 112, 106
Lau, Laue (thin forest) 72
Laub, Laube, Lauber, Laubner (leaf, foliage, arbor)
Laubach (forest brook) 77, 122
Laubenstein (lion mountain) 73
Laubheim, Laubheimer (swamp hamlet) 80, 123
Lauch, see Lau
Lauch, Laucher (leek, leek seller) 105

Lauck, Laucks (St. Luke) 131
Laudenslager, Laudenslayer, Laudenschlaeger, see Lautenschlaeger 151
Laue, see Lau
Lauenroth (lion clearing) 126
Lauenstein (lion mountain) 73, 122, see Loewenstein 122
Lauer, Laur, Laurer, Lauerman (tanner) 96
Lauf, Laufe (course) 122
Laufenberger, Lauffenberger 151 (waterfall mountain) 68
Laufenburgen, Laufenburger, Lauffenberger (waterfall castle) 73, 122
Laufer, Lauffer, Laufert (runner, fr Lauffen 122)
Lauffen (waterfall, places in Switzerland and Wurttemberg) 122
Laughner, see Lochner 151
Lauman, Laumann (forest dweller) 72
Laupheim 122, see Laubheim
Laur, see Lauer
Laus < Nikolaus 53
Lauss (boundary)
Laut, Lauth (loud) 115
Laut, Lauth (lute) 106
Lautenbach (swampy brook) 80, 77, 122
Lautenschlaeger, Lauteschlager, Laudenschlaeger (lute player) 96
Lauter (swamp) 80
Lauterbach (swampy brook) 80, 77, 122
Lautermilch (pure milk)
Lauterwasser (pure water)
Lauth, see Laut
Lauthans (noisy Johnny) 134

Lautringer (fr Kaiserslautern)
122
Lax (salmon) 115
Lazarus (NT name) 131
Leab, see Lieb 151
Leabhart, see Lephard 151
Leaderer, see Lederer 151
Leaderman, see Ledermann
151
Leap, see Lieb 151
Leapart, see Lephard 151
Leatherman, see Ledermann
151
Lebegut (Live well!) 116, 117
Leber (liver)
Leber (river name) 83
Leberecht (Live right!) 116
Leberknight, see Lieberknecht
151
Lebermann (dweller on the
Leber 83, also see
Liebermann)
Lebherz (dear heart) 151
Lebkucher (cookie baker) 96
Lebolt, see Leopold
Lech, Lechmann (dweller on
the River Lech, swamp) 80,
83
Lech, Lechner, Lechnir, see
Lehner
Lechliter, see Lichleiter
Leder, Lederer (leather, leather
worker) 96, 106, 105
Lederhos (leather breeches,
peasant) 112, 122
Lederkremer (leather
merchant) 105
Ledermann (leather worker) 96,
105
Ledig (single, free)
Leeb, Leeby, see Lieb, Liebe
151
Leer (empty)
Leffel, Lefler, Leffler, see
Loeffler
Lehder, see Leder
Lehfeld (tenant field) 84
Lehm, Lehmer (clay, ceramics
worker) 96, 106

Lehman, Lehmann (tenant),
see Lohmann
Lehmbeck (clay brook) 77,
122
Lehmkuhl (clay pond) 81,
122
Lemberg (clay mountain) 68,
122
Lehn, Lehen (fief) 122
Lehne (steep slope) 71
Lehner, Lehnerd, Lehnert,
Lehnerts, Lenerz,
Lehninger (tenant) 122
Lehnhoff (rented farm) 84
Lehnwald (forested fief) 71
Lehr (teaching)
Lehr (swamp) 80, 122
Lehrer, Lehrman, Lehrmann
(teacher, minister)
Lehrkind (pupil, apprentice)
Lehrmann (swamp dweller)
80
Leib, Leiber, Leibert (body)
Leibenguth (life and
property, a serf)
Leibheim (fr Leipheim) 122
Leibknecht (body servant)
Leibnitz (Slavic place name)
122
Leibrock (body gown) 112
Leichnam, Leichtnam
(corpse)
Leicht (light)
Leidhauser, see Leithauser
65
Leidhauser (taverner) 65
Leidig, see Ledig
Leidner, see Leitner
Leihkauf (loan purchase,
drink sealing a bargain)
Leihofer, Leihoffer (tenant)
92
Leim (clay)
Leimbach, Leimback (clay
brook, swamp brook) 80,
77, 122
Leimberg, Leimberger (clay
mountain) 68
Leimkuhler (clay pond) 80

Leinbach, Leinbacher,
Leinebacher (clay brook) 77,
122
Leinberger (fr Leinberg 122,
clay mountain) 68
Leine (leash)
Leineweber, Leinweber (linen
weaver) 96
Leinhardt, see Leonhard
Leinwand (cloth, mercer) 105
Leip, Leipp (fr Leipe 122), see
Leib
Leippold, see Leopold
Leis, Leiss, Leise, Leiser (soft,
softly) 115
Leisler, Leissler (wainwright)
96
Leist (last, schoemaker) 104,
106, 122
Leite, Leitner (dweller on a
slope) 71
Leitenberger (slope mountain)
71, 68, 122
Leiter (ladder)
Leiter (leader)
Leithausen, Leithaeuser,
Leithauser, Leitheuser
(occupant of house on slope)
71, 65
Leitheimer (fr Leitheim, hamlet
on a slope) 71, 123, 122
Leither, Leitmann, Leitzmann
(guide)
Leithiser, see Leithausen
Leitinger, see Leite
Leitner, see Leite
Lembach (swamp brook) 80, 77,
122
Lemberg (swamp mountain) 80,
68
Lembchen, Lembke, Lembcke,
Lemke, Lembeke (little
lamb) 91
Lemer, see Laemmer
Lemke, see Lembchen, also <
Lamprecht
Lemmenhoffer (lamb farm)
Lemmer, see Laemmer

Lemmlein (little lamb) 91
Lempke, see Lembchen
Lenard, Lennert, see
Leonhard 151
Lence, see Lentz 151
Lendeman, Lendemann
Lendler, see Laendler
Lener, see Lehner
Lenert, Lennert, see Lehnert
Lengfelder, Lengenfelder (fr
Lengfeld 122), see
Langenfelder
Lenhard, Lenhardt, Lenhart,
see Leonhard, Lehner
Lenhof, Lennhof, see
Lehnhoff
Lennerd, Lennert, see
Lenhard, Lehner 151
Lentz 122, Lenz, Lentzer
(spring 143, or < Lorentz,
St. Laurentius 131)
Leonhard, Leonhardt,
Leonhart, Leonard (lion +
strong) 48, 46
Leonhardi (son of Leonhard)
142
Leonhauser (lion house) 48,
65
Leopold, Lepold (folk +
brave) 46, 46
Lepart, Lepert, Lepperet,
Lephardt (leopard, or lion
+ strong) 48, 46
Lepper, Leppert (shoe
repairer, clothes patcher)
96
Lerch, Lerche, Lercher,
Lerge, Lerich (lark, joyful
person) 115, 122
Lerner (learner, pupil)
Lesch, Lesch, Lescher (one
who lives on the Lesch)
83
Leschke (Slavic: "forest
dweller")
Leser, Lesemann (reader)
Lesser (bloodletter)

Lilienthal, Lillienthal, Lilenthal (lily valley) 76, 122

Limbach, Limbacker (swampy brook [fr *lint*] 80, or see Leinbach

Limberger (fr Limberg 122, linden mountain), 89, 68, see Leimberger

Lime, see Leim 151

Limmat (Swiss river) 83

Limpert, see Lambert

Linck, Linke, Linker, Linkert (left, left-handed) 114

Lind, Lindt, Linde, Linder, Linders, Lindler, Lindner (dweller near the linden trees) 89

Lindauer (fr Lindau, swampy meadow) 80, 84, 122

Lindbeck (linden brook) 89, 77

Lindbeck (swampy brook) 80, 77

Linddorf (linden village) 89, 123, 122

Linddorf (swampy village) 80, 123

Lindeman, Lindemann, Lindemeyer, Lindemyer (dweller near the lindens) 89

Lindemann (dweller near the swamp) 80

Lindemuth (gentle disposition) 115

Lindenberg, Lindenberger (linden mountain) 89, 68, 122

Lindenfeld, Lindenfelder (linden field) 89, 84, 122

Lindenschmidt, Lindenschmid (smith under the linden trees) 89, 96

Lindenstrutt (fr Lindenstruth 122, linden swamp) 89, 80

Lindhorst, Lindhurst, Linhorst (linden hurst) 89, 72, 122

Lindler, Lindner, Lindt, see Lindeman

Lindober, see Lindauer

Linebaugh, see Leinebach 151

Lineweaver, see Leineweber 151

Lingelbach, Lingelback (mud brook) 77, 122

Lingenberg (muddy mountain) 68

Lingenfeld, Lingenfelder, Lingenfelter, Lingerfelt (swampy field) 84

Lingert, see Linhard

Linhard, Linhardt, Linhart, see Leonhard 151

Link, see Linck

Linneman, see Lindeman

Linnestruth, see Lindenstrutt

Lins, Linse, Linsen (lentil) 105

Linsenbiegler, Linsenbigler (fr Linsenbuehl) 68

Linsenmeyer, Linsenmyer (lentil farmer) 93

Lintner, see Lindeman

Lintz, Linz (fr Linz) 122

Lion, Lyons (fr French *lion*)

Lipmann, Lipp, Lippmann < Philipp 53

Lippelt, Lippolt < Leopold

Lippert, Lipphart, see Lebhart

Lisch 122, Lischer, see Lescher

List (intelligence, cunning, skill) 115, 122

Litinger (dweller on a slope), see Leitner

Litfass (wine barrel)

Little, see Luetzel 151

Litz, Litze (lace) 106, 112

Litzeldorf (little village) 123

Litzen, Litzmann < Ludwig 53

Lob, Lobe, Lober (praise, praiser)

Lobach, Lobeck (forest brook) 71, 77, 122

Lobauer (forest peasant) 71, 91
Lobaugh, see Lobach 77, 151
Loch (hole) 122
Lochbaum (hollow tree,
  boundary tree) 89
Lochner (dweller by a pond) 80
Lock (pond) 80
Lockermann (dweller by a
  swamp) 80
Loeb (fr Loebau 122, see also
  Loew)
Loeffler (spoon maker) 96
Loesch (extinguish), see Lesch
Loescher, Loeschner (stevedore)
Loesser, see Lesser
Loew, Loewe (lion) 48
Loewenberg (lion mountain) 48,
  68, 122
Loewenstein, Leuwenstein (lion
  mountain) 48, 73, 122
Loewenstern (lion star) 48
Loewenthal, Lowenthal (lion
  valley) 48, 76, 122
Loffler, see Loeffler
Lofink (wood finch) 115
Loh (flame)
Loh 122 (forest 71, swampy
  area 80), see Hohenloh
Lohaus (forest house) 71, 65,
  122
Lohaus (tanner's shop) 65, 122
Loher, Lohgerber (tanner) 96
Lohman, Lomann (forest man,
  tanner) 71, 96
Lohoefer (proprietor of the
  Lohoff) 92, 122
Lohmeyer (forest farmer) 71,
  93
Lohmuller (forest miller) 71,
  103
Lohn, Lohner, Lohnes, Loner,
  Lohnert (reward, rewarder;
  dweller on the Lahn) 83, 122
Lohr, Lohre, Lohrman,
  Lohrmann, Lorman (fr Lohr
  122, dweller on the Lohr 83)
Lombarth, see Lambart
Longacker (long field) 84, 151

Longanecker, Longenecker,
  see Langenecker 151
Longbrake, see Lamprecht
  151
Longnecker, see Langenecker
Longhoffer, see Langhoffer
  151
Loos, Loose (lot, fate) 122
Loos, Loose, Looser <
  Ludwig 53
Lor, see Lohr
Lorbach (laurel brook) 89,
  77, 122
Lorch, Lorche (place name)
  122
Lorentz, Lorenz (St.
  Lawrence) 131
Lortz, Lorz, see Lorentz
Losacker (field drawn by lot)
  84
Losch, Losche, Loscher,
  Loschert (costly leather,
  leather worker) 96
Lotz, Lots, Lotse (pilot)
Lotze < Ludwig 53, 54
Loudenschlager, see
  Lautenschlaeger 151
Louderback, see Lauterbach
  151
Loudermilk, see Lautermilch
  151
Loudiwick, see Ludwig 151
Loughman, see Lachman 151
Loughner, see Lachner 151
Lovenstein, see Loewenstein
  151
Lowdermilk, see Lautermilch
  151
Lowe, see Loewe 122, 151
Lowenhaupt (lion head) 149,
  151
Lowenstein, see Loewenstein
  151
Lowenthal, see Loewenthal
  151
Lower, see Lauer 151
Lowrentz, see Lorentz 151
Lubbe < Liutbert (people +
  bright) 46, 47, 53, 54

Lubeck, Lubecker (fr Luebeck)
122
Lubrecht < Liutbrecht (people
+ bright) 46, 47
Lucabaugh, see Luckenbach
151
Lucas, Luck, Lux (St. Luke)
131
Luchs (lynx) 115
Luck (St. Luke) 131
Luckabaugh, see Luckenbach
151
Luckenbach (swamp brook) 80,
77, 122
Luckenbill (swamp hill) 80, 67
Lucker (swamp dweller) 80
Ludeke, Luddecke, Lueddecke
< Ludolf 53, 54
Luden, Luder < Ludwig 53, 54
Ludewig, see Ludwig
Ludke, see Ludeke
Ludman, Ludemann < Ludolf
53, 54
Ludmer (loud + famous) 47, 47
Ludolf, Ludolph (loud + wolf)
47, 48
Ludowice (fr Ludowici, son of
Ludowicus, Latin for Ludwig
142, 151
Ludwig, Ludwig (loud + battle)
47, 46
Luebbe, Luebber, Luebbers,
Luebbermann, Luebke <
Liutbert (folk + bright) 46,
47, 53, 54
Luechow (place name) 122
Lueck, Luck (St. Luke) 131
Lueder, Lueders, Luedemann
(loud + army) 47, 46
Luedge, Luedke, Luetge,
Lutjen, Luetcke, Luetke <
Ludwig, Luthari (loud +
army), etc. 53, 54
Lueppert, see Lebhart
Luetze, Luetzmann < Ludwig
53, 54
Luetzel (little) 113
Luft, Lufft (air) 122

Lugenbeal, Lugenbeel,
Luginbill (lookout hill) 67,
151
Luger (deceitful) 115
Lukas (Luke) 131
Lummel (lout, bore) 115
Lump, Lumpe (rag, tramp)
115
Luneburger, Lunenburger (fr
Lunenburg) 121
Lunte (fuze, harquebusier)
107
Luppold, see Leopold
Lurz (awkward) 115
Lushbaugh (reed brook) 77,
151
Lustbader (pleasure bather)
Lustgarten (pleasure garden)
84
Lustig (merry) 115
Luterman (lute player) 96
Luther (loud + army) 47, 46
Luthold, Ludholtz (folk +
loyal) 46, 48
Lutjen < Ludolf, Luther, etc.
53, 54
Lutter < Ludwig 53, 54
Lutterbeck 122, see
Lauterbach
Luttig < Ludolf 53
Luttich (fr Liege 122)
Lutz, Lutze, Lutzel, Lutzens
< Ludwig 53, 54
Lutzel (little) 113
Luxemburg (a principality,
little castle) 121

M

Maag (kinsman) 119
Maas, Mass (Meuse) 83, 122
Maas (ThoMAS) 131
Macher, see Metzger 151
Machler, see Mackler
Macht (power) 46
Mack, Mag, Mak, Makh <
Markward 53

Mackler (broker)
Mader, Maeder, Maehder
(mower) 95
Mader (dye seller) 105
Madreiter (meadow clearing)
125
Maerker (observer, umpire)
Maertens, Maerten, see Martin
Maertz, Maerz (March) 143
Maessner, see Mesner
Mag (kinsman) 119
Magdeburger (fr Magdeburg
122, the Virgin's city) 122
Magenheim, Magenheimer (fr
Magenheim 122, kinsmen
hamlet) 123
Magenhoffer (fr Magenhof 122,
kinsman farm) 92
Mager (thin) 114
Magerfield (infertile field) 84,
151
Magnus (Latin, great) 141
Mahl, Mahle (meal, time)
Mahler (miller) 103
Mahler (painter) 96
Mahlstedt (parliament place)
122
Mahnke < Mangold
Mahr (swamp) 80
Mahrenholtz (swamp forest) 80,
72, 122
Maienshein, see Mayenschein
151
Maier, see Meyer
Mailender (fr Milan) 122
Mainfort (Main ford) 78, 122
Mainhard, see Meinhard
Maintzer, Mainzer (fr Mainz
122) 129
Mair, Maiers, see Meyer,
Meyers
Maisel, see Meisel
Maisner, see Meissner
Makell (stain, spot)
Mal (boundary)
Malchior, Malcher, see
Melchior
Maler (painter) 96

Maltz, Malz (malt, brewer)
96, 106, 122
Mance, see Mantz 151
Mandel, Mandell, Manndel
(almond), see Mantel
Mandelbaum (almond tree)
89
Manfred, Manfretz (man +
peace or protection) 94, 47
Mangel (lack)
Mangold < Managwalt, great
+ power) 46
Manhim, see Mannheim
151
Mann, Manne, Manns (man,
vassal) 94, or < Hermann
Mannalther (adult) 113
Mannbar (marriageable)
Mannhardt, see Meinhard
Mannheim, Mannheimer (fr
Mannheim, swamp hamlet
122)
Mannherz (man heart) 115
Mannlein (little man) 94
Mansfeld (fr Mansfeld) 122
Mansfield, Mansfeild, see
Mansfeld 151
Mantel (coat, fr Latin
mantellum) 112, 106
Mantel (fir tree) 89, 122
Mantler (coat dealer) 105
Mantz, Manz < St. Manitius)
131, see Mangold
Mar, Marr (swamp) 80
Marbach (swamp brook 80,
77, name of city 122)
Marburger (fr Marburg 122,
swamp castle) 80, 73
Marckel < Markwart 53
Marcus (St. Mark) 131
Marder (marten) 115
Margenthaler, see
Mergenthaler
Margot (famous + god) 47
Margraf (margrave) 109
Mark, Marck, Marks, Marx,
Marcus (St. Mark, name
of a pope) 134

Markel, Markels, see Markwart
Markhart (boundary + strong) 46
Markwart, Markward, Markword, Marckwart, Markwardt (guardian of the boundary) 47
Marner (mariner)
Marold (famous + loyal) 47, 48
Marquard, Marquart, Marquardt, see Markwart
Marsch, Marscher (marsh) 80
Marschall, Marschalk (horse + servant, marshall) 107
Marstaller, Marsteller (horse + stall, equerry) 107
Mart, Martin, Martens, see Martin
Marti < Martin
Martin, Martins, Marthin (St. Martin, name of pope) 134
Martinus (St. Martin) 141
Martini (son of Martinus) 142
Martinssen (son of Martin) 59
Marx, see Mark
Maschauer (swampy meadow) 80, 84
Maschbaum (swamp tree) 80, 89
Mass (measure, see Thomas)
Mathaus, see Matthaeus
Matheis, see Matthias
Matt, Matz, see Matthaeus
Matt (sloping meadow) 71
Matthaeus, Matthaeus (St. Matthew) 131
Matthias, Mattheiss, Matteis, Mattis, Mattice (St. Matthew) 131
Matthiesen, Matthyssen (son of Matthias) 59
Mattmueller (miller on the sloping meadow 84, miller on the Matte 83)
Matz < Matthaeus or Mattias) 53
Matzger, see Metzger 151
Mauer 122, see Maurer

Mauershagen (walled enclosure) 123
Maul, Maule (mouth, probably large or deformed) 114
Maul (mule) 91
Maultasch (distorted face) 114
Maurer, Mauer, Mauerer (mason, fr Latin *murus*) 100
Maus, Mauss (mouse)
Mauser (mouser)
Maut, Mauth, Mauthe, Maute, Mautz, Mauter (toll collector)
Max < St. Maximilian 131
May (May) 143
Mayenbaum (may tree, maypole) 89
Mayer, see Meyer
Mayerhoff, Mayerhoffer (fr Mayerhoff 122), see Meyerhoffer
Maynard, Maynerd, see Meinhard 151
Mayr, see Meyer
Mayerhofer, see Meyerhoffer
Mayse (titmouse) 115
Maytag (Mayday) 143
Mealy, see Muehle 151
Mechler, see Mackler
Meckel < Mechthild (power + battle) 46, 46, 53, 54, 122
Mecklenburg (German province) 121
Meder, see Mader
Meer (sea, swamp) 80, 122
Meerholtz (swamp forest) 80, 72
Meerman (swamp dweller) 80
Mees, Meese, Meesen (swamp) 80
Megenhardt (might + strong) 46, 46
Meher (mower) 95

Mehl, Mehle, Mehler (meal,
grist, miller) 106
Mehlmann (meal dealer) 105
Mehnert, see Meinhard
Mehr, Mehren, Mehring <
Merhold 53, 54
Mehrenholtz (swamp forest) 80,
72
Merhold (famous + loyal) 47,
48
Meichler (dweller near
stagnant water) 79
Meidenbauer (horse farmer) 91
Meier, Meiers, see Meyer,
Meyers
Meierhofer (fr Meierhof 122),
see Meyerhofer
Meineke, Meinecke < Meinhard
53, 54
Meinhard, Meinhardt, Meinert,
Meiner (might + strong) 46,
46
Meinhold (might + loyal) 46,
48
Meininger (fr Meiningen) 122
Meinke, Meinken < Meinhard
53, 54
Meinschein, see Meyenschein
Meinster, see Muenster
Meintzer, Meinzer, Meinz (fr
Mainz) 122
Meise (titmouse) 115
Meisel (mouse hawk) 115
Meisenbacher (swamp-water
brook) 80, 77, 122
Meisenhalder, Meisenhelder,
Meisenholder (songbird
owner, songbird seller) 105
Meisenheim (titmouse hamlet)
123, 122
Meisner, Meissner (fr Meissen)
122
Meissel (chisel) 106
Meister (master)
Meisterjan (Master John)
Meitzel (power)
Meixner, see Meisner

Melchior, Melcher, Melchers,
Melger, Melken (one of
Three Kings) 111
Meltzer, Melzer (malt maker,
brewer) 96, 105
Memminger (fr Memming
122 or Memmingen 122)
Mencken, Menke, Menken,
Menkel < Meinhard 53, 54
Mendel, see Mandel
Mendelbaum, see
Mandelbaum
Mendelsohn, Mendelssohn
(son of Mendel) 59
Menge (multitude, retailer)
105
Mengel, see Mangel
Mengeldorff, see Mengersdorf
Menger, Mengers (monger, fr
Latin *mango*) 105
Mengersdorf (mongers'
village) 123, 122
Menges, Mengs, Mengen (fr
Megingoz, might + Goth)
46, 53, 54
Menhard, see Meinhard
Menke, Mennecke, Menning,
see Meinhard
Mensch (human being)
Mensh, Mentch, see Mensch
151
Mentz, Menz, Mentze,
Mentzel, Mentzell,
Mentzel, Mentzl, Mentzer,
see Maintzer
Merbach (swamp brook) 80,
77
Merck, Merckel, Merckle,
Mercke, Merkle, Merklin
< Markwart 53, 54
Merfeld (marshy field) 80,
84, 122
Mergardt (swamp garden)
80, 84
Mergart (son of Merigarda)
60
Mergel, Mergl, Mergler
(marl, marl supplier, fr
Latin *margila*) 105

Mergenthaler (marl valley) 76, 122
Merkel, see Markwart
Merker (fr Mark Brandenburg) 121
Mermelstein (marble) 73
Mertel, see Marten
Merten, Mertens, Merthens, see Martin
Merts, Mertz, Merz, see Maerz
Mesmer, Mesner (sexton, fr Latin *mansionarius*) 110
Mess (mass)
Messbach (swamp brook) 80, 77
Messer (knife, knife grinder, cutler) 106
Messer (official measurer) 109
Messerschmidt, Messerschmied (cutler, knife maker) 96
Messing, Messinger, Mesinger (brass, brass worker 96, 106; fr Messing 122)
Messmer, Messmers, see Mesmer
Messner, see Mesmer
Meth, Methe (mead, taverner) 96
Methaus (tavern, taverner) 96
Metscher, see Metzger
Metschke < Matthaeus 53, 54
Metter (mead maker) 96
Metz (inhabitant of Metz 122), see Metzger, Matthias
Metzbower (butcher farmer) 102, 91, 151
Metzdorf (butchers' village) 102, 123, 122
Metzdorf (Mechthild's village) 123
Metzel, Metzler (butcher, fr Latin *macellarius*) 102
Metzger (butcher, fr Latin *matiarius*) 102
Meurer, see Maurer
Meusel (little mouse)
Mewes, Meves < Matthaeus 53, 54
Mey, see May

Meyer (farmer, dairy farmer, fr Latin *major domus*) 93
Meyerhoffer, Mayerhofer (farm managed by bailif) 93, 92
Meyers, Meyerson, see Meyer 164, 59
Meylaender, see Mailaender
Meyner (might + army) 46, 46
Meysel, see Meisel
Mezger, see Metzger
Michael, Michaels, Michaelis, Michaeles, Michel, Michele (St. Michael) 131
Michel, see Michael
Michel, Michels, Michler, Michelman, Michelmann (large) 113
Michelbach (large brook) 77, 122
Michelbach (St. Michael's brook) 77, 122
Michelfelder (large fields) 84, 122
Michelfelder (St. Michael's fields) 84, 122
Michelsen (son of Michel) 59
Mick, Micks, see Mueck
Middag, see Mittag 151
Middeldorp, Middendorf, see Mitterdorf
Middelstaedt (middle town)
Miers, see Meyer 151, 164
Miesbach (marsh brook) 80, 77, 122
Mil ..., mill ..., see Muehl
Milch (milk) 105
Milcher, see Melchior
Milchsack (milk bag)
Mild (generous) 115
Milhaus, see Muehlhaus
Milheim (mill hamlet) 123
Milhizer, Milheisler, see Muehlhaus
Milhous, Milhouse, Milhouser, see Muehlhaus 151

Millberg, see Muehlenberg
Millen (place name) 122
Miller, see Mueller
Millhaus, Millhauser < see
Muehlhaus
Millhof (mill farm) 92, 122
Millhouse, Millhouser, see
Muehlhaus 151
Millspaugh (mill brook) 77, 151
Millstein, Milstein (millstone)
73, 151
Milner, see Muehlner
Milroth (mill clearing) 126
Miltz (spleen)
Mincer, see Maintzer
Minch, Minnich, see Moench
Minchhoff (cloister farm) 92,
151
Minden (name of city) 122
Minderlein (of low rank)
Minehart, see Meinhard 151
Mineweaser (meadow on the
Main) 84, 151
Mingeldorf, see Mengersdorf
Minger, Mingers, see Menger
Mingersdorf, see Mengersdorf
Mink, Minke (Wendish, miller)
Minne (love)
Minnegerode, Minnigerode
(Minne's clearing) 126
Minnik, see Moench
Minster, see Muenster
Mintz, Mintze, Mintzes,
Mintzer, see Muentz,
Muentze, Muentze
Mire, see Meyer 151
Mischle, Mischler, Mitschler <
Michael
Misener, see Meisner
Misslich (awkward,
inconvenient) 115
Mitnacht, Mittnacht,
Mitternacht (midnight) 143
Mittag (midday) 143
Mittelberger, Mittenberger (fr
Mittelberg 122, middle
mountain) 68
Mitteldorf (middle village) 123

Mittelstadt, Mittelstaedt
(middle city)
Mittenberger (fr Mittenberg
122)
Mittendorf (in the middle of
the village) 123, 122
Mittenthal (in the middle of
the valley) 76
Mittermeier (middle farmer)
93
Mittersteiner (middle stone)
73
Mix, see Mueck
Mock (female wild boar, see
also Mack)
Moeglich (possible) 117
Moehle, Moehler, see
Muehle, Muehler
Moehm (aunt) 119
Moehlmann, Moellmann
(miller)
Moeller, Moellers, Moelleken,
see Mueller
Moench, Moenck (monk, fr
Latin *municus*) 110
Moenkeberg (monk
mountain) 68, 122
Moersberger (marsh
mountain) 80, 67
Moerschbacher (fr Moersbach
122, swamp brook) 80, 77
Moersdorf (swamp village)
80, 123, 122
Moeser, Moesinger (fr Moese
122, marsh) 80
Moessbauer (marsh farmer)
80, 93
Moessmer, see Messmer
Mohler, Mohlmann, see
Mahler, Mueller
Mohn (poppy)
Mohnberger (poppy
mountain) 68
Mohr, Moor, Mohrman,
Mohrmann (Moor, possibly
actor in miracle play 111)
Mohr (fen or bog) 80, 122
Mohrmann (dweller on a
fen) 80

Molden, Molder, Moldenhauer,
Mollenhauer (trough maker
96, fr Moldau 122)
Molk (milk, milk dealer) 106
Moll, Molle (heavy set) 114
Mollenhauer, Mollnauer, see
Molden
Moller, see Mueller
Molnar, Molner, see Mueller
Moltke (Slavic: young)
Moltmann (earthman, Adam)
Moltz, Moltz, see Maltz
Momma, see Mumma
Monat, Monath, Monnat
(month)
Monbauer (proprietor of the
Monhof, poppy farm) 91
Mondschein (moonlight)
Monich, Monick, see Moench
Montag (Monday) 143
Moon, see Mohn
Moor 122, Moore, see Mohr
Moos (fen, bog) 80, 122
Moosmann (dweller on a fen)
80
Morast (marsh, morass) 80
Morganstein, see Morgenstein
151
Morgedaller, see Morgenthaler
Morgen (morning) 122
Morgenroth (morning red) 148
122
Morgenstein (morning stone)
73, 148
Morgenstern (morning star,
mace) 108, 148, 122
Morgenthal, Morgenthaler
(morning valley) 76, 148, 122
Morgenthau (morning dew) 148
Morgott, see Margot
Moritz (St. Mauritius) 131, 122
Morman, Mormann (dweller on
the fen) 80
Morningstar, see Morgenstern
152
Morsberger, Morstein (swamp
mountain) 80, 68
Morsch (rotten, decayed)

Morschheimer (fr
Morschheim, rotten +
hamlet) 123, 122
Morstadt, Morstaedter (fen
city) 80
Mosbach (marshy brook) 80,
77, 122
Mosberg (marsh mountain)
80, 68, 122
Mosel (fr the Moselle) 83,
122
Moser, Mosemann (dweller
on a marsh) 80
Moser (place name) 122
Moses, Mose (OT name) 135
Mosmiller (marsh miller) 80,
103
Mosner (marsh dweller) 80
Moss, see Moos
Mossbach, see Mosbach 122
Mosser, see Moser
Mosshamer (bog hamlet) 80,
123
Mossmann (dweller on a
marsh) 80
Most (grape-juice, fr Latin
mustum)
Mott, Motte (moth)
Mous, see Maus 151
Mowrer, see Maurer 151
Much (marshy stream) 81,
122
Mueck, Muecke, Muck, Mick,
Micks, Mix (midge, gnat,
restless person) 115, 122
Mueckenberg (gnat
mountain) 68, 122
Mueckenfuss (gnat leg) 114
Muegge, see Muecke
Mueh (trouble, effort)
Muehl (mill)
Muehlebach (mill brook) 77
Muehleisen, Muehlseisen
(mill axel-iron)
Muehlenberg (mill mountain)
68
Muehlenstein (millstone) 73
Muehler, see Mueller

Muehlhaus, Muehlhause,
Muehlhausen, Muehlhauser
(mill house) 65
Muehlheim (mill hamlet) 123
Muehlhoff (mill farm) 92
Muehlke (little mill)
Mueller (miller, fr Latin
molinarius) 103
Muench, see Moench
Muencheberg (monk mountain)
110, 68
Muenster (minster, fr Latin
monasterium) 122
Muentz, Muentze, Muenz (coin,
minter) 106
Mugg, see Mueck
Muhl, Muhly, Muhler, see
Muehle, Muehler 151
Muhlbach muddy stream) 77,
see Muehlbach
Muhleisen, see Muehleisen
Muhlhaus, see Muehlhaus
Mulhauser, see Muehlhaus
Mulinari (miller, fr Latin
molinarius) 142
Mullendorf (mill village) 123
Muller, see Mueller
Mullhausen, see Muehlhaus
Mumma, Mumme
(masquerader)
Munch, see Moench
Mund, Mundt (guardian 47, see
Siegmund)
Mundelein (little guardian)
Munich, see Moench
Munk, Munke, see Moench
Munkshower (monk's meadow)
84, 151
Munster 122, see Muenster
Muntz, Munz, Muntzer,
Munzer, see Muentz
Murach (swamp river) 80, 79
Murbach (swamp brook) 80, 77,
122
Murdorf (swamp village) 80,
123
Murgenstern, see Morgenstern
151
Murlach (swamp pond) 80, 81

Murnau, Murner (swamp
meadow) 80, 84, 122
Muschel (mussel)
Musculus (Latin, muscle)
141
Muss < Dominicus,
Hieronymus) 131
Musse (leisure)
Musselman, Mussellmann
(Moslem, one who has
fought the Moslems)
Must, see Most
Muth, Muthe (courage,
disposition, mood) 46
Muth < Helmuth 53, 54
Mutscher, Mutschler,
Mutschke (baker of long
loaves) 96
Mutter (official measurer)
109
Myer, see Meyer 151
Mynhard, see Meinhard 151
Myrs, Myers, see Meyer 151
Myster, see Meister 151

N

Naas, Nass (wet, see Nase)
Nachbar, Nachbahr
(neighbor)
Nachlas (legacy)
Nacht (night)
Nachtigal, Nachtigall
(nightingale) 115
Nack 122, Nacke (nape of
neck) 114
Nader (sewer)
Nadler, Nadeler, Nadelmann
(needle maker) 96
Naegele, Naegeli (little nail,
clove) 105
Naff, see Neffe
Nafzger, Naffzer, Naftziger
(sleepy person) 115
Nagel, Nagell, Nagele Nagl,
Nagler (nail, nail smith)
96, 98, 106

Nagengast (stingy host) 96, 115
Nahrgan, Nahrgang (earning of
  nourishment, livelihood)
Nanamacher, see
  Nonnenmacher 151
Nangesser (probably fr
  Nongazzer)
Napfel, Nappel (an apple) 89
Nase, Nasemann (nose,
  promontory) 114, 74
Nass (wet), see Nase
Nassau, Nassauer (fr Nassau,
  swamp meadow) 80, 121
Nast (fr Ast, branch cutter) 95
Nastvogel (nest bird) 115
Nathan (OT name) 135
Natter (adder)
Nau, Nauer, Nauert, Nauerz
  (boatman, *nau* fr Latin
  navis)
Nauman, Naumann (new man),
  see Neumann
Naumburg (new castle) 122
Neander (Greek for Newmann)
  143
Nebel (fog)
Nebeling (fr land of fogs, cf.
  Nibelungen)
Needleman, see Nadelmann
  151
Neef, Neefer, see Neff
Neesemann (son of Agnes) 60
Neff, Neffe (nephew) 119
Nefzger, see Nafzger
Negele, Negle, see Naegele
Neher (ferryman)
Nehring (nutrition, subsistence;
  fr Nehring or Nehringen
  122)
Nehrkorn (fattening corn)
Neibauer, Neibuhr, see
  Neubauer
Neibling, Nuebling, see
  Nebeling
Neid, Neider, Neidert (envy,
  hater) 46, see also Neidhard
Neidenbach (stream brook) 83,
  77

Neidenberg (place name) 68
Neidhard, Neidhart,
  Neidhardt (hate + strong)
  46, 46
Neidig (envious) 115
Neidlinger (fr Neidling or
  Neidlingen) 122
Neifeld (new field) 84
Neighoff, see Neuhoff 151
Neihart, Niehart, see
  Neidhart
Neihoff, see Neuhoff
Neikirk, see Neukirk
Neimann, see Neumann,
  Niemann
Neimiller (new miller) 103
Neischwanger, see
  Neuschwander
Neisser (dweller near the
  Neisse River) 83
Neiswander, Neiswender,
  Neiswenter, Neiswinter,
  see Neuschwander 151
Neithard, see Neidhard
Nelde < Arnold
Nembhard (one who likes to
  take) 115
Nemeyer, see Niemeyer
Nemth, Nemetz, Nemitz, see
  Nimmitz
Ness (fr Nessen) 122
Nessel (nettle) 72
Nesselroth (nettle clearing)
  72, 126
Nessler (dweller in the
  nettles) 72
Nester (Greek, Nestor) 143
Nett, Netter (dweller on the
  Nette) 83
Nettelbladt (nettle leaf)
Netz (net, netz fisherman)
  106
Neu, Ney (new, new settler)
Neubach, Neubacher,
  Neubeck, Neubecker (new
  brook) 77

Neubauer, Neubaier (newly
arrived farmer, proprietor of
the Neuhof) 91
Neuber, Neubert, Neuberth, see
Neubauer
Neuberger (fr Neuberg 122,
new mountain) 68
Neuburger (fr Neuburg 122,
new castle) 73
Neudorff 122, Neuendorff (new
village) 123
Neuenschwander,
Neuenschwand 122, see
Neuschwander
Neufeld, Neufeldt (new field)
84, 122
Neugart, Neugarth, Neugarten
(new garden) 84, 122
Neugebauer, see Neubauer
Neuhart, Neuharth, see
Neidhart
Neuhaus, Neuhausen,
Neuhauser (new house) 65,
122
Neuhof, Neuhoff (new farm) 92,
122
Neukamp (new field) 84, 122
Neukirch (new church) 122
Neuland, Neulander (newly
cleared land) 125, 122
Neuman, Neumann (proprietor
of the Neuhoff)
Neumark (new boundary
marker) 122
Neumarkt (new market) 122
Neumauer (new wall)
Neumayer, Neumeier,
Neumeyer (new farmer,
proprietor of the Neuhof) 93
Neumeister (new master)
Neumyer, see Neumayer 151
Neun, Neuner (nine, ninth)
Neunuebel (nine evils)
Neupert, see Neubauer
Neuremberg, see Nuernberg
Neureuther (new clearing) 126
Neuschaefer, Neuschafer (new
shepherd) 95

Neuschwander,
Neuschwender (new
clearing) 126
Neuschwanger, see
Neuschwander
Neustadt, Neustater (new
city) 122
Newbauer, see Neubauer 151
Newberger, see Neuberger
151
Newfeld, see Neufeld 151
Newhagen (new enclosure)
155
Newhart, see Neidhart 155
Newhiser (see Neuhaus) 155
Newhof, see Neuhof 155
Newman, see Neumann 155
Newmeyer, see Neumeyer
155
Newmister, see Neumeister
155
Newstead, see Neustadt 155
Newwirth (new host) 155
Nibling, see Nebling
Nicewonder, see
Neuschwander 151
Nicholas, see Nikolaus
Nicht, Nichter (not, naught)
Nick < Nikolaus 53, 54
Nickel, Nickels (nickel, <
Nikolaus)
Nicodemus (St. Nicodemus)
131
Nicolai, Nicolay < Nikolaus
Nicolas, Nicolaus, see
Nikolaus
Nider ..., see Nieder
Nidorf, see Neudorf 155
Niebe (merry, lively) 115
Niebel, see Nebel
Nieber, see Neubauer
Niebuhr, Niebur, see
Neubauer
Nied, Niede (rivet, nail,
nailsmith) 106
Niedenthal, Niedentohl (low
valley) 76
Nieder (low)

Niederauer (fr Niederau 122, low meadow) 84

Niederhaus, Niederhausen, Niederhauser (fr Niederhausen 122, low house) 65

Niederhof, Niederhoff, Niederhuber (low farm) 92, 122

Niedermayer, Niedermeyer (proprietor of the Niederhof) 93

Niehaus, see Neuhaus

Niehof, see Neuhof

Niel, Nielmann (swamp, swamp dweller) 80

Nieman, Niemann, Niman, see Neumann

Niemand, Niemandt (no one)

Niemeier, Niemeyer, see Neumayer

Niemiller, see Neumiller

Niemitz, see Nimitz

Niemyer, see Neumayer

Niemoeller (proprietor of the new mill)

Nierendorf (lower village) 123, 122

Nierhaus (lower house) 65

Niermeyer, Niermyer, see Niedermayer

Nies, Niese, Nieser, Niess, Niessler, Niessmann (usufruct, also < Dionysius and Ananies)

Nighswander, see Neuschwander 155

Niklas, Niklaus, see Nikolaus

Nikolai, see Nikolaus

Nikolaus, Nikolas (St. Nicholas, name of a pope) 134

Nimann, see Nieman

Nimitz, Nimetz (Slavic: "the dumb one," German) 122

Nipp, Nipper, Nippert (dweller near water) 81

Niswander, see Neuschwander 155

Niswonger, see Neuschwanger 155

Nitchmann, see Nitsch

Nitsch, Nitszche, Nitschmann < Nikolaus 53, 54

Nitze < Nikolaus 53

Niwenhous, see Neuhaus 151

Nobel (noble, name of lion in Renard cycle)

Noble, see Nobel 151

Nodhart, see Nothart

Noes (place name) 122

Nofziger, see Nafziger

Nohrnberg, see Nuernberg 151

Nolder < Arnold

Noll, Nolls, Noller, Nollmann (heavy, simple person, hill) 115, 72

Nollendorf (hill village) 72, 123

Nolt, Nolte, Nolting, Noelting < Arnold 53, 54

Nongazzer (resident on nun alley) 65

Nonnenmacher, Nonemaker (pig castrator)

Noppenberger (woolnap mountain) 68, 122

Norbeck (northern brook) 77

Norberg, see Nordberg

Nord, Nordt, North (north)

Nordahl (north valley) 76

Nordberg (northern mountain) 68, 122

Nordbrook, Nordbruch (northern brake) 80, 122

Nordbruck (northern bridge)

Nordhaus, Nordhauser (fr Nordhausen 122, north house) 65

Nordheimer, Northeimer (north hamlet) 123

Nordhoff (northern farm) 92

Nordhus, see Nordhaus

Nordlingen, Nordlinger (fr Nordlingen 122)

Nordman, Nordmann
(northerner, Northman)
Nordorf (north village) 123, 122
Nordstrand (north beach) 122
Nordstrom (north stream) 77
North (north)
Noth (plight, hardship)
Nothard (battle + strong) 46,
46
Notte (nut) 89
Nottebom, Nottebohm, see
Nussbaum
Nowack, Nowak (Slavic: new
man)
Nuechterlein (moderate
drinker) 115
Nuernber, Nuernberger (fr
Nuremberg 122)
Nueschler (buckle maker) 96
Nuess, Nuessli, Nueslein,
Nuesslein (little nut) 89
Numeyer, see Neumeyer
Nummer (number)
Nunamacher, Nunnamacher,
see Nonnenmacher
Nungesser, see Nongazzer
Nurenberg, see Nuernber
Nushagen (nut hedge) 123
Nusholtz (nut wood) 89
Nussbauer, Nusbauer,
Nuszbaurn (nut farmer) 91
Nussbaum, Nusbaum,
Nussbaumer (nut tree) 89
Nusterer (maker of rosaries) 96
Nuswanger, see Neuschwanger
Nyenhuis, see Neuhaus
Nymann, see Neumann

O

Oakes, see Ochs 151
Oben (up above)
Obenauer (upper meadow,
beyond the meadow) 84
Obendorf, see Oberdorf
Obenheim (water hamlet) 80,
123 see Oberheim

Obenheyser (upper houses,
beyond the houses) 65
Ober (boss, superior)
Oberbeck (upper creek,
across the creek) 77
Oberberger (fr Oberberg 122,
upper montain, beyond
the mountain) 68
Oberdahlhof (upper valley
farm) 76, 92
Oberdorf, Oberdoerfer (fr
Oberdorf 122, upper
village, beyond the village)
123
Oberfehl, Oberfell (beyond
the swamp) 80
Oberfeld, Oberfeldt,
Oberfelder (upper field,
beyond the field) 84, 122
Oberheim (upper hamlet)
123
Oberheuser (upper houses)
65
Oberholtz, Oberholtzer
(beyond the forest) 72, 122
Oberkirch, Oberkirche (upper
church) 122
Oberkofler (upper monticule)
67
Oberkuhn (temerarious) 115
Oberlaender, Oberlander
(highlander, fr Oberland
122)
Oberle, Oberlin < Albrecht
Oberman, Obermann (boss,
superior)
Obermayer, Obermeyer,
Obermeier (chief bailiff)
93
Obermiller, Obermueller,
Obermuller (upper miller)
103
Oberndorf 122, see Oberdorf
Oberscheimer, Obersheimer
(upper hamlet) 123
Oberst (colonel) 107
Oberthaler (fr Oberthal,
upper valley) 76, 122
Obitz, see Opitz

Obmann (steward)
Obrist (see Oberst)
Obser, Obster (fruit grower or dealer) 89, 105, 143
Ochs (ox) 91, 149
Ochsenbacher (fr Ochsenbacher 122, ox brook) 77
Ochsenberger (fr Ochsenberg 122, ox mountain) 68
Ochsenfuss (ox foot) 114
Ochsenhirt (ox herder) 95
Ochsenreiter (ox clearing, ox rider) 126
Ochsner (ox raiser or seller) 95
Odenwald, Odewalt, Odewaelder (swamp mountains, mountains along Rhine) 121
Oechsele, Oechsle, Oechslin, Oechselin, Oexli (little ox) 149
Oechsener, see Ochsner
Oechsler, see Ochsner
Oechsli (see Oechsele)
Oefner, Oeffner (oven tender, oven maker) 98
Oehl (oil, oil dealer, fr Latin *oleum*) 105, 122
Oehler, Oehlers, Oehlert, Oehleret, see Ulrich, Eyler
Oehlstrom (eel stream) 77
Oelberg (Mount of Olives) 122
Oelhaf, Oelhafer (oil pitcher, oil dealer) 105
Oelken, Oelker (oil dealer) 105
Oellen, Oeller, Oelmann, Oellenschlaeger (oil maker) 96
Oertel, Oertli < Ortulf (point of sword + wolf) 46, 48
Oesch 122, Oescheler, Oeshler, see Esch, Eschelmann
Oesler (fr Oesel) 122
Oeste, Oester 122, Oesterle, Oesterlein, Oesterlin, Oesterling, Oestermann (easterly, man fr the east, see Oster)

Oestreich, Oestreicher, Oesterreicher (Austrian) 121
Oetting, Oettinger (fr Oettingen 122)
Oexler, see Ochsner
Ofenstein (oven stone) 73
Offenbach, Offenbacker (swamp brook) 80, 77, 122
Offenhauser (fr Offenhaus 122, swamp house) 80, 65
Offenstein (open stone) 73
Offer, Offerman, Offermann, see Opfermann
Offner, see Oefner
Oheim (uncle) 119
Ohl 122, Ohle < Odal (inherited property 47), see also Ahl
Ohl, see Oehl
Ohlbach 122, see Ahlbach
Ohlendorf, see Altdorf
Ohlenschlaeger, Ollenschlager (oil maker) 96
Ohler (oil dealer) 105
Ohlhausen (old houses) 65
Ohlhausen (swamp houses) 80, 65
Ohlhaver (last year's oats)
Ohlhoff (old farm) 92
Ohli, Ohliger, Ohlinger (oil dealer) 105
Ohlmacher (oil maker) 96
Ohlmann (old man)
Ohlmeyer (proprietor of the Ohlhoff) 93
Ohlschlaeger, see Ohlenschlaeger
Ohlweiler (old village) 123, 122
Ohlwein (old friend, see Alwin)
Ohm, Oheim, Ohms (mother's brother) 119
Ohne (without, see Ahn) 122
Ohnemann (without a husband)

Ohnesorg, Ohnisorg (without worry) 115
Ohnfeld (without a field) 84
Ohnhaus (without a house) 65
Ohnschild (without a shield)
Ohr (ear) 114
Ohrbach, see Auerbach
Ohrenschall (ear deafening noise)
Ohrle (little ear) 114
Ohrndorf, Orendorf (village on the Oren) 83, 123
Oldenburg (old castle, German province) 121, 122
Oldendorf, Ollendorf (old village) 123, 122
Oldhouse, see Aldhaus, Althaus 151
Oldhuis, see Althaus
Olenschlaeger, see Ohlenschlaeger
Olinger, Ollinger (fr Ollingen 122)
Ollrich, Olrick, see Ulrich
Olthof, see Althoff
Onangst, Ohnangst (without fear) 115
Opdebeek (on the brook) 70, 77
Openbrink (on the hill) 70, 74
Opfer, Opher (sacrifice, fr Latin *operari)*
Opfermann (sexton) 110
Opfertuch (sacrificial cloth)
Opitz < Albrecht 53
Oppenheim, Oppenheimes, Oppenheimer (open hamlet) 123, 122
Oppermann, see Opfermann
Oppert < Albrecht 53
Oppitz, see Opitz
Oppmann, see Obmann
Ordemann, see Ortmann
Ordner, see Ortmann
Orebaugh, see Auerbach 151
Orendorf, Orndorf (village on the Oren 83, swamp village 80, 123)
Orff < Ordolf (sword point + wolf) 46, 48

Orgelmann (organ player) 96
Orndorf, see Arndorf
Ornhold, see Arnold
Ornstein, Orenstein, see Arnstein
Ort, Orth, Ord, Oertli (place) 122
Ort, Orth (point of sword or spear 46, point of land)
Ortel, Ortell < Ortlieb, Ortwin, etc.
Ortlieb (point of sword + dear) 46, 48
Ortman, Ortmann, Orthmann, Ortmeyer (dweller at the end of the village) 94, 93
Ortner, see Ortmann
Ortwein (sword point + friend) 46, 48
Ortwig, Orwig (point of sword + battle) 46, 46
Osmann, see Ostmann
Ossenecker (ox field) 84, 85
Ossenfort (ox ford) 78
Ost (east)
Ostberg (east mountain) 68, 122
Ostendorf (east village) 123, 122
Oster (easter) 143
Osterberg, Osterberger (east mountain) 68, 122
Osterhaus (eastern house) 65
Ostericher (Austrian) 121
Osterle, see Oesterle
Osterling (easterner)
Osterloh (eastern forest, Easter fire) 122
Osterman, Ostermann, see Ostmann
Ostermayer, Ostermeier, Ostermeyer (eastern farmer) 93
Ostermueller (eastern miller) 103
Ostertag (Easter) 143
Osthaus (eastern house) 65
Ostmann (eastern man)

Ostreicher (Austrian) 121
Oswald, Ostwalt, Osswald (god
+ rule, English saint) 47, 71,
131
Otfried (treasure + protection)
47, 47
Otmar (treasure + famous) 47,
48
Ott, Otte, Odt, Utt (treasure)
47
Otten, Ottens < Otto 122
Ottendorf, Ottendorfer (Otto's
village) 123, 122
Ottenheim, Ottenheimer (Otto's
hamlet) 123
Otter (otter, otter hunter) 91,
122
Otterbach (swamp brook) 80,
77, 122
Otterbein (otter bone, otter leg)
Ottersheim (otter hamlet) 123

P

Pabst (pope, fr Latin *papa*)
110, 134, 143
Pabstmann (member of papal
party) 110
Pachmann, Pachmeyer (tenant
farmer) 93
Pacht, Pachter, Paechter
(tenant)
Packer, see Bacher
Packheiser (bake house) 65
Paebke (little priest) 110
Paetz 122, see Betz
Paetzsch, Paetsch < Petrus
Paff, see Pfaff
Paffenbach (priest's brook) 110,
77
Paffenroth (priest's clearing)
110, 126
Pagel, Pagels < Paulus
Pahnke (Slavic: young lord)
Painter (dweller in a fenced
inclosure)
Palmer (palmer)

Palzgraf, see Pfalzgraf
Palsgrove, see Palzgraf 151
Pamberg, see Bamberg 151
Pancer, see Pantzer 151
Panebaker, Pannabaker,
Pannabecker, see
Pfannenbecker 151
Pantzer, Panzer (breastplate,
fr Latin *pantex*) 108
Pape (priest, Latin *papa*)
110
Papel (poplar) 89
Papelbaum (poplar tree) 89
Papenberg, see Pappenberg
Papendorp (priest's village)
110, 123
Papp, Pappe, see Pape
Pappenberger (priests'
mountain, swamp
mountain) 80, 110, 68
Pappenheimer (fr
Pappenheim 122, priests'
hamlet, swamp hamlet)
80, 110, 123
Papst, see Pabst
Paris, Pariser (Parisian,
journeyman who trained
in Paris) 122
Parkent, Parmenter (fustian
dealer)
Parr (pair, couple)
Parris, see Paris
Part, Parth, Partz, see Bart
Pasch 122, Pasche (Easter
143, also fr French dice
game)
Paschke < Paulus 53, 54
Passaw, Passauer (fr Passau,
Latin *castra batava*) 122
Passmann (dweller in a
pass)
Pastorius (Latin for
Schaefer) 140
Pate, Path, Pathe (godfather,
fr Latin *pater*)
Patz, Patzer < Balthasar 53,
54

Pauck, Paucker, Pauckner
(drummer) 96
Paul, Pauls, Paulus (St. Paul,
name of pope) 134
Pauli, Pauly (son of Paulus)
142
Pauling, Paulinger, Paulmann
< Paulus
Paulitsch < Paulus
Paulus (St. Paul) 134
Pausch, see Baus
Pause (pause)
Paynter, see Painter 151
Peal, Pealer (see Buehl,
Buehler) 151
Pech 122, Peche (pitch, tar
maker) 96; see also Beck
Pechmann (tar maker) 95
Pechtle, see Bechtle
Peck, see Beck
Peel, Peeler, see Buehl,
Buehler
Peffer, Peffers, see Pfeffer
Peifer, Peiffer, see Pfeiffer
Peightel, see Bechtel 151
Peil, see Pfeil
Pelgrim, Pelegrim, Pellegrin,
see Pilgrim
Pelican (pelican, house name)
148
Peltz, Pelz, Peltzer, Peldner,
Peldtmann (pelt, hide
worker, fr Latin *pelis*) 96
Pennecker (little bear) 48
Penner (salt maker) 96
Pennypacker, Pennybaker, see
Pfannenbecker
Pepper, Peppermann, see
Pfeffer, Pfeffermann
Perger, see Berger
Perle (pearl)
Perlman (pearl dealer, possibly
Ashkenazic metronym for
"Pearl's husband")
Perlmutter (mother of pearl)
Pershing, Persing, Persinger,
see Pfirsich

Peter, Peters, Peterlein,
Peterke, Petrus (St. Peter)
131, 135
Peterly (son of Peter) 59,
142
Petersen, Peterson (son of
Peter) 59
Petri, Petry (son of Peter)
142
Petsch < Peter
Petz, Petts (bear, also <
Peter)
Petzold < Peter
Peukert (drummer, person fr
Peuker in Silesia) 96, 122
Pfaar 122, see Pfarr
Pfadenhauer (thread maker)
96
Pfaeffer (priest) 110
Pfaeffikon (priest village)
110, 127
Pfaff, Pfaffe (priest, fr Latin
papa) 110
Pfaffenberger (fr Pfaffenberg
122, priests' mountain)
110, 68
Pfahl (stake, fr Latin *palus*)
Pfaltz (Rhenish Palatinate,
from Latin *palatium*) 121
Pfalzgraf (palgrave, fr Latin
palatium + *graf*)
Pfanne, Pfanner (pan, pan
maker, fr Latin *panna)*
106
Pfannebecker (cake baker)
96
Pfannenstiel, Pfanstiel (pan
handle)
Pfanner (pan maker) 96
Pfannkuchen (pancake)
Pfannstiel, see Pfannenstiel
Pfarr (pastorate, fr Latin
parrochia) 122
Pfarrer (pastor) 110
Pfau (peacock) 115
Pfeffer, Pfeffermann (pepper,
seller of pepper, fr Latin
piper) 105
Pfefferkorn (pepper corn) 105

Pfeifenberger, Pfeiffenberger
(pipe mountain) 68
Pfeifer, Pfeiffer, Pfeiffers,
Pfeifere (fifer, fr Latin *pipa*)
96
Pfeil, Pheil, Pheyl (arrow, fr
Latin *pilus*, a javelin) 108
Pfeiler (arrow maker, fletcher)
108
Pfennig, Pfenning (penney)
Pfingst, Pfingstag, Pfingsten
(Pentecost, Whitesuntide)
143
Pfirsich, Pfersich (peach, fr
Latin *malum persicum*) 89
Pfister, Pfistner, Pfisterer
(baker, fr Latin *pistor*) 102
Pfitz, Pfitze, Pfitzer, Pfitzel
(flagellant)
Pfitzner, see Pfuetzner
Pflanz, Pflantz (plant, fr Latin
planta)
Pflaum (plumb, fr Latin
prunum) 89
Pflaumenbaum (plum tree) 89,
122
Pfleger (guardian, fosterer,
judge)
Pflueger (plowman) 91
Pflug (plow, plowman) 91
Pflug (a measure of plowland)
122
Pflugfelder (arable field)
Pfoersching, see Pfirsich
Pfoertner, Pfortner (gate
keeper, fr Latin *porta*)
Pfuetzner, Pfutzner (dweller by
a pond) 80
Pfuhl (puddle, fr Latin *puteus*)
80, 122
Pfund (pound), fr Latin *ponde*)
Pfutzner, see Pfuetzner
Pfyfer, see Pfeiffer
Ph ..., look under Pf
Pheidler (shirt maker) 96
Pheifer, Phifer, Phieffer, see
Pfeifer

Philip, Philips, Philipp (St.
Philip) 131
Philipi (son of Philip) 142
Philips, Philipson (son of
Philip) 59
Phister, see Pfister
Phyffer, see Pfeifer
Pichler, see Buehler
Pickel, Pickelman (pick) 106,
122
Pickli (little pick) 106
Piefer, see Pfeiffer
Piehl, Piel, Pihl, see Buehl
Piehler, see Buehler
Pieper, see Pfeifer
Pieters, Pieterse, see Peter
Pilger, Pilgrim, Pilgram
(pilgrim, fr Latin
peregrinus)
Pilgrim < Biligrim (sword +
helmet) 46, 46
Piller (sword + army) 46, 46
Piltz (mushroom, fr Latin
boleta) 105
Pinsel (artist's brush, fr
Latin *penicillus*)
Piper, see Pfeifer
Pister, Pistor, see Pfister
Pitsenberger, Pitzenbarger
(dweller near mountain
peak) 68
Plage (marshy grassland) 80
Planck (white)
Planckenhorn (white peak)
72
Platner, Plattner (sheet
metal worker, armor
maker) 108
Platte (small plateau)
Platz (place, village green, fr
Latin *platea*)
Pless, Plesse, Plessi < St.
Blasius 131
Plessing < St. Blasius 131
Pletsch, Pletscher, see
Platner
Plette, see Platner
Pletz (clothes patcher) 96

Ploeg, see Pflug
Plug, see Pflug
Plum, see Blum, Pflaum
Plumenstein (flower stone) 73
Poehlman, Poehlmann, see
    Pohlmann
Poehmer, see Boehmer
Poetzel, Poetzold, Poetsch <
    Peter
Poffenberger, see Pfaffenberger
Pogener, see Bogener
Pohl, Pohlner (Pole) 122
Pohl (pool, pond, swamp) 80,
    122
Pohl, Pohle, Pohler, Pohling <
    Paulus
Pohl (stake, fr Latin *palus*)
Pohlhaus (fr Pohlhausen 122,
    pond houses) 80
Pohlman, Pohlmann (dweller
    near a pool) 80
Poland, Polander (fr Poland)
    121
Poldermann (occupant of a
    polder)
Polmann, Pollmann, Pollner,
    Polner, see Pohlmann
Polther, Poltermann < St.
    Hippolytus 131
Pommer (Pomeranian) 121
Pommer (place name) 122
Pope, see Pape
Popp, Popps, Poppe, see Papp,
    Pappe
Porkholder, see Burghalter 151
Portz (place name) 122
Posner (fr Posen) 122
Possart, Possert, see Bosshart
Posthumus (posthumous)
Pot, Pott, Potts, see Bote
Potasch (potash maker) 96
Pothe, see Pot
Poth, see Bote
Potsdammer (fr Potsdam) 122
Potter (potter) 96
Pottgiesser (potter) 96
Potthast (potroast, porridge)
Powledge, see Paulitsch 151
Pracht (splendor) 122

Pradenhauer 96
Praetorius (Latin for
    Schultheiss) 141
Praeuner, see Braeuner
Prag, Prager (fr Prague) 122
Prahl, Prall (splendor,
    luxury)
Pramschufer, Pramschuefner
    (boat poler)
Prang, Prange (claw) 114
Pranger (pillory)
Praslaw (fr Breslau) 122
Prass, Prasse (glutton) 115
Precht, see Brecht
Prechtel < Helmbrecht 53,
    54
Prediger (preacher, fr Latin
    predicare) 109
Preis, Preiss, Preise, Preisz
    (praise, price, prize, fr
    Latin *pretium*)
Preising, Preisinger (fr
    Preisingen) 122
Preissle, Preissmann
    (shoelace maker) 96
Preller (shouter)
Presser, Pressler (fr Breslau)
    122
Presster, Prester, see
    Priester
Pretorius, see Praetorius
Preusch, Preuscher, see
    Preuss
Preuss, Preussner (Prussian,
    North German) 120
Prevost (prevost, fr Latin
    praepositus) 109
Price, see Preiss, Preuss
Prieber, Pryber < Pribislav
    (Slavic)
Priest, Priester (priest, fr
    Latin *presbyter*) 110
Printz, Prinz (prince, fr
    Latin *princeps*) 109, 122
Probst, Propst (provost, fr
    Latin *propositus*) 109
Prophet (prophet), fr Latin
    propheta) 135
Prost (simple) 115, 122

Prost (Prosit, a Latin toast)
  117
Pruner, Prunner, see Brunner
Pryss, see Preis
Puehl (pillow, fr Latin
  pulvinus) 106
Puetzbach (pond brook) 80, 77
Puhl (pool) 80
Puhlhoffer (farm by a pool) 80,
  92
Pulgram, see Pilgrim
Pullmann, see Pulvermacher
Pulver (powder)
Pulvermacher (powder maker)
Pundt, see Pfundt
Puntzius (Pontius Pilate,
  perhaps actor in morality
  play) 111
Pupper (doll maker) 96
Purpur (purple)
Putsch, Putscher (rioter)
Putz (finery, cleaning)

Q

Quade (wicked, dirty)
Qualbrink (agony hill) 74
Quandt, Quante (rascal) 115
Quandmeyer (rascal) 93
Quarengesser, Quarngesser
  (path along the Quern) 83,
  65
Quart (quart)
Quasebarth (glutton) 115
Quast (tassel, bather's whisk)
Quell (spring) 79, 122
Quenzer (card player)
Querfurth (fr Querfurth, city
  on the Querne) 83, 122
Querne (name of river) 83
Quetschenbach (plum brook)
  89, 77
Quick (alive, lively) 115
Quirmbach (fr Quernbach) 122
Quitman (quince dealer) 89,
  105

R

Raab, Raabe, see Rab
Rabanus (Latin for Rabe)
Rab, Rabb, Rabe, Raben,
  Rapp (raven)
Rabenau (raven meadow) 48,
  84, 122
Rabenecke (raven field) 48,
  85, 122
Rabenhorst (ravens' eyrie)
  48, 72, 122
Rabenstein (raven crag) 48,
  73, 122
Rach (vengeance)
Rachbach (muddy stream)
  80, 77
Rackensperger (muddy
  mountain) 80, 68
Radabaugh, Radebaugh,
  Radebach, see Rautebach
  151
Radebach 122, see
  Rautebach
Rademacher, Radmacher
  (wheelright) 96
Rademan, Radmann (marsh
  dweller) 80, see also
  Rathmann
Rader, Radner, Raderman,
  see Rademan
Radick < Radolf (counsel +
  wolf) 47, 48
Radke, Radtke < Conrad 53,
  54
Raeck, see Reck
Raeder, see Reeder
Raedermacher, see
  Rademacher
Raff, Raffer (scrawny person)
  114
Raffensberger, Raffensbarger
  (raven mountain) 48, 68
Raffschneider, see
  Reifschneider
Rafkamp (raven field) 48, 84
Rahder, see Rader
Rahl, see Rall

Rahm, Rahmm (cream) 122
Rahman, Rahmann (marsh
dweller) 80
Rahn (slender) 113
Rahn (brunet) 112
Rahnfelder, perhaps for
Rheinfelder
Raibold < Raginbold (counsel +
bold) 46, 46
Raichert, see Reichert
Rainard, Renard, see Reinhart
Raisbeck, Raischbeck (rapid
stream) 77
Rall (water rail) 115
Rambach, Ramsbach (swamp
brook) 80, 77, 122
Ramberg, Ramberger,
Ramsberg (raven mountain)
68, 122
Rame, Rahme, Ramm, see
Rahm
Ramer (creamer)
Ramler, Rammler (wether,
male hare)
Ramm (bear leek, *allium
ursinum*) 122
Rammelkamp (wether field) 84
Ramsau (meadow with bear
leek, *allium ursinum)* 84,
122
Ramsberg (raven mountain, or
mountain with bear leek
allium ursinum) 68, 122
Ramsburg (raven castle) 73
Ramsland (raven land) 48
Ramspacher, see Rambach
Ranck, see Ranke 122
Rand, Randt (edge of the
shield, shield) 46
Randolf (shield + wolf) 46, 48
Ranft (bread crust)
Rang, Rank (rank)
Ranke (tendril, climber, agile
person) 115
Rap, Rappe, Rab (black horse)
91
Raper, Rapert (counsel +
bright) 47, 47
Rapp, Rappe (black horse) 91

Rappolt < Ratbold (counsel +
bold) 47, 46
Rasbach, Rashpacker, see
Raschpacher 151
Rasch (swift) 115
Raschbacher, Raschpacker (fr
Raschbach 122, swift
brook)
Rat, Rath (counsel) 47
Ratenmacher, see
Rademacher
Rather, Ratherr (councilman)
159
Rathgeb, Rathgeber (advice-
giver)
Rathhauser (city hall) 65
Rathmacher, see Rademacher
Rathschild, see Rothschild
Ratmann, Rathmann,
Rattmann (councilman)
Ratner, see Radner
Ratschlag (advice)
Rattenauer (rat meadow, see
Reitenauer)
Ratz, Ratze (rat)
Rau, Raue, Rauh, Rauher
(rough, hairy) 115, 114
Raub, Rauber (robbery,
robber)
Raubach 122, Raubaugh, see
Rautebach, Rohbach
Raubenstine, see Rubenstein
151
Rauch (towsel haired) 112
Rauch (fish and meat
smoker) 96, 106
Rauchfass (incense burner)
106
Raudabaugh, see Rautebach
Raudabush, see Raudenbusch
151
Raudenbusch (rue bush, fr
Latin *ruta*)
Rauff (brawl)
Raugh, see Rau 151
Rauh, see Rau
Raum (room, space) 122
Raun, Rauner (mystery,
whisperer) 122

Raup, Raupp, see Raub
Rausbach, see Rauschbach
Rausch, Rauscher (rush,
   intoxication) 122
Rauschbach, Rauschenbach
   (bullrush stream) 81, 77
Rauschberg, Rauschenberg,
   Rausenberger (bullrush
   mountain) 81, 68
Rauschert (illegitimate child)
   119
Rauschkorb (reed basket) 106
Rauth (rod)
Rayser, see Reiser
Reach, see Reich 151
Read, see Ried 151
Reamer, see Riemer 151
Reaser, see Rieser 151
Reb, Reber, Rebert (grapevine,
   vintner) 106
Reback, see Rehbock 151
Rebein, see Rehbein 151
Reberg, Reberger (roe
   mountain) 68
Rebhahn, Rebhan, see Rebhuhn
Rebholtz (grapevine) 72, 122
Rebhoon, see Rebhuhn 151
Rebhuhn, grouse 115
Rebmann (vine dresser)
Rebsamen (grapeseed), see
   Ruebsamen
Rebstock (grapevine) 149
Rebuck, see Rehbock
Rechner (accountant) 169
Recht (right)
Rechter, Righter, see Richter
   151
Rechthand (right hand)
Reck, Recke (hero)
Reckenberger (fr Reckenberg
   122, marsh mountain) 80, 68
Reckenwald (marsh forest) 80,
   71
Recker, Reckers, Reckert,
   Reckman (dweller by a
   marsh) 80
Reckner, see Rechner

Rector (rector, see also
   Richter) 109
Redeman, Redemann (swamp
   dweller) 80, see also
   Rademann
Redenbaugh (swamp stream
   80, 77, 122), see also
   Reitenbach
Reder (councilman, see also
   Reeder) 109
Redmann, see Redemann
Ree ..., see Rie...
Reeb, see Reb
Reece, see Riess 151
Reed, see Riet 151
Reeder (shipowner)
Reep, Reeper, Reepschlaeger
   (rope, rope maker) 106
Rees, Reese, see Ries 151
Reeser, see Rieser 151
Regel (rule, fr Latin *regula*)
Regenhardt, see Reinhard
Regensburg (castle on the
   River Regen) 83, 73, 122
Regenstein (rain mountain,
   rock on the Regen River)
   83, 73, 122
Regenthal (Regen valley) 83,
   76, 122
Reger, Regert (heron, thin
   person) 114, 115
Reger (restless person) 115
Regler (monk in orders) 110
Regner (dweller on the
   Regen) 83
Regters, see Richter 151
Reh (roe) 122
Rehbein (roe bone)
Rehberg, Rehberger (fr
   Rehberg 122, roebuck
   mountain, see Reberg) 68
Rehbock (roebuck)
Rehder, see Reeder
Rehfeld (roe field) 84, 122
Rehfus, Rehfuss (roe foot)
   114
Rehorn (roebuck horn)
Rehkemper (roebuck field) 84

Rehkopf (roe head) 114, 149

Rehling (railing) 122

Rehm 122, Rem (strap cutter) 106, see also Reinmar

Rehman, Rehmann (marsh dweller) 80, see Raimann

Rehmeyer (marshland farmer) 80, 93

Rehwalt (roebuck forest) 71

Rehweg (roebuck path)

Reiber, Reibert (bath attendant, masseur) 96

Reibetanz (dance leader) 96

Reich, Reiche (empire, of the imperial party) 109, 122

Reich, Reicher, Reichert (rich) 115

Reichard, Reichhardt, Reichart, Reicharz (rule + strong) 46, 46

Reichel, Reichl, Reichle, Reichelt, Reichler < Reichard

Reichelderfer (Reichel's village) 151

Reichenbach, Reichenbacher (swamp stream) 80, 77, 122

Reichenbaugh, see Reichenbach 151

Reichenberg (swamp mountain) 80, 68, 122

Reichenecker (fr Reicheneck, swamp field) 80, 85, 122

Reicher, Reichert, see Reich

Reichman, Reichmann (rich man, imperial employee) 109

Reichter, see Richter 151

Reichwein (rule + friend) 46, 48

Reidenauer, see Reitenauer 151

Reidenbaugh, see Reitenbach 151

Reider, see Reiter 151

Reidnauer, see Reitenauer

Reif, Reiff (ripe, mature) 115

Reif (frost)

Reif (rope) 106

Reif, Reifen (ring, hoop) 106

Reiffschneider, Raiffschneider, Reifsnider, Reifsnyder (rope maker) 96

Reifschnieder, see Reiffschneider 151

Reifsnider, Reifsnyder, see Reiffschneider 151

Reighard, see Reichard 151

Reihart, see Reinhard

Reiland, see Rheinland 151

Reiman, Reimann (Rhinelander) 121, 151, 122

Reimar, Reimer, see Reinmar

Reimschneider, see Riemenschneider

Reimensnyder, Reimsnider, Reimensnyder, see Riemenschneider 151

Rein (clean, see Rhein)

Reinalt, see Reinhold

Reinart, see Reinhard

Reinbold < Reginwald (counsel + rule) 47, 46

Reincke, see Reinke

Reindollar, see Rheinthaler 151

Reineck 122, Reinecke, Reineke, Reinecker, Reinicker, see Reinke

Reiner, Reinert < Reinher (counsel + army) 47, 46

Reinfeld, Reinfelder 122, see Rheinfeld

Reinhard, Reinhardt, Reinhart, Reinheardt (counsel + strong) 47, 46

Reinheart, see Reinhard 151

Reinhold, Reinholdt, Reinholt (counsel + rule) 47, 46

Reinig, Reining, Reininger < Reinhard, Reinhold

Reinke, Reinicke, Reineke < Reinhart, Reinhold, etc.)

Reinknecht (stable boy, horse breeder)

Reinmar, Reimar (counsel + famous) 47, 47

Reinmuth (pure disposition)
115
Reinninger (fr Reining 122),
see Reinig
Reinohl, Reinoehl (pure oil, oil
dealer) 105, see Reinhold
Reinsch < Reinhold, Reinhard
Reinsfelder, Reinsfeller (fr
Reinsfeld 122), see Reinfeld
Reinstein 122, see Rheinstein
151
Reinthaler, see Rheinthaler
Reintzel, Reintzell, see Reinsch
Reinwald < Reginwald (counsel
+ rule) 47, 46, see
Rheinwald
Reis, Reiss (branch, faggot
gatherer) 95
Reis, Reise (journey, stone
slide)
Reisenweber, see Reusenweber
Reiser, Reisser, Rizer (traveler,
mercenary; dweller by a
stone slide)
Reiser (wood carver) 96
Reisfeld (stone slide field) 84,
122
Reisig, Reisiger, Reisinger
(dweller in the brush) 95
Reisig (armed for war) 107
Reising, Reissing, Reisinger
(knight on horseback) 107,
122
Reisman, Reissman, Reisner,
Reisler (soldier) 107
Reiss (journey, branch)
Reist, Reister (fr Reiste 122)
Reitberger (fr Reitberg 122,
bullrush mountain) 81, 68
Reitemeyer (clearing farmer)
126, 93
Reitenauer (fr Reitenau,
bullrush meadow) 81, 84
Reitenbach (bullrush brook) 81,
77
Reiter (rider, cavalryman) 107
Reiter (sieve) 106
Reith (clearing) 126, 122

Reitmeyer, see Reitemeyer
126, 93
Reitmueller (clearing miller)
126, 103
Reitnauer, see Reitenauer
Reitz, Reitzer (provocateur,
fr Reitz 122)
Reizer, see Reiser, Rieser
151
Remshard (marsh forest) 80,
72, 122
Renchler, see Rensch
Renck (vendace, a kind of
fish) 115
Rennenkampf ("Run into
battle!", aggressive person)
115, 116
Renner, Rennert (mounted
messenger)
Renninger, Reninger <
Reinhard
Renninger (place name) 122
Rennweg (path on mountain
ridge) 122
Renold, see Reinhold
Rensch, Renschler <
Reinhard, Lorentz
Rentner (pensioner)
Rentsch, Rentschler, see
Rensch
Rentz, Rentzel, Renz, see
Rensch
Rephann, see Rebhun
Repp, Reppe, Reppert (marsh
dweller)
Repphun, see Rebhuhn
Requardt < Rickward (rule +
guardian) 46, 47
Resch, Resh, Roesch, see
Rasch
Reser, see Rieser 151
Ress, Resse, Resse (swamp
dweller) 80
Rester (fr Resten) 122
Restar, Resta, see Rester
151
Reth (rushes) 81

Rethman, Rettmann (dweller at the rushes) 81

Rethmeyer, Rettenmeyer (farmer in the marsh) 81, 93

Rettberg (marsh farmer) 81, 68

Rettenburg (castle on the rushes) 81, 73

Retter, Reter (saver)

Rettig (radish, fr Latin *radix*) 105

Retz (dweller near swamp water) 80

Reu (remorse)

Reucher, Reuchert (meat or fish smoker) 96

Reudenauer, see Reitenauer

Reus, Reuse (eel trap) 106

Reusch, Reuschling (dweller in the reeds) 81, 122

Reusenweber (eel trap maker) 96

Reuss (Swiss river) 83

Reuss (Russian) 121

Reutenbach, see Reitenbach

Reuter, Reuther (cavalryman) 107

Reuter, Reuther (dweller in a clearing) 126

Reuthnauer, see Reitenauer

Rewold, see Rehwald

Rex (Latin for king) 109

Rey ..., see Rei and Rhei

Reybold, see Reinbold

Reydenauer, Reydenhower, see Reitenauer 151

Reyder, see Reiter 151

Reylandt, Reylender, see Rheinland 151

Reymann, see Rheinmann 151

Reyngold, see Reingold 151

Reynhart, see Reinhard

Reynolds, see Reinhold 151

Reys, see Reiss

Reyser, see Reiser

Reytenar, see Reitenauer 151

Reyter, see Reiter 151

Rezer, see Rieser 151

Rhein (Rhine) 83, 122

Rheinauer (meadow on Rhine) 83, 84

Rheinert, see Reinert

Rheinfeld (field on Rhine) 83, 84, 122

Rheingold (Rhine gold)

Rheinhard, Rheinhardt, see Reinhard

Rheinheim (hamlet on the Rhine) 83, 123

Rheinlaender, Rheinlender (Rhinelander) 121

Rheinstein (Rhine mountain, rhinestone) 83, 73, 122

Rheinstettler (fr Rheinstadt 122)

Rheinthal, Rheinthaler (Rhine valley) 83, 76, 122

Rheinwald (Rhine forest) 83, 71

Rhine, see Rhein 151

Rhinehart, see Reinhard 151

Rhinelander, see Rheinlander 151

Rhode, see Roth, Rode 151

Rhyner, see Reiner 151

Rhynhard, see Reinhard 151

Rice, see Reiss 151

Rich, see Reich 151

Richard, Richards, Richert, see Reichhard 151

Richman, see Reichmann 151

Richter, Richters (judge) 109

Richtersweil (judge's village) 109, 123

Richwein, Richwin, Richwien (rule + friend) 46, 48

Rick, Ricke, Ricker, Rickers, Rickert < Richard, Henrik

Rickel, Ricker, Rickert < Reichhard

Rickenbacher, Rickenback, Reichenbacher, Reickenbaker (fr Rickenbach 122, swamp brook 80, 77, 122)

Rickhoff (ridge farm) 68, 84

Rickmann (ridge dweller) 68

Rickter, Ricktor, Rictor, see
Richter 151
Ridder, see Ritter
Ridelsberg, Riddleberger,
Riddlespurger, see
Riedelsperger 151
Ridenauer, see Reitenauer 151
Ridenbaugh, see Reitenbach
151
Rider, see Reiter 151
Rieb, Riebe, Riep 122, see
Rueb
Riebman (turnip man) 105
Riebsame, see Ruebsamen
Riech, Riecher, Riechert,
Riechner < Richard
Rieck, Riecke, Rieckert <
Richard
Ried, Riedt, Riede, Reed (reed,
marshland) 81, 122
Riedel, Riedl, Riedling,
Ridelinger < Rudolf,
Ruediger 53, 54
Riedelsperger (Rudolf's
mountain) 53, 68
Rieder, Riedner (marsh
dweller) 81
Rieder (fr Rieden 122)
Riegel, Riegle, Riegelmann
(bolt, locksmith) 106
Rieger 122, Riegger, Riegert
(censurer), also < Ruediger
Riegler, Riegelman, Riegelmann
(locksmith, night watchman)
96, 109
Riehl < Rudolf 53, 54
Riehm, Riehme, see Riem,
Riemen
Riem, Riemen (strap, strap
cutter) 106
Riemann (Rhinelander) 121
Riemenschneider,
Riemenschnitter,
Riemschneider (strap cutter)
97
Riemer (strap cutter) 96
Rienhard, see Reinhard

Rienhof (farm on the Rhine)
83, 92
Rieper, see Reeper
Ries, Riese (giant) 149
Ries, Riese, Riess (timber
slide) 122
Riesberg (giant mountain) 68
Riesberg (timber slide
mountain) 68
Riesch < Rudolf 53
Riesenbeck (brook used for
logging) 77, 122
Riesenman (logger) 95
Rieser, Riesser, Reezer
(logger) 95
Riesinger, see Reisinger 151
Riet 122, Rieth 122, see
Ried
Riethmueller (miller on the
marsh) 81, 103
Rietweill (reed village,
marsh village) 81, 127
Rietwiese (marshy meadow)
81, 84
Rietz, Rietze < St. Mauritius
131, 122
Right, see Recht 152
Righter, see Richter 151
Rightmeyer, see Reitmeyer
151
Rightnour, see Reitenauer
151
Rightor, see Richter 151
Rigler, see Riegler
Rimbach (swamp-water
creek) 80, 122
Rinde (bark, bark collector)
95
Rinder (cattle) 91
Rindfleisch (beef, butcher) 96
Rindlaub (cattle foliage,
probably house sign) 149
Rindskopf (cow head) 114,
149
Rine, see Rhein 151
Rinecker, see Reinecker 151

Rinehard, Rinehart, Rinehardt, Rineheart, see Reinhard 151

Rinehimer, see Rheinheimer 151

Rineholt, see Reinhold 151

Rinestein, see Rheinstein 151

Ring, Ringe, Rings, Rinck, Rink (ring) 106

Ringel, Ringle, Ringeler, Rinkler, Ringelman (ring maker) 96

Ringelstein (place name) 122

Ringer (ring maker) 96

Ringgold, Ringold, see Rheingold

Ringsdorf (circular village) 123

Ringwald (encircling forest)

Rink, Rinker, Rinkert, Rinkler (clasp maker) 106

Rink, Rinker, Rinkert (round hill) 68

Ripley, Ripli < Ruprecht 53, 54

Rippart < Ruprecht 53, 54

Rippe (rib)

Rippe (swamp grass) 81

Rippel < Ruprecht 53, 54

Ripple, see Rippel 151

Risberg, see Riesberg

Risch (swamp) 80

Rischel (swamp dweller) 80

Rischenbeck (swampy brook) 80, 77

Rischhof (swamp farm) 80, 92

Rischstein (marsh stone) 80, 73

Riser, see Reiser, Rieser 151

Rising, Risinger, see Reising, Reisinger 151

Rismiller (swamp miller) 80, 103

Riss, Risse (gap, gorge) 122

Riss (swamp) 80, 122

Rissman (swamp dweller) 80

Risterholtz (bullrush forest) 81, 72

Ritenour (fen swamp) 81, see Reitenauer

Riter, Rither, see Reiter 151

Ritger, see Rutger 151

Ritmueller (miller on the marsh) 80, 103

Ritschard (fr Old French Richard)

Rittenauer (reed meadow) 81, 84

Rittenbach (reed brook) 81, 77

Rittenberg (reed hill) 81

Rittenhaus (reed house) 81, 65

Rittenhouse, see Rittenhaus 151

Rittenour, see Reitenauer 151

Ritter, Riter (knight) 107

Ritterbusch (knight's crest)

Ritterbush, Ritterpush, see Ritterbusch 151

Ritterman, Rittermann (trooper) 107

Rittmeister (cavalry captain) 107

Rittmeyer (reed farmer) 81, 93

Ritz, Ritzel (St. Euricius, St. Moritius, Henricius) 131

Ritzenberg (St. Moritz Mountain), 131, 68, 122

Ritzenthal (St. Moritz Valley) 131, 76

Ritzheim (St. Moritz hamlet) 131, 123

Ritzman, Ritzmann (servant of St. Moritz convent) 139

Rizer, see Reiser 151

Road, see Roth 151

Robacher, see Rohbach

Robertus (latin for Robert) 141

Robke, Robken < Robert 53, 54

Robling, see Roebling

Robrecht, see Ruprecht

Rock (gown) 112, 106

Rockefeller, Rockafeller < Roggenfelder (rye fields) 84

Rockenbach (rye brook) 77, 122
Rockenbauch (potbelly) 114
Rockenbaugh, see Rockenbach
151
Rockenbrod, see Roggenbrod
Rockenstihl (rye stalk, tall thin
person) 114
Rockstroh (rye straw)
Rodabaugh (clearing brook)
126, 77, 151
Rode (clearing) 126
Rodefeld (cleared field) 126, 84
Rodeheaver (clearing farmer)
126, 92, 151
Rodel, see Rudel
Rodemann (forest clearer) 126
Rodemeier, Rodemeyer (clearing
farmer) 126, 93
Rodenbach (clearing brook) 126,
77, 122
Rodenberg (cleared mountain)
126, 68, 122
Rodenhauser (fr Rodenhausen,
clearing houses) 126, 65
Rodenhiser, Rodenhizer,
Rodenizer, see Rodenhauser
151
Rodenstein 122, see Rotenstein
Roder (forest clearer) 126
Roder < Rodhari, famous +
army) 47, 46, 53, 54
Roder (place name) 122
Rodewald (cleared forest) 126,
71, 122
Rodman, Rodner (clearing
dweller) 126
Roeber, see Reber
Roebling < Robert
Roebling (fr Roeblingen, swamp
water) 80, 122
Roedeger, see Ruediger
Roedel (scribe, fr Latin *rotula*)
Roeder < Rother (famous +
army) 46, 47
Roeder, see Reeder
Roediger, see Ruediger
Roehl < Rudolf 53, 54
Roehm, see Rehm

Roehn, Roehner (rune) 122
Roehr (rushes) 81
Roemer (bragger) 115
Roemer (loving cup) 106
Roemer (Rome pilgrim)
Roenike, Roennecke <
Hieronymus (Jerome)
Roepke < Robert 53, 54
Roes (swampy ground) 80,
122
Roesberg, Rossberg (swamp
mountain) 68, 122
Roesberg (horse mountain)
68
Roesch, Roescher, see Rasch
Roeser (swamp dweller) 80
Roesler, Roessler,
Roesselmann, Roesemann
(carter) 96
Roesli, Roesslein (little
horse) 91
Roess, Roesser, Roessner, see
Roes, Roeser
Roetenbach (red brook) 77,
122
Roettger, see Ruediger
Roger (French, fr *Hrodoger*,
famous + spear) 47, 46
Rogge, Roggemann (rye, rye
dealer) 105
Roggenbrod (rye bread)
Roggenfeld, Roggenfelder
(rye field) 84
Roggenkamp (rye field) 84,
122
Roggensuess (rye sweet)
Roh, Rohe (raw)
Rohauer (cleared meadow)
126, 84
Rohback (clearing brook)
126, 77
Rohde (see Rothe, Rod)
Rohfeld (cleared field) 126,
84
Rohland, see Roland
Rohleder, Rohlehr (rawhide,
tanner) 96, 106

Rohlff, Rohlfs, Rohlfing, see
Rolf
Rohling < Rudolf 53, 54
Rohm, see Rahm
Rohman, Rohmann (dweller in
a clearing) 126
Rohn, Rohne, Rohner <
Hieronymus (St. Jerome)
Rohn, see Rahn
Rohr, Rohrs (reed, pipe) 81,
122
Rohrbach, Rorbach, Rohrback,
Rohrbacher, Rohrbeck (reed
brook) 81, 77, 122
Rohrbaugh, see Rohrbach 151
Rohrer (dweller by rushes) 81
Rohrig (swampy, covered with
reeds) 81
Rohrmann (marsh dweller) 81
Rohrmoser (dweller on the
reedy marsh) 81, 80
Roisch, see Reusch 151
Roland, Rolandt, Rolland
(illustrious + land) 126
Roland (cleared land) 125
Rolf, Rolff, Rolfes, Rolfers,
Rolfing < Rudolf 53, 54
Roller (carter) 95
Rombach, see Ronbach
Romer, see Roemer
Romisch (Roman)
Rommel, see Rummel
Rompf, see Rumpf
Romshower (tree trunk cutter)
95, 151
Ronbach (fallen tree brook) 89,
77
Roner (dweller among the
fallen trees) 89
Roorig, see Rohrig
Roos, Roosen, see Rose
Ropach, see Rohbach
Rosbach, Rosbeck (swamp
brook) 80, 77, 122
Rosdorf (swamp village) 80,
123, 122
Rose, Rosen (rose)
Rosenau, Rosenauer (swamp
meadow) 80, 84, 122

Rosenbach, see Rosbach
Rosenbalm (rose balm) 148
Rosenbauer (rose farmer,
horse farmer) 92
Rosenbaum (rose tree) 89,
148
Rosenberg, Rosenberger
(swamp mountain) 80, 68,
148, 122
Rosenblat, Rosenblatt (rose
leaf) 148
Rosenblit, Rosenbluth (rose
blossom) 148
Rosenblum, Rosenbloom (rose
blossom) 148, 151
Rosenbohm, Rosenboom 151,
see Rosenbaum
Rosenbower, see Rosenbauer
151
Rosenbusch (rosebush) 148
Rosenbush, Rosennbush, see
Rosenbusch 151
Rosencrans, Rosencranz,
Rosenkrantz (rosary) 106
Rosendahl, Rosendale,
Rosendall 122, see
Rosenthal
Rosendorf (swamp village)
80, 123
Rosenfeld, Rosenfelder,
Rosenfeldt (horse field) 84,
122
Rosenfeld (rose field) 84, 148
Rosenfield, see Rosenfeld
Rosengarden, Rosengarten
(rosegarden) 84, 122
Rosenhain, Rosenshein (rose
grove) 72, 122
Rosenhauer, see Rosenauer
Rosenhaupt (rose head)
Rosenheim, Rosenheimer
(swamp hamlet) 80, 123,
122
Rosenmueller (miller on the
Rosbach)
Rosensteel, Rosenstiel (rose
stem)
Rosenstein, Rosensteen
(swamp mountain) 80, 73

Rosenstern (rose star)
Rosenstock (rose bush)
Rosenthal, Rosenthall (swamp
   valley) 80, 76, 122
Rosenwald (swamp forest) 80,
   71
Rosenzweig (rose branch)
Rosfeld, see Rosenfeld
Rosli (little horse)
Rosner (carter)
Ross (steed, rose) 122
Rossau, see Rosenau
Rossbach, see Rosenbach
Rossenbaum, see Rosenbaum
Rossenberg, see Rosenberg
Rossenthal, see Rosenthal
Rosser (carter) 95
Rosskamm (horse dealer) 105
Rosskopf (horse head) 149
Rossler (carter) 95
Rossman, Rossmann (carter) 95
Rossnagel (horse shoe nail,
   blacksmith) 96, 106
Rotchild, see Rothschild 151
Rotenberg, Rotenberger (red
   mountain) 68, 122
Rotenburg (red castle) 73, 122
Rotenstein (carpenter's pencil)
Rotermund (red mouth) 114
Rotgerber (tanner) 97
Roth, Rothe, Rother (red)
Roth, Rothmann (clearing,
   dweller in a clearing) 126,
   122
Rothaar, Rother (red hair) 112
Rothacker (cleared field) 126,
   84
Rothacker (red field) 84
Rothage (cleared enclosure)
   126, 123
Rothenbacher (fr Rotenbach
   122, red brook) 77, 122
Rothenberg 122, Rothenberger,
   see Rotenberg
Rothenbuecher (fr Rotenbuch,
   red beech) 89, 122

Rothenburg, Rothenburger
   (fr Rothenburg 122, red
   castle) 73
Rothenheuser (fr Rothenhaus
   122, red house) 65
Rothenhoefer (fr Rothenhof,
   red farm) 92, 122
Rothermel (red sleeve) 112
Rothermund (red mouth) 114
Rothfus, Rothfuss (red foot)
   114
Rothgabe, Rothgeb, see
   Ratgeber
Rothhaas (red hare) 115
Rothholtz (red wood) 72
Rothhouse (red house) 65,
   see also Rathauser 151
Rothkamp (swamp field) 80,
   84
Rothkamp (cleared field) 84
Rothman, Rothmann
   (clearing dweller) 126, see
   also Ratmann
Rothmeyer, Rothmeier
   (clearing farmer) 126, 93
Rothrock (red gown) 112
Rothschild, Rothscheld (red
   shield, a house name) 149,
   158
Rothstein 122 (red
   mountain), see Rotenstein
Rott 122, Rotte, Rottman,
   Rottmann (troop, trooper)
   107
Rottmund, see Rothermund
Rotz, Rotzer (flax processor)
   95
Rouf, see Rauf 151
Rouland, see Roland 151
Rous, Roush, see Rausch 151
Roushenbacht, see
   Rauschenbach 151
Routh, see Rauthe 151
Rowland, see Roland 151
Royce, see Reuss 151
Rozen..., see Rosen 151
Rozencwaig, Rozencweig, see
   Rosenzweig 151

Rubenthal (turnip valley) 76
Rubert, see Ruprecht
Rubi, Ruby, Rubin, Rubins
  (ruby), see Rubinstein
Rubincam, Rubincamp (turnip
  field) 84
Rubinstein, Rubenstein (ruby)
  73
Rubenstien, see Rubenstein 151
Rubrecht, see Ruprecht
Rubright, see Ruprecht 151
Ruch, see Rauch
Ruck, see Rueck
Rucker, Ruckert < Ruediger 53,
  54
Rude < Rudolf 53
Rudegaire, see Ruediger 151
Ruckstuhl (chair with back)
Rudel, Rudell (pack, herd)
Rudi, Rudy < Rudolf, Ruediger
  53, 54
Rudiger, see Ruediger
Rudmann, Rudemann (leader of
  hounds, or < Rudolf)
Rudolf, Rudolph (illustrious +
  wolf) 47, 48
Rudolphi (son of Rudolf) 142
Rueb (turnip eater, turnip
  raiser or dealer) 112, 105
Ruebeck (turnip brook) 77
Ruebel (rape cultivator, fr
  Latin *rapum*) 91
Ruebenacker (turnip field) 84
Ruebenzahl (turnip tail,
  (Silesian spook)
Ruebsamen (turnip seed)
Rueck (jerk)
Rueckenbrot, see Roggenbrot
Ruecker, Rueckert (dweller on
  ridge)
Ruede (large hound)
Ruediger (illustrious + spear)
  47, 46, 39
Rueg, Rueger (reproof)
Ruehl, Ruehle, Ruel < Rudolf
  53
Rueppel < Ruprecht
Ruessel (trunk, snout)

Rueter (land clearer) 126,
  also error for Reuter
Ruetiger, Ruettiger,
  Ruettger, see Ruediger
Ruetsch (slide)
Ruf, Ruff, Roof (call), 151
  < Rudolf 53
Ruger, see Rueg
Ruh, Ruhe (rest)
Ruhl, Ruhle, Ruhling,
  Ruhlmeyer < Rudolf 53,
  54
Ruhland, Ruland, see Roland
Ruhm (fame)
Ruhrwein (stir wine) 116
Ruhsam (restful) 115
Rükeyser (dweller in a ridge
  house) 67, 65
Rulmann, Rullman < Rudolf
  53, 54
Rumbacker (fr Rumbach
  122) 77, 151
Rumbaugh, see Rumbacker
  151
Rummel, Rummler (hurly-
  burly) 115
Rump, Rumpf, Rumph (sieve
  in a gristmill) 106
Rumpf (torso) 114
Rumpel, Rumple (noise
  maker) 115, 151
Rund (round)
Rundberg (round mountain)
  68
Rung, Runge (wainwright)
  96, 106
Runkel, Runckel (marsh
  root) 81, 122
Runkelstein (reed mountain)
  81, 73
Runkhorst (swamp hurst) 81,
  72
Ruoff, see Ruff
Rupert, Ruppert, Rupertus,
  see Ruprecht
Rupp, Ruppel < Ruprecht 53,
  54

Ruppertsberger, Ruppersberger
(Ruppert's mountain) 68, 122
Ruprecht, Rupprecht (famous +
bright) 47, 47
Russ, Russe (rust), < Rudolf 53
Russel, see Ruessel
Rust (reeds, rushes) 81, 122
Rutger < Ruediger
Ruth, Rute (rod)
Ruth < Hrodomar (famous +
famous) 47, 47
Rutmann, Ruttmann, see
Rudmann
Rutschild, see Rothschild
Rutschman < Rudolf 54, 53
Ruttger, see Ruediger
Ruyter, see Reiter
Ryder, see Reiter 151
Rylander, see Rheinlander
Rynhart, see Reinhart 151
Rynthal (Rhine valley) 83, 76
Ryser, see Reiser, Rieser 151
Rysling, see Reisling 151
Ryther, see Reither, Reuther
151
Rytter, see Ritter 151

S

Saal (hall) 122
Saalig, see Selig
Saalwechter (hall waker)
Saat (seed, newly planted
grain) 122
Saatfeld (newly planted field)
84
Saatkampt, see Saatfeld
Sabel (saber) 108
Sach (thing, cause)
Sachs, Sachse (Saxon) 120
Sachmann, see Sackmann
Sack (sack) 122
Sackman (member of baggage
train) 107
Sacks, see Sachs
Saddler, Sadtler, see Sattler
Saefried, see Siegfried

Saeger (sawyer) 95
Saegmueller (sawmiller) 96
Saeli < Salomo
Saemann (sower) 95
Saemanshaus (sower's house)
65
Saemueller, see Seemueller
Saenger (singer, cantor) 96
Saeuberlich (clean) 115
Saffold, see Siegbald
Sager, Sagenmann (minstrel)
96
Sagmiller (sawmiller)
Sahl, see Saal
Saidemann, see Seideman
Sailer, see Seiler
Saks, see Sachs
Salbeck (swamp brook) 80,
77
Salberg (swamp mountain)
80, 68
Salfner, Salffner
Sali, Salli, Sally, Salley
(little Salomo)
Salinger < Salomo, also fr
Salingen 122
Salmann, Sallmann,
Sahlman (trustee,
custodian)
Salmann (hall man)
Salomo, Salomon, Salomon
(OT name) 135
Saltmann, see Salz
Saltner (forester, fr Latin
saltarius)
Salz, Saltzer, Salzer,
Saltzman, Saltzmann (salt
seller) 105, 122
Saltzberg, Salzberg (salt
mountain) 68, 122
Saltzgaver, Saltzgiver (salt
dealer) 105
Samann, see Saemann
Samenfink (seed finch) 115
Samet, Sameth, Sammet,
Sammeth (velvet dealer)
105
Samler, Sammler (collector)

Sammet, see Samet
Sampson (OT name) 135
Samstag (Saturday) 143
Samuel (OT name) 135
Sand, Sander, Sanders <
    Alexander, fr Sand 122
Sandberg (swamp mountain)
    80, 68, 122
Sandbower (swamp peasant)
    80, 91, 151
Sanderson (son of Sanders) 59
Sandhaus (swamp house) 80,
    65, 122
Sandhofer (fr Sandhof 122,
    swamp farm) 80, 92
Sandkuhler (fr Sandkuhl 122,
    swamp pool) 80, 80
Sandmann (swamp dweller) 80
Sandmeier (proprietor of the
    Sandhof, swamp farm) 80,
    93
Sanftleben (gentle life, bon
    vivant) 115
Sanftmut (gentle disposition)
    115, 139
Sanger, see Saenger
Sangmeister (choir leader)
Santen (fr Xanten) 122
Santer < Alexander, or fr
    Xanten
Santmeyer, Sandmeyers, see
    Sandmeier
Sarazin (Saracen)
Sartory, Sartorius (Latin for
    tailor) 141
Sass, Sasse, Sassen, Sasser,
    Sassman, Sassmann (Saxon)
    120, 122
Sattel (saddle) 106, 122
Sattelthaler (saddle valley) 76
Sattler (saddler) 96
Sattler (dweller on mountain
    pass)
Sauber, Sauberlich (clean, fr
    Latin *sobrius*) 115
Sauer, Saur, Sauers, Saure
    (river name, spring, swamp)
    80, 83
Sauerbier (sour beer) 112

Sauerbrei, Sauerbrey (sour
    pottage) 112
Sauerland ("southern land,"
    mountain range in
    Westphalia) 121, 122
Sauermilch (sour milk) 112
Sauerwein (sour wine) 112
Saul (OT name) 135
Saum (hem, boundary) 106
Saum (load, pack animal, fr
    Latin *suma*)
Saur, Saure, see Sauer
Sauter, Sautter, see Suter
Sax, Saxen, see Sachs
Sayler, see Seiler
Scammele, see Schemel
Schaab, see Schabbe
Schaadt, see Schad
Schaaf, see Schaf
Schaal, see Schall
Schabbe (shabby, skinflint)
    115
Schaber (scraper) 106
Schablein (shavings)
Schach (checkmate, wooded
    area) 122
Schacht (mine shaft) 122
Schacht, Schachtschneider
    (shaft maker) 96
Schacht (reed-bank) 81
Schachtel (box, case)
Schachter, Schachtner, see
    Schaechter
Schad, Schade, Schaden,
    Schadlein, Schadt (swamp
    water) 80
Schaeberle (scrapings)
Schaech, Schaecher (thief)
Schaechter (butcher) 96
Schaedel, Schadel (skull) 114
Schaefer, Schaefers,
    Schaeffer (shepherd) 95
Schaeffler, see Scheffler
Schaeflein (little sheep) 91
Schaefner, see Schaffner
Schaener, see Schoener
Schaenkel (leg) 114
Schaerer, see Scherer
Schaerf (sharp, sharpness)

Schaumloeffel (skimming spoon) 106
Schazel (little treasure)
Schechter, Schecter (Jiddish: slaughterer)
Scheck (dappled horse)
Schedel, see Schaedel
Scheel, Scheele, Scheeler, see Schiel, Schiele, Schieler
Scheeper, see Schaeffer
Scheer, Scheerer, Schehr, see Scher, Scherer
Scheermann, see Schermann
Scheermesser (shearing knife) 106
Scheetz, see Schuetz 151
Schef, Scheff, see Schief, Schiff
Scheffel (bushel) 106
Scheffel (*scabinus*) 109
Scheffer, Scheffers, see Schaefer
Scheffler (barrel maker)
Scheffner, see Schaffner
Scheib, Scheibe (disc, round pane) 106, 122
Scheid, Scheide, Scheidt (sheath) 106
Scheid (watershed, boundary) 122
Scheidecke, Scheidekke (dweller on a watershed or boundary) 122
Scheidel, Scheidler (arbitor)
Scheider, Scheidemann, Scheidmann (umpire)
Scheidt, see Scheit
Scheif, Scheiffler (crooked, askew)
Scheimer, Schaeumer (skimmer, cook) 96
Schein ..., see Schoen ...
Scheit, Scheiter (split log, woodcutter) 95
Scheithauer (log splitter) 95
Scheler, Schelbert (squinter) 114
Scheler (bark pealer) 95
Schell (bell, manacles) 106

Schellberg, Schellenberg, Schellenberger (swamp mountain) 80, 68, 122
Schellenschloeger, Schellenschlaeger (bell ringer)
Scheller (bell ringer, see Schaller)
Schellhaas (flushed, startled hare)
Schellhaus, Schelhaus (dirt house) 65
Schellhorn (trumpet, trumpeter) 96, 122
Schelling, see Schilling
Schellkopf (noisy person) 115
Schellmann (bell maker) 96
Schemel, Schemmel (footstool, fr Latin *scamillus*) 106
Scheneberg (reed mountain) 81, 68, see Schoenberg
Schenefeldt (reed field) 81, 84, 122, see Schoenfeld
Scheneman, Schenemann, see Schoenemann
Schenfeld, see Schenefeldt
Schenk, Schenck, Schenke (cup bearer, inn-keeper) 96
Schenkel, Schenckel (thigh) 114
Schenkemeyer (village taverner) 96, 93
Scheper, Schepers, see Schaeffer
Scheppler, see Scheffler
Scher, Scherr, Scherer, Sherer (barber, shearer, warper) 106
Scheraus (shearing house) 65
Scherf, Scherff, see Scharf, Scherflein 122
Scherflein (widow's mite)
Scherg, Schergh, Scherge (beadle, hangman's helper) 109
Schermann (shearer) 96

Schermesser, Scheermesser
(shearing knife, shearer) 106
Scherr, see Scher
Schertz, Schertze, Schertzer,
Scherzer (jester, jokester)
Schetzel (little treasure)
Scheu (shy) 115
Scheuer (tithe barn) 122
Scheuermann (barn supervisor,
barn builder)
Scheuermeyer (barn bailif) 93
Scheufler, Scheufeler (shovel
maker) 96
Scheunemann (barn supervisor)
Scheunemann (manager of a
tithe barn) 109
Scheurer (scourer, occupant of
a tithe barn)
Scheussler, see Schuessler 151
Schevaler (chevalier, cavalier)
Schey, see Scheu
Scheydt, see Scheit
Scheyer, see Scheuer
Schick (skill, dexterity, well
mannered) 115
Schieber, Schiebert (fr Schieben
122)
Schiedmann (arbiter)
Schief (crooked) 114
Schiefer, Schieffer (slater) 96
Schieferdecker (slater) 96
Schieffler (vacillator) 115
Schiel, Schiele (squinter) 114
Schiele, see Schule
Schierg, see Scherg
Schierman (marsh dweller 80,
boundry dweller), see also
Schermann
Schiermeister (worker in
charge of equipment)
Schiesser (baker's helper,
dweller on a steep slope) 96,
71
Schiff, Schiffe (ship)
Schiffbauer (ship builder) 96
Schiffer, Schiffmann (boatman)
149
Schiffhauer, see Schiffbauer

Schild, Schildt, Schiltz
(shield) 108, 106
Schilder (painter, shield
decorator) 96, 108
Schildhauer (shield maker)
108
Schildknecht (squire) 107
Schildkraut (thyssum)
Schildwachter,
Schiltwaechter (sentry)
107
Schilf (bullrushes) 81
Schiller (redish wine)
Schiller (squinter) 114
Schilling (shilling)
Schilling (freedman) 122
Schimel, Schimmel (white
horse)
Schimmelmann (greybeard)
112
Schimmelpfenig (miser) 115
Schimmelreiter (rider of a
white horse)
Schimpf, Schimpff (play,
amusement, entertainer)
96
Schinckel, see Schenkel
Schindel (shingle) 106, 122
Schindeldecker,
Schindelmann (roof
shingler) 106
Schindler (roofer) 96
Schine, see Schein 151
Schinkel, see Schenkel 151
Schipp (boat)
Schipper, Schippert, see
Schiffer
Schirach (Wendish: George)
Schirm, Schirmer (protector)
169
Schisler, Schissler, see
Schuessler
Schlachte (battle)
Schlachter, Schlahter
(slaughterer) 96
Schlade (reed-bank) 81, 122
Schlaechter (butcher) 96
Schlaegel, see Schlegel

Schlaffer (sleeper)
Schlag (blow)
Schlag (clearing, cf.
  Kahlschlag) 126
Schlagel, see Schlegel
Schlaich, see Schleich
Schlang (snake) 115, 149
Schlatter (swamp or marsh
  dweller) 80
Schlauch (wine bag, tube, hose)
  106, 122
Schlebach (sloe brook) 77
Schlebohm (sloe tree, wild
  plum tree) 89
Schlecht (simple, slight,
  straightforward) 115, 122
Schlechter, Schlechtermann
  (butcher) 96
Schlee, Schlehe (sloe) 89
Schlegel, Schlegl (mallet) 106,
  122
Schlegel (turnkey) 109
Schlegemilch (buttermilk 112,
  milk dealer 105)
Schlehdorf (wild plum village)
  89, 123, 122
Schleich, Schleicher,
  Schleichert (one who sneaks
  about or else walks in a
  stately fashion) 115, 122
Schleich (muddy place) 122
Schleier (veil maker) 106
Schleiermacher (veil maker) 96
Schleife, Schleiff (slip-knot)
  106, 122
Schleifer, Schleifner (grinder)
  96
Schleigh, see Schleich 151
Schlemmer (gormand, guzzler)
  115
Schlencker, Schlenker
  (shambler) 115
Schlesien, Schlesing,
  Schlesinger, Schlessinger
  (Silesian) 121
Schleucher, see Schleicher
Schleuder (sling shot) 107
Schley (fish dealer) 105, see
  Schlee

Schleyer, see Schleier
Schlicht, Schlichter (simple,
  smooth haired) 112
Schlicht (high flat area) 122
Schlick (mud, slime) 122
Schliemann (seller of
  freshwater fish) 105
Schliesser, Schliessers,
  Schliessmann (keeper of
  the keys, of the stores)
Schlimm, Schlimme (slight,
  simple) 115
Schlimp (diagonal)
Schlitt (sled)
Schlitz (muddy stream) 80
Schlitz (slit, slash) 112
Schloegel, Schlogel, see
  Schlegel
Schloss (lock, castle,
  locksmith) 106, 122
Schlosser (locksmith) 96
Schlossherr (chastelain) 96,
  see Schlosser
Schlossnagel (locknail) 106
Schlott, Schlotte, Slot (castle)
  122
Schlotter, Schlottman,
  Schlottmann (locksmith)
  96
Schlotterbeck (swamp brook)
  80, 77
Schlotterer (wobbler,
  doddering) 115, see also
  Schlatter
Schluecker, Schlucker
  (swallower, guzzler) 115
Schlueter, Schlueters
  (locksmith, keeper of the
  keys)
Schlumberger (gorge
  mountain) 68
Schlund, Schlundt (gorge)
Schluss (conclusion)
Schlussel, see Schluessel 151
Schluter, see Schlueter
Schmach (disgrace)
Schmaehling (slender person)
  113
Schmaek, see Schmeck

Schmaeussner, see Schmeiser

Schmahl, Schmahle, see Schmal

Schmal, Schmale, Schmall (narrow) 114

Schmalbach (narrow stream) 77, 122

Schmaltz, Schmalz, Schmalz (lard, tallow, candler) 105

Schmaus (banquet)

Schmeck (gourmet, taster) 115

Schmeiser, Schmeissner (thrower, slinger)

Schmeltz (enamel 106, 122, fr Schmeltz 122), see Schmaltz

Schmeltz (iron foundry)

Schmeltzer (melter, smelter, enameler) 96, fr Schmeltz 122

Schmerbauch (lard belly) 114

Schmerz (pain)

Schmick, Schmicke, see Schmuek

Schmid, Schmide, Schmids, Schmidt, Schmidte, Schmidts, Schmidtt, Schmidtz, Schmit, Schmith, Schmitt, Schmitte, Schmitz (Smith) 96

Schmidtbauer, Schmidtmeyer (smith farmer) 96, 92

Schmidtknecht (smith's helper) 96

Schmied, Schmiedt (smithy)

Schmieg (cuddle)

Schmierer (laugher, smiler) 115

Schmit, Schmitt, Schmitz, see Schmid

Schmittlein (little smith) 96

Schmoke, see Schmueck 151

Schmoller (pouter, sulker) 115

Schmollinger (tar boiler) 95

Schmolze, see Schmaltz

Schmueck, Schmuck (adornament)

Schmuecker (adorner) 96

Schmuecker (fr Schmueck, swamp) 122

Schmutz (dirt, filth)

Schnaack, Schnack (chitchat, nonsense)

Schnaack (deer fly)

Schnabel (snout, talkative person) 114, 115

Schnaebele (little snout) 114

Schnaid (trail cut through woods) 122

Schnaider, see Schneider

Schnall, Schnalle (buckle) 106, 122

Schnap, Schnaps (brandy)

Schnatter (chatterer, gabbler)

Schnauber (snorter) 115

Schnauffer (snorter) 115

Schnautz (snout) 114

Schnebele, see Schnaebele

Schneberger (fr Schneeberg 68, 122), see Schneeberg

Schneck, Schnecke (snail, snake, slow poke)

Schnee (snow)

Schneeberg, Schneeberger (fr Schneeberg 122, snow mountain) 106

Schneeganz (snow goose)

Schneehagen (snow enclosure) 123

Schneemann (snowman)

Schneeweiss (snow white) 112

Schneewind (snow wind)

Schneibly, see Schnaebele

Schneickburger (snail castle) 73

Schneid, Schneiden (mountain ridge)

Schneider (tailor) 104

Schneiderjohann (tailor John) 104

Schnel, Schnell (swift, active) 115

Schnellbacher (fr Schnellbach 122, rapid brook) 77

Schnellenbach (fr
Schnellenbach 122), rapid
brook 77
Schnellewind (strong wind)
Schnellmann (fast man, active
man) 115
Schnepf, Schnepfe, Schnepp,
Schneppe (snipe, weakling)
115
Schneyder, see Schneider
Schnider, see Schneider 151
Schnitter (reaper) 95
Schnitzel (chip, wood carver)
106
Schnitzer, Schnitzler, Schnizler
(cutter, wood carver) 96, 122
Schnor, Schnorr (cadger,
peddler) 105
Schnuck (small sheep) 91
Schnur (daughter-in-law) 119
Schnur, Schnurer, Schnurman
(string, string maker) 106
Schober, Schobert (haystack)
122
Schoch (hay stack)
Schock, Schoek, Schockmann
(swamp) 80
Schoedel, see Schaedel
Schoeff (assessor) 109
Schoeffler, see Scheffler
Schoemaker, see Schumacher
151
Schoemburg (beautiful castle)
73
Schoen, Schoene, Schoeny 151,
Schoener, Schoenert
(beautiful, handsome) 115,
122
Schoenau, Schoenauer
(beautiful meadow) 84, 122
Schoenbacher (fr Schoenbach
122, beautiful brook) 77
Schoenbaum (beautiful tree) 89
Schoenberger (fr Schoenberg
122, beautiful mountain,
shiny mountain) 68, 157
Schoenbild (beautiful picture)
Schoenbruck (beautiful bridge)

Schoendorf (beautiful village)
123, 122
Schoeneck (beautiful field)
85, 122
Schoenemann, Schoenmann
(beautiful man) 115
Schoener (fr Schoeningen
122), see Schoen
Schoenfeld, Schoenfeldt,
Schoenfelder (beautiful
field) 84, 122
Schoenhaar (beautiful hair)
112
Schoenhals (beautiful throat)
114
Schoenhardt (beautiful
forest) 72, 122
Schoenhof (beautiful forest)
92, 122
Schoenholtz, Schoenholtzer
(beautiful forest) 72, 122
Schoenknecht (beautiful
servant)
Schoenleben (the good life)
Schoenmann, see
Schoenemann
Schoenmannsgruber (fr
Schoenmann's valley) 76
Schoenthal (beautiful valley)
76, 122
Schoenwald, Schoenewalt
(beautiful forest) 71
Schoenweiss (beautiful
white) 112
Schoepf (scoop, place for
drawing water)
Schoerck, see Schubert
Schofer, Schoffer, see
Schaefer
Schoff (shed)
Schoffstal (sheep fold)
Schofner, see Schaffner
Schol, Scholle, Scholl (soil,
farmer, clodhopper)
Scholler (farmer, clodhopper)
Scholt, Scholtz, see Schultz
Schomaker, Schomakers, see
Schumacher
Schomann, see Schumann

Schombach, see Schoenbach,
  Schaumbach
Schomberg (beautiful mountain)
  68
Schomburg 122, Schomburger,
  see Schoemburg,
  Schaumburg
Schon, Schone, see Schoen
Schon ... , see under Schoen ...
Schonbach, see Schoenbach
Schonberg, see Schoenberg
Schonfeld (beautiful field) 84
Schonfield, see Schonfeld 151
Schopf (shock of hair) 112
Schopp 122, Schoppe (measure
  of wine)
Schorbach (dirty stream) 77,
  122
Schorch (fr French: Georges)
Schornstein (chimney)
Schott, Schotte (curds) 112, 105
Schott (bulkhead) 122
Schott (Scot) 122
Schotter (gravel)
Schotthofer (dairy) 92
Schoultz, see Schultz 151
Schoumburg, see Schaumburg
  151
Schour, see Schauer 151
Schrader, see Schroeder 151
Schram, Schramm, Schramme
  (scratch, abraision, wound)
Schranck, Schrank (cupboard,
  wardrobe) 106
Schranne (crack in glacier)
Schraub (screw) 106
Schrecengost, Schrecongost,
  Schreckengaust, Schrengost
  (Frighten the guest!) 116
Schreck (jump, fright) 122
Schreck (muddy ground) 80
Schreffler (bloodletter) 96
Schreiber, Schreiver (scribe) 96
Schreier (town crier) 96
Schrein, Schreiner (cabinet
  maker, fr Latin *scrinarius*)
  99
Schrempff (cut, wound)

Schreyder (gristmiller) 96
Schreyer, see Schreier
Schriber, see Schreiber 151
Schrimpf, Schrempf (cut,
  scar) 114
Schroeder, Schroeter,
  Schroter, Schroder,
  Shroder, Shrader (tailor)
  104
Schroff (rugged) 115
Schroll (clod, clodopper)
Schrott (bruised grain,
  groats) 106, 122
Schu (shoe, shoemaker) 96,
  104
Schub (push, shove)
Schubdrein (Shove it in!) 116
Schubert, Schuberth
  (shoemaker) 104
Schuch, Schuchard,
  Schuchart, Schuchardt
  (shoe, shoemaker) 96, 104
Schuchman, Schuchmann
  (shoemaker) 104
Schuck, Schucks, Schucker,
  Schuker, Schuckermann
  (shoe, cobbler) 96, 104
Schude, Schuder, Schudt,
  Schudy, see Schutt
Schuebel, Schueble (bushel)
  122
Schuele, Schuelle, see Schule
Schueler, Schuehler,
  Schueller, see Schuler
Schuenemann, Schuenmann
  (barn man)
Schuerer, Schuermann
  (scourer)
Schuessel, Schuessler (bowl,
  bowlmaker, fr Latin
  scutella) 106
Schuett, Schuette (rubble)
  122, see Schuetz
Schuetz (marksman) 107,
  122
Schuh (shoe, shoemaker)
  106, 104
Schuhl, see Schule

Schuhmacher (shoemaker) 104
Schuhmann, see Schumann
Schuhriem, Schuhriemen
(shoestrap, shoe lace) 106
Schuld, Schuldt (guilt, debt)
Schuldenfrei (debt free) 115
Schulder, see Schulter
Schuldheis, see Schultheiss
Schule, Schull (school,
synagogue, fr Latin *scola*)
Schulenberg (hidden mountain)
68, 122
Schulenburg (hidden castle) 73,
122
Schuler, Schueler, Schuller
(pupil)
Schulhoff (school yard) 92
Schulius (Latin for Schule) 141
Schulkind (school child)
Schullehrer (school teacher)
Schulmann, Schulmeister
(teacher)
Schult, see Schuld
Schult, Schulte, Schultes, see
Schultheis
Schulteis, see Schultheis
Schulter, Schulther, Schulters
(shoulder) 114
Schulter (debtor)
Schultheis, Schultheiss (village
magistrate) 109
Schultz, Schulz, Schulze, see
Schultheis
Schumacher, Schumaker, see
Schuhmacher
Schuman, Schumann, see
Schuhmacher
Schumer (cheat) 115
Schumm, see Schuhmacher
Schumpeter (Cobbler Peter)
104
Schunemann, see Scheunemann
Schunk, Schunke (shank,
thigh) 114
Schupp (scale)
Schuppen (shed)
Schurman, Schurmann (dweller
by a pond 80), see also
Scheuermann

Schurtz, Schurz (apron,
skirt, shirt) 106
Schuss, Schusz (shot)
Schuss (very steep slope) 122
Schussele, see Schuessel
Schuster (shoemaker, fr
Latin *sutor*) 104
Schut, Schutt, Schutte
(rubbish, rubble)
Schutz, Schutze (watchman,
guard), see Schuetz
Schwaab, Schwab, Schwabe,
Schwaber (Swabian) 120
Schwabeland, Schwabenland,
Schwabland (Swabia) 120
Schwabline (little Swabian)
120, 151
Schwaeher (brother-in-law)
119
Schwager (brother-in-law)
119
Schwaiger, see Schweiger
Schwalb, Schwalbe (swallow)
115
Schwalb (dweller near the
Schwalb, swamp) 83
Schwalbach (swamp brook)
80, 77, 122
Schwall, Schwalls (swamp)
80, 122
Schwalm (name of river,
swamp water) 80, 83
Schwamb, Schwamm,
Schwam (sponge) 106
Schwan (swan) 48, 149
Schwander, Schwandner,
Schwandter, Schwandtner
(occupant of a clearing
126, fr Schwand 122)
Schwandt (clearing, see
Schwander) 126, 122
Schwanebeck, Schwanenbeck
(swan creek) 48, 77, 122
Schwanfelder (fr Schwanfeld
122, swan field) 48, 84
Schwanger (pregnant)
Schwank, Schwanke (swing,
farce)
Schwantz (tail)

Scrivers, see Schreiber 151
Sebald, see Siegbald 151
Seacrist, see Sigrist 151
Seafred, Seafret, Seafrett, see
  Siegfried 151
Seager, see Sieger 151
Seagle, see Siegel 151
Sebald, see Siegbald 151
Sebastian (St. Sebastian) 131
Sebeniecher (seven oaks) 89
Sebert, see Siegbrecht
Sebold, Seboldt, Seabold,
  Seabolt, see Siegbald
Seckel (satchel, satchel maker)
  106
Seckinger (person fr Seckingen)
  122
Secrest, Secrist, see Sigrist
Sedlmayer, see Seddelmeyer,
  see Sattelmeyer 151
See (lake) 122
Seebach, Seebacher (lake
  brook) 80, 77, 122
Seeberg, Seeberger (lake
  mountain) 80, 68, 122
Seefeld, Seefeldt (lake field) 80,
  84, 122
Seefret, see Siegfried 151
Seeger, Seegar, Seger, see
  Sieger 151
Seegmiller (sawmiller) 103, 151
Seegrist, see Sigrist
Seekamp (lake field) 80, 84,
  122
Seel (soul)
Seel (swamp) 80, 122
Seelhorst (swamp hurst) 80, 72
Seelig, see Selig
Seelmann (swamp dweller) 80
Seemann (seaman)
Seemann (dweller on a lake)
  80
Seemueller (miller on the lake)
  80, 103
Seethaler (fr Seethal, lake
  valley) 122
Seewald (lake forest) 80, 71
Sefeldt, see Seefeld
Sefret, see Siegfried 151

Sefues < Josephus
Segbolt < Siegbald 151
Segel (sail) 106
Segeler, Segler (sailor, sail
  maker) 96
Seger, see Sieger 151
Segfried < Siegfried 151
Segmond, see Siegmund
Sehl (swamp) 80, see also
  Seel
Sehlhorst (swamp hurst) 80,
  72
Seib (sieve) 106
Seibald, see Siegbald
Seibel, see Siegbald
Seibert, Seipert < Siegbert
Seibold < Siegbald
Seibrandt < Siegbrand
Seidel, Seidell (mug, pint)
  106
Seideler, Seidler, Seidelmann
  (mug maker) 96
Seidemann, Seidenman,
  Seidman, Seidenspinner
  (silk worker) 96
Seidenschnur (silk thread)
  106
Seidner (silk worker) 96
Seif, Seifensieder (soap
  boiler) 106, 96
Seifert, Seiffert, Seifarth,
  Seifferth < Siegward
Seigel, see Siegel 151
Seigler, see Ziegler 151
Seil, Seile, Seiler (rope
  maker) 106
Seilback (fr Seilbach 122,
  rope brook), see Selbach
Seiler (rope maker) 96
Seip, Seipel, Seipell, Seippel,
  Sippel < Siegbald
Seippert < Siegbert
Seiss (sythe) 106
Seitz, Seiz, Seitzer < Siefried
Seivert, Seivers, see
  Siegfried, Siegwart
Sekler (sack maker) 96
Selbach (swamp brook) 80,
  77, 122

Selde (house, shelter) 65
Seldenreich (fortunate) 115, see
  Seltenreich
Selig (fortunate, blessed) 155
Seligman, Seligmann (blessed
  man) 155
Sell, Selle 122, Seller, Sellner,
  Selman, Sellmann (marsh
  land) 80
Sellmayer (farmer on the
  marsh) 80, 93
Selmer (hall + famous) 47
Selpert (hall + bright) 47
Seltenreich (seldom rich) 115,
  see Seldenreich
Seltzer, Selzer (salt merchant,
  meat and fish salter) 105, 96
Seman, Semans, see Saemann,
  Seemann 151
Semmel, Semmler, Semler
  (blond) 112
Semmel, Semmler, Semler
  (white roll baker) 96
Senck, Senk, Senkler
  (inhabitant of a burned off
  clearing) 126
Sendel, Senderling (swamp
  dweller) 80
Sender < Alexander 53, 54
Sender (dweller in a burned
  clearing) 126
Sendldorfer (swamp village) 80,
  123
Senf (mustard) 105
Senfelder, Senffelder,
  Sennfelder (mustard field) 84
Senft (gentle) 115
Senftleber, see Sanftleben
Seng, Senge (burned off land)
  84, 122
Sengebusch (burned shrubland)
  72
Senger (singer) 96
Sengeysen (scorching iron) 106
Sengstake (Burn the poker!,
  stoker) 116, 96
Senkel (lace) 106
Senn (Swiss shepherd) 95

Sennewald (shepherd's
  forest) 95, 72
Sennhauser (occupant of
  shepherd's hut) 95, 65
Sens (reed grass) 81
Sensabaugh, Sensebaugh
  (reed brook) 81, 77, 151
Sensenmann (reaper) 95
Senstack, see Sengstake
Sentheim, see Sontheim
Seppel, Seppler, Seppi <
  Josef, Giuseppi 53, 54
Sermatt (fr Zermatt) 122
Setmayer, see Settelmann
Settelmann, Settleman
  (dweller on a mountain
  saddle)
Settelmeyer, see Settelmann
Setzer, Setzler (compositor)
  96
Seuberlich, see Saeuberlich
Seubert, Seuberth < Siegbert
Seubold < Siegbald
Seuer, see Saeuer
Seuffert, Seufried < Siegfried
Seuter (shoemaker, fr Latin
  sutor) 104
Sevalt < Siegbald
Sevart, Severt, Sewrt <
  Siegwart
Severin (St. Severin) 131,
  122
Sewalt, see Seewald 151
Seybel < Siegbald
Seybert < Siegbert
Seybold, Seybolds < Siegbald
Seydel, see Seidel
Seydelmann (mug maker) 96
Seydelmann (silk worker) 96
Seydensticker (silk
  embroiderer) 96
Seydler, see Seydelmann
Seydt, see Seide
Seyfer, Seyfert, Seyvert,
  Seyferth, Seyfarth,
  Seyfardt < Siegwart
Seyfreet, see Siegfried 151

Seyfrid, Seyfrit, Seyfritz,
   Seyfried, Seyfriedt <
   Siegfried
Seyl, Sylar, see Seiler 151
Seyler, see Seiler
Seymond < Siegmund,
   Sigismund
Seyppel < Siegbalt
Sh ..., see under Sch
Shade, Shadlein, see Schad,
   Schadlein 151
Shafer, Shaffer, Shaefer,
   Shaeffer, see Schaeffer 151
Shaller, see Schaller 151
Shambaugh, see Schaumbach,
   Schambach 151
Shanebacker, see Schoenbacher
   151
Shanefelter, see Schoenfelder
   151
Shaner, see Schoener 151
Shank, see Schenk 151
Shantz, see Schantz 151
Shauder, see Schauder 151
Shauer, see Schauer 151
Sheaffer, see Schaeffer,
   Schiefer 151
Shealy, see Schiele 151
Sheats, Sheets, Sheetz,
   Sheatsen, see Schuetz,
   Schuetzen 151
Sheeler, Sheely, see Schieler,
   Schiele 151
Sheildknight, Scheldknight, see
   Schildknecht 151
Shenk, see Schenk 151
Shepperd, see Schaefer 152
Sherman, see Schermann 151
Shiller, see Schiller 151
Shilnite, see Schildknecht 151
Shimelman, see Schimmelmann
   151
Shindle, see Schindel 151
Shirer, see Scheurer 151
Shissel, Shissler, see Schuessel,
   Schuessler 151
Shmal, Shmall, see Schmal 151
Shnyder, see Schneider 151

Shoemaker, see Schumacher
   151
Shoffner, see Schaffner 151
Sholl, see Scholl 151
Shonfeld, see Schoenfeld 151
Shoney, see Schoene 151
Shonik, see Schoeneck 151
Shrader, see Schroeder 151
Shriner, see Schreiner 151
Shriver, see Schreiber 151
Shroder, see Schroeder 151
Shubert, see Schubert 151
Shuler, see Schueler 151
Shults, Shultz, see Schultz
   151
Shumaker, see Schumacher
   151
Shuman, see Schumann 151
Shutts, see Schutz 151
Sibert < Siegbert
Sibold < Siegbald
Sichel (sickle, fr Latin
   sicilis) 106
Sichelstiel (sickel handle)
   106
Sicher (secure, fr Latin
   securus)
Sieb, Siebe (sieve) 106, 122
Siebelt < Siegbald
Sieben (seven)
Siebeneichen (seven oaks)
   89, 122
Siebensohn (seven sons)
Sieber, Siebers (strainer,
   siever) 106
Siebert < Siegbert
Siebold, Sieboldt < Siegbald
Sieck (sick)
Sieck (marsh) 80, 122
Siecrist, see Sigrist 151
Siedel (settler, boiler)
Siedentop (boiling pot) 106
Siefer, Sieffert, Siefferts,
   Sieverts, Sievers, Siewers,
   see Siegwart
Sieg (victory) 46, 122
Sieg (river name, swamp)
   80, 83

Siegbald (victory + bold) 46, 46
Siegbert, Siegbrecht (victory +
bright) 46, 47
Siegbrand (victory + sword) 46,
46
Siegehrist, see Sigrist 151
Siegel, Siegal, Siegler, Siegle,
Sigle (seal, fr Latin *sigillum*)
106
Siegel < Siegfried, Siegward,
etc. 53
Siegenthaler, Siegenthahler
(victory valley)
Sieger, Siegert (winner)
Siegfried (victory + protection)
Siegle, Sigle, Siegal, Sigle, see
Siegel 151
Siegler, see Siegel, Ziegler
Siegman, Siegmann (victor) 46
Siegmund, Sigismund (victory
+ guardian) 46, 47
Siegrist, see Sigrist
Siegwald (victory + rule) 46, 46
Siegwart, Siegworth (victory +
guardian) 46, 47
Siehdichum (Look around!) 116
Siemer, Siemering < Siegmar
(victory + famous) 46, 47
Sieppert < Siegbert
Sievers, Sievert, Sieverts <
Siegwart
Sieweart, see Siegwart 151
Siewers, see Sievers 151
Sigel, Sigl, Siegel, Sigler, see
Siegel, Siegler
Sigfritz < Siegfried
Sights, see Seitz 151
Sigman, Sigmon, see Siegman,
Siegmund
Sigmund, see Siegmund
Sigrist, Sigrest (sexton, fr
Latin *sacrum*) 110
Sigwalt, Siewald < Siegwald
Sigwart, see Siegwart
Sihler, see Seiler 151
Silbaugh, see Selbach 151

Silber, Silbers, Silbert,
Silver, Silvers (silver,
silver smith)
106
Silberberg, Silverberg (silver
mountain) 68, 148, 122
Silberhorn (silver horn)
Silbermann, Silverman
(silver smith) 96
Silbermetz (silversmith) 96
Silbernagel, Silvernail (silver
nail) 106
Silberstein, Sillverstein
(silver stone, silver
mountain) 73, 122
Silberzahn (silver tooth)
Siler, see Seiler 151
Silver, see Silber
Simeon (OT name) 135
Simmel (baker of white rolls)
106
Simmermann, see
Zimmermann 151
Simon, Simons (NT name)
131
Singer, Singert, see Saenger
Singhaus (concert house) 65
Singvogel (song bird) 115
Sinn (mind, idea)
Sinn (swamp water) 80
Sipart, see Siegbert
Sipe, see Seib
Sipp, Sippen (kinsman) 119
Sippel, Sipple < Siegbald
Sirach (OT name) 135
Siskind, see Suesskind
Sites, see Seitz 151
Sitzer (sitter)
Sivert < Siegwart
Siwald, see Seewald,
Siegbald 151
Sl ..., see under Schl ...
Slagle, see Schlegel 151
Slater, see Schlatter 151
Slaubaugh (meadow brook)
84, 77, 151
Slaybaugh (blackthorn brook)
89, 77, 151

Slauch, see Schlauch 151
Slaughter, see Schlechter 151
Slaymaker, see Schleiermacher 151
Slechter, see Schlechter 151
Slegel, see Schlegel 151
Slemaker, see Slaymaker 151
Slemmer, see Schlemmer 151
Slicher, see Schleicher 151
Slosser, see Schlosser 151
Slotman, see Schlosser 151
Sluss, see Schluss 151
Sly, see Schley 151
Sm ..., see Schm ...
Small, see Schmal 151
Smick, see Schmueck 151
Smit, Smith, see Schmidt 151
Smith, see Schmidt 151
Smoke, see Schmuck 151
Smouse, see Schmauss 151
Sn ..., see under Schn ...
Snavel, see Schnabel 151
Snavely, see Schnaebele 151
Sneckenberger, see Schneckenberger 151
Snee, see Schnee 151
Sneider, see Schneider 151
Snell, see Schnell 151
Snider, Sniders, see Schneider 151
Snively, see Schnaebele 151
Snyder, Snyders, Snyderman, see Schneider 151
Soeldner (mercenary, fr Latin *solidarius*) 107
Soeller (fr Soell 122)
Soeller (balcony, fr Latin *solarium*)
Soeter (shoemaker) 104
Sohn, Sohns (son) 119
Sol (mud, bog) 80
Soldan, see Soltan
Soldier, see Soeldner 151
Soldner, see Soeldner 151
Solms (swamp water) 80, 122
Solomon, see Salomo 151
Soltan (sultan)
Solter, see Saltzer

Soltmann, see Salz, also inhabitant of Solt 122
Sommer, Somer, Sommers (summer)
Sommerfeld 122, Sommerfelt (summer field) 84
Sommerfield, see Sommerfeld 151
Sonderman, Sondermann (swamp dweller) 80
Sondheim (swamp hamlet) 80, 123, 122, see Sontheim
Sonn (sun)
Sonnefeld, Sonnenfeld (sun field) 84, 122
Sonnenberg (sun mountain) 68, 122
Sonnenleiter, Sonnelitter (fr Sonnenleite, sunny slope) 71
Sonnenschein (sunshine) 122
Sontag, Sonntag (Sunday) 143
Sontheim, Sontheimer (south hamlet) 123, 122
Sooter, see Sutter 151
Sorber (Sorbian) 121
Sorg, Sorge (care, worrier) 115, 122
Sorgenfrei (care free) 115
Sower, see Sauer 151
Spaar, see Spahr
Spaengler, see Spengler
Spaeth, Spaet, Speth (late, tardy) 155
Spahn (swamp) 80
Spahr (sparrow) 115
Spaight, see Spaeth 151
Spainhour, Spainhower, see Spanhauer 151
Span (chip)
Spange (buckle, bracelet) 106
Spangenberg, Spangenberger (swamp mountain) 80, 68, 122
Spangler, see Spengler 151
Spanhauer (chip hewer) 95
Spanier (Spaniard) 121

Spann 122, see Span
Spar, see Spahr
Sparenberg (sparrow mountain)
  68
Sparr (rafter) 122
Spath, see Spaeth
Spatz (sparrow, urchin) 115
Specht, Spaecht (woodpecker)
  115
Speck (lard, pork seller) 105
Speck, Speckmann (raised path
  through a bog, corduroy
  road) 65, 122
Speelmann, see Spielmann
Speer, Speers, Speert (spear)
  107, 108
Speicher, Speichert (granary, fr
  Latin *spicarium*) 122
Speidel (woodcutter's wedge)
  95, 106
Speier, see Speyer
Speight, Speights, see Spaeth
  151
Speis, Speiss, Speise, Speiser
  (food, victualer) 106
Speismann (victualer) 96
Speker, see Spieker 151
Spelmann, Spellmann, see
  Spielmann 151
Spener (needle maker) 96
Spengler, Spengel (tinsmith) 96
Sperber (sparrow hawk) 115
Sperling (sparrow) 115
Sperre, Sperry (baricade,
  closing) 151, 122
Spessart, Spessard (mountain
  range, swamp forest) 80, 72,
  122
Speyer (city on Rhine) 122
Spicer, see Speiser 151
Spidel, Spidelle, see Speidel
  151
Spiecher, see Speicher 151
Spiegel (mirror, fr Latin
  speculum) 106, 122
Spieker (large nail, spike) 106
Spieker (granary) 122

Spielacker (field drawn by
  lot) 84
Spielberg (lookout mountain,
  fr Latin *specula*) 68, 122
Spieler (player, gambler)
Spielmann, Spillman
  (minstrel) 96
Spies, Spiess (spear, spit,
  spit-shaped field) 108, 106,
  122
Spies (swamp) 80
Spigel, see Spiegel 151
Spiller, see Spieler 151
Spindel, Spindler (distaff,
  spinner, distaff maker)
  106
Spingler, see Spengler 151
Spinnenweber, Spinneweber
  (spinner-weaver) 96
Spinner, Spinnler (spinner)
  96
Spittel (hospice) 122
Spittelmayer (hospice
  overseer) 93
Spittler (worker in a
  hospice) 96
Spitz, Spitzer, Spitzner
  (point, dweller near a
  peak) 122
Spitznagel, Spitznagle (sharp
  nail) 106
Spitznas (pointed nose) 114
Spohn, see Span
Sponheimer (city name) 122
Spoon, see Span 151
Spoonhour, see Spanhauer
  151
Spott, Spotz (ridicule)
Sprecher (speaker)
Spreckels (marsh dweller) 80
Sprengel (diocese) 122
Sprenkel, Sprenkle, see
  Sprengel
Springer, Sprenger,
  Springmann (jumper, dan-
  cer 96, fr Springen 122)
Springfeld (spring field) 84
Spuecher, see Spiecher

Spuhler (spool maker) 96
Spur (spoor)
Spyker, see Spieker
Staab, see Stabe
Staadt 122, see Stadt
Staal, see Stahl
Stabe (staff)
Stablein (little staff) 151
Stabler, see Staebler 151
Stack < St. Eustachius 131
Stackhouse, see Stockhaus 151
Stackman, Stackmann, see
 Stockmann 151
Stadel, Stadeli (stable, barn)
 122
Stadelman, Stadelmann (barn
 supervisor) 96
Stadelmayer, Stadelmeier (barn
 steward) 96
Stadler, Stadtler, Stattler (barn
 supervisor) 96, 122
Stadt, Stadtler, Statler
 (townsman) 122
Staeblein (little staff)
Staebler (staff-carrying official)
 109
Staeheli, Staehle, Staehli,
 Staehler, Steheli, Steely,
 Stelly (steel, blacksmith) 96
Staempfli, see Stempel
Staerk (strength)
Staetler (townsman)
Staffel (step, rung) 122
Stahl, Stahle, Stahler, Stahley,
 Stahlmann, see Staehli
Stahlschmit (steel smith) 96
Stahr (starling) 115
Staiger, see Steiger
Stalden (steep path) 65
Staley, see Staeheli
Stall, Stallmann, Stalling (stall,
 barn, stableman) 122
Staltzfus, see Stoltzfus
Stambach, Stambaugh (stump
 brook) 77, 122
Stamberg, Stammberger (stump
 mountain) 68, 122
Stamgast (regular guest)
Stamitz, see Steinmetz 151

Stamm, Stam (stem, trunk)
Stammler (stutterer) 114
Stampf, Stampfel, Stampfl
 (stamp, tamper) 106
Stampf (steep path) 65
Stanback (stone brook) 77,
 151
Stance, see Stantze 151
Stand, Stand, Stant
 (condition)
Stang, Stange, Stanger (pole,
 stick, spear) 106
Stantze (stamp, die) 106
Stapf, Stapp (step)
Star, Stahr, Starr (starling)
 115
Starck, Stark, Starke,
 Starker (strong)
Startz, see Stortz 151
Stassen < St. Anastasius 131
Stattler, see Stadtler 151
Staub, Staube, Stauber
 (dust)
Stauch (jolt)
Staud, Staude, Staut, Staudt
 (shrubs, underbrush) 72
Staudehauer (brush clearer)
 72, 95
Staudemeyer (proprietor of
 the Staudehoff) 72, 93
Stauffer (mug maker) 96
Stauffer (crag dweller)
Staup, see Staub
Stauss, see Steiss
Stayner, see Steiner 151
Stealy, see Staeheli 151
Stebbins < St. Stephan 131
Stecher, Stechler (engraver)
 96
Steckel, Stecker (swamp) 80
Stedler, Stedeler, see
 Stadtler
Steely, see Staeheli 151
Steenfeld, see Steinfeld
Steer, Steere, see Stier 151
Steermann (cattle raiser) 91,
 151
Steffen, Steffel, Steffens,
 Steffy, see Stephan

Steinmetz, Steinmets (stone cutter) 96, 100

Steinmeyer, Steinmeier (proprietor of the Steinhoff) 93

Steinseiffer, Stainsayfer (stony brook) 77

Steinthal (stone valley) 73, 76

Steinwald (stone forest) 73, 71

Steinwand (stone wall) 73, 122

Steinway, see Steinweg 151

Steinwedel (stony ford) 73, 78, 122

Steinweg (stony path) 73, 65, 122

Steinwyk (stone village) 73, 123

Steiss (rump) 114

Steitz (fuller, cloth cleanser) 96

Steli, Stelly, see Staeheli 151

Stell (frame, holder)

Steller, Stellmach, Stellmacher, Stellmann (wainwright, cartwright) 96

Stelling (marsh dweller 80, fr Stellingen 122)

Stellwagen, Stellvagen (stage coach)

Stelly, Stelley, see Staeheli 151

Steltz, Stels, Selzer, Stelzner (stilts, walker on stilts or crutches) 114, 106

Steltzfuss (wooden leg) 144

Stemm, Stemmer, Stembler, Stemler, Stemmler (marsh dweller) 80

Stempel, Stemple (stamp) 106

Stenbaugh, see Steinbach 151

Stendal 122, see Steinthal

Stengel, Stengle, Stenglein (stalk)

Stenhouse, Stenkamp, see Steinhaus, Steinkamp 151

Stentz, Stenzer < Polish: Stanislaw

Step, Stepf, see Stapp, Stapf

Stephan, Stephann, Stephans, Steffen, Steffe, Stephanus

(St. Stephen, name of pope) 134

Stephani, Stephany, son of Stephan 142

Steppe (quilt) 106

Sterb (Die!) 116, 117

Sterchi, Sterki (strength), see Stuerki

Stern, Sterne (star)

Sternberg, Sternberger (swamp mountain) 80, 68, 122

Sternfeld (swamp field) 80, 84, 122

Sternglass (star glass, telescope)

Sternheim, Sternheimer (swamp hamlet) 80, 123

Sternkamp (steer field) 84, 122

Sternthal (swamp valley) 80, 76, 122

Stettiner, Stettinius (fr Stettin) 122, 141

Stettler, see Staedtler 151

Steubesand (fine sand)

Steuer (dowry, steering, tax, tax collector) 109

Steuernagel (tiller)

Steyer, Steyert (fr Styria, Steiermark) 121

Steyger, see Steiger

Stich (stitch, tailor) 104, 122

Stichel, Stichler (engraver, stylus) 106

Stichling (stickleback) 115

Stichter (founder)

Stick, Stickeler (embroiderer) 106, 122

Stickelbach (stickleback brook) 115, 77

Stiebel (dust)

Stief (steep)

Stiefel, Stieffel, Stieffler (boot, boot maker) 104, 106

Stieg (staircase) 122

Stiegel, Stiegler, Stiegman,
Stiegmann (stile, dweller
near a stile) 122
Stier, Stierle (bull, steer) 91
Stierhoff (steer farm) 92
Stierlin, Stierlin (little steer)
91
Stiermann (keeper of breeding
bulls) 91
Stiernkorb (beggar's basket)
Stiffler, Stifler, see Stiefel
Stigall, Stigler, see Stiegel 151
Stiger, see Steiger 151
Still, Stille, Stilling, Stillmann
(tranquil person) 115
Stillwagon, Stillwagoner, see
Stellwagen 151
Stindler (fisherman) 96
Stinefield, see Steinfeld 151
Stiner, see Steiner 151
Stinnes < Augustinus 131
Stirn (forehead) 114
Stob, Stober (bath attendant)
96
Stock (stick, tree trunk) 122
Stockhausen (tree trunk
hamlet) 65, 122
Stockmann, Stockmeister
(jailor) 109
Stockmann, see Stuckmann
Stockschlaeger (whipper)
Stockstill (stockstill, very quiet)
115
Stoehr, Stoer, Stoerr, Sterr
(sturgeon catcher 91 or
dealer 105), see also Stehr
Stoekel, Stoeklin (little stick)
Stoff (stuff)
Stoffel, Stoffels < Christoff 53
Stoffer, see Stauffer
Stolte (proud) 115
Stoltfus, Stoltzfuss (limper)
114
Stoltz, Stoltze, Stoltzer, Stolz
(proud) 115
Stoltzenbach (proud brook) 77,
122
Stombaugh, see Stambach 151

Stombler, see Stammler 151
Stone, Stoner, see Stein,
Steiner 152
Stoneburner, see
Steinbrenner 152
Stonefield, see Steinfeld 152
Stonesifer, see Steinseiffer
151, 152
Storch, Storich, Storck, Stork
(stork) 114
Storm, see Sturm
Stortz (tumble, crash)
Stotler, see Statler 151
Stottlemeyer, Stottlemire,
Stottlemyer, see
Stadelmeyer 151
Stotz (log, clumsy person)
115
Stoudemeyer, Stoudemaier,
Stoudemire, see
Staudemeyer 151
Stoudt, Stout, see Staude
151
Stouffer, Stoupher, see
Stauffer 151
Stoup, see Staub 151
Straatmann, see Strattmann
Strabel, see Strobel
Strack (stiff, inflexible) 115
Strackbein (stiff leg) 114
Straecker, see Strecker
Strahl, Strahle 122, Strale
(ray of light, arrow)
Straight, see Streit 151
Strait, see Streit 151
Strasbaugh (road brook) 65,
77, 151
Strasburg, Strasburger,
Strassburger (fr
Strassburg) 122
Strass (road, highway, fr
Latin *strata*) 122, see
Strassner
Strasser, Strassner,
Strossner (dweller on a
highway) 65

Strattmann, Stratmann, Strathmann (dweller on the street or road) 65
Straub, Straube (towseled) 122
Strauch (bush, shrub) 122
Straup, see Straub
Straus, Strauss (fight)
Strausbaugh, see Strasbaugh
Strauss (bouquet)
Strauss (ostrich, probably a house name) 49
Streck, Strecker (stretcher, stretch of land)
Strecker (torturer) 96
Streckfuss (Stretch leg!) 116
Streich (strike, blow)
Streif, Streiff (stripe)
Streif (mounted patrol) 107
Streisand, see Streusand
Streit 122, Streith, Streiter (struggle, struggler)
Streng, Strenger (strict) 115
Streusand (blotting sand)
Stricker, Strickert, Strickler, Strickmann (knitter) 96
Stricker (poacher)
Strickler, see Stricker
Striegel, Strigel, Striegler (curry comb) 106
Strite, see Streit
Strobank (straw bench)
Strobar, Strohbart (straw beard) 122
Stroebel, Strobel, Strobel (disheviled)
Stroessner, see Strassner
Stroh, Stro (straw) 122
Strohacker (straw field) 84
Strohbeck (straw brook) 77
Strohmann, Stromann, Strohmayer, Strohmeyer, Stromier (straw man, straw dealer) 105
Strohschneider (straw cutter)
Strom, Strohm (stream, current, river) 79
Stromann, see Strohmann
Stromenger, Strominger (straw dealer) 105

Strosnider (straw cutter) 151
Strouse, see Strauss 151
Strub 122, Strube, Strubel, Struble, Strubler (disheviled) 112
Strubhar (tousle haired) 122
Struck, Strucke, Struckmann (dweller in the bushes) 72
Strueve, see Strub
Strumpf, Strumpfer, Strumpfler (stocking maker) 106
Strunck, Strunk (stalk, stump, stocky man) 114
Struth (swamp) 80, 122
Struvel, Struwel, see Stroebel
Stube (heated room, bather) 96
Stuber (bath attendant) 96
Stuck, Stucke, Stucker, Stuckers, Stuckert (dweller on stump-covered ground)
Stuckey, see Stucki 151
Stucki (tree stump)
Stude, see Staude
Studebecker, Studebaker, Stuttenbecker (shrub brook) 72, 77
Studenroth (brush clearing) 72, 126
Stuebe, see Stube
Stuehler (chair maker) 106
Stuerzebecker (tumbling stream) 77
Stuhl, Stuhlmacher, Stuhldreher, Stuhlmann, Stuhlman, Stulman (chair, chair maker) 96, 106
Stull, see Stoll
Stultz, see Stoltz
Stum, Stumm, Stumli (mute) 114
Stump, Stumpe, Stumpel, Stumpf, Stumpff (blunt) 115
Stuntz, Stunz (stump, small barrel)

Stupp, Stupf (step, stoop)
Sturm (storm, violent person) 115
Sturmer (warrior) 107
Sturtz (plunge, fall, steep slope) 71
Sturtzbach (rapid stream) 77
Sturzenegger (field on a steep slope) 71
Stutz (support)
Stutzmann (defender)
Stuver (heavy-set man) 114, see Stuber
Styer (fr Steiermark) 121, 151
Sucher (searcher, hunting assistant) 91
Sudbrok, Sudbrook (muddy brake) 80
Suder, Sudermann (one dwelling toward the south, name shortened fr one of the following)
Suderode (south clearing) 126, 122
Sudheim (south hamlet) 123, 122
Sudhoff (south farm) 92, 122
Suehn (penitence, penance, reconciliation) 138
Suender, Sunder (sinner) 138
Sues, Suess 122, Suesse (sweet) 115
Suesskind (sweet child) 115
Suessmann (sweet man) 115
Suestrunk (sweet drink)
Suetterlin, see Suter
Sugarman, Sugerman, see Zuckerman 151
Sultzbach, Sulzbacher (swampy brook) 80, 77, 122
Sulz (salt lick, salt worker) 96
Sulzer, Sulzmann (maker of jellied meat) 96
Sumwalt, see Zumwald 151
Sundheim (south hamlet) 123, 122
Surland, see Sauerland 151

Suskind, Sussman, see Suesskind, Suessman 151
Suter, Sutor, Sutter (shoemaker, fr Latin *Sutor*) 104
Sutorius (latinization of Sutor) 141
Sutter (swamp) 80, see also Suter
Sutterlin (little shoemaker) 104
Sutterlin (little swamp) 80
Sw ..., see under Schw ...
Swaggert, see Schweiger 151
Swarts, Swartz, see Schwartz 151
Swartsback, Swarzbaugh, see Schwartzbach 151
Swarzwelder, see Schwartzwaelder 151
Swearer, see Schwoerer 151
Sweetser, see Schwytzer 151
Sweigert, Sweigart, see Schweiger 151
Swerdlin, see Schwertlein 151
Swiger, Swigger, Swiggert, see Schweiger 151
Swindel, Swindall (swindle, swindler) 151
Swinehart (strong as a wild boar) 151
Switzer, see Schweitzer 151
Swob, Swope, Swopes, see Schwab 151
Swyger, Swygert, see Schweiger 151
Sybel, Seybold < Siegbald 151
Sybert, see Siegbert 151
Syder, Sydnor, see Seider, Seidner 151
Syfrett, Syford, see Siegfried 151
Sygrist, see Sigrist 151
Syler, see Seiler 151
Sylvester, see Silvester 151
Symon, see Simon 151

T

Tabb, Tabbert < Dietbert (people + famous) 46, 47

Taescher (purse maker) 96

Taffner (fr Taffingen, marsh village) 80, 122

Taich, see Teich

Tallebach, Telebach (muddy brook) 80, 77

Tanhauser (forest house, fir house) 89, 65

Tanhof, see Tannhoeffer

Tannebaum, Tannenbaum (fir tree) 89

Tannenberger (fr Tannenberg 122, fir mountain) 89, 65

Tannenzappf (pine cone)

Tanner (dweller among the firs) 89

Tannhoeffer (fr Tanhof 122, farm among the firs) 89, 92

Tants, Tantz, Tantzer (dance, dancer) 96

Tapfer (brave) 115

Tapp, Tapper (tap maker, taverner) 96, 106

Tappert (wearers or makers of long coats, fr Latin *tabardum*) 106

Tasch, Tascher, Taschner, see Taescher

Tatelbaum, Dattelbaum (date tree) 89

Taub, Tauber (deaf, deaf man) 114

Taub, Taube (dove) 115

Taubenfeld (dove field) 84

Taubenheim (dove + hamlet) 123, 122

Taubenslag (dove cote) 151

Tauber, Taubert, Taubermann (cock pigeon, pidgeon raiser or seller) 105, 143

Tauber (name of river) 83

Taubner, Taubman, Taupmann, see Tauber

Tauchinbaugh (Jump in the brook!) 116, 77, 151

Tausch (barter, trickster)

Tausendschoen (thousand beautiful [thanks?]) 117

Taxler (badger hunter) 91

Taylor, see Schneider 152

Teagle, see Tiegel 151

Teale, see Thiel 151

Tederick < Dietrich

Teel, see Thiel 151

Tegler, Tegele (tyler, brickmaker, fr Latin *tegula*) 96

Teich, Teichner (pond, dweller by a pond) 80, 122

Teichgraeber (pond digger, ditch digger) 80

Teichmueller (miller on the pond) 80, 103

Teitelbaum, see Dattelbaum

Teitz, see Dietz 151

Telebach, see Tallebach

Teller, Tellermann (dish, dishmaker, fr Latin *talea*) 106

Tempel (temple, synagogue)

Tenberg, Tennenberg, Tennenbaum, see Tanberg, Tannenberg, Tannenbaum

Tenner, see Danner

Teobald, see Theobald 151

Tepel, Teppel < Dietmar

Tepper (potter) 96

Tesch, Tesche, see Taescher

Tessler, see Tischler

Tester, Testor, see Textor

Teubel, see Teufel

Teuber, Teuber, Teubner, see Tauber

Teufel, Teufell (devil)

Teufer (baptist)

Textor, Textur (Latin for Weber) 141

Thal, Thalberg (valley, valley mountain) 76, 68, 122

Thaler (coin from Joachimsthal)

Thalmann (valley man) 76, 94

Thanhouser, see Tannhauser
151
Thankappan, see Tarnkappe
Theil (part)
Theiss, Theissen < Matthias
Theobald, Thebald (folk + bold)
46, 46
Therman, see Thurmann 151
Theus < Matthaeus or
Timothaeus
Thiel, Thiele, Thielemann,
Thielman < Dietrich 53
Thiemer < Dietmar
Thierfelder 122 (animal field)
84, 122
Thiergarten (zoo, animal park),
84, 122
Thiess, Thiesse, Thiessen 122
< Matthias
Thilo < Dietrich 53
Thiringer, see Thueringer
Thoene < Antonius 53, 54
Tholde < Berthold 53, 54
Thom < Thomas 53, 54
Thomas, Tomas (St. Thomas)
131
Thons, Thonis, Thonges < St.
Anthonius
Thor (door)
Thormann (gate keeper)
Thorwart (door keeper)
Thron 122, Throne (throne)
Thueringer (Thuringian) 120
Thuermann, Thurman (door
man)
Thurm (tower, fr Latin *turris*)
Thurmherr (lord of the tower)
Thussing, see Tussing
Thyssen < Matthias 53, 54
Tibbet < Theobald 53, 54
Tice, see Theiss 151
Tiebendorf, see Tiefendorf 151
Tiede, Tiedebohl, Tiedeman,
Tiedemann, Tidemann <
Dietbald 53, 54
Tiefenbach (deep brook) 77, 122
Tieffenbrunn (deep well) 79,
122

Tiefendorf, Tiebenderf (deep
village) 123, 122
Tiegel (saucepan, crucible, fr
Latin *tegula*) 106
Tielmann, Tilman, Tillman <
Dietrich 53, 54
Tier (animal)
Tierdorf (animal village) 123
Tiess < Matthias 53, 54
Tietz, Tietzer < Diedrich 53,
54
Tiffenderfer, Tiffendarfer, see
Tiefendorf 151
Tilgen, Till < St. Ilgen 131
Till, see Diehl
Tillich < Dietrich 53, 54
Tillinger, see Dillinger
Tillmann, see Tilgen
Tilly < Dietrich 53, 54
Tilo < Dietrich 53, 54
Timmer (timber, carpenter)
98, 106
Timmerman, Timmermann,
see Zimmermann
Timothaeus, Thimothee (St.
Timothy) 131
Tischler, Titshler, Tischer,
Tisher, Tischmann
(cabinet maker, fr Latin
discus) 106, 98
Tisher, see Tischler 151
Titshler, see Tischler 151
Titus (Latin name) 141
Tobel, Tobler (wooded gorge)
122
Tochtermann (son-in-law)
119
Tod, Todt (death, godfather)
119
Toennies < St. Anthonius
Toepfer, Toepfner (potter) 96
Toerrenberger, see
Duerrenberger
Togend, see Tugend
Tolde < Berthold 53, 54
Toll, Tolle (mad) 115
Toll < Berthold 53, 54

Toller, Tollmann, Tolner (toll collector) 109

Toltzmann, see Tolde

Tombaugh (at the brook) 70, 77, 151

Tonner, see Donner

Tonnewan (barrel, cooper) 106

Tontz, see Tantz 96, 151

Topfer (potter) 96

Topp (forelock, pigtail) 112

Topper (potter) 96

Torbeck (at the brook) 70, 77

Torfstecker (peat digger) 95

Torgler, Torkler (wine presser) 96

Totenberg (swamp mountain) 80, 68

Totenberg (godfather's mountain) 68

Toubman, see Taubman 151

Trachsler, see Drechsler

Trachtehengst (packhorse, dray horse) 106

Trager (porter, carrier)

Tran (whale oil) 105

Tranck (drink)

Trapp (bumpkin) 115

Trapp (bustard) 115

Traub (grape, vintner)

Traugott (Trust God!) 116, 140

Traut, Traud, Traudt, Trauth (dear) 48, 115

Trautmann, Troutman (confidant) 48, 115

Trautwein (dear friend) 48, 48, 115

Traxel, Traxler, see Drechsler

Treger, see Trager

Treibel (mallet, cooper) 106

Trepp, Treppe (stairs)

Tressler, see Drechsler

Tretler (treader or treadmill)

Treutel, Treuttle (sweetheart) 48, 115

Treutlen, see Treutel 25

Trexler, see Drechsler

Triesler, see Drechsler

Trimbach (place name) 122

Trinkauf (Drink up!) 116

Tritt (step)

Trockenmiller (dry miller) 103

Troester (draff)

Troester (comforter)

Troll (goblin)

Trommler (drummer) 96

Trompeter, Trumpeter (trumpeter) 96

Trootman, see Trautmann 151

Tropf (drop, simple person) 115

Trost (helper, comfort)

Trott, Trotter, Trottman (wine presser) 96

Trotz (defiance)

Trout, see Traut 151

Troutman, see Trautmann 151

Troxel, Troxell, Troxler, see Drechsler 151

Truckenbrodt (dry bread, baker) 96

Truckenmiller, see Trockenmiller

Trueb (sorrowful) 115

Truman, Trueman, see Trautman

Trumm (end of field)

Trump, Trumph (trump, drummer) 96

Trumpeter, see Trompeter

Trunk (drink)

Trutmann, see Trautmann 151

Tsahn, see Zahn 151

Tschantz, see Schantze

Tschudi (judge) 109

Tschudi (foolish, tense person) 115

Tsvetshen, see Zwetschen 151

Tuch, Tuchman, Tuchmann (mercer) 106

Tuerenberger, see Duerrenberger

Tuerner (tower keeper, fr Latin *turris*)

Tullius (Latin name) 141
Turban < St. Urbanus 131
Turinger, Thurringer, see
    Thueringer
Turn, see Thurm
Turnbach (tower brook) 77
Turnbaugh, see Turnbach 151
Turnipseed, see Ruebsamen
    152
Tussing (French, Toussaints)
Tysen, Tyssen, Tyson, see
    Theissen

U

Uberhoff (upper farm) 70, 92,
    122
Uebel (evil, irascible obstinate
    person) 115
Ueber (over)
Ueberholtz (upper forest,
    beyond the forest) 70, 72,
    122
Ueberroth (upper clearing,
    beyond the clearing) 70, 126,
    122
Uehlein (little owl) 115
Uffer, Ufner (dweller on the
    shore)
Uhl, Uhle, Uhll (owl) 115, see
    Ulrich
Uhland (lancer) 107
Uhlefelder, Uhlfelder (swamp
    field) 80, 84
Uhlenbeck (swamp brook) 80,
    77
Uhlenberg (swamp mountain)
    80, 68
Uhler, see Aulmann
Uhlich, Uhlig, Uhlik, Ulich,
    Uly < Ulrich 53, 54
Uhlmann, Ullmann (dweller
    near the elms) 89
Uhrich, Urich, see Ulrich
Uhrmacher (clock maker) 96
Ulbrich < Uodalbrecht,
    inheritance + bright) 46, 47

Ulbright, see Ulbrich 151
Uli < Ulrich 53, 54
Ullman, Ullmann, see Ulrich
Ulmer (dweller by the elms)
    89
Ulmer (inhabitanht of Ulm)
    122
Ulrich, Ullrich, Ulrik
    (inherited property + rule)
    46, 46
Umbach, see Ambach
Umbaugh, see Umbach 151
Umbreit (unwilling,
    incapable) 115
Umholtz (at the forest) 70,
    72
Unangst, see Ohnangst
Unbescheiden (indiscrete,
    unknowledgeable) 115
Unclebach, see Unkelbach
    151
Underkoffler, Underkofler,
    Underkaufer (middleman),
    see Unterkofler
Underweg (underway)
Unfried (disturber of the
    peace) 115
Unfug (mischief, impropriety)
    115
Ungeheuer (monster)
Unger, Ungerer (Hungarian)
    121
Unkel, Unkle (toad)
Unkelbach (toad brook) 77,
    122
Unold, Unhold (monster,
    fiend)
Unrat, Unrath (rubbish)
Unrau, see Unruh
Unruh (disquiet) 115
Unselt, Unseldt, Unsoeld,
    Unsoelt (tallow dealer)
    105
Unstruth (swamp on the
    One) 79, 80, 83
Unterberg (below the
    mountain) 68, 122

Unterdenerd (under the earth)
70
Unterkofler (lower monticule)
67
Unterwalden (among the
forests, below the forests) 70,
71, 122
Unverferth (unafraid) 115
Unversagt, Unferzagt
(undaunted) 115
Uphoff (on the farm) 70, 92,
122
Urbach 122, see Auerbach
Urban (St. Urbanus, name of
pope) 134
Urich, Urick, see Ulrich
Urman, Urmann, see Uhrman
Utli, Utley < Ulrich 53, 54
Uts, Utz < Ulrich) 53, 54

V

Search also under W

Vaibel, see Weibel
Vaïhinger (fr that city) 122
Valck, Valck, see Falk
Valenstein, see Wallenstein
Valentin (St. Valentine) 131
Vannamacher, see
Wannemacher 151
Vass, see Fass
Vassler < St. Gervasius 131
Vat (barrel, < St. Servatius)
131
Vater (father) 119
Vaught, see Vogt 151
Veit, Veicht < St. Vitus 131
Velte, Velten 122 < St.
Valentin 131
Venator (Latin, hunter) 141
Verner, see Werner
Verber, see Faerber
Vetter, Vetters (cousin,
kinsman) 119
Vetterli (little cousin) 119
Veydt, see Weide

Victor (Latin, victor, name of
pope) 134
Viebig, Viebing (cattle path)
Viehmann (husbandryman)
91
Viehmeyer (cattle farmer) 93
Viehweg, Vieweg (cattle
path) 65
Viereck (quadrangle) 122
Vierengel (four angels, house
name) 149
Vierheller (four pence) 112
Vietor (Latin: traveler) 141
Vincent (St. Vincent) 131
Vink, see Fink
Vitzthum 122, see Witzthum
Vleeschower, see
Fleischhauer 151
Voegele, Voegeli, Voegelein
(little bird)
Voelcker, Voelker, Voelkner,
see Volker, Volkner
Voelkel < Volkmar
Vogel, Vogl, Vogle (bird) 115
Vogeler, Vogler, Voegeler
(fowler)
Vogelgesang (birdsong)
Vogelmann (fowler) 115
Vogelpohl (bord pool) 80, 122
Vogelsang, see Vogelgesang
Vogelstein (bird mountain)
68
Vogt 122, Vogts, Voegt,
Voigt, Voight (governor, fr
Latin *advocatus)* 109
Volk, Volck, Volcks (nation,
folk)
Volkel, Voelkel < Volkmar
Volkenstein, see Wolkenstein
Volker, Volcker, Volkner
(people + army) 46, 46,
also short for any of
following
Volkhart, Volkert (folk +
strong) 46, 46
Volkmann (people + man)
46, 94
Volkmar (people + famous)
46, 47

Voll, Volle, Voller, Vollers (full)
Vollbert, Vollbrecht (full +
bright) 47
Vollenweide, Vollenweider, see
Fuellenweide
Vollmer, Volmer, Volmar, see
Volkmar
Vollmerhausen (Volkmar's
houses) 65
Vollprecht, Volpert, see
Vollbrecht
Voltz, Volz, see Foltz
Vom Berg (fr the mountain)
70, 68
Vom Hoff (fr the court) 70, 92

In seeking a name preceded by
von, look under the base name,
i.e. von Hagen
appears under Hagen.

Von Berg (fr the mountain) 70,
68
Von Burg (fr the castle) 70, 73
Von Busch (fr the bush), see
Busch 70, 72
Vonderheid, Vonderheide (fr
the heath) 70, 84
Vonderhorst (fr the hurst) 70,
72
Von der Lind (fr the linden)
70, 89
Von der Weyt (fr the meadow)
70, 84
Vonhagen (fr the enclosure) 70,
123
Vonholt (fr the forest) 70, 72
Vonniederhauser, Von
Niederhaeuser (fr the lower
houses) 70, 65
Von Paris (Parisian,
journeyman who trained in
Paris) 70, 122
Vonwald (fr the forest) 70, 71
Vorhenne (trout) 115
Vorhoff (atrium, before the
farm) 70, 92, 122
Vorman, see Fuhrmann

Vorm Walt (in front of the
forest) 70, 71, 122
Vornfeld (before the field)
70, 84
Voss (fox) 115
Vosse < Volkmar
Vosshage (fox enclosure) 123,
122
Vought, see Vogt 151
Vries (Frisian) 121
Vulkner, see Volkner

W

Waag 122 (scales), see Wage
Waber, Waeber, see Weber
Wachenhut (sentry, guard)
Wachenschutz (guard) 107
Wachs, Wax, Wachsmann
(wax dealer) 105
Wachsmuth (bright mind)
115
Wachtel (quail) 115
Wachter, see Waechter
Wacker (brave, watchful) 115
Waechter, Wachter
(watchman)
Waeger (official weigher) 109
Waesche (washing,
bleaching) 106
Waffenschmidt (armorer) 108
Waffler, Wafler, Waffelaer
(armorer) 108
Wage (scales) 106
Wageman (official weigher)
109
Wagener, see Wagner
Wagenfuehr (carter) 95
Wagenhorst (marshy hurst)
80, 72, 122
Wagenknecht (carter's
helper) 95
Wagenmann (wainwright) 96
Wagenseil (wagon rope,
carter) 106

Waggener, Waggner, Waggoner, see Wagner 151

Wagner, Wagener, Waagner, Wagenaar (wainright) 106

Wahl 122, Wall, Waal (choice)

Wahlberg (marsh mountain) 80, 68, 122

Wahlenfeld (marsh field) 80, 84

Wahrheit (truth, informant, guarantor) 115

Wahrlich (honest) 115, 117

Waibel, see Weibel

Waiblinger (fr Waibling 122)

Waid 122, Waidner, see Weid, Weidner

Waidmann, Waitmann, see Weidmann

Waitz, see Weitzen

Walbaum (walnut tree) 89

Walber, Walberd, Walbert, Walbrecht (battlefield + bright) 46, 47

Walbrecher (wall breaker)

Walburg (battlefield + protection) 46, 47, see also Waldburg

Walch, Walcher (foreigner, non-German) 145

Walchensee (foreigners' lake) 145, 80, 122

Walcker, see Walker

Wald, Waldt, Walde, Walt (forest) 71, or < Oswald

Waldbauer (forest farmer) 71, 91, 94

Waldberg (forest mountain) 71, 68, 122

Waldbrand (forest clearing) 71, 126

Waldburg, Waldburger (fr Waldburg 122, forest castle) 71, 73

Waldeck, Waldecker (fr Waldeck 122, forest place, German province) 71, 85

Walden (forests) 71

Waldenberger (forest mountain) 71, 68

Waldhausen, Waldhauser (fr Waldhausen 122, forest houses) 71, 65

Waldkirch (forest church) 71, 122

Waldman, Waldmann 122, Waldner (forester, giant)

Waldmeier, Waldmayer (forest farmer, proprietor of the Waldhof) 71, 93, 94

Waldmueller (forest miller) 71, 103

Waldorf (forest village) 71, 123, 122

Waldschmidt, Waldschmitt (forest smith, one who smelts his own ore) 71, 96

Waldsee (forest lake) 71, 80, 122

Waldvogel (forest bird, carefree person) 71

Walheim (swamp hamlet) 80, 123, 122

Walk, Walker (fuller) 96

Wall (rampart, fr Latin *vallum*) 122

Wallach (gelding) 122

Wallendorf (marsh village) 80, 123, 122

Wallenhorst (marsh hurst) 80, 72, 122

Wallenser (Waldensian, fr Wallensen 122)

Wallenstein (fortified mountain) 73, 122

Wallenstein (foreigners' mountain) 145, 73, 122

Waller, Wallner (pilgrim)

Wallerstein (pilgrims' mountain) 73, 122

Walliser (Swiss fr Valais) 145, 121

Wallner (forest warden) 71

Wallrodt (marsh clearing) 80, 126, 122

Walpert (battlefield + brilliant) 46, 47

Walsch (Romance) 145

Walser, see Walliser

Walstein, see Wallenstein
Waltemeyer, Waltimyer, see
　Waldmeyer
Walter, Walters, see Walther
Walther, Walthers (rule +
　army) 46, 46
Walthorn (waldhorn) 96, 106
Waltmann, see Waldmann
　(forest dweller, giant) 71
Waltz, Walz, Waltze 122,
　Waltzer, Walzer (roll, roller,
　or < Walther)
Wambach, Wambaugh (marsh
　brook) 80, 77, 151
Wambold (hope + bold) 46, 122
Wamser, Wambescher (jerkin
　maker) 96
Wand (cliff)
Wandel (Vandal) 121
Wandel (change)
Wanger (fr Wangen, damp
　sloping meadow) 71, 122
Wankel (fickle) 115
Wankmueller (miller off the
　beaten path) 103
Wann, Wanne 122 (vat) 106
Wannamacher, Wannemacher,
　Wannermacher (winnowing
　basket maker, vat maker, fr
　Latin *vannus*) 96
Wannamaker, see
　Wannamacher 151
Wanner (tub maker) 96
Wantz (bedbug)
Wapner, see Waffner
Wardmann (watchmann)
Warm (warm)
Warmkessel (warm kettle,
　cook) 106
Warmuth, see Wermuth
Warner (warner)
Warnke, Warnecke, Warneche,
　Warnek, Warneke <
　Wernher
Warnold (guard + loyal) 47, 48
Warschauer (fr Warsaw) 122
Warshauer, see Warschauer
　151

Wartburg (lookout mountain)
　47, 73, 122
Warth, Warthmann,
　Wartmann (lookout) 47
Waschke < Slavic: Vadislav
Wasp (wasp)
Wasser (water) 122
Wasserkrug (water jug) 106
Wasserman (waterman)
Wasserzieher (bath
　attendant) 96
Waterman, see Wassermann
　151
Watsack (clothes bag) 106
Watte (wadding, padding)
Wattenbach (swamp stream)
　80, 77, 122
Waxler, see Wechsler 151
Wayer, see Weiher, Weyer
　151
Weabel, see Weibel 151
Weaver, see Weber 151
Webel (sergeant) 107, see
　Weibel
Weber, Webert, Webber,
　Webner, Webling (weaver)
　96
Wechsler (money changer) 96
Weck, Wecker, Weckerle,
　Weckler, Weckerli,
　Weckerlin, Weckerling
　(baker or seller of rolls)
　96
Weckesser (roll eater)
Wecter, see Waechter 151
Wedekind (forest child) 72
Wedel (whisk) 106, 122
Wedemann, Wedemeyer,
　Wedemayer (forest
　dweller, forest farmer) 72,
　93
Weg, Wege (way) 65, 122
Wegand, see Weigand
Wegener, Wegner, see
　Wagner
Weger, Wegerlein (weigher)
Wegmann (dweller on a
　roadway) 65

Wegner, see Wagner
Wegstein (guide post) 73
Weh, Wehe (woe, pain) 117
Wehmeyer, see Weidemeyer
Wehn, Wehner < Werner 53,
54, 122
Wehner, see Wagner
Wehr, Wehrs (defense) 122
Wehrl, Wehrle, Wehrli, Wehrly
< Werner 53, 54
Weibel, Weible 151 (village
authority) 109, 107
Weichert < Wighard (battle +
brave) 46, 46
Weicker, Weickert, see
Weichert
Weid 122, Weit, Weidt, Weide
122 (pasture) 84
Weidebach (brook through
meadow or willows) 84, 77
Weidemann, Weidemeyer
(meadow man 84), see also
Weidmann
Weidenauer (fr Weidenau 122,
pasture meadow) 84, 84
Weidenbacher (fr Weidenbach
122, meadow brook) 84, 77
Weidenmeyer (pasture farmer)
84, 93
Weiderholt, see Wiederholt 151
Weidmann, Wideman (hunter)
Weidner (dweller on a pasture
84), see also Weidmann
Weier 122, see Weiher
Weierbach (fish pond brook) 77,
122
Weiermiller (fish pond miller)
77, 103
Weigand, Weygant (warrior)
107
Weigel, Weigels, Weigelt,
Weigle < Weigand 53, 54
Weigert, see Weichert
Weihaus, see Weinhaus 102, 65
Weiher 122, Weier (fish pond,
fr Latin *vivarium*)
Weihrauch (incense) 105
Weil 122, Weile, Weill (village,
fr Latin *villa*) 127, 148

Weiland, see Wieland
Weiler, Weilert (inhabitant
of a villa) 127
Weiman, see Weinmann
Weimar, Weimer, Weimert
(fr Weimar 122, holy
spring) 79
Wein, Wyn (wine, wine
dealer) 102, 105
Weinacht (Christmas) 143
Weinberg (vineyard) 102, 68,
122
Weinberger (vintner) 102, 68
Weinblatt (grape leaf) 102
Weinbrenner (brandy
distiller) 102, 96
Weiner, Weiners, see
Wagner
Weinfeld (vine field) 102, 84
Weingard, Weingarden,
Weingart, Weingarten 122,
Weingartz (vineyard) 102,
84
Weingartner, Weingaertner,
Weingertner (vintner) 102
Weinglass (wine glass) 106
Weinhandl (wine dealer) 102,
105
Weinhard (friend + strong)
48, 46
Weinhaus (tavern) 102, 65
Weinheimer (fr Weinheim
122, swamp hamlet) 80,
102, 123
Weinholt (friend + loyal) 48,
48
Weinhouse, see Weinhaus
102, 65, 151
Weininger (fr Weiningen
122)
Weinkauf, Weinkop (wine
seller, drink to confirm a
sale) 102, 105
Weinland (wine country) 102
Weinmann (wine merchant)
102, 105
Weinreb (grape) 102
Weinreich (friend + rule) 68,
46

Weinstein (wine mountain) 102, 73

Weinstock (grape vine) 102, 149

Weintraub, Weintrob (grape, wine dealer) 102, 149

Weintraut (friend + dear) 48, 48

Weir, see Weiher

Weirauch, see Weihrauch

Weis, see Weiss

Weisaecker, Waisacker (white field) 84, 85

Weisbacher, Weissbacher, Weisbeck, Weissbecker (fr Weissbach 122, white brook) 77

Weisberg (white mountain) 68

Weisborn, Weisborrn (white spring) 79

Weisbrod, Weisbord, Weisbrot, see Weissbrot

Weise (wise) 115

Weiselberger, see Wieselberger 151

Weisenmiller, see Weissmiller

Weiser (guide, wise man)

Weisfeld, Weisfeldt (white field) 84

Weisgarber, Weisgerber, see Weissgerber

Weishaar, see Weisshaar

Weishaupt, Weisshaupt (blond, white hair) 112

Weishart, see Weisshart

Weismantel, see Weissmantel

Weiss, Weisse, Weisser, Weissert (white, blond) 112

Weissbach, Weissenbach (white brook) 77

Weissbart (white beard) 112

Weissberg, Weissenberg, Weissberger (white mountain) 68

Weissbrot, Weissbrodt (white bread) 106

Weissenberger (fr Weissenberg 122, white mountain) 68

Weissenborn (white spring) 79, 122

Weissenburg (white castle) 73, 122

Weissenfeld (white field) 84, 122

Weissgerber, Weissergerber (tanner of white leather) 97

Weisshaar (white hair, blond hair) 112

Weisshardt, Weisshart (white forest) 72

Weisskirch (white church) 122

Weisskittel (white smock, baker) 122

Weisskopf (white head, blond head) 112

Weissler (whitewasher) 96

Weissman, Weissmann (white man, white-haired man) 112

Weissmantel (white cloak) 106

Weissmueller, Weissmiller (miller of white flour) 103, 162

Weissmut (wise disposition) 115

Weitenauer (fr Weitenau 122, broad mead) 84

Weithenbach (broad brook) 77

Weitmann, see Weidmann

Weitzel, Weitzell (wheat seller) 105

Weitzen (wheat, wheat dealer) 105

Weitzenkorn (wheat grain, wheat dealer) 105

Weitzman, Weitzmann (wheat dealer) 105

Weksler, see Wechsler 151

Welck, Welk (faded, withered)

Welcker, see Walker

Welder, see Schwarzwaelder 151

Welenbach (swampy brook) 80, 77

Welhoeltzer (swampy forest) 80, 72

Wellbrock (swamp brake) 80, 80

Welle, Wellen (well, faggot, faggot gatherer) 95

Welle (marshy ground) 80, 122

Wellemeyer (marsh farmer) 80, 93

Weller, Wellner (clay or loam mason) 96

Wels, Welss (catfish) 115

Welsch, Welsh, Welch (Romance) 145

Welschhan (turkey) 145

Welter, Weltner, Weltz (fr Welt 122), see Walther

Wendel, Wendl (Vandal, Wend) 121

Wendelmuth (vacillating) 115

Wendelspiess (Turn the spit!, cook) 96

Wenger 122, Wengert, see Wanger

Wenholt, see Weinholt

Wenig (few, small)

Weniger (fewer, less)

Wenner, Wennert < Werner 53, 54

Wentz, Wentzel, Wentz, Wenzel < Werner 53, 54

Weppler (armed soldier) 107

Weppner (armorer) 108

Werbel (legendary minstrel)

Werber (entrepreneur, recruiter)

Werdebaugh (river island creek) 77, 151

Werdmann, see Wertmann

Werdmueller (miller on river island) 103

Werele, Werle, Werli, Werlin, Werlein < Werner 53, 54

Werfel, see Wurfel 151

Werkmeister (foreman)

Wermuth (vermouth) 105

Wernegerode (swamp clearing) 80, 126, 122

Werner, Wernher, Warner (protection + army) 47, 46

Wernicke, Wernecke < Werner 53, 54

Wert, Werth (island in river)

Werthamer, Wertheimer (German city) 122

Wertmann, Werthmann (dweller on river island)

Wertmueller (miller on river island) 103

Wertsch, see Wirtsch

Wesbrot, see Weissbrot

Weschenbach (laundry creek) 77

Weschler (fuller) 96

Wess, Wessberg, see Weiss, Weissberg

Wessel 122, Wessels, Wessell, Wessels < Werner 53, 54

Wessner, see Wiessner

Westendorf (west village) 123, 122

Westenfeld, Westerfeld (west field) 84, 122

Westerkamp, Westkamp (west field) 84

Westfal, Westfalen (fr Westphalia) 121

Westhoff (west farm, now sometimes Westcourt in America) 84

Westinghouse (house toward the west) 65, 151

Westphal, Westphale, see Westfal 151

Wetter (weather, name of river meaning "swamp") 80, 83

Wetterau (meadow on the Wetter) 83, 84

Wettstein, see Wetzstein

Wetzel, Wetzler < Werner 53, 54

Wetzikon (Werner's village) 127
Wetzstein, Wettstein
  (whetstone, knife grinder)
  73, 106
Wexermann (forest farmer)
Wexler, see Wechsler 151
Wey ..., see Wei ...
Weydenhauer (willow cutter)
  89, 95
Weydenmeyer, see Weidemeyer
Weydner, see Weidner
Weyer 122, Weyher, see
  Weiher
Weyerhausen (house on fish
  pond) 65
Weygel, see Weigel
Weyhinger, see Vaihinger
Weyl, see Weil
Weyland, see Weiland
Weyrauch, Weyhrauch, see
  Weihrauch
Weys, see Weiss
White, see Witt, Weiss 151,
  152
Whitehard, see Weishard 151
Whiteman, see Wittmann,
  Weidmann 151
Whitesel, Whitesell, Whytsell,
  see Weitzel 151
Wibel, see Weibel 151
Wice, see Weiss 151
Wichert, Wichart < Wighard
Wichmann, see Wiechmann
Wicker, Wickert, see Wichert
Wickes < Ludowicus 53, 54
Widder (ram) 91, 149
Wideman, Widman, see
  Weidemann, Weidmann 151
Widemeyer, Widemayer, see
  Weidemeyer 151
Widener, see Weidner 151
Widerholt, see Wiederholt
Widmann, see Wittmann,
  Weidmann
Widmer, see Wittmann
Widmeyer, Weidemeyer
Wiechert < Wighard

Wiechmann < Wigman
  (battle + man) 46, 94
Wied 122, Wiede (withe,
  willow tree) 89
Wiedbach (swamp brook) 80,
  77
Wiederholt (repeated,
  opponent)
Wiederkehr (return)
Wiedersprecher (gainsayer)
Wiedkamp (pasture field) 84,
  84
Wiedmann, see Weidemann
  151
Wiedmayer, see Weidemeyer
Wiedner < see Weidner
Wiegand, Wigand, see
  Weigand
Wieger, Wiegert, Wiegner
  (official weigher) 109
Wiegman, Wiegmann
  (weigher) 109
Wiel, Wiele (marsh) 80
Wieland (name of legendary
  smith)
Wiemer, Wiemers < Wigmar,
  war + famous) 46, 47
Wien, Wiener, Wieners (fr
  Vienna, Viennese) 122
Wienholt, see Weinholt
Wienke < Wignand (battle +
  brave) 46
Wier, see Weyher 151
Wies, Wiese (meadow) 84
Wiesbaum (hay pole) 84, 89
Wiesel (weasel) 115
Wieselberger (fr Wieselberg
  122, weasel mountain) 68
Wiesenbacher (fr Wiesenbach
  122, meadow brook) 84,
  77
Wiesenthal (meadow valley,
  bison valley) 84, 76, 122
Wiesenthauer (bison
  meadow) 84
Wiesman, see Wiesner
Wiesner, Wiessner (dweller
  on the meadow) 84

Wiess, see Wiese, Weiss

Wiest (fr Wieste 122), see Wuest 151

Wigand, see Weigand 151

Wigener < Weigand

Wighard (battle + strong) 46, 46

Wightman, see Weidmann 151

Wiland, see Wieland

Wilbert (determination + bright) 46, 47

Wilcke (little William) 53, 54

Wild, Wilde, Wilder (wild, game) 115

Wildberg 122, Wiltberger, Wildenberger (wild mountain) 68

Wildenmut, Wildermuth (wild disposition) 115

Wilder, Wilderer (hunter, poacher)

Wilderbach (wild stream) 77

Wildfang, Wilfong (tended forest, game, prey, tomboy)

Wildhengst (wild stallion)

Wildheyt (wildness)

Wildschuetz (hunter, poacher)

Wilfong, see Wildfang

Wilgar, Wilger (determination + spear) 46, 46

Wilhelm, Wilhelms, Wilhelmus (determination + helmet) 46, 46, 136

Wilhelmi (son of Wilhelm) 142

Wilk, Wilke, Wilkes, Wilkens, Wilkins, Wilkie, Willikin < Wilhelm 53, 54

Will, Wille (will, determination) 46

Willem, Willems < Wilhelm

Willich, Willig (willing) 115

Willikon (Wilhelm's hamlet) 127

Williram (will + raven) 46, 48

Willkom (Welcome!) 117

Willmann, Willmanns, Wilmann (determination + man) 46, 94

Willmer, Willmers, Wilmer, Wilmers (determination + famous) 46, 47

Willner, Wilner (poacher)

Willoch < Wilhelm

Willowby, see Wilderbach 151

Willpert (determination + bright) 46, 47

Wilt, see Wild

Wiltrout < Wiltrud (determination + beloved) 46, 48, 151

Wimer, Wimmer, see Widmer

Wimmler (marsh dweller) 80

Winckler, Winckelmann, see Winkler

Wind (wind) 122

Windemuth, Windermuth, see Wendelmuth

Winder, Winders, see Winter, Winters 151

Windisch (Wendish, Slavic) 121

Windmiller, Windmueller (proprietor of a windmill) 103

Winebarger, see Weinberger 151

Winebrener, Winebrenner, see Weinbrenner 151

Winecoff, see Weinkauf 151

Winegard, see Weingard 151

Winfurth (fr Weinfurth) 122

Winhart (friend + strong) 48, 46

Winholt (friend + loyal) 48, 48

Winkel (corner, angle, wooded valley) 122

Winkelmeyer (farmer in wooded valley 93, or fr Winkel 122)

Winkler, Winkelman, Winkelmann (store-keeper) 105

Winter 122, Winters, Winders (winter)

Winter, see Wintzer
Winterberg (winter mountain)
68, 122
Wintermantel (winter coat)
112, 106
Winterstein (winter mountain)
73, 122
Wintner (vintner) 102
Winz 122, Winzer (vine
dresser) 102
Wipbold, Wippel < Wigbald
(battle + bold) 46, 46
Wipert < Wigbert (battle +
bright) 46, 47
Wirbel (whirl, vertebra)
Wirt, Wirth (host, proprietor)
96
Wirthlin (little host) 96
Wirtsch < Wirt
Wirtz, Wuertz (spice) 105
Wisbrod, see Weissbrod 151
Wischel (wiper) 96
Wise, see Wiese, Weiss 151
Wishard, Wishart, see
Weisshart 151
Wismatt (white meadow) 84
Wisner, Wissner, see Wiessner
Wissant (bison, auerochs)
Wissel, Wissels < Werner 53,
54
Wissler, see Wechsler
Witsel < Ludwig or Wiegand
53, 54
Witt, Witte (white)
Wittbecker (fr Wittbeck 122,
white brook, forest brook) 77
Wittekind, see Wedekind
Wittenbach (white brook, or
forest brook) 77, 122
Wittenberg (white mountain)
68, 122
Witthauer (woodchopper) 95
Witthof (forest farm) 92
Witthuhn (white chicken)
Witthuhn (grouse, forest hen)
Wittich (legendary hero)

Wittmann, Wittmer
(manager of church
propety, or see
Weidmann)
Wittmayer, Wittmayer,
Wittmyer (manager of
glebe land) 93
Wittstadt (white city) 122
Wittwer (widower)
Witz (wit, intelligence 115,
or < Witu, forest 72)
Witzel < Wiegand 53, 54
Witzthum (manager, fr Latin
vice-dominus) 109
Woeber, Wobner, Woebner
see Weber
Woefel, Woefele, Woelffle
(little wolf 48), see
Wolfhart
Woelpert (wolf + bright 48,
47, or rule + bright 46,
47)
Woerbel, see Werbel
Woerner, see Werner
Wohl (well-being)
Wohlfart, Wohlfahrt,
Wohlfert (welfare)
Wohlfart, Wohlfahrt <
Wolfhart
Wohlfeil (inexpensive)
Wohlgemut, Wohlgemuth,
Wohlmut (happy
disposition) 115
Wohlleben, Wohleben (the
good life)
Wohlschlaegel (wool cleaner)
106
Wohner (occupant)
Wolbert < Walbrecht
Wold, see Wald
Wolf 122, Wolfe, Wolff, Wolfs
(wolf 48), or < Wolfgang,
Wolfhart
Wolfart, Wolfarts 122,
Wolfahrth, see Wohlfart
Wolfer, Wolfers, Wolfert <
Wolfher (wolf + army 48,
46), or Wolfhart

Wolffanger, Wolfanger (wolf catcher)
Wolfgang (wolf + gait)
Wolfhart (wolf + strong) 48, 46
Wolfkamp, Wolfkampf (wolf field) 48, 84
Wolfram (wolf + raven) 48, 48
Wolfshagen (wolf's enclosure) 48, 123, 122
Wolfskehl (wolf's throat) 122
Wolhandler (wool dealer) 105
Wolk (cloud)
Wolkam (wool comb) 106
Wolkenstein (clouds mountain)
Wollenhaupt (wool head) 112
Wollenmacher (Woolmaker) 96
Wollenschlaeger (wool beater) 96
Wollenweber, Wolweber (wool weaver) 96
Woller, Wollner, see Wollenschlaeger
Wollf, see Wolf
Wollhuter (maker of wool hats) 96
Wolpert < Walbrecht
Wolter, Wolters, see Walther, Walthers
Woltmann, see Waldmann
Woltz, see Waltz
Wool, Wolle (wool) 105, 106
Woolmaker, see Wollenmacher 151
Woost 122, see Wuest 151
Workman, see Werckmann 151
Worms, Wormser (fr Worms) 122
Worst, see Wurst
Wrangel (querulous) 115
Wrighter, see Reiter 151
Wucher, Wucherer (usurer)
Wuellner, see Wollner
Wuensch (wish, Wendish)
Wuerfel (dice, gambler)
Wuertemberger, Wuerttemberger (fr Wurttemberg) 121
Wuertz (spice) 105

Wuest, Wueste (desert, wasteland)
Wuetrich (maniac) 115
Wulf, Wulff, see Wolf, Wolff
Wulfhart, see Wolfhart
Wuller (woolworker) 96
Wullwever (wool weaver) 96
Wund (wound, wounded)
Wunder (wonder, miracle)
Wunderlich, Wunderlick, Wunderli, Wonderlich (quaint, odd, eccentric) 115
Wunsch, see Wuensch
Wurfel, Wuerfel (dice)
Wurst, Wurste (sausage) 106, 106
Wurster (sausage maker) 96
Wurttemberger, Wurttenberger (fr Wurttemberg 122, reed mountain) 81, 68
Wurtz, Wurts, see Wuertz
Wurz 122, see Wuertz
Wurzburg, Wurtzburger (fr Wurtzburg 122, swamp castle) 80, 73
Wust, see Wuest
Wycoff, Wyckoff (wine seller) 102, 105
Wydman, see Weidmann
Wygand, see Weigand
Wygart, see Weingard
Wyl, see Weil
Wyman, Weinmann (wine seller) 102, 105
Wyngarde, Wyngartner, Wyngaarden, see Weingard, Weingaertner
Wynkoop, see Wycoff
Wys, Wyss, see Weiss

X

Xander < Alexander

Y

For Y see under J.

Yaeger, Yager, see Jaeger 151
Yahr, see Jahr 151
Yakeley, see Jaeckli 151
Yauch, see Jauch 151
Yeager, Yager, see Jaeger 151
Yenny, see Jenny 151
Yetter, see Jeter 151
Yingling, see Juengling 151
Yingst, see Juengst 151
Yoder, see Joder 151
Yonce, see Jantz 151
Yongman, see Jungman 151
Yonker, see Junker 151
Yoos, see Jost 151
Yorden, see Jordan 151
Yost, see Jost 151
Youngblood, see Jungblut 151
Younginger, see Junginger 151
Yuengling, see Juengling 151
Yung, see Jung 151
Yungmann (young man) 151
Yunker, see Junker 151
Yustus, see Justus 151

Z

Zaber, Zaberer (fr Zabern) 122,
129
Zach 122, Zacharias (OT name)
135
Zachringer, Zaehringer,
Zahringer (Swiss dynastic
name)
Zaehringen (fr Celtic
Tarodunum) 129
Zaharias (OT name) 135
Zahl (numer)
Zahler (teller, payer, debtor)
Zahm (tame, domestic)
Zahn (tooth, dentist) 114, 96
Zahringer, see Zachringer
Zaiss, see Zeiss

Zang 122, Zange (tongs,
torturer, tooth puller) 106
Zanger (lively, merry) 115,
see Saenger 151
Zangmeister, Zangmaster
(choir master) 151
Zank, Zanck, Zanker
(quarrel, quarreler) 115
Zant (tooth) 114
Zapf (tap, taverner) 106
Zarncke (Slavic: black) 112
Zart (tender) 115
Zauberbuehler, Zouberbuhler,
see Zuberbiller
Zaun, Zuner (fence, fence
maker) 106, 122
Zech, Zechman (tippler) 115,
122
Zeder (cedar) 89
Zedler (scribe) 96
Zeh (toe) 114
Zehenbauer (tithe farmer) 91
Zehender, Zehnder, Zehnter
(tithe collector) 109
Zehn, Zehner (ten, tenth)
Zehntbauer, see Zehenbauer
Zehr (nourishment) 106
Zeidler (honey gatherer) 95
Zeigenfuss (goat foot) 114,
151
Zeiger (hand of clock)
Zeigler, see Ziegler 151
Zeil, Zeile (line)
Zeiss (gentle, tender) 115
Zeit (time)
Zeitler, see Zeidler
Zell (cell, fr Latin *cella*) 122
Zeller, Zellner (dweller near
a shrine or cell)
Zellhofer (farm near a shrine
or cell) 92
Zellner, see Zoellner
Zelt, Zelter (tent, tentmaker)
96
Zelter (palfrey)
Zenger (lively person) 115
Zenker (quarreler) 115

Zentgraf, Zentgraft (village
  magistrate) 109
Zentner (hundredweight) 114
Zentz < St. Vincentius 131
Zepp, see Zapf
Zepperfeld, Zeppenfeldt
  (threshing floor) 84
Zercher, see Zuericher
Zermatt (at the meadow, Swiss
  village) 122
Zetel (marsh) 80
Zettel (scrap of paper, note)
  122
Zettelmeyer, Zettlemoyer, see
  Seddlemeyer 151
Zettler, see Zedler
Zeumer (bridle maker) 96
Zeuner (fence maker) 96
Zickafoose, Zickefoose (Shake a
  leg!) 116, 151
Ziebli, Zieblin, see Zuebli
Ziege, Ziecke (goat) 91
Ziegel, Zieggel, Zigel, see
  Zuegel 151
Ziegenbein (goat leg) 114
Ziegenmilch (goat milk) 106
Ziegler, Zigler, Zeigler, Zieglert
  (tile setter or maker, fr
  Latin *tegulum*) 96, 101
Ziel (goal)
Zielke (little goal)
Zieman < Sigmann (victory +
  man) 46, 94
Zier (decoration) 115, 106
Zigenfuss (goat leg) 114
Zigler, see Ziegler
Zilber, see Silber 151
Zimmer, Zimmerli (timber,
  carpenter) 106
Zimmermann, Zimermann
  (carpenter) 96, 98
Zinder (silk worker) 96
Zink (cornet player) 96
Zinn, Zinner (pewterer) 96
Zinser (payer or receiver of
  rent)
Zipfel, Zipfler (peak, peak
  dweller)
Zipperer (thresher) 95

Zircher, see Zuericher
Zirkel (district) 122
Ziskind, see Sueskind 151
Zittrauer, Zittrower
  (trembling mountain) 68
Zobel (hair-knot, girl) 112
Zobrist (uppermost)
Zoeller, Zoellner, Zeller (toll
  collector, fr Latin
  telonarius) 109
Zoll (toll, fr Latin *teloneum*)
  122
Zoll (club, log)
Zollbrueck (toll bridge) 122
Zoller, Zollner, see Zoeller,
  Zoellner
Zollikoffer, Zollicoffer (place
  in Switzerland) 122
Zollinger (fr Zolling 122)
Zollmann, Zoellner (toll
  collector) 109
Zopf (forelock) 112
Zorbach, Zorbaugh (at the
  brook) 70, 77
Zorn (anger, also a place
  name) 122
Zouberbuhler, see Zuberbiller
  151
Zuber (wooden bucket) 106
Zuberbiller (bucket hill)
Zubly, Zuebli, Zueblin
  (mountain stream, fr
  Latin *tubus*)
Zuchtmann (disciplinarian)
Zucker, Zuckermann (sugar
  seller) 105
Zuegel (bridle) 106
Zuend (fuse, harquebusier)
  107
Zuend (at the end [of the
  village]) 70
Zuendl (fuse, kindling, fire
  tender)
Zuericher, Zuercher (Swiss fr
  Zurich) 122, 129
Zuern, see Zorn
Zug (city in Switzerland) 122
Zugel, see Zuegel
Zulauf (throng)

Zumbrun, Zumbrunn, Zum
  Brunnen (at the well) 70, 79
Zumbusch (at the bush) 70, 72
Zumdahl (at the valley) 70, 76
Zumlaub (at the foliage) 70
Zumstein, Zumstain (at the
  stone) 70, 73, 122
Zumwald (at the forest) 70, 71,
  122
Zunder (tinder, punk,
  harquebusier)
Zunft (guild)
Zupfer (wool or flax puller) 96
Zurbrueck (at the bridge) 70
Zurbuechen (at the beeches)
  70, 89
Zurcher, see Zuericher
Zurheide (to the heath) 70, 84,
  122
Zuskin, see Sueskind
Zwaig, see Zweig
Zwantzig, Zwanzger,
  Zwantziger (twenty)

Zweback, see Zwieback 151
Zweck (nail, target, goal) 122
Zweibrucker, Zwebricher (fr
  Zweibruecken) 121, 122
Zweifel (doubt)
Zweig (branch, twig,
  taverner) 96
Zweigle (little branch, graft)
Zweigler (dweller at a
  crossroads)
Zwetsch, Zwetschen (plum)
  89
Zwickel (gusset)
Zwicker (excutioner)
Zwiebach (zwieback)
Zwiebbler (onion seller) 105
Zwiffler, see Zwiebbler
Zwigart, see Schweiger 151
Zwinger (castle) 122
Zwirn (thread) 105, 106
Zygler, see Ziegler 151